Not of Un   *e:*

Canceled Saint   ...s in the
Liturgical Cale   ...anges of 1969

Compiled and edited by
Michael Murphy

*Dedicated to my loving wife, Pam, whose love and patience
has allowed me to follow my creative spirit.*

*In loving memory of my grandmother, Dolores, and my
mother, Mary, for teaching me to be a faithful Catholic.*

Published in the United States by Saint Anastasia Press

© 2023 Michael Murphy

Cover picture (paperback) - *Saint Peter Catholic Church (Millersburg, Ohio)
- Stained Glass, St. Christopher - Detail.* By Nheyob, 18 Apr. 2015,
commons.wikimedia.org/wiki/File:
Saint_Peter_Catholic_Church_(Millersburg,_Ohio)_-
_stained_glass,_St._Christopher_-_detail.jpg.

Library of Congress Cataloging-in-Publication Data:

ISBN: 979-8370-03784-9 (ISBN-13)

First Printing: January 2023

Printed in the United States of America

Not of Universal Importance

Not of Universal Importance

Contents

Introduction

> *For there shall be a time, when they will
> not endure sound doctrine; but, according
> to their own desires, they will heap to
> themselves teachers, having itching ears:
> And will indeed turn away their hearing
> from the truth, but will be turned unto
> fables. But be thou vigilant, labor in all
> things, do the work of an evangelist, fulfill
> thy ministry. Be sober. [2 Tim. 4:4-5]*

From the Protestant Reformation of the 16th century until the eve of the Second Vatican Council, Catholics increasingly lived within their communities of Catholic neighborhoods, Catholic schools, and Catholic hospitals. Both events triggered theological, political, intellectual, and cultural turmoil, with the Reformation dividing Catholic Europe, and the latter caused doctrinal, political, academic, and cultural upheaval inside the Catholic Church.

They embraced their faith, attended Mass, received the sacraments, and they adhered to Saint Paul's warning, to "...be not conformed to this world; but be reformed in the newness of your mind, that you may prove what is the good, and the acceptable, and the perfect will of God" [Rom. 12:2].

The Second Vatican Council changed this when the Council fathers sought to embrace the secular world and to become ecumenical with the other religions of the world. "This sacred Council has several aims in view: it desires to impart an ever-increasing vigor to the Christian life of the faithful; to adapt more suitably to the needs of our own times, those institutions which are subject to change; to foster whatever can promote union among all who believe in Christ; to strengthen whatever can help to call the whole of mankind into the household of the Church. The Council, therefore, sees particularly cogent reasons for undertaking the reform and promotion of the liturgy" ([Sacrosanctum Concilium] SC 1).

> *"[It is an error to believe that] Christ did not teach a determined body of doctrine applicable to all times and all men but rather inaugurated a religious movement adapted or to be adapted to different times and places." - Pope Pius X, Lamentabili Sane (1907), The Syllabus of Errors, No. 59.*

> *"The Council also desires that, where necessary, the rites be revised carefully in the light of sound tradition and that they be given new vigor to meet the circumstances and needs of modern times." – Pope Paul VI, Sacrosanctum Concilium (1963)[2].*

Modernism

Pope Pius X tried to warn the Church of the errors of modernism in his encyclical, *Pascendi Dominici Gregis[3]*, given at St. Peter's, Rome, on the 8th day of September 1907, the fifth year of his Pontificate. "The office divinely committed to Us of feeding the Lord's flock has especially this duty assigned to it by Christ,

---

[1] Pius X. *"Lamentabili Sane* (1907)." New Advent | Catholic Library, 3 July 1907, www.newadvent.org/library/docs_df07ls.htm.

[2] Paul VI, "*Sacrosanctum Concilium (1963).*" The Vatican | Documents of the Second Vatican Council, www.vatican.va/archive/hist_councils/ii_vatican_council/documents/vat-ii_const_19631204_sacrosanctum-concilium_en.html.

[3] Pius X. *"Pascendi Dominici Gregis.*" The Vatican | The Holy Father, 8 Sept. 1907, www.vatican.va/content/pius-x/en/encyclicals/documents/hf_p-x_enc_19070908_pascendi-dominici-gregis.html.

namely, to guard with the greatest vigilance the deposit of the faith delivered to the saints, rejecting the profane novelties of words and oppositions of knowledge falsely so-called. There has never been a time when the Catholic body did not require the supreme pastor's vigilance. Wherefore we may no longer be silent, lest we should seem to fail in Our most sacred duty, and lest the kindness that, in the hope of wiser counsels, we have hitherto shown them, should be attributed to forgetfulness of Our office" ([Pascendi Dominici Gregis] PDG 1).

"...the Modernists (as they are commonly and rightly called) employ a very clever artifice, namely, to present their doctrines without order and systematic arrangement into one whole, scattered and disjointed one from another, so as to appear to be in doubt and uncertainty, while they are in reality firm and steadfast...." (PDG 4).

"It remains for us now to say a few words about the Modernist as reformer. From all that has preceded, some idea may be gained of the reforming mania which possesses them: in all Catholicism, there is absolutely nothing on which it does not fasten. Reform of philosophy, especially in the seminaries: the scholastic philosophy is to be relegated to the history of philosophy among obsolete systems, and the young men are to be taught modern philosophy, which alone is true and suited to the times in which we live. Reform of theology; rational theology is to have modern philosophy for its foundation, and positive theology is to be founded on the history of dogma. As for history, it must be written for the future and taught only according to modern methods and principles. Dogmas and their evolution are to be harmonized with science and history. In the Catechism, no dogmas are to be inserted except those that have been duly reformed and are within the capacity of the people. Regarding worship, the number of external devotions is to be reduced, or at least steps must be taken to prevent their further increase, though, indeed, some of the admirers of symbolism are disposed to be more indulgent on this head. Ecclesiastical government requires to be reformed in all its branches, but especially in its disciplinary and dogmatic parts. Its spirit with the public conscience, which is not wholly for democracy; a share in ecclesiastical government should therefore be given to the lower ranks of the clergy and even to the laity, and authority should be decentralized. The Roman Congregations, and especially the index and the Holy Office, are to be reformed. The ecclesiastical authority must change its line of conduct in the social and political world; while keeping outside the political and social organization; it must adapt itself to those which exist in order to penetrate them with its spirit. With regard to morals, they adopt the principle of the Americanists that the active virtues are more important than the passive, both in the estimation in which they must be held and in the exercise of them. The clergy are asked to return to their ancient lowliness and poverty, and in their ideas and action to be guided by the principles of modernism; and there are some who, echoing the teaching of their Protestant masters, would like the suppression of ecclesiastical celibacy. What is there left in the Church which is not to be reformed according to their principles? (PDG 38)"

Ecumenism[4]

Faith and Order, a modern ecumenical group, had its first major meeting in 1927. A delegation traveled to the Vatican to invite Pope Pius XI to attend the summit. The Holy Father greeted the pilgrims warmly and applauded the spirit that drove them to seek unity. But, at

---

[4] https://www.catholic.com/magazine/print-edition/pope-pius-xi-and-ecumenism

the same time, he flatly refused to go and barred any Catholics from going.

While no Catholics attended the conference, 450 persons from ninety various denominations did. The agenda included debates about unity, ecclesiology, sacraments, and ministry. Unsurprisingly, no progress was made. Doctrinal disputes were barely considered, and disagreements between "high church" and "low church" viewpoints prevented the conferees from reaching an agreement on the character of the ecumenical movement. Finally, the essential aspect of the conference was that it took place at all.

This was the scenario in which Pius XI found himself when he set out to compose *Mortalium Animos.* He forcefully condemned the faults he saw manifested in the ecumenical movements of the time. He acknowledged that these initiatives appeared to be decent and honorable on the surface. But, he cautioned: "In reality beneath these enticing words and blandishments lies hid a most grave error by which the foundations of the Catholic faith are completely destroyed" ([Mortalium Animos] MA 4).

He then went on to describe the errors. First, people who supported these initiatives denied the Church of Christ's apparent actuality, claiming that the genuine Church is exclusively invisible: "They understand a visible Church as nothing else than a federation composed of various communities of Christians, even though they adhere to different doctrines that may even be incompatible with each other" (MA 6).

Second, he critiqued efforts to downplay the contradictions seen in many Christians' views. They allowed direct inconsistencies inside their invisible "Church of Christ" by claiming that only a few teachings, or "fundamentals," require unity of belief. They dismissed these distinctions and conflicts as unimportant: "They add that the Church in itself, or of its nature, is divided into sections; that is to say, that it is made up of several churches or distinct communities that still remain separate and, although having certain articles of doctrine in common, nevertheless disagree concerning the remainder.... Controversies, therefore, they say, and longstanding differences of opinion that keep asunder till the present day the members of the Christian families, must be entirely put aside and from the remaining doctrines a common form of faith drawn up and proposed for belief" (MA 7).

Because of these fallacies, the Holy Father rejected these efforts at "pan-Christianity," as he dubbed them: "This being so, it is clear that the Apostolic See cannot on any terms take part in their assemblies, nor is it anyway lawful for Catholics either to support or to work for such enterprises" (MA 8).

The modernists at the Second Vatican Council accepted that which had been forewarned. Accordingly, ecumenism was embraced in the Pastoral Constitution on the Church in the Modern World, *Gaudium et Spes,* promulgated by Pope Paul VI on the 7th day of December 1965. "...the Catholic Church gladly holds in high esteem the things which other Christian Churches and ecclesial communities have done or are doing cooperatively by way of achieving the same goal. At the same time, she is convinced that she can be abundantly and variously helped by the world in the matter of preparing the ground for the Gospel. This help she gains from the talents and industry of individuals and from human society as a whole. The Council now sets forth certain general principles for the proper fostering of this mutual exchange and assistance in concerns which are in some way common to the world and the Church" ([Gaudium et Spes] GS 4).

This decision runs contrary to the magisterium of the Catholic Church, which teaches infallibly, "*extra ecclesiam nulla salus*," or, "outside the Church, there is no salvation." This is affirmed in the *Catechism of the Catholic Church*, paragraphs 846-48. How should we interpret this declaration, which the Church Fathers frequently repeat? Positively, it signifies that all salvation comes from Christ, the Head, through the Church, his body:

"Basing itself on Scripture and Tradition, the Council teaches that the Church, a pilgrim now on earth, is necessary for salvation: the one Christ is the mediator and the way of salvation; he is present to us in his body, which is the Church. He himself explicitly asserted the necessity of faith and Baptism and thereby affirmed at the same time the necessity of the Church, which men enter through Baptism as through a door. Hence, they could not be saved who, knowing that the Catholic Church was founded as necessary by God through Christ, would refuse either to enter it or to remain in it".

Conclusion

The Second Vatican Council merely called for the *pruning* of the liturgical calendar, not to take a chainsaw to it. The modernists saw to the latter along with the obfuscation of the liturgical seasons as they had been known since the early days of the Christian Church. The reader will see how beautifully the liturgical year once flowed, with each season beginning with a period of penance and preparation. Advent prepared to soul for Christ's birth at Christmas. Septuagesima provided for a smooth transition from the joyful Christmas to the penitential season of Lent. Lent prepares the soul for a joyful Easter. Pentecost revisits Christ's three-year mission among us here on earth. The Feast of Christ the King is the exclamation point at the end of the liturgical year, at which time we begin they year again with Advent. It was all so perfect and so simple.

The embracing of the modern world has led to the destruction of the Catholic way of life. Catholic schools, which remain after dwindling attendance over multiple generations, have become secularized and teach worldly morals not aligned with official Church teachings. Catholic hospitals struggle to remain Catholic under constant pressure to provide care not in line with the Magisterium. Most modern Catholics have received poor catechesis, do not know magisterial Catholic morals and beliefs, and have been led astray by self-serving "pastors." Most believe they can be "cafeteria Catholics" and choose which beliefs they wish to follow and which teachings of Christ agree with their personal chosen lifestyles. These progressive Catholics boast that Jesus ate with sinners, but they do not remember that he always chastised them to "go and sin no more."

The Catholic Church was once the leader in setting morals for the world. Now, the Church follows the world in its immorality. Weak clerical leadership fails to defend the faith for fear of hurt feelings or perception that they are not being "pastoral." Instead, they promote "all are welcome" while driving away faithful Catholics. The pews are emptying, the parishioners remaining are aging, and churches are closing. Young people are not attracted to 1970s folk music and vestments. They desire authentic Catholicism that lifts them spiritually. The promised springtime never came. We were warned.

"One of the weaknesses of the postconciliar liturgical reform can doubtless be traced to the armchair strategy of academics, drawing up things on paper which, in fact, would presuppose years of organic growth. The most blatant example of this is the reform of the Calendar: those responsible simply did not realize how much the various annual feasts had influenced Christian people's relation to time. In redistributing these established feasts throughout the year according to some historical arithmetic—inconsistently applied at that—they ignored a fundamental law of religious life."

~ Joseph Cardinal Ratzinger (Pope Benedict XVI), *The Feast of Faith: Approaches to a Theology of the Liturgy*

The Church Year Before the Second Vatican Council

"Enter into the temple of God that thou mayest have part with Christ unto life everlasting" (Rite of Baptism). So we have the privilege of having "part with Christ" through baptism. Why does this matter?

Jesus is both the Son of God and the Son of Man. We are adopted as God's children through baptism and become "other Christs." The mysteries of Jesus' life on earth — his incarnation, birth, life, sufferings, death, and glorious resurrection — are mysteries we know. Through our baptism, we became a part of Jesus and are now a part of all the mysteries of His life. We share His mysteries when we are united with Him. This is done every time we make the sacred sacrifice of the Mass because that is when Christ, in the form of a man, presents Himself to His Father, and all the mysteries of His earthly life are remembered.

But since the vast mysteries of Christ limit even the finest of our minds, we must consider and practice each of these holy truths separately. God permits us to do this because of His loving goodness. Christ reenacts the sacred mysteries of His earthly existence every year in His Church. He now experiences them in unison with all of the living members of His Mystical Body rather than alone. The mystical Christ, or Christ and His followers, reenacts the enigma of Christ's incarnation, crucifixion, death, and resurrection every year. The Church Year, often known as the Liturgical Year, has this purpose.

The Incarnation and the Redemption are the two great mysteries at the center of all the happenings during our Lord's life on earth. The Church Year thus has two primary halves or periods. The Incarnation or Christmas Period and the Redemption or Easter Period may be referred to as such. Advent kicks off the Christmas

Season, which lasts until Septuagesima Sunday, while Septuagesima kicks off the Easter Season, which lasts until the next Advent.

We go through these two liturgical seasons every year, and we ought to take the time to become more intimately joined with Christ in His holy mysteries every year. We will try our best to immerse ourselves as deeply as we can in the mysteries of Christ this year to honor our heavenly Father even more through Him.

The Incarnation and The Redemption

The celebration of the feasts of the Liturgical Year is the best method to actively participate in learning about the mysteries of the Incarnation and Redemption.

The Liturgical Year is split into two sections: the Incarnation Period, which is marked by the celebrations of Christmas and Epiphany, and the Redemption Period, which is marked by the celebrations of Easter and Pentecost. She will record the times spent in preparation, celebration, and extension associated with each of these feasts. After Pentecost, the Church and each member will grow in their relationship with Christ via the power of the Holy Spirit. As a result of their leadership and intercession, the saints' feast days throughout the year inspire and benefit us.

It must be understood that the feasts of the Liturgical Year not only commemorate but also reenact the hallowed mysteries of Christ's life and death. Therefore, living the Liturgical Year is crucial to the Christian life because of this internal reality — the development of the members of Christ through participation in Christ's mysteries. Abbot Marmion writes so clearly on this matter that he is here quoted:

> Although it is always the same Savior, the same Jesus, pursuing the same work of our

sanctification, each mystery is a fresh manifestation of Christ for us; each has its special beauty, particular splendor, as likewise its grace.

The Fathers of the Church speak more than once of what they call the *vis mysterii*, the virtue, and signification of the mystery being celebrated. So, in each of Christ's mysteries, we may apply to Christians what St. Gregory of Nazianzen said of the faithful at the feast of Easter: "We cannot offer a gift more pleasing to God than to offer ourselves with a perfect understanding of the mystery."

Some there are who see nothing in celebrating Christ's mysteries beyond the perfection of the ceremonies, the beauty of the music and liturgical ornaments, and the harmony of the ritual. There is all this, and that is excellent.

It is a psychological law of our nature that we should pass from the visible to the invisible. These outward elements have their use, but we must not exclusively stop at them; they are but the fringe of Christ's garment; the virtue of the mysteries of Jesus is above all interior, and it is this virtue that we must seek before all.

Each of Christ's mysteries, representing a state of the Sacred Humanity, thus brings us special participation in His divinity. For example, at Christmas, we celebrate the birth of Christ upon the earth; we sing that "wonderful exchange" which was made in Him between the Divinity and Humanity. He takes human nature from us to make us partakers of His divine nature, and each Christmas, worthily celebrated, is for the soul, by a more abundant communication of grace, like a new birth of divine life. Upon Calvary, we die to sin with Christ; Jesus gives us the grace to detest more deeply all that offends Him. During Paschal time, we participate in that liberty of soul, in that more intense life for God, of which He is the model in His Resurrection. On the day of His Ascension, we ascend with Him to heaven, to be like Him, by faith and desire, with the heavenly Father, *in sinu Patris*, in the intimacy of the divine sanctuary.

Following Christ Jesus in all His mysteries, uniting ourselves to Him, we share, little by little, but indeed, and each time more fully and deeply, in His divinity and His divine life.[5]

Incarnation Period

In this period, you will read about the mystery of the incarnation of the Son of God. You will see how Christ in His Church lives the sacred mysteries of His birth and childhood again and how He manifests Himself to the world.

There are in the Christmas Period three different stages:

1. The time of preparation for the coming of Christ is Advent;
2. The celebration of Christ's coming from Christmas to the feast of the Epiphany;
3. The continuing of the celebration through the time after Epiphany.

In studying this period, you should try not only to learn about the truths of our holy faith, which it contains but also to have a part in them through living day by day in close union with Christ in His Church.

---

[5] Marmion, Columba, and the Nuns of Tyburn convent. *Christ in His Mysteries*. London: Sands: 1923. Print.

The First Sunday of Advent

Nearly two thousand years ago, the Son of God was born of the Blessed Virgin Mary in Bethlehem. The long-promised Messiah came to redeem mankind. We know that Abraham and Isaac and Jacob, David and the prophets, and the people of Israel and Juda hoped for His coming. What the birth of our divine Savior in Bethlehem meant to the people who knew Him in His coming, this His coming means to us this Christmas, for we need the Redeemer as intensely as did the patriarchs of old. We need to be freed from our sins, and we want to grow increasingly closely united with God our Father. Since we can come to the Father only "through Christ our Lord," we pray earnestly for His coming during Advent.

"Stir up thy might, we beseech thee, O Lord, and come," we pray with the priest in the Collect of the Mass for the first Sunday of Advent. We ask Christ to come to deliver us from the sins that threaten to separate us from Him. Of course, the dangers are different for each Catholic joining with the Church in this prayer today. But God knows each of us, young and old, and He knows the temptations besetting us now.

God will be pleased with our prayer for His aid, but He also wants us to do something to help ourselves. What this is, He tells us in the Epistle. Through St. Paul, He reminds us that we should rise up from our passivity and indifference and go to work with all our heart and strength to do God's will. Our heavenly Father tells us we should "put on Jesus Christ." God wishes to see in us a reflection of His divine Son's charity, humility, and obedience.

We want to do as God tells us, and we ask Him in the Gradual to teach us how we can "put on Christ" in our life now. "Show, O Lord, thy ways to me: and teach me thy paths."

In the Gospel, our heavenly Father reminds us of the glorious coming of Christ, which will take place at the end of the world. Then we shall be glad of our efforts to please Him. Those who have been united with Christ during their life on earth will be united with Him in His glory.

Encouraged by the word of God, we bring to the altar at the Offertory our earnest resolutions to "put on" the charity of Christ, especially during this first week of Advent, and we place our trust in God that He will help us to keep our resolutions.

During the Canon of the Mass, we try to enter as closely as we can into the celebration of the holy Mysteries, for we hope to be cleansed from our sins and strengthened in His grace through the Sacrifice of Christ. When we receive Christ in holy Communion, we have a more intimate part in His holy life. Christ will live in us, and we in Him.

Now we can truly "put on the Lord Jesus Christ." Living in Him, we shall love our heavenly Father with His love. And we shall love our neighbors, parents, brothers, and sisters, all with whom we live, in Christ and through Him. His divine charity will fill up our littleness. By His grace, we shall be obedient, kind, truthful, honest, and pure in all our thoughts, words, and actions.

So "we may with becoming honor prepare for the approaching solemnities of our redemption" (Postcommunion).

The Second Sunday of Advent

During the hundreds of years before the coming of Christ, God sent His prophets to encourage His people with the promise of the Messiah to come. During Advent, our heavenly Father reminds us from time to time that Christ will come to us this Christmas to save and sanctify us if we persevere in preparing for His coming. Today, in the Introit of the Mass, God tells us that "the Lord shall make the glory of his voice to be heard in the joy of (our) heart." We want to keep on in our preparation for Christmas, doing all that God expects of us, but we know that we are likely to weaken in our good resolution. Therefore, we ask God today to "stir up our hearts to make ready the ways of (His) only-begotten Son" (Collect). We ask God, too, that through the coming of Christ this Christmas, we may come to serve God with purified minds. When our thoughts are right and pleasing to God, our words and actions will be so. We need God's help to keep our thoughts as will please Him.

In the Epistle, our heavenly Father tells us, through St. Paul, how our minds and thoughts should be. He would have us be "of one mind, one towards another, according to Jesus Christ." The mind of Jesus Christ was filled with charity toward all, not merely toward some, but toward all. And this is the mind our Heavenly Father wishes to see in us — "that with one mind and with one mouth (we) may glorify God and the Father of our Lord Jesus Christ" (Epistle). When all the children of God are gathered about the altar on Sunday to offer to Him with the priest the Sacrifice of His divine Son, our Lord Jesus Christ, God wishes to see us all united in charity. Only then are we pleasing to God.

It is a great and sublime thing for us to put aside all willful sin — all uncharitable thought and feeling, all selfishness — and, united in charity with all, to go up the altar of God with our gifts. Happy in this thought, we sing: "I rejoiced at the things that were said to me: we shall go into the house of the Lord. Alleluia."

Today in the Gospel, Jesus tells us the works that He does. "The blind see, the lame walk, the lepers are cleansed, the deaf hear, the dead rise again, the poor have the Gospel preached to them.' Jesus is the same "yesterday and today and forever." In Galilee and Judea,

"He went about doing good." Today throughout all the world, He gives sight to the blind, hearing to the deaf, and health to the sick. Not only does He heal sick bodies, but He also gives strength to sickly souls and even restores souls that have been dead in sin to life. He sees the weakness of souls: our blindness to some of His truths, our deafness to His word, our lameness in walking in His way. God, and only God, can cure our sick souls and make us rugged, healthy children of our heavenly Father.

At the Offertory, we remind God of our confidence in His power and goodness. "O God, turning thou wilt bring us life." In the Secret, we again place all our confidence in God's mercy: "...whereas we have no merits to plead in our favor, do thou succor us by thy protection."

Last week we began our preparation for Christ's coming. We resolved to "put on the Lord Jesus Christ" and to show the charity and humility, and obedience of Christ in our conduct. Today at the Offertory, we also bring to the altar our victories and failures. Since we are sorry for our sins, God will know how to turn even our failures to His honor and glory. We also place on the altar our resolutions for this coming week. The time is not long before Christmas, and we have much to do to make our lives ready for a closer union with Christ.

There are many things to distract our thoughts from God, and we must watch against them. In the Postcommunion today, we will ask God to teach us to think little of the things of earth and to love the things of heaven.

The Third Sunday of Advent, or Gaudete Sunday

"The Lord is nigh." For two weeks, the children of God have been laboring, through prayer and penance, to purify their souls and make them ready for the coming of Christ. Sometimes this has called for heroic courage and generosity. Today our Father in heaven, who has been watching our efforts during Advent, encourages us greatly and urges us to be glad and joyous. "Rejoice in the Lord always: again, I say, rejoice. Let your modesty be known to all men: for the Lord is nigh" (Introit).

Through all the Church, there is rejoicing today. Rose-colored vestments replace the violet, and the organ is heard again in the churches. There is deep joy and peace in the hearts of those who have been trying earnestly to prepare for Christ's coming. Once, the Chaldeans overcame the Jews and forced them to go to Babylon as captives. For about seventy years, the people of God remained in captivity, and they repented sincerely for their sins during this time. In His own time, God "turned away the captivity of Jacob" and brought His people safely back to Jerusalem. If, by the grace of God, we have been preserved from the captivity of mortal sin, which makes us exiles from God's kingdom, let us rejoice and thank God. If we have been so unfortunate as to offend God by grievous sin, we know that, in the Sacrament of Penance, God frees His children from captivity and restores them to places of honor in His kingdom. We know that our salvation is in the hands of God, and we cry out to Him: "Stir up thy might, O Lord, and come: that thou mayest save us. Alleluia."

While the Jews were captives in Babylon, they sent money to Jerusalem for the priest there to buy victims and offer sacrifice to the Lord. At the Offertory, we bring our gifts, which we have been preparing for the past week. Self-conquests, acts of virtue, acts of penance, whatever the good we have done, we place it on the altar and offer our minds, hearts, souls, and bodies again to God. Only in this way can we fully have part with Christ in His sacrifice, for He offers Himself entirely to His heavenly Father.

Hundreds of years before our Lord was born, the prophet Isaias foretold to the people of Israel that God would one day found a glorious kingdom. He said to them, "Say to the faint-hearted, take courage and fear not: behold our God will come and save us" (Communion). In the Mass today, Christ in His Church speaks these words to us, and in holy Communion, He comes to us to make them true. In His strength, we shall be strong to persevere in preparing for "the coming festival." Throughout the day, the coming week, and throughout our lives, He will be with us to help us.

In the Gospel today, our heavenly Father directs us to "make straight the way of the Lord." Therefore, if you expect to share in the spiritual joys of the great feast you are about to celebrate, you must earnestly strive by prayer and penance to make the crooked ways straight. We understand what it means to be crooked in our dealings with our associates, and we heartily despise this practice. But, if our living is not as straight and clean as we wish, is it not because we do not "Keep our hearts and minds in Christ Jesus our Lord"?

At the close of the Mass, the priest, acting as Christ, bids all of us, "Ite, missa est." "Go forth," he says, "to your work or mission." Each of us then will go from Mass today to the particular work we must do to "make straight the way of the Lord" in our hearts. We go out to this work fearlessly and with joy, for we know that our Savior will soon come to us to unite us more intimately with Himself. "The Lord is nigh."

Ember Week in Advent

From the early centuries, the Church has set aside a week at the beginning of each of the four seasons as a time of prayer, penance, and renewal of spirit. These weeks are called ember weeks. By their observance, the Church wishes to consecrate each of the seasons to God.

In the Masses of the ember days during Advent, the thought of the coming Savior is most important. We shall consider the texts of the Masses for Wednesday, Friday, and Saturday and try to enter into the spirit of the Church in the observance of these ember days. The Mass for Wednesday is sometimes called *"Missa aurea"* or the "golden Mass," for it celebrates the holy mystery of the Incarnation. In the Epistle, we read the words of the prophet Isaias, spoken about seven hundred years before the coming of Christ, "Behold a virgin shall conceive and bear a son, and his name shall be called Emmanuel." In the Gospel, St. Luke tells of the fulfillment of this prophecy. The angel Gabriel, sent from God, announces to the Blessed Virgin that she is to become the mother of God. The Annunciation is the beginning of the mystery of our redemption.

In the Mass for Friday, Isaias speaks to us again, describing the Redeemer who is to come. He will be born of the family of Jesse, the father of David. He will be filled with the spirit of God, for He is the very Son of God. He will know us all as we are and will not consider what men think of us. The more we understand the infinite greatness of Christ, the more we shall long for His coming to us.

God was present in His power and majesty in the tabernacle in the desert and later in the temple at Jerusalem. Two golden cherubim were shielding the ark of the covenant in the Holy of Holies. The cherubim's wings guarded a golden slab called the Oracle or Mercy Seat, for God directed and guided His people from this place. Only the high priest ever entered the Holy of Holies, and he beheld God's majesty only as a cloud that rested over the ark of the covenant. The psalmist expressed the people's longing to see God's face. "Come, O Lord, and show thy face to us, thou that sittest upon the cherubim: and we shall be saved."

Jesus Christ, our Savior, is the manifestation of God to men. Happy were they who looked upon the face of Christ. Happy are we who, although we do not see God with our bodily eyes, can touch Him and be made to live His very life through the Mass and the sacraments.

The only thing that can weaken or destroy our unity with God is sin. Therefore, we beg to be delivered from this great evil in the Collect of Saturday. We confidently ask for deliverance from sin through the coming of our Redeemer.

The Lessons for Saturday, with one exception, are wen from Isaias. In them, the prophet foretells the joy of the kingdom of Christ, "'Then shall the eyes of the blind be opened, and the ears of the deaf shall be unstopped. Then shall the lame man leap as a hart, and the tongue of the dumb shall be free; for waters are woken out in the desert, and streams in the wilderness" (Second Lesson). How often, in the sacraments, we have drunk from these water-saving streams and have been refreshed and strengthened! "He shall feed his flock Me a shepherd: he shall gather together the lambs with his arm, and shall take them up in his bosom, the Lord our God" (Third Lesson). We have known, each of us, the strength and sweetness in the heavenly Food with which our divine Shepherd nourishes us. He feeds us with His very life.

Realizing better how good God has been to us in letting us live after His coming and making us members of Christ in His Mystical Body, we offer the Sacrifice of Thanksgiving with all the devotion we are capable of.

During these last days before the coming of our Savior, let us make our prayers of the beautiful "O Antiphons," "O Emmanuel, our King, and Lawgiver, the expected of the nations and their Savior, come to save us, O Lord our God" (Antiphon, December 23).

The Fourth Sunday of Advent

From the day of the fall of our first parents, mankind had looked forward to the coming of the Redeemer, for in Him, they would be born again to life in God as Adam and Eve lived before their sin. Patriarchs, prophets, and holy men and women of Israel and Juda longed to see the day of His coming. But generation after generation passed, and the Redeemer was still the Promised One. Then nearly two thousand years ago, a man who preached stern lessons of penance to the people came into the country around the river Jordan. He was John the Baptist, sent by God to prepare men for the coming of the Messiah. The word of St. John to the people was that they should do penance for their past sins and turn away from sin in the future. Only sin blocked the way of the Lord into their hearts and lives.

Christ will come as truly to us in the Mass of Christmas as He came in Bethlehem over nineteen hundred years ago. Today the Church warns us, through the words of St. John the Baptist, to prepare ourselves for His coming. "Prepare ye the way of the Lord, make straight his paths. Every valley shall be filled, every mountain and hill shall be brought low, the crooked shall be made straight; the rough ways plain." The Church also renews to us the promise He made to the people of Judea, "And all flesh shall see the salvation of God."

Everyone in the secret of his own heart knows how greatly he needs the Savior to take away his sin and heal the wounds sin has made in his soul. We want to remove from our lives every obstacle that will interfere with God's grace flowing into our souls. We want to be healthy branches on the Vine, which is Christ- animated by the same Life which is His and thereby bringing forth fruits to the honor and glory of our heavenly Father. We know this is the life a Christian should live, but in our weakness, we fall away from a generous, courageous serving of God.

Therefore, with all our hearts, we join with the priest in today's Collect. "Stir up, O Lord, we beseech thee, thy power and come; and with great might succor us: that, by the help of thy grace, that which is hindered by our sins may be hastened by thy merciful indulgence."

In the Epistle for today, St. Paul reminds us that the Lord sees us just as we are and judges us with justice. Only what is wholly true and sincere counts with God. Should we be fearful because of our sins, we are confident at the thought that we are offering to our heavenly Father a Victim wholly pleasing to Him in the holy Mass. Jesus Christ is our powerful Mediator with His Father. We pray earnestly at the Secret, "Favorably regard, we beseech thee, O Lord, these present sacrifices, that they may profit us both unto devotion and salvation."

If you would prepare the way for the coming of Christ as did St. John, you must, like him, be a person of principle, not "a reed shaken with the wind" (Matt. 11:7), the plaything of whims, and victim to human respect, nor "a man clothed in soft garments," always seeking your comfort, and a slave to your lower tendencies, but, like St. John, an angel before the face of Christ our Lord.

The Vigil of the Nativity of Our Lord

"This day you shall know that the Lord will come and save us; in the morning you shall see his glory." This is the joyous announcement the Church heralds to all her children in the Introit of today's Mass. Therefore, each one must do his part today to prepare all things for Christ our King's coming. Then we can fulfill the word which the Church speaks to her children today: "The Lord cometh! Go ye out to meet him, and say: How great is his dominion, and of his kingdom, there shall be no end: he is the mighty God, the Ruler, the Prince of Peace. Alleluia!" (Lauds). And in the evening, at Vespers, the Church sings joyously, "Or ever the sun be risen, ye shall see the King of kings coming forth from the Father, as a bridegroom out of his chamber."

The Nativity of the Lord

"Glory to God in the highest, and on earth peace among men of good will" (Luke 2:14). There are certain days which are kept in every family-days which all the children come home to celebrate. Such a family reunion is a dim image of the glorious feasts celebrated in the family of God. One of the most loved and beautiful of these feasts is the birthday of Christ, our Elder Brother. This feast we celebrate today, in union with all other members of God's family, in heaven and on earth. For weeks the Church has been preparing for this day. Indeed, hundreds and hundreds of years ago, she planned certain parts of the celebration. From the words of the prophets, the Gospels, the sermons of holy men, and the songs some of her children have composed, she has collected beautiful passages about the coming of Christ. Through the hours of the night and day, she will praise God in these songs, chants, and prayers, now preparing for the holy sacrifice of the Mass and prolonging the joy of the holy Sacrifice.

Before midnight, priests and monks gather in choiring God's praises in the office of Matins. If we cannot be present at this holy office, we can at least unite in spirit with those praying it. The prayers are strong in gladness and joy for the greatness of our Savior, who is come. "For unto us a Child is born, and unto us, a Son is given: and the government is upon his shoulder, and his name shall be called Wonderful, Counsellor, the Mighty God, the Everlasting Father, the Prince of Peace" (First Lesson).

All should rejoice. "Rejoice, O thou that art holy, thou drawest nearer to thy crown! Rejoice, O thou that art sinful, thy Savior offereth thee pardon" (Fourth Lesson). In this office, the Church reminds us of our great dignity as children of God and urges us to live in a manner becoming this dignity. "Learn, O Christian, how great thou art, who hast been made partaker of the divine nature" (2 Pet 1: 4) and "fall not again by corrupt conversation into the beggarly elements above which thou art lifted" (Sixth Lesson).

At the midnight Sacrifice, through the world, there arises the joyous song of the Introit, commemorating the eternal birth in heaven of the Son of God. In this Mass, we have in mind, especially the divinity of Christ, begotten of the Father from all eternity and equal to the Father in all things. Because our Redeemer is truly the Son of God, he united human nature with divine nature when He became man. Through Christ, we are united with God. In the Secret of this Mass, we pray that this mystery may be realized in us.

At the Offertory, we place the gifts we prepared during Advent on the altar, and we give ourselves again wholly to God. Then, at the words of Consecration, the bread and wine are changed entirely into the Body and Blood of our divine Savior. And we, whom the bread and wine represent, we, too, are changed.

Christ comes to us in holy Communion to perfect our union with Him and to give us strength that we may deserve "by worthy conversation to attain unto fellowship with him" (Postcommunion).

Immediately after the midnight Mass, the Church sings Lauds in praise of God. Then, at dawn, the little office of Prime is said, and the second Mass of Christmas is celebrated. Over and over in the prayers of the Mass, we ask that, through the mystery of the Son of God becoming man, we may share in His divinity and live now as children of God should.

In the third Mass, we have ever before our minds the divinity of our Savior, "begotten of the Father from all eternity," and we turn to Him with confidence that He will save us from our sins and unite us ever more closely with our heavenly Father.

Through Terce, Sext, None, and Vespers, the Church praises God and thanks Him for His infinite goodness in sending His divine Son to be our Redeemer, for "all the ends of the earth have seen the salvation of our God" (Responsory, Sext). The praises of men are united with the adoring songs of the angels. "This day the Christ is born: this day the Savior is appeared: this day the angels sing praise in the earth and the archangels rejoice: this day the righteous are glad and say: Glory to God in the highest. Alleluia" (Antiphon, Second Vespers). In her final evening prayers at the close of Christmas Day, the Church praises Christ, our Lord and Savior.

> Jesu, the Virgin-born, to Thee
> Eternal praise be given,
> With Father, Spirit, One and Three,
> Here as it is in heaven. Amen.
>
> (Hymn at Compline)

The Feast of the Holy Name of Jesus

"In the name of Jesus, let every knee bow, of those that are in heaven, on earth, and under the earth: and let every tongue confess that the Lord Jesus is in the glory of God the Father" (Introit). Thus, in today's liturgy, the Church honors the holy name of Jesus. Even the impious forces of hell, Heaven and earth acknowledge and praise His sacred name. The name of the Savior was decreed from all eternity. It is through the name of Jesus that we are to reach our salvation. In loving gratitude to our heavenly Father for giving us His only-begotten Son to be our Savior, we praise the most holy name of Jesus and acknowledge its power in all nations. "Save us, O Lord, our God! and gather us from among the nations: that we may give thanks to thy holy name, and may glory in thy praise" (Gradual).

St. Peter, when asked by what power he cured an infirm man, said to the Jews, "By the name of our Lord Jesus Christ of Nazareth, whom you crucified, . . . by him this man standeth before you whole" (Epistle). Therefore, in the name of the same Jesus Christ, we offer God a perfect tribute of praise, thanksgiving, reparation, and petition in the holy sacrifice of the Mass.

Through the power of the name of Jesus, we hope to have our names made truly immortal. In the Postcommunion, we pray that as God's grace is poured out upon us, "we may rejoice that our names are written in heaven, under the glorious name of Jesus, as a pledge of eternal predestination. Through the same Lord."

There will be numerous opportunities for each of us to honor the holy name of our Savior. At home, school, work, and recreation, we can show by our words and conduct the reverence we have for the name of Jesus. In honoring the Holy Name, we are observing God's second commandment and proving our love for our divine Savior, who bears the name Jesus. "I will glorify thy name forever; for thou, O Lord, art sweet and mild" (Offertory).

The Epiphany of Our Lord Jesus Christ

When the Son of God became man and was born of the Blessed Virgin Mary in a stable in Bethlehem, most of the Jews knew nothing of His birth. They paid no attention to the rumors that shepherds watching on the hillsides near Bethlehem had seen a vision of angels and heard their voices telling of the birth of the Savior in the city of David. Days passed, and men went about their business in Jerusalem without a thought that nearby, in a lowly stable, was the Child for whose coming all the patriarchs and prophets had longed. Priests and doctors in the temple and Herod in his palace had other thoughts in their minds than the coming of the Messiah.

Then one day, there came into Jerusalem a strange procession. Three wise men from different countries rode into the city on their camels. They sought King Herod and said, "Where is he that is born king of the Jews? For we have seen his star in the east and are come to adore him."

The words of the wise men troubled King Herod. What would it mean for him that another should be king of the Jews? His heart was hardened because of his evil life, and he thought only of his worldly concerns. So Herod immediately sent the chief priests and scribes to find out where the promised Messiah was to be born. "In Bethlehem of Juda," they answered him, "for so it is written by the prophet: And thou, Bethlehem, the land of Juda, art not the least among the princes of Juda; for out of thee shall come forth the ruler that shall rule my people Israel" (Gospel).

Hearing this word, the wise men joyfully went their way, following the star until it rested over the cave where the Child was. "And entering into the house, they found the child with Mary, his mother, and falling down they adored him. And opening their treasures, they offered him gifts: gold, frankincense, and myrrh" (Gospel).

By the grace of God, the wise men knew that Christ was God, and they adored Him. The divinity of Christ had been made known to peoples from the lands far to the east and to the people of Jerusalem. Christ had manifested Himself.

A few days ago, Jesus Christ came again to the world on Christmas Day. He came into the hearts of all those members of His kingdom who welcomed Him. It is fitting that He, the Son of God, should be made known to the world. Today He wills to manifest Himself not in the form of a babe born in Bethlehem but in His Mystical Body, the Church. He wills that in all His members, His divinity should appear, manifesting to the world that He who lives in His Mystical Body, the Church, is Christ, the eternal Son of the Most High God.

We can show Christ in our conduct only when we are united with Him in our lives. That is when we truly live in Him. The name Jesus means Savior, and the name Christ, the Anointed One, or the high priest. It is particularly in His supreme act as high priest – in the Sacrifice of the Cross that Jesus saves us. And it is through union with Christ in His Sacrifice that we are transformed into "other Christs" and receive the grace and strength to show Him forth in our daily lives.

On this feast of the Epiphany, and during the time after the Epiphany, we will try to know Christ better and make Him known to others so that they too may know and adore Him, truly God, as He is truly man.

Today, with the royal wise men of the East, we see Him in His epiphany, not as a leader of great power and majesty, but as a helpless babe wrapped in swaddling clothes and lying in a manger.

With the living faith of the holy Magi, the wise men, we adore this King of the universe. We, the Mystical Israel, acknowledge the divinity of Christ our King, and we cry out to Him in the liturgy of the Mass, "Lift up thy eyes round about and see: all these are gathered together: they are come to thee" (Epistle). We bless Him for His mercy. He is come to teach us the way to His eternal kingdom. We have not perhaps this world's wealth to offer Him as our tribute of honor, but we make a complete offering of ourselves that He may present us to His heavenly Father as co-victims with Him in the holy Sacrifice.

In a spirit of gratitude to God for the gift of His divine Son, who is come to be Himself our offering, we pray in the Secret of the Mass, "Graciously regard, O Lord, we beseech thee, the gifts of thy. Church: in which are offered now no longer gold, frankincense, and myrrh, but he whom those mystic offerings signified is immolated and received, even Jesus Christ thy Son our Lord."

The Feast of the Holy Family

Once, in Palestine, there lived a family that never dwelt upon this earth before or since. The head of this family was Joseph, a just man selected by God from among all men to be the foster father of His Son. The spouse of Joseph was Mary, the purest and most beautiful of all creatures, chosen from all eternity to be the Mother of "the Word made flesh,"; and the Son of Mary is the Son of the Most High God. So today, we celebrate the feast of the Holy Family, praising and thanking God for having shown us in the lives of Jesus, Mary, and Joseph the picture of perfect family life and begging Him to bless our homes and our families so that they, too, may be holy.

In the Introit of the Mass today, we rejoice with Mary and Joseph for their happiness in having been called to be the mother and the foster father of the Son of God. Then turning to Jesus, in the Collect, we ask Him for the grace to imitate the virtues of the Holy Family so that one day we may share their joy in heaven.

What does it mean to practice the virtues of the Holy Family, to live in our family a life that is pleasing to God? Jesus Christ, speaking to us in the Epistle through His Apostle St. Paul, tells us what we must do. He tells us of the charity which must rule all our words and actions. The virtues of the true Christian family are mercy, benignity, humility, modesty, and patience. Mercy and benignity will help us be good, generous, and kind to our fathers and mothers and brothers and sisters. Humility and modesty will teach us to let others have the first honors and the choice of pleasures and comforts; they will teach us to imitate Christ, who came not "to be ministered unto, but to minister" (Matt. 20: 28). Patience will help us to bear with others and to forgive them if they should injure us. "But above all these things," says St. Paul, "have charity, which is the bond of perfection."

The Gospel for today tells of the finding of the Child Jesus in the temple. "And he went down with them, came to Nazareth, and was subject to them... And Jesus advanced in wisdom, age, and grace with God and men." Jesus, obedient to Mary and Joseph, is the divine Exemplar whom we are to follow. Let us try by the generosity and wholeheartedness of our obedience to please Jesus and to grow more like Him.

As Jesus grew "in wisdom, and age, and grace with God and men," so must you. Perhaps you are now about the age of Jesus when He went down to Nazareth with Mary and Joseph. It is the will of God that each year, each month, and each day should see you becoming more Christ-like. Your conduct can be truly Christ-like only if you are united with Christ by grace and living His life. Join earnestly with Holy Church in the Postcommunion today. "Let us whom thou dost refresh by thy heavenly sacraments, O Lord, ever follow the example of thy holy Family; so that at the hour of our death thy glorious Virgin Mother and blessed Joseph may be near us, and we may be found worthy to be received by thee into eternal dwellings: Who livest and reignest."

The Second Sunday After the Epiphany

"Let all the earth adore thee and sing to thee, O God" (Introit). In His epiphany, Christ manifested Himself to the wise men as the Son of God. They knew that He was divine, and they worshiped Him. During the time after the Epiphany, the Church keeps before us, particularly the blessed truth that Christ is God. In the Gospel for today, we see Him performing His first miracle. When Jesus changes water into wine at the wedding feast of Cana, He proves that He has divine power over the things of earth. "All things were made by him: and without him was made nothing that was made" (John 1:3). Jesus Christ, born in poverty in the stable of Bethlehem, is the eternal Son of God, who rules heaven and earth. Today, Catholics join in the hymn of praise, "Let all the earth adore thee and sing to thee, O God."

Rarely in the Gospels do we see our Blessed Lady, and still more seldom do we hear her speak. Today St. John not only shows us the Blessed Virgin in all her graciousness, but he also records her very words. Amid the merrymaking and feasting in Cana, the Mother of Christ notices the scarcity of wine and, having spoken of it to her Son, goes to see that the bride and groom are spared all embarrassment. So did our Lady show the tenderness of her love for the children of men, her concern for their most minor cares. With the Blessed Virgin, love of neighbor was allied to love of God and zeal for His glory.

Mary said to the waiters, "Whatsoever he shall say to you, do ye." During the years at Nazareth, she had seen Him whom she knew to be the Lord of the universe, obeying her slightest wish and that of St. Joseph. There doubtless, she had often listened to His words about His heavenly Father, and she knew that the supreme purpose of her divine Son was to accomplish in all things the will of the Father. Therefore, "I came down from heaven, not to do my own will, but the will of him that sent me" (John 6:38). Our Mother would have all men share in the peace which comes from an entire submission of our will to the will of God; so she says to us today, "Whatsoever he shall say to you, do ye."

In the holy Mass today, let us place our will upon the altar, submitting it wholly to the will of God. The water that the priest mingles with the wine at the Offertory represents us, while the wine represents Jesus Christ. Let us beg of our Lord, who once changed water into wine, to grant that we may be wholly changed into Him. So may we "be made partakers of his divinity who has deigned to become a partaker of our humanity" (Offertory prayer).

The Third Sunday after the Epiphany

"Lord, I am not worthy that thou shouldst enter under my roof; but only say the word, and my servant shall be healed" (Gospel). Today we are a part of the multitude following Jesus as He comes down the mountain and enters the city of Capharnaum. Here we meet a centurion, grieving greatly because his servant "lieth at home sick of the palsy" (Gospel). At our Lord's assurance that He will come and heal him, the centurion pleads his unworthiness and strongly manifests his ardent faith in the divine power of Christ. The prayer of the centurion is the prayer of a respectful servant, humble but confident of His Master's mercy and power.

In the person of the centurion, we present ourselves at the holy Sacrifice. If he had reason to plead unworthiness, how much more have we when the Lord of heaven and earth comes to us at the Sacrifice Banquet! He is not merely our guest but our food and our life.

Filled with the thought of our unworthiness, we pray in the Collect, "Almighty and eternal God, graciously look upon our weakness: and stretch forth the right hand of thy majesty for our protection." Therefore, let us carefully heed God's instruction in the Epistle and Gospel.

Jesus Christ, true God and true man, is the Head of our race. He merited for us the grace of being made children of God, and He wills that we should live in charity toward all. In the Epistle for today, Christ tells us, through St. Paul, that we must do good to all, both friends and enemies. "To no man render evil for evil." The kingdom of Christ is the kingdom of peace. For the sake of Christ, we must love even those who seek to harm us; so we shall not be "overcome by evil, but (shall) overcome evil by good." Peace with our neighbor is the condition that God has placed for the acceptable offering of the holy Sacrifice. "If therefore thou offer thy gift at the altar, and there thou remember that thy brother hath anything against thee; Leave there thy offering before the altar, and go first to be reconciled to thy brother: and then coming thou shalt offer thy gift" (Matt. 5:23-24).

Let us pay our homage to Christ's divinity by giving up, for His love, every slightest feeling of ill will toward another. If someone has done us an injury, then in forgiving him from our heart, we can prove so much more our love for Christ. Aware of our need for forgiveness, let us cry out, "Lord, I am not worthy that thou shouldst enter under my roof; say but the word and my soul shall be healed."

The Fourth Sunday after the Epiphany

"Love, therefore, is the fulfilling of the law" (Epistle). Holy Church consoles us with the thought that love and the law are ones that we need but to possess true love of God and neighbor to fulfill the law. She would have us realize that to observe all the commandments is not an impossibility, as it may seem at times, but that despite our weakness, God's grace and love in our hearts will do what is impossible for us alone.

To help us understand better how God's divine power and strength can make us do what we could not hope to do alone, the Church presents a picture of the helpless disciples on a stormy sea, saved by their all-merciful and all-powerful Master. Like the disciples, many of us who are present at the holy sacrifice of the Mass today are amid a great tempest. Our souls may be grieved at the loss of temporal possessions, we may be unresigned to the death of a dear one, or numerous temptations may assault us. Yet, in all these trials, we seek consolation from our Savior in the Eucharistic Sacrifice. We are not fighting alone, for Christ is mindful of us and our necessities. In the holy Mass, we are made strong in Him. He may not return our lost wealth, restore life to the body of our beloved one, nor remove our temptations, but we experience, as did the disciples, a great calm.

Is there a storm in your soul? Hear our Lord say, "Why are you fearful, O ye of little faith?" (Gospel) Confidence in God will bring great peace to your soul.

Love of God was given to you in Baptism. Are you keeping it alive and strong, causing it to grow daily and thrive, or is it growing weak through lack of nourishment? If we love God, we will keep His commandments. Is your love for God outwardly active? Does it show itself in the love of our neighbor?

Place yourself and the trials and temptations that disturb you on the altar as an Offertory gift at holy Mass today. Unite your offering with the divine Victim so that it may be acceptable to our heavenly Father.

The Fifth Sunday after the Epiphany

The kingdom which Christ came to establish is His Church. From the Gospel for today, we learn something about this kingdom that we need to remember. Perhaps we have sometimes been surprised and even shocked to find any evil within the Church, to see Catholics whose lives were not all they should be. However, we need not be surprised at this condition, for Jesus Himself has told us in advance that it would be so.

Like the man in the Gospel, Jesus sows "good seed in his field." He sows in the hearts of His followers the seed of His truth and His own divine life. But meanwhile, the enemy-that is, the world, the flesh, and the devil sows the hearts of men the cockle of false teaching.

The cockle appears among the blades of wheat; it spoils the beauty of the field and perhaps even hinders the growth of the wheat.

The divine Sower permits both to flourish, however. "Suffer both to grow until the harvest." In the design of God, evil, too, has a purpose. It is permitted to exist to purify the good, for the virtue of good persons is tested and strengthened by opposition. The necessary separation will be made only at harvest time, at the Last Judgment. The goodwill then receives their reward, and the wicked, everlasting punishment.

Let us try to be good wheat in God's field, straight, strong, and beautiful. In the holy Mass and in the sacraments, we receive the life and energy we need to grow in Christ, unchanged by the cockle pressing about us.

How can we know whether Christ's seed is growing within us? "By their fruits, you shall know them" (Matt. 7:16). Our words, actions, and conduct will reveal and express our life. Indeed, we who have lived with our Lord ought to show to all with whom we come in contact the gentleness, the sympathetic understanding, and the great charity of Christ. Therefore, let it be said of each of us, as St. Peter once said, "Thou also wast with Jesus the Galilean ... for even thy speech doth discover thee" (Matt. 26: 69, 73).

The Sixth Sunday after the Epiphany

"The Lord hath reigned; let the earth rejoice" (Introit). Today, as for the past three Sundays, we children of God sing out these words of the Introit with joy. In the days of King David, when the enemy assailed God's Chosen People, God fought on the side of the Israelites, and they were, of course, victorious. "Sion heard and was glad: and the daughters of Juda rejoiced" (Introit). Looking back to the first Sunday of Advent, we know that through the coming of Christ, we have been strengthened and made victorious over the enemies of our souls. For whatever victories we have gained and all the graces of this Christmas Period, let us thank the Lord today.

In the Epistle, St. Paul tells of his gratitude to God for how the Thessalonians had turned from worshipping idols to serving the one true God. He looks upon these people as specially chosen by God, for the Holy Ghost worked great wonders in them, teaching them to see and love the word of Christ as taught by St. Paul. Indeed God has been infinitely generous in His graces to us. Therefore, we will offer the Eucharistic sacrifice today with a deep feeling of thanksgiving for God's graces. With confidence, let us ask that this oblation may "cleanse, renew, govern and protect us" so that we may be more pleasing to God.

As a member of Christ's Mystical Body, it is your privilege to draw freely from the fonts of grace and sacraments so that you may live in closer union with Christ. The more Christ-like you become, the greater your influence as an apostle of Christ will be. Good example always has more effect on the lives of others than numerous books, much talking, and hours of preaching. If your life is holy, you will unconsciously be an inspiration and example of good to others. Remember that it is the blessed obligation of every child of God to live to give glory to his heavenly Father.

Redemption Period

From the following outline, we can understand the principal divisions of the Easter, or Redemption, Period and the unique object or character of each division:

- **Septuagesima** (time of remote preparation): Via our relationship with the Redeemer, we come to understand our depravity and our need for atonement.

- **Lent** (time of near preparation). Atonement for sin through steadfast repentance in harmony with our Savior's atoning service.
- **Passiontide** (time of immediate preparation): Taking part in the conflict at Golgotha between the Prince of Life and the Prince of Death by working to fulfill Christ's passion.
- **Eastertide** (celebration): By conquering sin and living a renewed or enhanced life of grace, we can participate in the beautiful resurrection of Christ, His ascension, and the Holy Ghost's descent.
- **Pentecostal time** (prolongation): Participation in the life of the Church, the Mystical Body of Christ; personal sanctification. The Redemption is applied in the Church to the soul.

All the Mystical Body of Christ members bid farewell to the Alleluia, symbolic of the Christmas Season's delights, and turn their steps toward the mountainous routes that lead to Easter on the eve of Septuagesima during Vespers, the Church's solemn evening liturgy. Thousands of people are adjusting to their parts in this stage of life's theater, which is real life. Young people, maidens, and even small children are together with old men and women. They gather from all over the world and from all levels: kings and queens, businessmen and laborers, educators and students, bankers and beggars, clergymen of all orders, cardinals, bishops, and parish priests, with the Vicar of Christ on Earth serving as their leader. Everyone is taking their positions quietly since they are all actors in the exquisite mystery play of our redemption.

In this ongoing drama, we all have a part to play. There is also no practice. We start right away, on

Septuagesima, by adhering as closely as we can to the direction provided by the Holy Spirit, especially at Mass and other sacraments.

Septuagesima Sunday

"So run that you may obtain" (Epistle). The divine Householder, Jesus Christ, calls us to work in His vineyard today. His call is heard throughout the entire world and is addressed to all social classes. The significant task of raising us up to Himself, for which He took on human form, is about to start. He does not, however, labor on his own. He is generous and lavish with His graces, but in exchange for the reward of eternal life with Him, He asks for our collaboration, our readiness to suffer, to work, and perhaps even to die with Him.

Today, as Christ observes His vineyard – the hearts of Christians – He sees that some are oblivious to His call because they are preoccupied with their own interests. Others, given over to sensuality and self-indulgence, will not work when fasting and penance are required; still, others, following dreams of celebrity, have little time for spiritual matters.

But happily, many people are eager, hopeful, and joyful to be accepted as worthy of working and suffering alongside Him after rejoicing in His birth and the manifestations of His divinity. Therefore, they do not view Septuagesima as the beginning of a gloomy period. On the contrary, they look forward to Easter, knowing they will be united with Christ in His suffering, death, and beautiful resurrection. Therefore, they diligently get ready to work in the Master's vineyard.

How are we to carry out the tasks assigned to us by the Christian life itself? We learn from the Epistle of St. Paul. We must race to gain the prize, not lagging or following the herd with curiosity and indifference, but as joyful athletes dressed in the shining armor of self-denial and penance.

Take note of the holy Church's tender care on this day. She embodies the role of a mother with her kind, appropriate cautions. The joyous mysteries of our Savior's life have just been revealed to us by her. She now reminds us that there is work to be done, a race to run, and a battle to be won and that not every day can be a day of joy and feasting. The Lenten season will start in a few weeks. To get ready for the splendors of Eastertide, we must experience the painful mysteries of Christ's life. Our Mother wants us to enter the penitential season gradually, so she does not want us to do so abruptly during the Septuagesima season.

If you want to use the season of penance well, you must first ignite the desire to do so in your soul. Consider the current state of the church. Plan your actions so that you can sprint and win the prize. Have you made the most of the recent happy season? Have there ever been instances when you let worldly pleasures steal your spiritual joy? Ask our Lord to ignite virtuous desires in your soul when He visits you this week in Holy Communion.

Sexagesima Sunday

"Arise, O Lord, help us and deliver us" (Introit). The goal and significance of the Redemption are for man to reach up to God, which is an enormous task far beyond our limited abilities. Therefore, Christ continues His holy mission of reconciling man to God while living in the Church as the Redeemer. Each year, He calls all the members of His Mystical Body to join Him in His penance and suffering so that they, too, may share in His triumphant resurrection and ascension into heaven.

The Church issues a second, emphatic exhortation to penance today. In the Epistle, St. Paul describes the labors he underwent, the lofty graces he received, and the challenging tribulations he faced. It takes supernatural power to defeat the forces of evil and advance the kingdom of Christ within the soul. God promises that this will not be lacking. "My grace is sufficient for thee: power is made perfect in infirmity (Epistle). And we have a lot of infirmities. We lay our weaknesses on the altar of sacrifice in faith that God would strengthen us for His glory and work in us.

The primary time for sowing in the Christian calendar is Lent. We need to cultivate the soil of our hearts to make room for the grace seed, just as we would in the vineyard. It is necessary to remove all of the pebbles and stones. The seed of God's word must be fostered by the light of God's grace and our genuine, earnest efforts if it is to bear fruit a hundredfold, just as the seed needs sunlight and moisture for its growth. When the Sower Himself visits us, we will recommit ourselves to His love and service. We shall attend the Sacrifice Banquet with vigor and purpose, resolved to purify. We will move forward with strength in Him who says, "My grace is sufficient for thee," assisted by His divine power and grace which He instills in us.

So, all that is left is for each of us to work with God's grace. You must apply the benefits of the Redemption to yourself if you want to benefit from it. Make it a goal to live each day more fully in the spirit of the Church since doing so will enable you to experience the work of the Redemption in yourself. The Redemption's work is still being done for you this year. Do you approach this season with zeal and resolution, determined to strengthen and purify your spirit? Ask God for help earnestly, keeping in mind that you cannot succeed alone. Every day, minor flaws almost imperceptibly enter into our work. If we do not regularly evaluate our actions in light of God's significant Sacrifice for us, selfish tendencies will continue undetected and unrepaired. Participating regularly in holy Mass will provide us with a wealth of assistance and power if we are sincere in our pursuit of holiness. Consider what in your life needs to be fixed before starting your Lenten preparations.

Quinquagesima Sunday

"Now there remain faith, hope, charity, these three; but the greatest of these is charity" (Epistle). The Church wants to ensure we understand how vital charity is before we begin the holy season of Lent because without it, no matter how many penances we complete, they will be for nothing. St. Paul writes in today's Epistle, "If I should distribute all my goods to feed the poor, and if I should deliver my body to be burned, and have not charity, it profiteth me nothing." Our love for God is inversely correlated with the merit of our good deeds.

The Church wants us to understand that today, no amount of penance or sacrifice will be of any use to us if we lack the virtue of charity, which St. Paul refers to as the "queen of virtues." The other virtues are the outgrowth of charity. Since faith and hope will not be present in heaven, charity is called "the greatest of them." There will be no need for faith because we can see it, and hope will be unnecessary because all of our desires will be fulfilled. But charity will endure and be perfected.

"Charity envieth not, is not provoked to anger, thinketh no evil, beareth all things, endureth all things." These are some of the requirements of charity that St. Paul sets forth before us. We conclude that the perfect application of the law of charity will result in our perfection as Christians.

But how do we know we are charitable? Maybe our love for God is not as rational as our love for our parents. "If you love me, keep my commandments," our

Lord Himself has commanded (John 14:15). Herein lies the test. The first three commandments are directed at God, while the rest are directed at our neighbor. As a result, "if any man says, I love God, and hateth his brother; he is a liar." (1 John 4:20).

Do we pray and resist when tempted because we do not want to disobey God's laws? Finally, there is charity. We have charity if we sin due to weakness, but we are remorseful and vow not to do so again. By loving and being patient with our neighbor, we will undoubtedly please God if we constantly seek to obey His will. In the same way, God loves us; He created and redeemed him. Offer the Eucharistic sacrifice frequently during Lent to experience the lovely connection of charity that binds you to Christ and your friend in Christ.

Our preparation for Lent is complete as of this day. Keep in mind that the effectiveness of our penances and works depends on the extent of our charity. On the last Sunday before Lent, Christ invites us to go to Jerusalem with Him. He says, "All things shall be accomplished which were written by the prophets concerning the Son of man, for he shall be delivered to the Gentiles, and shall be mocked, and scourged, and spit upon; and after they have scourged him, they will put him to death; and the third day he shall rise again" (Gospel). We must pray for clarity to understand and charity to endure when faced with the mystery of suffering. Let us plead, "Lord, that I may see," just like the blind man in the Gospel.

We must resist feeling scared or depressed due to this program of suffering and atonement. If it does, our repentance is not motivated by kindness or God's love. In the Tract today, we join King David in saying: "Sing joyfully to God all the earth; serve ye the Lord with gladness. ... He made us, and not we, but we are his people and the sheep of his pasture." We can only hope for the grace to be abundant and joyful in our Lenten penances if we regularly unite with Christ in His Sacrifice. In the Postcommunion, it is clear where to look for the power and light needed to triumph. "We beseech thee, almighty God, that we who have received this heavenly food may by it be safeguarded from all adversities."

Ash Wednesday

"Blow the trumpet in Sion, sanctify a fast" (Epistle). The mystical Christ, the Church, begins a forty-day fast from the world and its pleasures to renew God's kindness for the entire world. She also continues the great redeeming task. Millions of men and women join together in confessing their sins, making amends, and pleading for forgiveness as they humble themselves before the omnipotent majesty of God. The Lenten fasts and prayers aim to enhance the soul's life and purge it of previous sin.

So that Christ may reign supreme in the soul, a determined struggle must be fought against the world, the flesh, and the devil. However, this enormous effort cannot be accomplished solely through corporeal penance; spiritual discipline must also be practiced in addition to physical fasts. The prophet Joel encourages us in the lesson to experience deep inner anguish that manifests as fasting. In the Gospel, Christ promises this reward, "But thou, when thou fastest, anoint thy head and wash thy face, that thou appear not to men to fast, but to thy Father who is in secret: and thy Father who seeth in secret will repay thee."

The First Sunday in Lent

"He shall call upon me, and I will hear him" (Introit). Loud and clear is the cry to arms over the face of the earth. Loyal members of the King's army, we march to war, eager for service, alive with the hope of victory.

Away with pleasure and self-seeking in our lives. On to battle, to days of fasting, self-restraint, and penance. God's angels and saints are accompanying the mighty army, offering protection from the cunning snares of the enemy. The personal fear of each individual is swept aside in the might and courage of the King who leads, a noble Leader who asks of His subjects no test of fidelity which He has not endured. "He shall call upon me and I will hear him: I am with him in tribulation (Tract).

In company with our Leader, we learn that our first duty is resisting temptations. Satan will suggest that our Lenten practices are too arduous, that our health cannot stand the strain, that we are foolish to deprive ourselves of legitimate pleasures, that our companions will laugh at us, and that we have not the courage to persevere. But in all these temptations, we trust Him who conquered that we might conquer. "The Lord will overshadow thee with his shoulders and under his wings, thou shalt trust" (Offertory).

We must wage constant and relentless warfare against Satan to gain eternal life. Alone we are helpless, but if we enroll ourselves in the army of Christ, with Him as our Leader, we need have no fear. The holy season of Lent is intended to make us capable of fighting courageously for Christ. Armed with penance and mortification, we will fearlessly open a battle against the powers of darkness. Jesus promises always to be near to give an encouraging word, a helping hand, protection, and final triumph.

Resolve today on a definite act of self-denial which you will practice this week. Then, in the holy Mass, ask for special help to be faithful in keeping your resolution so that you may wage a successful battle against the evil spirit.

The Second Sunday in Lent

"Let it not be vain for you to rise up early, before the light: for the Lord hath promised a crown to them that watch" (Invitatory, Matins). A week of Lenten penance is over, and we need to renew our courage today so we may enter vigorously upon the second week of Lent. However, our nature rebels against penance, and we beg God in today's Collect "to keep us, both within and without; that we may be protected in the body from all adversity, and made pure in mind from every evil thought."

Lent is a time not only of atoning for our sins through penance but also of extraordinary efforts to live a genuinely Christian life. In the Epistle, St. Paul exhorts us to a life of sanctity. "We pray and beseech you in the Lord Jesus that as you have received of us how you ought to walk and to please God, so also you would walk."

The life to which Christ calls us in Baptism and He wishes us to live with special intensity during Lent is not easy or comfortable. It is a life of vigorous striving against the world, the flesh, and the devil. It is a life of renunciation of the devil with all his works and pomps. But it is more than a renouncement of evil. It is a strong embracing of good. It is a relentless, persistent devotion to Christ. To encourage us, Christ sometimes reveals Himself to us so that we may see more of the infinite beauty and majesty of Him whom we love. In the Gospel today, we read of the transfiguration of Christ. Peter, James, and John, who were later to behold Jesus in His dreadful agony, now see Him transfigured in glory and hear a voice out of the cloud saying, "This is my beloved Son, in whom I am well pleased: hear ye him." Overwhelmed with the vision of Christ transfigured, St. Peter cried out, "Lord, it is good for us to be here" (Gospel). And it is good for us to be at the holy Sacrifice, in which God is glorified, and we are transfigured through Christ our Lord.

By offering ourselves in union with the divine Victim of the cross, we shall be lifted up and drawn to God. In return, Christ will give us His most sacred Body and Blood to nourish us and strengthen our union with Him in this life. In this way, we shall be transformed into Christ-we shall share in the transfiguration of Christ. And when we appear before our Father in judgment, He will see His own divine image in us. He will show us the commendation, "This is my beloved son, in whom I am well pleased."

Through Baptism, we first became sons of God. If we have lost the right of sonship through sin, we must regain it with a sincere confession and a solid resolve to live better. Today's liturgy urges us to strive, particularly for the virtue of purity, if we would be like God. How guarded are you in your thoughts? In your choice of magazine stories and present-day books? In the movies you attend? How will the recollection of your baptism and the fact that you are a member of Christ's Mystical Body help you to respect your body and to preserve purity? Of what value is bodily mortification? Partake frequently of the Bread of Life that "maketh virgins and martyrs."

The Third Sunday in Lent

"My eyes are towards the Lord, for he shall pluck my feet out of the snare; look thou upon me, and have mercy on me, for I am alone and poor" (Introit). This cry of the holy Church voices the spirit of Lent. Many dangers encompass us. Satan, endeavoring to keep his court, is alarmed and angered at his losses during the penitential season. He comes to the battle with reinforcements (Gospel), and our only hope is to keep our eyes on the Lord. "To Thee, O Lord, have I lifted up my soul: in Thee, O my God, I put my trust" (Introit). Today's Gospel scene strengthens our hope: Jesus casts out a devil from a seemingly helpless individual, for the "same was dumb" and could not even ask for help.

Christ not only freed Satan's poor victim, but when the multitudes wondered, and the Pharisees scoffed and committed the frightful blasphemy of calling Christ the prince of devils, He also openly professed His divinity. Moreover, he made clear that it is only the God-Man who, in His name, can cast out devils. Why then need we fear, for do we not daily ask and expect all help through our Lord Jesus Christ?

Trusting in the divine strength, we dare not only do penance for our past sins but also turn today with fresh vigor to living a genuinely Christian life, a "putting on of Jesus Christ." In the Epistle, St. Paul urges us to do this very thing. "Brethren: be ye followers of God as most dear children." Not only in the shunning of evil does the Christian life consist, but also in a vigorous reaching out toward good. "Walk then as children of the light; for the fruit of the light is in all goodness, and justice, and truth" (Epistle).

This theme of a positive serving of God appears in the Gospel also. "He that is not with me is against me, and he that gathereth not with me scattereth. Blessed are they who hear the word of God, and keep it."

The Offertory and Communion verses express the joy to be found in the service of God. For the positive pursuit of holiness, as for works of penance, the source of our strength is in God. So, we pray with the Church, "We beseech thee, almighty God, look upon the desires of thy lowly servants: and stretch forth the right hand of thy majesty to be our defense" (Collect). "May this Victim, O Lord, we beseech thee, cleanse us from our sins, and sanctify the bodies and minds of thy servants for the celebration of this Sacrifice. Through our Lord Jesus Christ, who livest and reignest with thee in the unity of the Holy Ghost, God, world without end. Amen" (Secret).

On the first Sunday of Lent, you enrolled yourself under the standard of the King of Justice. As this season of prayer and penance advances, the powers of Satan become more bitter against our Leader, and his attacks on you may become more personal and frequent. Therefore, be always on your guard and watch your senses closely. Try to unite yourself more closely with our Savior in the holy sacrifice of the Mass today, for you will be victorious through Him. Christ, Himself tells us that Satan's workers are so crafty and powerful that without the help of God, it would be impossible for us to resist.

The Fourth Sunday in Lent, or Laetare Sunday

"Rejoice, O Jerusalem, and come together, all you that love her; rejoice with joy, you that have been in sorrow" (Introit). The joy the Church would have us feel today is the reward of the struggle and labors of the weeks of penance. Already we participate with Christ in the liberty of a victor. "We are not children of the bondwoman, but of the free; by the freedom wherewith Christ hath made us free" (Epistle). In the Gospel, Christ shows us the multitude sustained by the miraculous bread. In the Eucharistic Bread lies our strength in weariness.

Our blessed Lord looks upon us who, like the multitudes on the mountainside, have come to Him. He sees us feeding upon the love of self, love of ambition. He sees us trying to stifle the hunger for the supernatural life by empty and vain pleasures and amusements. He sees us also in our better moments when, cooperating with His grace, we try to live as He would have us. He knows we are hungry for the Bread of Life, His life, and His love. And Jesus, in His priests, takes the bread and, giving thanks to almighty God, says to us: "Take ye, and eat. This is my body" (Matt. 26:26).

The Church, in her liturgy, wishes to fill you with gladness so that you may courageously continue your preparation for Easter. You have reason to rejoice if you have kept Lent in the spirit of the Church. Holy Communion will give you the strength to persevere in your good resolutions during the remaining days of Lent. Do you make your sacrifices more pleasing by offering them union with Christ during the Mass? Have you any cause to rejoice for how you have spent the first half of Lent? During the holy Mass today, place yourself in spirit with the Apostles at the Last Supper and ask them to obtain a greater love for holy Communion.

Passiontide

> Forth comes the Standard of the King:
> All hail, thou Mystery ador'd!
> Hail, Cross! on which the Life Himself
> Died, and by death our life restor'd.
> (Vexilla Regis)

Christ encourages all His followers to share in His suffering during His holy passion and death on the Sunday before Lent. "Behold, we go up to Jerusalem, and all things shall be accomplished which were written by the prophets concerning the Son of man. For he shall be delivered to the Gentiles, and shall be mocked, and scourged, and spit upon: and after they have scourged him, they will put him to death, and the third day he shall rise again" (Gospel, Quinquagesima). We have tried to better our lives during Lent and prepare ourselves for this oneness with Jesus Christ in His sufferings.

We are aware that some saints have had the grace to share in Christ's suffering to the extent that they have suffered the five wounds in their hands, feet, and sides; other saints have endured the anguish of the crowning with thorns. These remarkable graces are destined for a select few; God does not intend for everyone to go through these difficulties.

All Christians are welcome to participate in a sharing of Christ's passion, nevertheless. The divine mysteries of our redemption are repeated during these Passiontide days, especially during Holy Week. However, the Christ who now suffers, dies, and then rises again is the Mystical Christ, Christ in all of His members. The degree to which we live in solidarity with Christ in His Church by the spirit of the Church for each day is the degree to which we partake in His restoration of the sacred mysteries.

Because we know that Christ is the magnificent Victor over sin and death, we experience triumph and victory even in our sufferings alongside Him. He enables us to find victory in Him.

> Salvation's spring, blest Trinity,
> Be praise to Thee through earth and skies:
> Thou through the Cross the victory
> Dost give; oh, also give the prize!
> (Vexilla Regis)

Passion Sunday

> Hail, Cross! thou only hope of man,
> Hail on this holy Passion-day!
> (Hymn, Second Vespers)

Death entered the world due to man's sin, and man himself shut the doors to endless life. However, He, who is Life itself, underwent death after becoming a man, bringing life back to the human race. Today, the Church, the mystic Christ, begins the season of Passiontide, during which the agony and death of the Messiah are remembered and reenacted.

The Church expresses her sorrow for Christ's suffering by omitting the *Gloria Patri* from the psalms *Judica me* and *Lavabo*, shrouding the statues of the saints and the chant used. The liturgy for this day inspires sadness but not despair because it all carries a theme of impending victory.

In the Introit, we pray with King David, "From the unjust and deceitful man deliver me, for thou art my God and my strength." We place our confidence in God that He will bless our efforts at self-conquest.

Under the Old Law, the high priest would enter the Holy of Holies once a year and sprinkle the blood of the goat offered as atonement for the sins of the people (Lev. 16). In the New Law, Christ Himself, our divine High Priest, "by his own blood entered once into the holies, having obtained eternal redemption" (Epistle).

Let us enter this year's Passiontide season bravely and tenderly, firm in our faith in the infinite holiness and strength of Christ, our High Priest. By reflecting on it and remaining steadfast in your Lenten penances, ask God for a correct understanding of Christ's suffering and the grace to share in it to the extent you can.

We can only learn to live in Christ by dying to ourselves first. We only genuinely have life to the extent that we link with Christ. Let us mortify ourselves via the Lenten penances so we can rise to life with Christ through the death of self. Let us be aware that seeking oneness with Christ requires self-denial and sacrifice rather than self-indulgence and pleasure. Are we becoming more capable of resisting the need to pamper ourselves? How do we respond to other people's requests? How can we deal with the difficulties and sorrow that life brings us? In the holy Sacrifice, you offer yourself daily as a victim in conjunction with Christ Himself. In the holy Communion, you beseech Him to teach you to die to yourself and live for Him alone.

The Seven Sorrows of Our Blessed Lady

"O all ye that pass by the way, attend and see if there be any sorrow like to my sorrow" (Tract). Holy Church, in her liturgy on Friday in Passion Week, compassionates our Blessed Lady in her suffering. Let us, her children, meditate upon her seven sorrows.

- **The prophecy of holy Simeon.** "Simeon blessed them, and said to Mary his mother: Behold, this child is set for the fall, and for the resurrection of many in Israel, and for a sign that shall be contradicted; and thy own soul a sword shall pierce, that, out of many hearts, thoughts may be revealed" (Luke 2:34-35).

- **The flight into Egypt.** "Behold an angel of the Lord appeared in sleep to Joseph, saying: Arise, and take the child and his mother, and fly into Egypt: and be there until I shall tell thee. For it will come to pass that Herod will seek the child to destroy him" (Matt. 2:13).

- **The loss of Jesus in the temple.** "They came a day's journey, and sought him among their kinsfolks and acquaintance. And not finding him, they returned into Jerusalem, seeking him" (Luke 2:44-45).

- **The meeting of Jesus carrying the cross.** "'And bearing his own cross, he went forth to that place which is called Calvary" (John 19:17).

- **The death of Jesus.** "There stood by the cross of Jesus, his mother... Jesus ... said: It is consummated. And bowing his head, he gave up the ghost" (John 19:25, 30).

- **Taking her dead Son down from the cross.** "When it was evening, there came a certain rich man of Arimathea, named Joseph. ... He went to Pilate and asked for the body of Jesus. Then Pilate commanded that the body should be delivered. And Joseph taking the body wrapped it up in a clean linen cloth" (Matt. 27:57-59).

- **The burial of Jesus.** "Now there was in the place where he was crucified, a garden; and in the garden, a new sepulcher, wherein no man yet had been laid. There ... they laid Jesus" (John 19:41-42).

Let us focus on Mary's sufferings during the death of her heavenly Son today. She was supposed to participate in saving our souls from the beginning of time. The curse pronounced on the serpent, "She shall crush thy head, and thou shalt lie in wait for her heel" (Gen. 3:15), was about to be fulfilled. The prophecy of Simeon, "Thy own soul a sword shall pierce," was soon to be realized. Show compassion for your mother, whose soul is broken by the inhumane suffering inflicted upon her cherished Son. Join your struggles, hardships, and sorrows with hers so that they will be more appealing to your Redeemer. Think about your mother's pain and love as she accepted the mutilated body of Jesus from Joseph of Arimathea. What appropriate way can you offer today to honor Mary, the Mother of Sorrows, and your Mother?

"Thou art sorrowful and worthy of tears, O Virgin Mary, standing near the cross of the Lord Jesus, thy Son, the Redeemer" (Gradual).

Palm Sunday

Glory and praise to Thee, Redeemer blest!
To whom their glad hosannas children poured.
Hail, Israel's King, hail! David's son confessed!
Who comest in the name of Israel's Lord.

(Gloria, Laus)

To complete that magnificent triumphant parade of our King into Jerusalem, we, the members of Christ's Mystical Body, join the Hebrew youth today. Undoubtedly, our Savior was joined by a diverse crowd as He made His regal entrance into the city of David. So, likewise, the Apostles and Christ's followers were surrounded by the vast crowd, including Hebrew children and women waving palm branches, travelers, merchants, priests, Pharisees, scribes, and ancients.

Some people might have just been in awe of Christ's might, while others genuinely believed He was the Messiah and exalted Him. The Pharisees may have been present out of concern for losing the honor that generally goes along with such celebrations. Many others simply participated in this notable parade since they were followers. They agreed with the majority; therefore, they joined the crowd against Christ not too many days later. These followers joined the armies of God one day, then joined the armies of Lucifer the next.

We will enter Sion today in triumphant procession with Christ. Because of the sincerity of our praise, love, and honor, we will resemble some of the Jews of His time. He is our King and will destroy the influence of the dark prince within our souls. Shall we be like the unfaithful Jews? Shall we today sing, "Hosanna to the Son of David," and tomorrow cry, "Crucify Him! Crucify him"? Our faith will compel us to follow Him in all of His suffering until we reach the heights of Golgotha as knights of His royal guard. We will declare His victory over the world and sin there beside Him.

Thee their poor homage pleased, O gracious King!
Ours too accept the best that we can bring.

(Gloria, Laus)

The Hebrew children praised and honored God, which pleased Him. At the holy Mass, offer oneself as a sacrifice. Your plans for mortification during Holy Week should be brought as presents. Offer your oblation during the Consecration in connection with the priceless Body and Blood of Jesus so that God may accept it. Ask for the grace to be true to Him and to join heart and soul in the spirit of the Church during these days of sadness and mourning when Jesus Christ, King of kings, comes to you in Holy Communion to be your nourishment and strength.

Holy Thursday

"For as often as ye eat this Bread and drink this Cup, ye do show the Lord's death till He comes" *(Matins)*.

"And the day of the unleavened bread came, on which it was necessary that the pasch should be killed. And he sent Peter and John, saying: Go, and prepare for us the pasch, that we may eat. But they said: Where wilt thou that we prepare? And he said to them: Behold, as you go into the city, there shall meet you a man carrying a pitcher of water: follow him into the house where he entereth in. And you shall say to the good man of the house: The master saith to thee, Where is the guest chamber, where I may eat the pasch with my disciples? And he will show you a large dining room, furnished; and there prepare."

"And they going, found as he said to them, and made ready the pasch. And when the hour had come, he sat down, and the twelve apostles with him. And he said to them: With desire, I have desired to eat this pasch with you before I suffer. For I say to you, that from this time I will not eat it, till it is fulfilled in the kingdom of God."

71

Good Friday

> O holy God, O holy strong One,
> O holy immortal One, have mercy upon us.
> (Adoration of the Cross)

"And they took Jesus and led him forth. And bearing his own cross, he went forth to that place which is called Calvary, but in Hebrew Golgotha, where they crucified him, and with him two others, one on each side, and Jesus in the midst. ... The soldiers, therefore, when they had crucified him, took his garments and they made four parts, to every soldier a part) and also his coat. Now the coat was without seam, woven from the top throughout. They said then one to another: Let us not cut it, but let us cast lots for it, whose it shall be; that the scripture might be fulfilled, saying: They have parted my garments among them, and upon my vesture, they have cast lots. And the soldiers indeed did these things."

"Now there stood by the cross of Jesus his mother, and his mother's sister, Mary of Cleophas, and Mary Magdalen. When Jesus, therefore, had seen his mother and the disciple standing whom he loved, he saith to his mother: Woman, behold thy son. After that, he saith to the disciple: Behold thy mother. And from that hour, the disciple took her to his own. Afterward, Jesus knowing that all things were accomplished, that the scripture might be fulfilled, said: I thirst. Now there was a vessel set there full of vinegar. And they, putting a sponge full of vinegar about hyssop, put it to his mouth. Jesus therefore, when he had taken the vinegar, said: It is consummated. And bowing his head, he gave up the ghost" (Gospel).

"Greater love than this no man hath, that a man lay down his life for his friends" (John 15:13). This Christ did for each of us personally, and He would have done so had there been no other souls than ours to be redeemed. He asks us, in turn, to take the cross for our standard.

Whether we will or not, crosses will enter our lives. If we carry them unwillingly, the burden will become heavier; if we accept them as coming from God, they will not only become lighter but will also be the means of our being united more closely with Christ that we "may have life, and may have it more abundantly" (John 10:10).

Holy Saturday

"He is not here, for he is risen, as he said" (Gospel). We should keep in mind that in the early days of the Church, the services that we now observe on Holy Saturday actually took place on Saturday night and lasted until dawn on Sunday morning and that they were specially tailored to the baptism of the catechumens who were to be admitted into the Church. This will help us to get into the spirit of today's service. It was customary to spend this Saturday in fasting, prayer, and spiritual vigilance at the tomb of our Lord until Easter morning.

The blessings and the Mass make up today's two portions of the liturgy. The former involves blessing the fresh flame lit by a flint at the church's entryway. Next, the Easter candle, the triple candle, and all the lamps and candles in the church are lit from this fire. The reading of the Twelve Prophecies, which the Church intended to serve as guidance for the catechumens who were to be baptized this evening, comes after the blessing of the Easter candle. Finally, the Litany of the Saints is sung while the baptismal font is blessed.

The joyful Easter celebration then begins after the Mass. The altar is decorated with flowers, the statues' violet coverings are removed, the priest is dressed in white, the Gloria is sung, and the bells ring out once more to announce the Lord's resurrection. The Church cries out repeatedly, "Alleluia, alleluia," to her risen Lord.

Even if your tasks might take longer than usual today, you should try to remain remarkably tranquil. Join the Mystical Body as a whole in anticipating the joyful resurrection of its Head, Christ. By receiving a thorough purification from sin in the Sacrament of Penance, you can prepare your heart to partake generously in the promises of the risen Savior. Your genuine and joyous involvement in our risen Savior's victory will be symbolized for you on Easter morning.

Easter Sunday

"I arose, and am still with thee, alleluia" (Introit). Christ is risen in triumph. Christ, the spotless Victim, has conquered death and is risen as He said. Behold Christ Jesus coming forth from the tomb in His glorified humanity! Hear the song of joy and gladness with which the Church greets our risen Christ, our triumphant High Priest.

"Christ, my hope, is risen" (Sequence). "This is the day which the Lord hath made. Let us rejoice and be glad in it" (Gradual). "Christ rising again from the dead, dieth now no more, death shall no more have dominion over him" (Rom. 6:9). Life has conquered death, heaven has conquered hell, Christ the King reigns supreme.

> In this great triumph death and life
> Together met in wondrous strife,
> The Prince of Life, once dead, doth reign.
> (Sequence)

We are one with Christ; His resurrection is our resurrection; His joy, our joy; His triumph, our triumph.

> Christ; innocent and undefiled,
> Sinners to God hath reconciled
> (Sequence)

The holy women brought the news of the resurrection to the world. Out of love for the Master, they went to the tomb to anoint His sacred Body with sweet spices. The angel of God was there to comfort and console them, and it was from him they heard the glad tidings which they later proclaimed to all they met, "He is risen, he is not here" (Gospel).

The Church in the Epistle for today shows us how to celebrate this feast of the Resurrection. "Purge out the old leaven, that you may be a new paste." Let us enjoy this feast "not with the old leaven, nor with the leaven of malice and wickedness; but with the unleavened bread of sincerity and truth." Let us leave our past sinful ways as Christ left the tomb and let us become a new paste so that Christ our Master may work in our souls through grace.

From what particular faults of your past life have you resolved to turn away? What evil tendency is holding you back from perfect union with Christ? Strive to live a new life that you may share in the eternal resurrection. "As Christ is risen from the dead by the glory of the Father, so we also may walk in newness of life" (Rom. 6:4).

Eastertide

The days after the Resurrection were wonderful for the Apostles and disciples of Christ, and they are always glorious days for all who are united with Christ in His Mystical Body. Let us consider first the joy of the Apostles and followers of our Lord.

Their divine Master, whom they had seen suffering and humiliated, even to the death of the cross, had shown that sufferings and death had no power over Him, for He had risen in glory from the tomb. His five sacred wounds were the glorious scars of a mighty victory. The Apostles knew that He whom they loved and followed was the very Son of God, infinite in power and majesty.

And Jesus Christ, triumphant over sin and death, loved His own with infinitely tender love. He was with them often during the forty days before His ascension, conversing with them, eating with them, and filling their hearts with love for Him.

"Was not our heart burning within us, whilst he spoke in the way, and opened to us the scriptures?" So exclaimed the happy disciples to whom our Lord appeared as they went on their way to Emmaus.

"It is the Lord," John cried out for joy when he and the others in the ship saw a Man standing at dawn on the shore of the sea of Tiberias and heard Him say, "Children, have you nothing to eat?" And the impetuous Peter, impatient of the slowness of the boat, leaped into the sea that he might come sooner to Jesus.

"My Lord and my God" was Thomas' strong act of faith as he beheld for the first time the risen Christ.

Blessed as these Apostles and disciples were with the vision of Christ triumphant, they were no more privileged than we. "Blessed are they that have not seen and have believed," was our Lord's gentle rebuke to the doubting Thomas. Jesus Christ, risen from the dead, thought not only of those whose happy lot it was to be with Him in Palestine but also of all other men and women, of all places and in all times. Christ had accomplished the work of man's redemption by His sufferings, death, and glorious resurrection. Once more, man could enjoy the union with God that our first parents experienced. The moment of Christ's triumph was when the world had been waiting since God had promised Adam and Eve that He would send a Redeemer. Never in all time could there be another such Victor.

During the days of Eastertide, Christ in His Church often reminds His members of the triumph in which they share. "The Lord hath brought you into a land flowing with milk and honey, alleluia," the Church sings in the Introit on Easter Monday. We think of the gladness the Israelites, after years of wandering in the desert, came to the land God had promised to Abraham, Isaac, and Jacob at length. At our baptism, we were brought into the blessed land of promise, wherein we enjoy the liberty of the children of God. Our Elder Brother has purchased this land for us with His precious Blood, and He is our victorious Leader. United with Him, we need not fear the power of any enemy, for He is the strong and mighty Lord.

"If you be risen with Christ, seek the things that are above, where Christ is sitting at the right hand of God, alleluia; mind the things that are above, alleluia." This is the word of the holy Church to us in the Communion verse of the Mass for Easter Tuesday. The Mystical Body of Christ has grown through the renewal of our redemption mysteries this year. And now it must continue to grow. This is the concern of each member. It is for each of us who have shared in the mystery of Christ's glorious resurrection to prove by our lives that we are united with Him.

As the Apostles and disciples were filled with joy at the resurrection of Christ, so we rejoice, too, and we look ahead to the joys of eternal life with Christ. The theme of the Mass on Easter Wednesday is joy. "Sing ye to the Lord a new canticle; sing to the Lord all the earth" (Introit). In the Gospel for today, St. John tells us of the morning when, wearied from their night's fishing, the disciples came to the shore to find that Jesus had prepared breakfast for them. "As soon then as they came to land, they saw hot coals lying, and a fish laid thereon, and bread." Every morning Jesus invites us to break our fast with the Bread which will sustain us through the day and life. In the Postcommunion for today, we ask God that we may experience the effects of holy Communion by being more completely transformed into Christ. "May we be cleansed, O Lord, we beseech thee, from our old nature, and may the reverent reception of thy sacrament make of us a new creature" (Postcommunion).

Loyal disciples of Christ, we long to see His kingdom extended to include all peoples. In the Collect for Easter Thursday, we ask that the baptized of all nations may "be one by faith in their minds and by love in their good deeds." So may it be said of us, as God's Chosen People of old, "They praised with one accord thy victorious hand, O Lord, alleluia" (Introit).

"And behold I am with you all days, even to the consummation of the world" (Gospel, Easter Friday). Living nearly two thousand years after Christ spoke these words to His Apostles, we are experiencing their fulfillment. He "who died once for our sins, the just for the unjust, that he might offer us to God" (Epistle), renews His Sacrifice daily and offers us to His heavenly Father with Him. Living in the Church, He acts through her sacred liturgy, praising and glorifying His Father and sanctifying the souls of men.

On Easter Saturday, St. Peter speaks to us as he did to the early Christians, urging us to put all malice and envy out of our lives and seek only our divine Savior. "If so be," St. Peter says, "you have tasted that the Lord is sweet." And he reminds us that, united with Christ in Baptism, we share in His priesthood and can "offer spiritual sacrifice acceptable to God by Jesus Christ" (Epistle). The offering we bring to the altar in the holy sacrifice of the Mass, where united with the priest, we offer ourselves with Jesus Christ to our heavenly Father. In the Communion verse today, St. Paul reminds us that we who have been made sharers in the life of Christ must show Him forth in our daily life. "All ye who have been baptized in Christ, have put on Christ, alleluia."

Low Sunday

"Put ye on the Lord Jesus Christ" (Rom. 13:14). The first Sunday after Easter is sometimes called Low Sunday, as it marks the closing of the Easter octave, which opened with such splendor. It is also sometimes called White Sunday, for in the early days of the Church, on this Sunday, the newly baptized Christians laid aside the white robes which they had worn since their baptism on Easter Sunday. From this time on, they were to remember that they must show forth Christ in the whiteness and purity of their lives. At their baptism, they had "put on the Lord Jesus Christ," and they must never cease to be clothed in Him.

On Easter Sunday, we were all raised into closer union with Christ according to the measure of God's giving of grace and our correspondence with it. It is for us now to live more completely in Christ, letting His thoughts and His will determine ours. In the Collect, we pray for the grace to show forth in our life and conduct the effects of our participation in the mystery of Christ's resurrection.

"Peace be to you" were the first words of Jesus to His Apostles after His resurrection. The peace which Christ gives is His grace a sharing in His life. Sin alone can separate us from Christ and cut us from participation in His life. Sin alone can deprive us of real peace. After Jesus, risen from the dead, greeted His Apostles with the words, "Peace be to you," He breathed upon them and said to them: "Receive ye the Holy Ghost. Whose sins you shall forgive, they are forgiven them; and whose sins you shall retain, they are retained" (Gospel). In the Sacrament of Penance, we can have our sins forgiven and return to or be strengthened in the peace of Christ, that is, in His divine life.

Let us thank God for giving us the Sacrament of Penance, and let us often receive this sacrament humbly and earnestly. Not only are our sins forgiven in confession, but we also receive special sacramental graces, which will help us avoid sin in the future. Moreover, with infinite tenderness, Christ heals the wounds sin has made in our souls and gives us the pledge of His assistance in times of temptation.

At the Offertory today, place on the altar your resolution to prepare earnestly and lovingly for the Sacrament of Penance and to go to confession often and regularly as a means of bringing you into closer union with God.

In the Postcommunion today, we ask God that the holy mysteries of the Sacrifice, which He gave us to "ensure our salvation," may be "a remedy for us both now and in the time to come." Through the divine strength we have received in the holy Sacrifice, we shall be able to show forth in our life and conduct the effects of our celebration of the mystery of Christ's glorious resurrection.

The Second Sunday after Easter

"I am the good shepherd" (John 10:11). In the Mass for the second Sunday after Easter, the Church calls us to join with all the members of the Mystical Body and with Christ Himself, our Head, in praise of our heavenly Father for all His goodness. "The earth is full of the mercy of the Lord, alleluia" (Introit). Everything about us, especially all the growing things, the new buds, and blossoms on the trees, speak to us of the goodness of Him who is Life itself. We remember that, through His divine Son's sufferings, death, and glorious resurrection, He rescued His people "from the perils of eternal death," and we beg Him to bring us safely to the happiness of everlasting life.

To enjoy in eternity this blessed life of union with God, we know we must live in union with God in this present life. St. Peter reminds us how we must live in today's Epistle — "Christ suffered for us, leaving you an example that you should follow his steps." To follow Christ and live as He lived is the life program for every Christian. If we are to follow Him and live as He lived, we must ever try to know Him better. How shall we come to know Christ better — to know how He looks at things and how He speaks and acts? When two of the disciples were on their way to Emmaus on the first Easter day, Jesus joined them and talked with them as they walked along the way. "But their eyes were held, that they should not know him" (Luke 24:16). Then, at their request, Jesus "he went in with them, and it came to pass when he reclined at table with them, that he took the bread and blessed and broke and began handing it to them" (Luke 24:29-30). And "the disciples knew the Lord Jesus in the breaking of bread" (Alleluia Verse). In the "breaking of bread" in the holy sacrifice of the Mass, we, too, will come to know the Lord Jesus.

In the Sacrifice Banquet, our divine Shepherd comes to be Himself, our nourishment, and our very life. Jesus says of Himself, "I am the good shepherd; and I know mine and mine know me" (Gospel). He knows each of us. He knows us intimately, our strengths and weakness, desires and temptations. "Who his own self bore our sins in his body upon the tree: that we, being dead to sins, should live to justice: by whose stripes you were healed" (Epistle).

Let us offer the holy Sacrifice as often as possible and come to the Banquet table where Christ breaks the heavenly Bread for His disciples. There He will know and speak with us and give us presents, and He will bind us more closely to Himself.

The Third Sunday after Easter

"Shout with joy to God, all the earth, alleluia" (Introit). So there was great joy among the Apostles when

81

Christ, risen from the tomb, came and went among them. By His resurrection, He had shown that He is God and that nothing — not even death itself — can have power over Him. So the members of Christ's Mystical Body rejoice with Him today for His glorious triumph and call on all the things of earth to exult and be glad.

But it is not enough for us merely to rejoice in Christ's victory. During the years of our life here, we must work at perfecting our union with God so that we shall be ready when God calls us to participate in eternal rejoicings. In the Gospel today, we hear Christ telling His disciples that there will be days of sorrow and lamenting ahead for them; days when they will no longer see Him with them; days when they will be working alone for the spread of His kingdom in the face of the scorn and persecution of the world. But Jesus tells His Apostles, too, that their "sorrow shall be turned into joy." He says to them, "So also you now indeed have sorrow but I will see you again, and your heart shall rejoice; and your joy no man shall take from you."

We who live almost two thousand years after Christ spoke these words have perhaps known their truth in our lives. We know that people sometimes scorn the Christian way of living. Those who are faithful to Christ in all the details of their life, who will not compromise honesty for the sake of money or political honor; who will not read a bad book even though it is popular; who dare to denounce the impure movie which is drawing crowds; who assist at holy Mass daily and frequent the sacraments; those who, in short, are trying with all their hearts and souls to grow in Christ, for the greater glory of their heavenly Father will often meet scorn and criticism and a kind of petty persecution from the world. But their "sorrow shall be turned into joy."

To live as Christ would have us live and to merit the joy which "no man shall take from (us)," we stand in constant need of His graces. Hence, we ask God in the Collect today, "Grant that all who are counted of the Christian faith may abhor whatever is contrary to that name, and strive after that which becomes it." So St. Peter tells in the Epistle how we should strive, "Refrain yourselves from carnal desires which war against the soul, having your conversation good among the Gentiles: that whereas they speak against you as evildoers, they may, by the good works, which they shall behold in you, glorify God in the day of visitation."

By our conversation and the conduct of our lives, we may be the means God uses to show others the Catholic faith's truth, beauty, and strength. We may be the means of bringing to the Good Shepherd some of the "other sheep" He would also have in His fold. Since we can show forth Christ in our conversation and actions only according as we are united with Him, let us earnestly pray in the Postcommunion, "May the sacraments which we have received, O Lord, we beseech thee, be unto our souls a quickening food and to our bodies protection and aid."

The Fourth Sunday after Easter

"Sing ye to the Lord a new canticle, alleluia; for the Lord hath done wonderful things, alleluia" (Introit). Holy Church invites all her children to praise God for the beautiful things He has wrought in souls during this Paschal season. Many Catholics, inspired by God's grace during this holy time, are determined now to live more intensely in the spirit of the Church. Each of us, doubtless, is resolved to make our life correspond! with our high vocation as a Christian, that is, "another: Christ." Afraid lest amid temptation we may forget the attractions of the Christ-life and be drawn into worldliness, we pray to God in the Collect, "O God, ... grant that thy people may love what thou dost command and desire what thou dost promise."

St. James, who knew our Lord intimately and who saw the cheapness and nothingness of worldly enjoyments compared with the grace of God, tells us in the Epistle, "Dearly beloved, every best gift, and every perfect gift, is from above, coming down from the Father of lights."

As our divine Savior often reminded His Apostles that the time was drawing near when He would leave them to go to His Father, He continues now to remind the members of His Mystical Body that the time will come when they will be with Him in everlasting glory. We are destined not only for our life in this world. There is also an eternity of glorious life awaiting us if we are ready to receive it. "Life everlasting in Christ Jesus our Lord" is the reward of a life of grace in this world.

To be united with Christ in eternity, we must first be united with Him in this life. "O God, who by communion in this venerable sacrifice hast made us partakers of the one supreme Godhead," we pray in the Secret. We are partakers of God's life through participation in the holy Mass and the sacraments, which have their source in the Eucharistic Sacrifice. Therefore, through frequently assisting at holy Mass, we will try to live more and more in Christ for the glory of our heavenly Father.

The Fifth Sunday after Easter

The theme of the Mass for the fifth Sunday after Easter is that we should declare our deliverance from sin not only in song but also in our daily lives. In the Epistle, St. James states emphatically, "Be ye doers of the word, and not hearers only, deceiving your own selves." He insists that active charity, purity of life, and restraint from evil words must be the fruits of one's faith. In the Offertory, we praise God, "who hath set (our) soul to live," and in the Communion, we are urged to "show forth His salvation from day to day."

Of ourselves, we cannot hope to accomplish this manifestation of Christ in our daily lives, but we are not alone. God, our all-wise and all-powerful Father, will always help us. Christ reminds us of this in the Gospel. "If you ask the Father anything in my name, he will give it to you ... and I say not to you, that I will ask the Father for you: for the Father himself loveth you, because you have loved me and have believed that I came out from God."

If we are proud, irritable, uncharitable, and jealous in our contact with others, we are not manifesting Christ to the world, however loudly we may proclaim our devotion. "In this is my Father glorified," said our Lord in His last talk with His disciples, "that you bring forth very much fruit, and become my disciples" (John 15:8).

If we would enjoy the benefits of membership in Christ's Church fully, we must strive after those things by which we live in Christ. The liturgy teaches us this lesson. "Be ye doers of the word, and not hearers only." God has shown us His favor by giving us unique means to work for His glory and our salvation. Baptism was a gift of God, for which we must make returns by working for the eternal home to which it gives us a right. Confirmation strengthened us that we might champion the cause of Christ through a Christ-like life.

You can do much good if you accept St. Paul's challenge to spirituality. "Therefore, let us feast, not with the old leaven, nor with the leaven of malice and wickedness; but with the unleavened bread of sincerity and truth" (I Cor. 5:8). Additional strength to work for God through labor for your fellow creatures will come to you in frequent participation in the holy Sacrifice. Each day of your life will then be blessed with the grace that makes you ready to forget yourself and eager to serve your neighbor, in whom you find our Lord and Savior Himself.

Thus, your efforts to share in the work of restoring all things in Christ will be most helpful. "Grant us, O Lord, whom thou hast filled with the strength of this heavenly banquet, both to desire what is right and to obtain what we desire" (Postcommunion).

The Ascension of Our Lord

"Ye men of Galilee, why wonder you, looking up to heaven? Alleluia. He shall so come as you have seen him going up into heaven, alleluia, alleluia, alleluia" (Introit). Like the Apostles, we stand in wonderment today at the mystery of Christ's glorious ascension. The Church addresses us in the Introit with the words the angels spoke to the Apostles as they beheld their divine Master raised up from their midst and taken into heaven.

"Oh, clap your hands, all ye nations; shout unto God with the voice of exultation." All over the world today, the members of Christ join in this glorious triumphant chant. Our Savior, Jesus Christ, God, and man, has wrought the work of redemption for the glory of His heavenly Father and our eternal happiness. He has prayed to His Father, "I have glorified thee on the earth; I have finished the work which thou gavest me to do, and now glorify thou me, O Father, with thyself, with the glory which I had before the world was with thee" (Gospel, Vigil of the Ascension).

Today this prayer of Christ is fulfilled. Clothed in His glorified humanity, He "was taken up into heaven, and sitteth at the right hand of God" (Gospel). As God, Jesus Christ is equal to His Father in all things; as man, He is in the highest place in heaven next to God.

As members of Christ's Mystical Body, we share in His exultation. Today He raises us up with Him, for, as St. Leo says, "There where the Head has gone before, the Body is called to follow." Seated at the right hand of God, Jesus Christ continues His office of mediator and daily offers Himself and us with Him as a pleasing oblation to His eternal Father. As we grow in union with Christ, we shall share in the glory of the new Jerusalem when Christ presents the fullness of His Mystical Body as a tribute to His Father on the final day.

Today in the Offertory, in union with the priest, give yourself, your mind, your heart, your will, all that you are and have, as an offering to God. Then at the Consecration, when Christ offers Himself to His eternal Father, unite your offering with that of the divine Victim and, "calling to mind... his glorious ascension into heaven," pray with added fervor, "Most humbly we implore thee, almighty God, cause these our mystic offerings to be brought by the hands of thy holy Angel unto thy altar above, before the face of thy divine majesty, that those of us who, from this sharing in the heavenly sacrifice, shall receive the most sacred Body and Blood of thy Son may be filled with every grace and heavenly blessing. Through the same Christ our Lord. Amen" (Canon).

Whitsunday or Pentecost

Preparation for Pentecost. Through His sufferings and death, His glorious resurrection and ascension, Jesus Christ redeemed us; He made it possible for us to become sharers in the life of the Blessed Trinity as our first parents were before they sinned. In the plan of God, the actual birth to a new life, in each person's case, is the work of the Holy Ghost.

As the Apostles spent the days after our Lord's ascension in prayer and preparation for the coming of the Holy Ghost, so now we spend the nine days between Ascension Thursday and Pentecost Sunday in earnest prayer that the Holy Ghost will make us more His own at His coming this Pentecost Sunday.

Cleanse all sin and affection for sin from your heart, and prepare yourself through prayer that the Holy Ghost may make you His own forever. Plan a definite program, deciding precisely what prayers you will say each day, what acts of self-denial you will perform, and what gifts you will offer at the Offertory during the Masses of this novena so that you may receive the gifts of the Holy Ghost in their fullness. Then, ask the grace to persevere in your intention during each holy Mass.

The feast of Pentecost. "But the Paraclete, the Holy Ghost, whom the Father will send in my name, he will teach you all things, and bring all things to your mind, whatsoever I shall have said to you" (Gospel). The hour has come for the fulfillment of God's promise of the Holy Ghost. Jews from every country of the Gentile world have flocked to Jerusalem, and the Apostles and disciples are gathered in the Cenacle, the room where the Last Supper took place. Here they are united with Mary in prayer for the coming of the Paraclete. There is a spirit of expectation throughout the city; the divine Spirit has begun His work by instilling this warning into souls.

Suddenly a mighty gust of wind sweeps over the city fills the room where the disciples are gathered, and brings with it tongues of fire, which rest on their heads. Thus, the Living Fire, the third Person of the Blessed Trinity, comes to take possession of their hearts. "Go, teach all nations," Jesus had said to His Apostles, and now He supplies them with the light and strength to do this.

In the hearts of the multitude, too, the Holy Ghost places a longing for the truth. Moved by the Holy Spirit, they gather around the Cenacle, which houses the newborn Church, and shout with a loud noise for the Apostles. The Apostles "began to speak with divers tongues, according as the Holy Ghost gave them to speak... And ... the multitude were confounded in mind, because that every man heard them speak in his own tongue" (Lesson).

Today's liturgy is joyous because of the guiding presence of the Holy Spirit in the Church. "The Spirit of the Lord hath filled the whole earth, alleluia" (Introit). Therefore, eagerly and hopefully, we unite in prayer for the coming of the Holy Ghost: "Alleluia, alleluia! Send forth thy Spirit and they shall be created and thou shalt renew the face of the earth" (Alleluia Versicle).

What will Pentecost mean to you? It will mean the gifts of the Holy Ghost as far as you can receive them. If you take to the Fount of Life, a vessel filled almost to the brim with worldliness and self. Then there will be little room for the inpouring of the Holy Spirit. But if your heart has been emptied of sin, of the world, of self, if you are trying to live as St. Paul taught the early Christians to live, then fear of the Lord will fill you with a dread of sin; piety will make you love God as a father; knowledge will show you clearly the will of God; fortitude will be your strength in every trial and temptation; counsel will clear away your doubts; understanding will make you more alive to the mysteries of faith, and wisdom will give you a greater desire for the things of God.

Offer yourself to the heavenly Father at holy Mass, praying that your heart may be cleansed from sin and filled with the Holy Spirit.

Trinity Sunday

"Blessed be the holy Trinity and undivided Unity; we will give glory to him because he hath shown his mercy to us" (Introit). With this song of praise, the holy Church prepares to offer the holy Sacrifice in honor of the Most Blessed Trinity. Every blessing the Church gives is granted in the name of the Holy Trinity. Each psalm of the breviary terminates with the Gloria Patri in praise of the triune God.

Baptism makes us members of Christ's Mystical Body in the name of the Blessed Trinity. "Going, therefore, teach ye all nations; baptizing them in the name of the Father, and of the Son, and of the Holy Ghost" (Gospel). The Church prays for the dying: "Go forth, O Christian soul, out of this world, in the name of God, the Father almighty, who created thee, in the name of Jesus Christ, the Son of the living God, who suffered for thee, in the name of the Holy Ghost, who sanctified thee." "Delight, O Lord, his soul in thy sight, ... for though he may have sinned, he did not deny the Father, the Son, and the Holy Ghost."

The supreme tribute of praise to the holy Trinity is the holy sacrifice of the Mass. "For from the rising of the sun even to the going down, my name is great among the Gentiles, and in every place there is sacrifice, and there is offered to my name a clean oblation: for my name is great among the Gentiles" (Mal. 1:11).

The mystery of the Most Holy Trinity is so great that our minds can never understand it. With St. Paul, we cry out, "O the depth of the riches of the wisdom and of the knowledge of God! (Epistle). Although we do not understand the mystery of three Persons in one God, we know the love of the Father, Son, and Holy Ghost for us, and we love Them in return and adore Them, who in unity all perfect live and reign the one true God forever and ever.

The fact that God should reveal to us this heavenly secret of the adorable life of the triune God shows us how much He loves us. In gratitude for His love, we praise Him in the holy Mass. "Blessed be God the Father, and the only-begotten Son of God, and also the Holy Spirit; because he hath shown his mercy to us" (Offertory). As we chant these words of the Offertory, we bear to the altar our lives, our powers, our labors, our joys, our sorrows, and our hopes, dedicating them to the glory of the holy

Trinity. We mean to praise and bless God not only in our words but also in all the actions of our lives.

When God gives Himself to us in holy Communion, we pray that through the blessings of the adorable Trinity, we may be saved in soul and body, to share in the eternal hymn of praise to God the Father, God the Son, and God the Holy Ghost. "Grant, O Lord our God, that the reception of this sacrament and the confession of the holy and eternal Trinity and of its undivided Unity may profit us to the salvation of body and soul" (Postcommunion).

The Feast of Corpus Christi

> Sion, lift thy voice and sing,
> Praise thy Savior, praise thy King;
> Praise with hymns thy Shepherd true.
> (Sequence)

A great gladness fills our minds as we rise today. Eager to join in the praise Sion, the Church is giving Christ in the Eucharist; we prepare to celebrate "our" Mass. We assemble our gifts for the Father lovingly and humbly: our gratitude for Christ in the Eucharist, sorrow for any irreverence or indifference shown to the Blessed Sacrament, and self-denials and acts of virtue that we have prepared.

At church, we join with the priest as he enters "in unto the altar of God." There Christ says to us, "As the living Father hath sent me, and I live by the Father; so he that eateth me, the same also shall live by me" (Gospel). For Christ to live in us, we must first die to ourselves. On the paten with the Host, we place our gifts, all we have and are: our strength, our hearts, our minds, our souls. We pray that "we may be made partakers of his divinity who vouchsafed to become a partaker of our humanity."

Soon in the person of the priest, Christ speaks again the sacred words: "This is My Body. This is My Blood.?' The bread and wine, symbols of our offerings, have been wholly changed into Christ. Through the priest, we join with Christ, our High Priest, in offering to God the Father the perfect Victim, His divine Son. "Through him and with him and in him" we glorify the Father. Then with love immeasurable, Christ fulfills His promise and gives Himself to us that we may live by Him.

With Christ abiding in us, we go out to the day's work. Christ in our memories, in our hearts, in our minds, on our lips, in our actions; Christ in us and we in Him! Firm in His strength, we triumph over temptations. Throughout the day, we seek to live by Him, mindful of St. Paul's words, "Whether you eat or drink, or whatsoever else you do, do all to the glory of God" (I Cor. 10:31). When night comes, we would still hold close to Christ. Confidently we join with Mother Church in the prayers of Compline, "Into thy hands, O Lord, I commend my spirit."

The Sundays After Pentecost

Editor's note: The traditional Roman Missal includes fifty-three Sunday Masses and the other Sunday Masses (enough for each week of the year). Depending on how early or late Easter falls in a given year, there may be as few as six Sundays following Epiphany and as many as twenty-four Sundays following Pentecost. When this happens, the prayers and readings from the Sunday Masses that were not said during the Time after Epiphany are said on the Sundays between the twenty-third and twenty-fourth Sundays after Pentecost (the twenty-fourth Sunday after Pentecost is always said on the Sunday immediately before the First Sunday of Advent). The proper chants of the twenty-third Sunday (Introit, Gradual, Alleluia, Offertory, and Communion) are repeated on these "Resumed" Sundays after Epiphany. The twenty-third Sunday after Pentecost is omitted if there are fewer than twenty-four Sundays after Pentecost.

The Mystical Christ must become more powerful than ever before. Therefore, deepening and strengthening the Christ-life in every soul is necessary as it is brought into unity with Christ. Until "we all meet into the unity of faith, and of the knowledge of the Son of God, unto a complete man, unto the measure of the age of the fullness of Christ," this is the aim of time (Eph. 4:13). The Holy Ghost is responsible for achieving this lofty goal inside the Church and within each Church member.

After Pentecost, Christ, our King, calls us to His side, especially those of us who have received the rights and obligations of full citizenship in His kingdom in the Sacrament of Confirmation. We must actively participate in Christ's conflict with the world, the flesh, and the devil. Each of us is given instructions as to the work we are to accomplish by the Holy Ghost, the Spirit of Jesus. If we fail to do this work, we fail Christ our King and leave a weak place on the battleline.

The Holy Ghost will illuminate our minds with His wisdom and His will strengthen our wills with His fortitude, so we need not be the least bit concerned that we may not be able to achieve what God wants of us. Regardless of how uninformed, timid, or weak we may perceive ourselves to be. Because we have received the sacraments of baptism and confirmation, we have the right to request and expect this of Him. Remember how an angel of God once battled with Jacob and would not let go until he blessed him? (Gen. 32:23-30). Confidently pray to God for the power you require to overcome the temptations that test you.

The Holy Spirit "reneweth the face of the planet" annually. The Church expands yearly via the holy, life-giving work of the Holy Spirit, and each member of the Church experiences a fuller life of grace in proportion to the extent of God's grace-giving and that person's cooperation. Therefore, you must labor diligently and joyously this year to cooperate with the Holy Spirit in the sanctification of your soul for the honor of God. "In this, you bring out great fruit, and in this, my Father is exalted" (John 15:8).

What does this mean to you? What would it require of you, given your unique circumstances this year? Knowing will not be difficult if you pay attention to what Christ is trying to teach you via the Church's liturgy. The Holy Ghost, also known as the Spirit of Wisdom and Understanding, is fully aware of all the circumstances around your character and your tendencies, areas of strength, social circle, temptations, aspirations, and wants. He is aware of both your cowardice and charity. He also recognizes how cooperating with the graces He desires to grant you during this time will enrich the beauty and perfection of the entire Mystical Body of Christ and enable you to produce virtue-based fruit. "If anyone loves me, he will keep my word, and my Father will love him, and we will come to him, and will make our abode with him" (John 14:23).

The Changes Made After the Second Vatican Council

The Consilium and *Coetus 1*

Fr. Somerville-Knapman writes, "the Vatican Council's constitution on the liturgy, *Sacrosanctum Concilium*, was promulgated by Paul VI on December 4, 1963. Little time was lost in its implementation. With the motu proprio *Sacram Liturgiam* of January 25, 1964, Pope Paul VI erected a committee to revise all the liturgical rites, called the *Consilium ad exsequendam Constitutionem de Sacra Liturgia* (Consilium), "the committee for carrying out the constitution on the Sacred Liturgy." The committee's first president was Cardinal Giacomo Lercaro of Bologna, and its secretary was the controversial Fr. Annibale Bugnini, C.M.

The Consilium is arguably the most ambitious but ill-starred committee in the Church's history. Its membership was large and international in its spread. Its initial 42 members (later 51) were primarily bishops; more than 200 official consultors and unofficial advisers were assisting them. Despite the use of working groups, plenary sessions of the Consilium were unwieldy and procedurally flawed."[6]

The twenty-eight study groups, or *coetus*, were each given a specific task to complete as part of the enormous process of updating the liturgical texts. Every coetus had a relator, a secretary, a few consultors—generally no more than five or six—and occasionally one or two advisors. Each coetus' relator organized the group's work and authorized its official contributions, and schemata, to the other *coeti*. The schemata (outlines)

---

[6] Somerville-Knapman, OSB, Hugh. "The Strange Birth of the Novus Ordo." *Catholic Herald*, Catholic Herald, 14 Feb. 2020, catholicherald.co.uk/the-strange-birth-of-the-novus-ordo.

provide a progress report for the group, including the questions posed to the participants and their responses. In addition, they include the liturgical texts that the coetus had written since the previous report. In addition, the schemata provide a contemporaneous record of the revision work's various stages.

Coetus 1: De Calendario was the Consilium group entrusted with revising the Church's calendar. The members of this group were:

- **Fr. Agostino Amore, OFM**—(Italy) Professor of Ancient History of the Church, Antonianum, Rome [a.k.a. the Pontifical University of Saint Anthony, and as Pontifical Athenaeum Antonianum]
- **Fr. Annibale Bugnini, CM**—(Italy) Secretary of the Council for the Implementation of the Constitution on the Liturgy— *Coetus Relator*
- **Fr. Ansgarius Dirks, OP**—(Netherlands) Professor of Liturgy, Dominican Liturgical Institute, Rome— *Coetus Secretary*
- **Msgr. Pierre Jounel**—(France) Professor of Liturgy, Catholic Institute of Paris
- **Canon Aimé Georges Martimort**—(France) Professor of Liturgy, Catholic Institute of Toulouse
- **Fr. Adrien Nocent, OSB**—(Belgium) Professor of Liturgy, Pontifical Liturgical Institute, Rome (Sant'Anselmo)
- **Fr. Herman Schmidt, SJ**—(Netherlands) Professor of Sacred Liturgy, Pontifical Gregorian University, Rome
- **Dom Rombaut Louis René van Doren, OSB**—(Belgium) Abbot of the Abbey of Mont César, Louvain, Belgium

- **Msgr. Johannes Wagner**—(Germany) Director, Liturgical Institute, Trier [a.k.a. German Liturgical Institute (DLI) in Trier)

The *Centre de Pastorale Liturgique* (CPL), which was established on May 20, 1943, on the grounds of the *Éditions du Cerf* publishing business (belonging to the Dominicans), included three members of this group: Martimort, Bouyer, and Jounel. At its foundation meeting, Dom Lambert Beauduin[7] was present. This group of activists, known as the CPL, saw themselves as part of the (pastoral) Liturgical Movement, which Dom Beauduin famously started. The first congress, which was titled "Pastoral Liturgy Studies" and took place in January 1944, made this fundamental idea of "pastoral liturgy" (and not just "liturgy") clear. Fr. Aimé-Georges Martimort's 1945 letter to the CPL outlined the significant modifications in liturgical matters resulting from the Second Vatican Council. And the central figures of the CPL—namely: Louis Bouyer, Pierre Jounel, Pierre-Marie Gy, Joseph Gélineau, Bernard Botte, Joseph Lécuyer, etc.—would become the great voices during the Council and in its implementation[8].

As reported by Dr. Kwasniewski in the *Sanctoral Killing Fields* article, Fr. Cassian Folsom, O.S.B., founder of the Benedictine monastery in Norcia and a professor of liturgy at Sant'Anselmo in Rome, delivered a paper entitled *Summorum Pontificum and Liturgical Law*, at the London Oratory on December 13, 2013, in which he said the following: "...Concerning the calendar, and especially the superabundant growth of the sanctoral

---

[7] Belgian monk Lambert Beauduin OSB (August 5, 1873–January 11, 1960) established the abbey that is now known as Chevetogne Abbey in 1925. He was a key figure in the Belgian liturgical movement and the forerunner of the restoration of the liturgy in Europe. The future Pope John XXIII, Angelo Roncalli, declared in 1957 that Beauduin was responsible for his ecumenical vocation.

[8] Society Saint Plus X. (2020, April 23). *50 Years of the New Mass: The National Center for Pastoral Liturgy (12)*. FSSPX.News. Retrieved from https://fsspx.news/en/news-events/news/50-years-new-mass-national-center-pastoral-liturgy-12-56289.

cycle, there has always been [the] need of periodic pruning. But in the 1970 Missal, the pruning was so radical that the original plant is sometimes unrecognizable."

Fr. Pierre Jounel, a member of Coetus I, reflects in his *Memoirs*[9], "I prefer to say nothing, or little, about the new calendar, the handiwork of a trio of maniacs who suppressed, with no good reason, Septuagesima, and the Octave of Pentecost and who scattered three-quarters of the Saints hiddledy-piggledy, all based on notions of their own devising! Because these three hotheads obstinately refused to change anything in their work and because the pope wanted to finish up quickly to avoid letting the chaos get out of hand, their project, however insane, was accepted! (Bouyer, pp. 222-223)."

Pope Paul VI published the motu proprio *Mysterii Paschalis* on February 14, 1969. It altered the liturgical festivals of Jesus Christ and the saints in the General Roman Calendar as well as the liturgical year of the Roman Rite. By signing this document, Pope Paul VI set the rules for restoring the liturgical year that the Second Vatican Council established. He also "approved[d] by Our apostolic authority...the new Roman Universal Calendar...and similarly the general norms concerning the arrangement of the liturgical year."

The reception of *Mysterii Paschalis* was contrasted. Despite an almost universal application, it received severe criticism from lay sources such as the *New York Times*, which questioned the axing of popular feast days such as Saint Valentine's Day or the feast of Saint Bernard and in the Catholic press generally. Those of the clergy and faithful whose view of worship and

[9] Bouyer, Louis, and Peter Kwasniewski. *The Memoirs of Louis Bouyer: From Youth and Conversion to Vatican II, the Liturgical Reform, and After*. Translated by John Pepino, English Lang. Ed., Kettering, OH: Angelico Press, 2015. Print.

religion generally had been devotional were disconcerted. However, the cofusion was also due in part to surprise and a lack of preparation[10] (Bugnini, p. 315).

The Changes to the Catholic Liturgical Year Before Vatican II[11]

In addition to the significant changes and alterations to the Holy Week Liturgies in the 1955 Missal, there were also a few other noteworthy changes. With the Advent of the 1955 Calendar, Pope Pius XII instituted the feast of "St. Joseph, the Worker" on May 1st (moving the feast of "Saints Philip and James" from May 1st, where it had been since the sixth century, to May 11th). In doing this, he also suppressed the Patronage of St. Joseph that – since Pope Pius IX's decree of September 10th, 1847 – had been celebrated on the second Wednesday after the Octave of Easter. In 1954, Pius XII also instituted the Feast of the Queenship of the Blessed Virgin Mary on May 31st; to make room for it, he moved the Feast of St. Angela Merici to June 1st.

The year 1955 saw some of the most significant changes to the Church's Liturgy since the Council of Trent. In *Cum nostra hac aetate* (March 23rd, 1955), Pius XII *abolished* 15 Octaves in addition to the Octave for the Dedication of a Church and particular octaves for patrons of various religious orders, countries, and dioceses. He also abolished roughly half of all vigils, leading to the removal of the liturgical vigils of the Immaculate Conception, Epiphany, All Saints, and for all of the Apostles except Saints Peter and Paul. The total number of liturgical vigils was now reduced to seven.

---

[10] Bugnini, Annibale. *The Reform of the Liturgy, 1948-1975.* Translated by Matthew J. O'Connell. Collegeville: Minnesota, Liturgical Press, 1990. Print.
[11] Plese, Matthew. "The Traditional vs. Modern Catholic Calendar." *The Fatima Center*, 6 June 2022, fatima.org/news-views/catholic-apologetics-170.

These vast changes affected both the Temporal and Sanctoral cycles.

Additional changes in 1960 under John XXIII include the removal of most saints on the calendar twice. For instance, the Feast of the Finding of the Holy Cross, the second feast of St. Agnes commemorating her apparition to her parents, and the Feast of St. John before the Latin Gate were all removed. These changes were incorporated in the 1962 Missal; however, a priest may still choose to offer a votive Mass for those saints on those traditional feast days.

Changes Made by the Consilium Following the Second Vatican Council

In the writings[12] of Fr. Jounel, he states that their primary objectives were to alter the sanctoral list to enrich and purge it and assign the saint's memorial to the anniversary day of their passing, in line with traditional practice.

The commemoration of their anniversaries is where the cult of the martyrs started, and this tradition persisted up to the eleventh century. But Ado of Vienne had added a few arbitrary dates to his martyrology back in the ninth century, and these gradually made their way into the calendar. The factors that influenced the selection of dates starting in the seventeenth century were occasionally relatively unimportant. In particular, there was a desire to fill the voids left by the Lenten weeks at the close of the nineteenth century. There was a need to go back to the original sources.

The Roman Church frequently celebrates Eastern saints on the same day their feast is commemorated in

---

[12] Jounel, Pierre. "The General Roman Calendar of 1969", *The Liturgy and Time: The Church at Prayer, an Introduction to the Liturgy, vol. 4.*, pp. 126–127. Collegeville, MN: Liturgical Press, 1985. Print.

their place of origin, thanks to the restoration of the old custom. However, the deaths of Saint Benedict, Saint Gregory the Great, and Saint Thomas Aquinas, whose anniversaries usually fall in Lent, have had their feast days moved to other days that have long been associated with their remembrance as exceptions to the rule.

It may appear contradictory to choose to remove saints from the list while simultaneously adding to it. The reformers first lowered the number of saints recommended being commemorated to less than 180 to accomplish their purpose. First to be dropped were the names of individuals whose mere existence was in doubt (John and Paul, Ursula, Catherine, Felix of Valois, etc.). The celebrations of the local Roman martyrs, about whom Gregory the Great only knew the *nomen-locus-dies* (name-place-day) that meant so much to him, and the founders or foundresses of the city's old temples were also left out (Prisca, Sabina, Chrysogonus, etc.). However, the reformers preserved the names of the major Roman martyrs (Fabian, Cornelius, Sixtus I, Agnes, etc.) and the patrons of the basilicas that pilgrims now visit (Cecilia, Sebastian, Pancratius, Nereus, Achilles, etc.). Thus, the calendar retains part of the ambiance of ancient Rome.

Most of the names that have been dropped, as the Council suggested, are those of the numerous saints whose legacy is exclusively perpetuated in a small area or a particular religious family. The titles of saints representing different parts of the world have been introduced due to their suppression, including Saint Peter Chanel, the sole saint from Oceania, and the martyrs from the United States, Canada, Japan, and Uganda. All the centuries, from the martyrs of the Neronian persecution to Saint Maximilian Kolbe, are represented in the calendar, just as all the continents today have witnesses.

Not all of the saints listed on the Roman Calendar are honored similarly. The majority of them are optional in commemoration. Thus, the devotion of the saints is legitimately accessible for veneration by the Christian people.

Tradition dictates that several calendars, including diocesan, regional, and calendars used by specific religious orders and communities, may be used in addition to the General Roman Calendar. Additionally, it is acceptable to honor the memory of any saint named in the Roman Martyrology on days when no memorial is required. Because of this, a revision of the Martyrology from 1584 is now required.

The Roman liturgy relies not only on the calendar to revive the devotion of the saints. Additionally, it depends on the revised Mass and Liturgy of the Hours formularies and the celebration's more lenient rules. The hagiographical readings and the Mass prayers highlight each saint's spiritual message.

Even though many changes occurred before Vatican II, they pale compared to the changes made after it. With the introduction of the *Novus Ordo*, more than 300 saints[13] were removed from the General Calendar, as calculated by Dr. Peter Kwasniewski in his *New Liturgical Movement* article *The Sanctoral Killing Fields: On the Removal of Saints from the General Roman Calendar*[14]. Significant among the faithful were the many devotions to the saints. The many devotions to the saints were significant among the faithful. People like Saint Telesphorus, the Forty Martyrs of Sebaste, Saint Anicetus, Saints Cletus and Marcellinus, the Seven

---

[13] An exact count is not possible because numerous saints, particularly martyrs, include groups of un-named and un-quantified companions.

[14] Kwasniewski, Peter A. "The Sanctoral Killing Fields: On the Removal of Saints from the General Roman Calendar." *New Liturgical Movement*, Church Music Association of America, 16 Nov. 2020, www.newliturgicalmovement.org/2020/10/the-sanctoral-killing-fields-on-removal.html.

Holy Brothers, Saint Thecla, Saint Placid, Saint Ursula, and Saint Barbara are no longer well-known among Catholics. These saints provided a stirring and enduring witness to our ancient Faith. They were a source of great inspiration and role models for us all during difficult times. All of them, and more, were removed from the liturgical calendar, leaving all parishes named after such saints orphaned and with no patronal feast day remaining on the universal calendar.

While the Sanctoral Cycle underwent hundreds of changes in 1969, the Temporal Cycle underwent significant changes with the introduction of the *Novus Ordo* Mass. These modifications included the following:

- Eliminating Septuagesima entirely, allowing the Alleluia to be used until Ash Wednesday. Unfortunately, this modification made easing into Lenten penance much more difficult.

- Making it unnecessary to veil statues and images during Passiontide.

- Replacing *Time After Epiphany* and *Time After Pentecost* with an oddly named "Ordinary Time" season that is divided in half and appears to be unrelated to the Liturgical Year. Such a shift shattered the "three cycles with seven seasons" Temporal Cycle that had existed for centuries. (Remember the theological significance of the numbers three and seven in our Faith.)

- Shifting several temporal feast days, such as the Feast of Christ the King (from the last Sunday of October to the final Sunday before Advent) and the Feast of the Holy Family (from the Sunday after January 6th to the Sunday in the Octave of Christmas).

The changes made after Vatican II also affected how we refer to feast days. In 1969, the ranking of feast days was changed to solemnities, feasts, memorials, and optional memorials. In the 1962 Missal, we had First-, Second-, Third-, and Fourth-Class feast days. But for centuries before the 1962 Missal, up until the changes made by Pope Pius XII in 1955, the ranks of feast days were, from least to most important: Simple, Semi-double, Lesser Double (also known as Double), Greater Double, Double of the Second Class, and lastly Double of the First Class.

One change not approved (thankfully!) was the elimination of Ash Wednesday. "Annibale Bugnini and his crew tried to get rid of Ash Wednesday so that Lent could begin on a Sunday (justified partially by an alleged statement of Leo the Great, later proven fictitious). However, Pope Paul VI put his foot down in an uncharacteristic move, refusing to scrap Ash Wednesday[15]."

---

[15] Ostrowski, Jeff. "Bugnini Wanted to Eliminate Ash Wednesday!" *Corpus Christi Watershed*, 29 Dec. 2013, www.ccwatershed.org/2013/12/29/bugnini-tried-to-eliminate-ash-wednesday.

The Renewal of the Liturgical Year and the Roman Calendar after the Second Vatican Council[16]

The guidelines for understating the reform of the Liturgical Year and the Calendar were contained in the fifth chapter of the constitution Sacrosanctum Consilium. However, the indications contained in this regard were very brief. In it, without going into details, it was requested:

- The revaluation of Sunday so that other solemnities are not put before it;
- the review of the Liturgical Year, recovering its original character and particularly the centrality of the Pascal mystery;
- the pre-eminence of the temporal cycle over the saints;
- the restoration of the baptismal and penitential elements of Lent;
- the inclusion in the Calendar of only those saints of genuinely universal importance, reserving the rest for particular calendars.

This reform was developed in several phases. The first and most important was carried out by Coetus I of the *Consilium ad exsequendam constitutionem de sacra liturgia* that renewed the Liturgical Year and the Roman Calendar. The Consilium reviewed his work in its fifth and seventh plenary sessions, which took place from April 26-30, 1965, and October 6-14, 1966. This reform passed to a second stage on April 18, 1967, when the result sent to Pope Paul VI for his opinion was accepted.

---

[16] Goñi, Beásoain P. J. A. *La Reforma Del Año Litúrgico Y Del Calendario Romano Tras El Concilio Vaticano II*. Roma: Ed. Liturgiche, 2011. Print.

In addition to making his observations, he handed it over to the Sacred Congregation for the Doctrine of the Faith and the Sacred Congregation for Rites for examination. The renewal of the Liturgical Year and Roman Calendar entered its final stretch in June and July 1968 when a commission was made up of members of the Sacred Congregation for the Doctrine of the Faith. The Consilium studied the contributions of Pope Paul VI and the Congregation, giving its final form. It was approved by the Pope on February 14, 1969, and promulgated by the Sacred Congregation for Rites on March 21 of the same year.

Coetus I separately analyzed Advent, Christmas, Lent, the Easter Triduum, the Easter season, the Sundays after Epiphany, the Sundays after Pentecost, and the litanies and ember days.

Season of Advent

Regarding the Advent season, Coetus I wondered whether it should be considered the beginning or the end of the Liturgical Year. This is reflected in the questionnaire prepared after the first meeting of Coetus I. "Should the season of Advent be considered the beginning of the liturgical year, so that it is a preparation for the feast of the Nativity of the Lord, or should it be considered the conclusion of the liturgical year, so that it is established in an eschatological sense?"

They agreed that Advent would be the beginning of the Liturgical Year and would run from the first vespers of its first Sunday (the closest to November 30) until the hour of none on December 24. The liturgical year begins on the first Sunday of Advent and runs from the first vespers of this Sunday to the Ninth Vigil of Christmas. (Some would prefer that Advent be the conclusion of the liturgical year and be established in an eschatological sense). This approach to Advent by Coetus I the Consilium accepted me at its fifth plenary assembly.

The liturgical year in liturgical books begins on the first Sunday of Advent. A show of hands accepted this principle. But, on the other hand, they presented Advent as a time of joyful waiting, so it should lose the penitential character that it had at that time. So, on their Sundays, the Gloria should be said (in the Tridentine Missal, the Gloria was suppressed during this time). The time of Advent is not a time of penance but instead of joyful expectation. Accordingly, on Sundays, it is said, *Gloria in excelsis.*

As we shall see, the Sacred Congregation for the Doctrine of the Faith did not share this vision of Advent, which is why, finally, the Gloria was not re-incorporated into Sunday Advent masses.

Season of Christmas

At Christmas time, the Coetus I raised in its first meeting the possibility of commemorating the Motherhood of the Virgin Mary, the imposition of the name of Jesus, and the beginning of the civil year on the octave of Christmas. The day on which to celebrate the feast of the Baptism of the Lord was also questioned, proposing that it remain as it was, that is, on January 13th, or else set to the Sunday after Epiphany (January 6). Thirdly, they proposed that the Episcopal Conferences be granted the power to transfer the Epiphany of the Lord (January 6) to the following Sunday, where this feast was not mandatory. And finally, they questioned when the Christmas season should end: *Should the season of Christmas be closed after Vespers (Completorium) of the Sunday following Epiphany, or should it be said after Vespers (Completorium) on January 13?*

With the answers of the members of Coetus I and also of the XVII, to which, as we said, they had sent the questionnaire, they agreed on the following:

- The Christmas season would begin with the first vespers of December 24 and would end on the Sunday after the Epiphany with the celebration of the Baptism of the Lord. Until then, it ended on January 13, the eighth of the Epiphany, the day on which the feast of the Baptism of the Lord was celebrated. This configuration disappeared because the octave of the Epiphany was suppressed.

- On the day of the Octave of Christmas, the Circumcision of the Lord would no longer be celebrated in order to commemorate the Maternity of the Virgin Mary, as it seems that the Roman liturgy originally celebrated it[17]. In addition, the beginning of the year and the imposition of the name of Jesus on the Son of God, which would occur the same day, could be evoked in the prayer of the faithful.

- The feast of the Holy Family could be moved to the Sunday that falls between January 1ˢᵗ and 5ᵗʰ, occupied at that time by the feast of the Holy Name of Jesus, which would be suppressed in the renewed calendar. Until then, in the calendar in use, it was celebrated on the Sunday after the Epiphany, but on that day, they wanted to fix the feast of the Baptism of the Lord.

---

[17] Botte, Bernard, "La première fête mariale de la liturgie romaine (The First Marian Feast of the Roman Liturgy)" *Ephemerides Liturgicae*, vol. 47, no. 6, 1933, pp. 425–30. Roma: Edizioni Liturgiche.

- Finally, they established that the transfer of the Epiphany feast could be allowed, where it was mandatory, to the following Sunday.

Baptism of the Lord

For pastoral reasons, it is absolutely desirable to celebrate the Baptism of the Lord on Sunday. However, unless the commemoration of the Lord's Baptism is celebrated at home, most of the faithful will continue to ignore this fact of salvation. Therefore, the Sunday following the feast of the Epiphany will be more appropriate.

Holy Family

As the commemoration of the Baptism of the Lord is assigned to the first Sunday after Epiphany, the feast of the Holy Family must be removed from this Sunday. Therefore, and after the suppression of the feast of the Holy Name, the Sunday between January 1st and 5th remains vacant.

This Sunday may be assigned the Gospel of the first Sunday after Epiphany (the same Gospel as the feast of the Holy Family). For the rest of the mind, this Sunday may be called the second Sunday after Christmas or the Sunday of the Holy Family. The Sunday service and Mass can be adjusted a little along with the delay of the Holy Family.

There is no significant disadvantage in the fact that the Gospel of the Child Jesus in the Temple is read before the feast of the Epiphany because the exact chronology of the life of God is not always preserved in the liturgy.

Epiphany

In many countries, Epiphany is not a civil holiday, and therefore the Epiphany feast is celebrated without precept. Accordingly, it seems that the territorial ecclesiastical authorities should be granted the possibility of assigning the feast of the Epiphany to the following Sunday, except if the sixth day of January falls on a Sunday. In those regions, the Baptism of the Lord was on the sixth day of January. Together with the Eastern churches, it can be celebrated. On Sunday, both the Epiphany and Baptism of the Lord are celebrated at the same time, using a proper formula in which both mysteries are commemorated at the same time. The question remains to be resolved as to when the period (cycle) of the Nativity should conclude: after Epiphany, after the first Sunday after Epiphany (Baptism of the Lord), or after the Second Sunday (the first miracle of Christ).

The Consilium, in its fifth plenary assembly, approved all of these provisions agreed in Coetus I to establish January 1, the eighth day of Christmas, as the feast of the Motherhood of the Virgin Mary and to commemorate on that same day the imposition of the name of Jesus as well as the beginning of the civil year.

It was decided to celebrate the B.V.M. and the name of Jesus, or the imposed name of Jesus, but nothing has been established about the name of this day (the eighth day of Christmas). But, equally, the beginning of the civil year must be considered, at least in the prayer of the faithful.

There was no consensus on the other issues (Holy Family, Baptism of the Lord, when Christmas time ends), so it was determined that they would continue to be studied. Regarding the possibility of moving the Epiphany celebration to the following Sunday, where it was not mandatory, they requested the pertinent authorization from the authorities responsible for this matter.

Coetus I provided a solution to the pending issues at the beginning of December 1965, specifically in schema 132 of the 3rd day of that same month and year: they proposed that the feast of the Holy Family be celebrated on Sunday of the octave of Christmas, and when there is no Sunday, on December 29; and they agreed that the Christmas season would conclude on the Sunday after Epiphany with the feast of the Baptism of the Lord.

> The season of Christmas runs from the 1st Vesper of Christmas until the 2nd Vesper of the Sunday 1st after the feast of the Epiphany.
> [...]
> The Sunday below the eighth day of Christmas is the Sunday of the Holy Family of Jesus, Mary, and Joseph (see Appendix I). If it is not observed on a Sunday, the festival falls on December 29.

The Consilium gave its definitive *placet* to Christmas time in its seventh plenary assembly, not without debating the possibility of adopting another date for the Feast of the Holy Family since Coetus I had proposed other alternatives to the Sunday of the octave of Christmas such as on Sunday that falls between January 2 and 5, or May 1, or that each Episcopal Conference establishes it on the date it deems most appropriate.

Fathers are asked to choose one of these four possibilities for celebrating the feast of the Holy Family, namely:

> 1) on the Sunday below the Octave of Nativity as proposed in the schema;

2) on Sunday between the 2nd and 5th of January;

3) May 1;

4) to be celebrated at a time when the bishops' conferences will best see it.

Now, as we see in the following diagrams, the idea of placing it on the Sunday of the octave of Christmas («*Dominica in fra octavam Nativitatis fit dominica de sancta Familia*» [The Sunday on the eighth day of Christmas is the Sunday of the Holy Family]) prevailed because, although chronologically out of date, "it highlights the mystery of the incarnation, which introduces the Son of God into the fullness of humanity through the family" (Guano), and because the Christmas celebration calls and gathers numerous families around to the domestic home; for all of which it is very suitable for opportune pastoral developments[18].

Regarding the transfer of the feast of the Holy Family to December 29, when there is no Sunday in the octave of Christmas, there was no continuity. In the first later schemas, it was indicated that when there was no Sunday, the votive mass of the Holy Family could be celebrated on December 29 to 31 («*Dominica infra octavam Nativitatis fit Dominica de Sancta Familia Iesu, Mariae, Ioseph. Si dominica non habetur, Missa votiva de s. Familia celebrari potest a die 29 ad 31 decembris.*» [*The Sunday below the eighth day of Christmas is the feast of the Holy Family of Jesus, Mary, and Joseph. If it is not observed on Sunday, the votive Mass of St. The family can be celebrated from December 29 to 31.*]) but later, this rubric was suppressed. In such a way, in the renewed Roman Calendar published in 1969, nothing was said in this regard. It was the following year, in the typical edition of the Roman Missal, where it was indicated that when there was no Sunday in the octave of Christmas, the feast

---

[18] Bugnini, *Reform.*

of the Holy Family would be celebrated on December 30: «*Dominica in fra octavam Nativitatis, vel, ea deficient, die 30 decembris: Sanctae Familiae Iesu, Mariae et Ioseph*» [*Sunday on the eighth day of Christmas, or, if they fail, on December 30: Holy Days of Jesus, Mary, and Joseph*].

Season of Lent

Regarding Lent, Coetus I began planning when this liturgical season should begin and when the ashes should be imposed.

- Should the 4th day of Ashes be retained as the beginning of Lent, or should the 4th day of Ashes be suppressed and the three days that follow, the beginning of the 4th day of Lent be replaced by Sunday 1st in Lent (or on 1st Vespers of this Sunday)?

- Whether the ashes are to be laid on the Sabbath after Vespers 1 Sunday, on Sunday itself, or on the 2nd day after Sunday I?

They agreed, not without some contrary opinion, that the season of Lent begins on the first Sunday of Lent instead of Ash Wednesday so that the number forty of biblical resonance would be maintained, counting from that Sunday to Holy Thursday. However, ash could continue to be imposed on that day, either on the initial Sunday itself or the following Monday. In this way, the primitive tradition regarding this liturgical season was recovered, the traces of which are found in the Tridentine Missal, specifically in the prayer over the offerings of the first Sunday of Lent («*Sacrificium quadragesimalis initii solemniter immolamus*» [*We solemnly offer the sacrifice of Lent*]), and in the Tridentine Breviary where, although the Calendar marked the beginning of the Lenten season on Ash Wednesday, the Lenten texts were not used until first Sunday of Lent, so the corresponding rubric said: "On this and other Fridays up to the Ninth Sabbath inclusive, everything is counted as on the previous Fridays after Septuagesima, except those that are considered proper."

Lent

Almost all consultors of group 1 (with two or three contradicting) and all consultors of group 17 (On special rites in the liturgical year) opt for Lent to begin on the 1st Sunday of Lent. And indeed, not because of vain archeology, but because of the typology of forty days: Jesus fasted for 40 days and 40 nights in the desert, Moses was 40 days, and 40 nights on Mount Zion, Elijah walked for 40 days and 40 nights up to Mount Horeb (the readings of the first week of Lent).

In calculating from 1st Sunday of Lent up to the fifth day of Holy Week inclusive, Sundays not being excluded, there are forty days of penance before the three holy days. That is why in ancient times, Lent was prayed from the 1st Sunday of Lent (as is still done today in the Ambrosian rite), traces of the beginning of which are still found in the Liturgy of this Sunday: The ordinary for the season of Lent does not begin from the day of the 4th of Ashes, but from this Sunday: the day of the 4th of Ashes and the third in the following days the Office is performed "for a year."

It may be objected that there are no longer 40 days of fasting if Lent begins with Sunday the 1st of Lent and the Sundays are included in the number (for he does not fast on Sunday).

The answer to this difficulty is: (1) a fast (in the strict sense) is generally where the world is reduced to a few days; (2) Even on Sundays, I will fast from sins and vices and worship the neighbor. Thus, a more accurate or perfect sense of fasting can be more easily taught.

A more incredible difficulty arises from the contrary secular practice of beginning with Lent ends on the day of the 4th of Ashes, in which the more severe practice of fasting and abstinence prevails, and "carnival."

Another difficulty is connected with this: if Lent begins at home on the 1st of Lent, when are the ashes to be blessed and put on? Some propose that the blessing and the imposition of ashes should be kept on their day "because custom is stronger than laws."

Others propose the 2nd day after the 1st Sunday (into which the obligation of fasting and abstinence could be transferred) or the sabbath after the 1st Vespers of the 1st Sunday.

The Sunday (whose Office begins at 1 Vespers, the Sabbath) seems incompatible with this rite of ashes.

The Consilium accepted the proposal of Coetus I regarding Lent in its fifth plenary assembly, leaving to the Episcopal Conferences the choice of the day of imposition of ashes as well as the configuration of the days that are distant from Ash Wednesday to the first Sunday. of Lent, mainly where the traditional seasonal masses typical of this liturgical season are celebrated.

May it please that the period of Lent begins from the first Sunday, leaving the power of the Episcopal Conferences to indicate the day of ashes or the imposition of ashes, either on the 2nd day after Sunday the 1st or on the 4th day preceding Sunday, if cut now, or on another day or several days before the 1st Sunday, so that the day from Are the days of the 4th Ash Wednesday to the 1st Sunday of Lent a time to prepare for Lent?

I like: 11
I like it, keeping the four days of ashes: 3
I do not like it: 3

None (white): 1
The arrangement of the days from Ash
Wednesday 4th to Sunday 1st is left to the
Episcopal Conferences, especially where
stations are celebrated.

As we shall see, Pope Paul VI and the Sacred
Congregation for the Doctrine of the Faith favored Lent
beginning on Ash Wednesday. And so, it remained in the
definitive configuration of the Liturgical Year.

On the other hand, as reflected in schema no. 174
of August 1, 1966, they agreed to suppress the time of
Passion that in the Calendar in use comprised the last two
weeks of Lent, thus giving a terminological unit to the time
of preparation for Easter.

As it now prevails, the season of the Passion shall
be abolished so that there may be a series of six Sundays
in Lent, the sixth of which is called "In the Passion or the
Palms."

Paschal Triduum

On the configuration of what was then called the
sacral Triduum, the Coetus I debated, on the one hand,
with what name it should be designated and, on the other.
Yes, it began with the Mass of the Lord's Supper on Holy
Thursday or, on the other hand, with Good Friday itself,
the Thursday that precedes it is a day of preparation for
the Triduum.

Is it acceptable to call the three days that
remember Christ crucified, buried, then resurrected (i.e.,
the 6th day of the Passion, Holy Saturday, Resurrection
Sunday) three days of Easter?

Whether the beginning of this is to be considered
the Mass on the 5th day of the Lord's Supper (so that the
Chrism Mass is like the conclusion of the solemn Lent),

or does this three day start from the 6th day of the Passion so that the 5th day of the Lord's Supper is considered a festive day, preparatory to the three days Easter?

They first adopted that the sacred Triduum is to be called the Easter Triduum and be made up of Good Friday, Holy Saturday, and Resurrection Sunday. However, there was no agreement on including the Mass of the Lord's Supper on Holy Thursday in the Triduum as preparation for it.

Easter Triduum

For centuries now, in the liturgical laws, the three last days of the Holy Week have been designated by the name of the sacred Triduum (cf. red code n. 75). According to the Fathers — but the sacred Triduum was understood to be the three days which commemorate Christ fixed on the cross, buried and resurrected, that is, the 6th day, the Sabbath, and the Sunday after the Resurrection.

So that it may be more easily explained to the faithful that Easter includes the death, self-purification, and resurrection of Christ, the name of the Three Holy Days, or rather the Three Days of Easter, should be restored to these three days (Friday, Saturday, and Sunday).

It is debated among the consultants whether the beginning of this Triduum should be the Vespertine Mass at the Lord's Supper or whether this Triduum should begin on Friday the 6th in the Passion (and Friday the 5th is a festive day by which the three days of paschal are prepared).

Reasons for the 1st sentence: "According to ancient tradition, the narrative of the Lord's Passion always (until 1955) included the institution of the Eucharist (in fact, in ancient times, it also included the message of the resurrection). And the Paschal Supper indeed is, as the Synoptic Gospels say, an antitype of the leadership of the Lamb in the old nativity scene. Furthermore, the Passover had an ancient beginning Easter from synthesis. So it would be helpful and good to give the 5th holiday an aspect of penitential particularities.

The Consilium, in its fifth plenary assembly, gave its approval to the restructuring of the Easter Triduum (Friday, Saturday, and Sunday), and they agreed that the Mass in Cena Domini should also be part of the Triduum.

It was requested that appropriate means be found so that the mysteries of Christ's burial and his descent into hell would be presented to the faithful on Holy Saturday.

Season of Easter

Regarding the structuring of Easter time, Coetus I raised, on the one hand, the possibility of suppressing the octave of Pentecost so that Easter time would end on Pentecost Sunday after II Vespers, and, on the other hand, suggested that the seven Sundays of Easter, with the degree of celebration of the class, be named by progressive numbering accompanied by the indication "after Easter," including Sunday after Ascension and Pentecost Sunday. Furthermore, they wished to grant the Episcopal Conferences the power to move the Feast of the Ascension of the Lord from Thursday of the sixth week of Easter to the Sunday afterward.

- May it please us to suppress the octave of Pentecost to end the Easter period?
- Is there after Vespers (*Completorium*) of Pentecost Sunday?
- Is it acceptable that all the Sundays of the Easter season, including the Sunday after the Ascension and the Sunday of Pentecost, should be counted as "after Easter" so there would be seven Sundays after Easter?

- Would you like all Sundays of the Easter season to be celebrated as 1st class Sundays?
- Should the feast of the Lord's Ascension be assigned for the entire Church on the Sunday before Pentecost, or, having assigned the feast of the Ascension of the Lord to the day after Easter, should the competent territorial authorities be granted the opportunity for local needs, to replace the feast of the Lord's Ascension on the following Sunday?

They decided that the Paschal time would recover its old configuration, an extension of Easter for fifty days that culminated with the feast of Pentecost. For this reason, the octave of Pentecost, which was introduced into the Roman liturgy in the seventh century, would be suppressed, and the Sundays that make up this time would be designated "II, III, IV... of Easter" instead of "II, III, IV... after Easter". Moreover, even the Sunday of Pentecost could be added to its title, "Sunday VIII of Easter," to show that this time is an eighth of weeks of the feast of Easter. In addition, it could be moved to the following Sunday in those places where the Ascension was not a civil holiday.

Pentecost

Already in the 3rd century, it seems, Easter is regarded as a festival of fifty days or seven weeks (Pentecost). Hence it is read in the *Gelasian Sacramentary* (ed. Mohlberg, n. 637): *"Almighty and everlasting God, who willed the paschal sacrament to be kept in mystery for fifty days."* These fifty days begin on Easter Sunday and are completed on the fiftieth day or the day of Pentecost. In all Eastern rites, the Easter season closes in the evening, on the day of Pentecost. Therefore, these two things are proposed:

119

1. The Octave of Pentecost should be suppressed (by two advisers of a different opinion), and Pentecost should be regarded as the seal of the paschal season. When the day of Pentecost was no longer understood at first as the fiftieth day of the Easter season but as the annual festival of the descent of the Holy Spirit, an eighth was added.

2. That the Sundays of the Easter season should be counted:
   - Sunday (1) of Easter or Resurrection
   - Sunday 2nd, 3rd, 4th, 5th, 6th, 7th of Easter (or: Paschal)
   - Sunday (Day) Pentecost or Sunday 8th of Easter (Paschal), and so it is considered the eighth of the weeks of the Easter season.

Ascension

In many countries, Ascension is neither a feast of precept nor a civil feast. Therefore, for these regions, the possibility should be given to the territorial ecclesiastical authorities so that the Office and the Mass can be carried out on the following Sunday.

The Consilium ratified the proposal of Coetus I for the Easter season in its fifth plenary assembly.

1. May it be pleased that the eighth day after Pentecost should be suppressed so that the period of the Paschal should be fifty days according to the venerable tradition, retained by some of the formulas of the octave for the days between the Ascension and Pentecost so that there may be a spiritual preparation for Pentecost and a prayer may be made for the coming of the Holy Spirit?

Likes: 10

Dislikes: 5

Please proceed as follows: 1

I like it: 1, but let the brightness shine the following day.

2. Is it acceptable that the Episcopal Conferences can transfer the feast of the Ascension to the following Sunday in countries where this feast is no longer celebrated?

Like: 13

Dislike: 5

As we shall see, the Sacred Congregation for the Doctrine of the Faith welcomed the suppression of the octave of Pentecost as long as the euchological forms of those days were used for the fairs from the Ascension to Pentecost, forming a liturgical «*novenario[19]*» preparation for the descent of the Holy Spirit.

Sundays after Epiphany and Pentecost (Sundays «per annum»)

Coetus I focused on the first session of the Sundays after Epiphany and Pentecost, which were later called per annum. Next, Coetus I focused on the three Sundays preceding Lent, Quinquagesima, Sexagesima, and Septuagesima, which formed the so-called Septuagesima time, as well as the day to fix the feast of the Holy Trinity, proposing the Monday after Pentecost.

---

[19] In some cultures, the most common forms of observance after the deceased has been laid to rest are a *novenario* (nine days of prayer, which can include Masses or just rosaries) or a *triduo de misas* (three masses on three consecutive days).

Around the time of the Septuagint, the following solutions are proposed: a) or the names and formularies of the Sundays of Sept. they are kept, it is removed; yet the penitential character of this time; b) or the time of the Septuagint is suppressed, but the formularies are used at another time; c) or the time of the Septuagesima is suppressed, but the formularies (with no minis removed and in a penitential character: it is said Gloria, Alleluia, etc.) are added to the last three Sundays before Lent, omitting, if necessary, other formularies "after Epiphany."

Coetus I determined that the time from Septuagesima Sunday to Lent should lose its proper denomination and penitential character (suppression of the Gloria and the Alleluia; the purple color of the liturgical clothes) so that these features would stand out in Lent.

The Period after Epiphany to Lent

The period of the Septuagesima presents a difficulty. It would please all the Consultors if the time of the Septuagesima were suppressed as to the name and the penitential character (only one feeling otherwise). The penitential character of the time of the Septuagesima or Pre-Lent (suppression of Glory and Alleluia, violet color) is complicated for the faithful to understand, except with many explanations. The external signs of the penitential season are now used, as in Lent, but they are not bound to particular penance as in Lent. To the mind of the Constitution "*de sacra Liturgia,*" the organization of the liturgical year should be made more apparent, suppressing the penitential character of this season.

As regards the names of Septuagesima, Sexagesima, and Quinquagesima, since these names are also used separately by some brothers, we must proceed cautiously in this matter and promote conversations about this matter and others. Regarding the formularies of these Sundays, this question depends on Coetus XI (on readings in the Mass) and Coetus XIV (on songs in the Mass).

Feast of the Trinity

And regarding the transfer of the feast of the Holy Trinity to the Monday after Pentecost, there were different opinions: some considered it correct, others opted for the suppression of this feast since the entire liturgy is Trinitarian, and others were inclined to keep it as it was, particularly for ecumenical reasons since in some Eastern Churches this feast is celebrated.

Since the whole Liturgy is Trinitarian, especially the baptismal liturgy, most of the Consultors wished that the feast of the Trinity should be suppressed or transferred to the second day after Pentecost. An objection was made against the suppression because some of the separated brethren celebrate this feast, or at least call this Holy Trinity Sunday.

The Consilium, in its fifth plenary assembly, decided to suppress the time of Septuagesima as penitential time. Is it acceptable to suppress the period of Septuagesima as a penitential period, leaving untouched the question of formularies, which belongs to those to further study?

> I like: 12
> Dislikes: 3
> Please, according to the method: 1: time remains for the steps to Lent.
> None (white): 1

Some have expressed a desire that, by suppressing the almost penitential character of this season, the preparatory character for Lent should be preserved. And on the feast of the Holy Trinity, the Consilium agreed that it should remain on the Sunday after Pentecost.

May it please that the feast of SS. Trinity Sunday after Pentecost?

> Likes: 13
> Dislikes: 3
> None: 2

In the first schemas, the future Sundays per annum [Ordinary Time] were divided into two groups: time from Epiphany to Lent and time after Pentecost, as in the Tridentine Calendar. In the schema n. 132 of December 3, 1965, proposed to group the Sundays of this last block in two ways: 1-4 Sundays after Pentecost, 5-15 Sundays after the Apostles, and 16-25 Sundays after the Cross; or: 1-11 Sundays after Pentecost; 12-22 Sundays after the Assumption of the Virgin Mary and 23-25 Sundays after the Feast of All Saints (November 1).

For the Sundays after Pentecost, consider the extension of this season based on the division.

A	B
Sundays after Pentecost	Sundays after Pentecost
I-IV (4 Sundays)	I-XI (11 Sundays)
Sundays after Apostles	Sundays after the Assumption of the BVM
V-XV (11 Sundays)	XII-XXII (11 Sundays)
Sundays after the Cross	Sundays after the Feast of All Saints
XVI-XXV (10 Sundays)	XXIII-XXV (3 Sundays)

However, the proposal did not satisfy, so a progressive numbering was adopted, from 1 to 24, on the Sundays after Pentecost. "For the Sundays after Pentecost, a continuous progressive numbering from 1 to 24 is retained."

Finally, as reflected in schema n. 328 of November 27, 1968, the traditional denomination (Sundays after Epiphany and Sundays after Pentecost) was abandoned, uniting both groups under a single name: *Tempus per annum*, with a continuous numbering, from 1 to 34, of the Sundays and weeks.

Tempus per annum [Literally "Time per Year" or Ordinary Time]

Ordinary Time (Latin: *Tempus per annum*) is the portion of the Roman Rite's liturgical year that does not coincide with the two major seasons of Christmastide and Eastertide or the corresponding preparatory seasons of Advent and Lent. Thus, the intervals between Eastertide and Advent and Christmastide and Lent are referred to as Ordinary Time. The *Solemnity of Christ the King* is observed on the final Sunday of Ordinary Time. The word "ordinary" as it is used in this sentence derives from the ordinal numbers used to identify or count the weeks, which run from the first week of ordinary time in January to the 34th week, which starts near the end of November. In English, however, the word *Ordinary* has the misplaced connotation of plain or vanilla.

In the *usus antiquior,* the Sundays of the first period were identified as *Sundays after Epiphany* and those of the second period as *Sundays after Pentecost.* These terms were dropped as a result of the decision by the Consilium (and endorsed by Pope Paul VI) to regard all of Ordinary Time as a single unit.

Besides the seasons having their own character, which has been dealt with above, thirty-three or thirty-four weeks are found in the circle of the year, in which the peculiar aspect of the mystery of Christ is not celebrated; but rather the very mystery of Christ is remembered in its totality, especially on Sundays. A period of this kind is called "time per year." The period of the year, in its earlier part, begins on the 2nd day, which follows the 1st day after Epiphany, and continues until the 3rd day before Quadragesima [Lent] inclusive; It is then resumed in its other part, on the 2nd day after Pentecost Sunday and explicitly before the 1st Vespers of Sunday 1st Advent.

Litanies and four seasons [Ember Days]

Coetus I questioned the opportunity to maintain the obligatory nature of the litanies, both major and minor, and the day that the four epochs [Ember Days] should be celebrated, proposing March 21, June 21, September 21, and December 21.

- Would it please that both major and minor litanies be celebrated "optionally"?
- Would you like the Four Seasons to be arranged, so they are celebrated at the beginning of each of the four seasons (or around the 21st of March, June, September, and December)?

Initially, they agreed that each Episcopal Conference would set the time, the mode, and the most appropriate way to celebrate the litanies and the four seasons in each territory according to their own idiosyncrasies. This is how it appears in the first configuration of the Calendar prepared by Coetus I.

The major and minor litanies seem to be left to the territorial ecclesiastical authorities, both as to the time and the manner or form of performing them. Subsequently, as shown in schemas no. 132 of December 5, 1965, and n. 174 of August 1, 1966, decided to suppress the major litanies celebrated on April 25, as it is a local Roman festival that is well adapted to a Western calendar but does not make sense in other latitudes. In addition, that day was left free for the feast of the apostle and evangelist St. Mark. The minor or rogation litany and the ember days could be established by each Episcopal Conference on the days and in the manner convenient to the needs of each place, according to its own idiosyncrasy.

The older Litany (April 25) is suppressed. The lesser litanies are celebrated on the days and in the order established by the Episcopal Conferences, according to local circumstances, as votive celebrations that are not connected with a particular liturgical season. Likewise, as votive celebrations, the Ember Days are ordered to be organized by the Conferences of Bishops. With the number of places joined even less than now and connected with all the times, these celebrations will be able to take place.

To carry out the reform of the Calendar, Coetus I established criteria based on number 111 of the conciliar constitution *Sacrosanctum Concilium*: "So that the feasts of the saints do not prevail over the mysteries of salvation, let the celebration from many of them to particular Churches, nations or religious families, extending to the whole Church only those that commemorate saints of truly universal importance." The Consilium approved these principles in its fifth plenary session. Furthermore, they established: that saints from different regions should appear in the Roman calendar — such as the Japanese, Canadian, and Ugandan martyrs — to manifest the universality of the holiness of the Church and prevent the Roman Calendar was still Mediterranean; that the festivals of devotion be reduced, that is, those that do not commemorate an event or a mystery in the life of Christ, the Virgin or a saint; that efforts should be made to inscribe the saints in their *dies natalis [birthday]*; and, finally, that all the apostles and evangelists be present, those ancient martyrs with universal worship or of importance for the whole Church and who belonged to all states of ecclesial life, the significant doctors and it would be necessary to see if the minors should also have independent celebrations, and the most important saints whose spirituality or apostolate has spread throughout the Church.

1. In reviewing the calendar, Saints (or groups of Saints) taken from different countries should be retained or added to it to show that sanctity is spread throughout the whole Church. For example, the Roman calendar seems not a Mediterranean calendar. So, in sowing, they would be, e.g., Japanese, Canadian, and Ugandan martyrs.

2. The feasts which do not commemorate some deed or mystery of the Redeemer's life or any of the Saints are to be reduced, especially if they are duplicates of other feasts.

3. Several Saints may be inserted in the calendar on the same day, and then, if they are assigned to the "*ad libitum*" *[optional]*, one of the several may be chosen, whose Mass shall be celebrated. Therefore, the Office said, but in the Mass of one, the commemoration of the others shall not be made.

4. Regarding the different orders of Saints, the following has been proposed in particular:

    a. All the Apostles, who are the foundation of the Church, and the Evangelists should be retained in the calendar of the whole Church.

    b. They should be retained or included among the older martyrs:

        i. those who had universal worship or were of universal importance for the life of the Church;

      ii. selected from all groups of clerics and faithful.

  c. Older teachers must be retained; We will discuss the minors in detail.

  d. Those Saints are to be retained for the whole Church, those who hold the importance of the whole salt in front of them because of a particular form of spirituality or apostolic side, raised by them and spread throughout the Church.

Later they would be synthesized into these four principles: reduce the number of devotional festivals, subject to the critical examination of the historical data of the saints inscribed in the Calendar, choose important saints for the whole Church, reconsider the date set for the celebration of each saint and make the saint list more universal. Guided by these principles, the Lord's feasts, the Virgin Mary's feasts, and the saints inscribed in the Calendar were revised.

Feasts of the Lord

The festivals that celebrate the mysteries of redemption linked to the temporal cycle, that is, Christmas (December 25), Epiphany (January 6), Easter, Ascension, and Pentecost, were maintained according to the legacy of the liturgical tradition. However, where they were not civil holidays, it was allowed to move the Epiphany and Ascension festivities to Sunday.

As we have seen when speaking of time itself, Coetus I proposed the date change of the festivals of the Holy Family, the Baptism of the Lord, and the Holy Trinity.

    • The Corpus Christi feast would continue to be celebrated on the Thursday after

Trinity Sunday, although allowing the Episcopal Conferences the power to fix it on another more appropriate day.

- The Feast of the Corpus Christi remains the 5th day after Sunday of the Holy Trinity due to the possibility of the Episcopal Conferences choosing another day more suitable.

- Regarding the Feast of the Sacred Heart of Jesus, it was initially thought to fix it on the 3rd Sunday of Pentecost, receiving the denomination of "Sunday of the Sacred Heart of Jesus."

- The feast of the Sacred Heart of Jesus is connected with the 3rd Sunday after Pentecost, which therefore becomes "Sunday of the Sacred Heart of Jesus."

- But finally, it stayed on its traditional date: the Friday after Sunday II after Pentecost.

- The Feast of the Sacred Heart of Jesus remains the 6th Sunday after the 2nd Sunday after Pentecost.

- The feast of Jesus Christ, King of the Universe, previously celebrated on the last Sunday of October, would occupy the last Sunday of the Liturgical Year to show that history is heading toward Christ as its fullness.

- The last Sunday before Advent becomes "the Sunday of our Lord Jesus Christ, the Universal King," suppressed and therefore another feast of the last Lord, which is now assigned to October.

As we shall see, the Sacred Congregation for the Doctrine of the Faith was not in favor of this transfer. Although finally, it was accepted. The feasts of the

Presentation (February 2) and the Annunciation (March 25) ceased to be considered feasts of the Virgin Mary to be feasts of the Lord. The first of these appeared as such from the first schema of the Calendar (schema no. 109 of September 25, 1965): «*In Praesentatione Domini.*» The second was still a Marian feast in that schema, «*In Annuntiatione B.M.V.,*» but from the following one (schema no. 132 of December 3, 1965), it was already called «*Annuntiatio Domini.*»

The feast of the Most Precious Blood of Christ (July 1) was suppressed, leaving its euchological form among the votive masses. The Feast of the Most Precious Blood is to be proposed to be suppressed and kept only as a "devotion" since the worship of the same Blood of the Lord is most important, and in its proper place, at the time of the Passion. The Mass can be kept well between the votives.

Similarly, the feast of the Holy Name of Jesus was suppressed as such being included in the celebration of the eighth of Christmas where the Gospel refers to the inscription of the name of Jesus, since it was then, eight days after his birth, when being circumcised they gave him his name (cf. Lk 2, 16-21). However, the Missal would include a votive mass dedicated to the Holy Name of Jesus.

Festivities of the Virgin Mary

1) The Coetus I included in the first schema of the Calendar, schema n. 109 of September 25, 1965, the following Marian feasts: those feasts that celebrated the mysteries of the life of the Virgin Mary: Annunciation of the Virgin Mary (March 25), Visitation of the Virgin Mary (July 2), Assumption of the Virgin Mary (Aug. 15), Nativity of the Virgin Mary (Sept. 8) and Immaculate Conception of the Virgin Mary (Dec. 8); the feast of the

Presentation of the Lord (February 2), which ceased to be a Marian feast to become a feast of the Lord, as it was initially.

- A memorial of Mary on the Octave of Christmas, as we explained when speaking of the changes made to the feast of the Circumcision of the Lord (January 1), replacing the feast of October 11.
- And the following devotional festivals: Our Lady of Lourdes (February 11), Seven Sorrows of the Virgin Mary (September 15), and Our Lady of the Rosary (October 7).

The other Marian feasts present in the Tridentine Calendar were suppressed: the Seven Sorrows of the Virgin Mary (Friday before Palm Sunday), as it was a duplication of the feast of September 15; Queenship of Our Lady (May 31); Our Lady of the Snows (August 5), which was a local celebration, the Dedication of St. Mary Major of Rome, with legendary content; Most Holy Name of the Blessed Virgin Mary (September 12), because its content is included in the Nativity of the Virgin Mary (September 8), thus eliminating a duplicate; Our Lady of Mercy (September 24), as it is considered a particular festival, and the Presentation of the Blessed Virgin Mary (November 21), as it is based on the apocryphal gospels and its Eastern content (honoring the initial sanctity of Mary) is already celebrated in the West on the feast of the Immaculate Conception of the Blessed Virgin Mary (December 8).

As we shall see, in the end, the Dedication of St. Mary (August 5) was included in the penultimate schema (schema no. 260 of November 30, 1960), and the Presentation of the Blessed Virgin Mary (November 21), in the final version at the expressed wish of Pope Paul VI. The Sacred Congregation for the Doctrine of the Faith also asked that the latter be re-registered. In addition, this Congregation requested, without success, that the feast of the Most Holy Name of the Blessed Virgin Mary (September 12) be included again in the Calendar; however, it remained only as a votive ass of the Missal.

2) In the following schema, n. 132 of December 3, 1965, the Feast of the Annunciation (March 25), as had happened with the Presentation (February 2), became the Feast of the Lord, recovering its Christological title: Annunciation of the Lord.

As a novelty, this schema distinguishes between the parties whose celebration was considered obligatory and those that were not. Among the first would be: Immaculate Conception of the Blessed Virgin Mary (December 8), Nativity of the Blessed Virgin Mary (September 8), Visitation of the Blessed Virgin Mary (July 2), Maternity of the Blessed Virgin Mary (January 1) and Assumption of the Blessed Virgin Mary (August 15). And they were listed as free: Apparition of Lourdes (February 11), Queenship of Our Lady (May 31), Our Lady of Sorrows (September 15), and Our Lady of the Rosary (October 7).

The schema indicated that, although Our Lady of Mount Carmel and the Immaculate Heart of the Blessed Virgin Mary were not included in the Calendar, they would remain only as votive masses of the Missal. Finally, however, both ended up being part of the Roman Calendar. The first figure from the fifth schema, collected in the second annex of schema no. 154 of May 3, 1966, and the second was incorporated into the final text, as we will see, at the request of the Sacred Congregation for the Doctrine of the Faith, being fixed on the Saturday after the solemnity of the Sacred Heart of Jesus (in the Tridentine Calendar it had been inscribed on August 22).

As we shall see, the Sacred Congregation for the Doctrine of the Faith was also not in favor of moving the

Feast of the Motherhood of the Virgin Mary from October 11 to January 1. However, in the end, they accepted the change.

3) In the third schema of the Calendar, schema n. 138 of December 30, 1965, the feast of Queenship of Our Lady (May 31) was included.

4) In the seventh version of the Calendar, schema n. 188 of September 22, 1966, which was to be presented to the Consilium for approval at its seventh plenary assembly that took place from October 6 to 14, 1966, the feast of the Visitation of St. Mary Virgin was transferred from July 2 to May 31, as the conclusion of the Marian month, the celebration of Queenship of Our Lady inscribed on that day being suppressed.

As we shall see, the Sacred Congregation for the Doctrine of the Faith was not in favor of changing the date for the feast of the Visitation of the Blessed Virgin Mary or suppressing the feast of the Queenship of Our Lady. So, finally, they accepted the transfer of the Visitation of the Virgin Mary to May 31 and managed to include the Queenship of Our Lady in the Calendar, but on August 22, as if it were an octave of the feast of the Assumption of the Blessed Virgin Mary, instead of May 31.

The Merits of the Saints[20]

While we might deserve graces for others via our prayers and good acts on earth, the Church teaches that the merits of the saints in heaven are incomparably more potent in attaining the graces and benefits we require. As a result, the traditional orations invoke the merits of the saints at least 200 times throughout the liturgical year. An oration will typically request something from God by "the assistance of their merits," "merits and prayers," "merits and intercession," or "merits and example."

The merits of the saints accompanied the soul into virtual oblivion in Paul VI's Missal orations. The revisers substituted new orations for the old ones that highlighted merits in 30 cases. The revisers removed the phrase "merit" from 21 other orations to the saints that they kept, and just three of the thirteen orations where it still appears in the revised Missal are mandatory.

Why virtually eliminate the concept of saints' merits? One possible explanation is the modern (and modernist) propensity to deny any actual boundary between the natural and supernatural orders, presenting religion as basically horizontal. One of the reviser's criticisms of the ancient saintly orations was that they were "too abstract," incapable of offering an attainable ideal of virtue for the modern man.

A typical outcome is the new Collect in honor of St. Gertrude the Great, which piqued [Fr. Cekada's] curiosity in researching new orations in the first place. Both the old and new Latin versions begin with the same phrase: "O God, who didst make a delightful dwelling for thyself in the heart of the holy virgin Gertrude..." However, the rest of the prayer has been rewritten:

---

[20] Cekada Anthony. *Work of Human Hands: A Theological Critique of the Mass of Paul Vi.* Philothea Press 2010.

Old Text	New Text
by her	*by her*
merits and	
intercession	*intercession*
do Thou mercifully	*do Thou mercifully*
wash away from	*enlighten*
our hearts the stains [of sin]	*the darkness of our hearts*
and grant that we may rejoice	*that we may joyfully*
[with her]	*experience Thee working*
in [heavenly] fellowship.	*and present within us.*

The prayer's entire perspective was altered: "enlightenment" and "joy" are part of modern man's experience, but merits, the stains of sin, and heavenly communion are not; therefore, the notions vanished.

Ecumenism was undoubtedly another motivation for abolishing merit. While the Church teaches that we might deserve for ourselves and others, traditional Protestantism claimed that human nature was so depraved that nothing could be merited. Remove the word from saints' orations, and another ecumenical hurdle is removed.

The Disappearance of Miracles

As theologians such as St. Robert Bellarmine have remarked, miracles are so inextricably linked to the Catholic religion that they cannot be separated from it. The Church's life, made illustrious by the remarkable lives of the saints, is a constant testament to the fidelity of miracles.

Some ancient orations, like those celebrating St. Fidelis of Sigmaringen and St. Augustine of Canterbury, simply mention the miracles performed by these saints. Other orations mention specific miracles, such as St. Raymond of Peñafort walking on water, St. Scholastica's soul ascending to heaven in the form of a dove, the fire of love in St. John of God's heart being so great that he emerged unscathed from rescuing the sick from a burning building, or St. Frances of Rome conversing with her Guardian Angel.

Needless to add, these miracles have all been hidden to make the prayers better suited to "the mindset of contemporary man," according to Fr. Carlo Braga, C.M. [21, 22] Expressions of the extraordinary or miraculous are "typical of a certain historical hagiography."

Such arguments may have led to the abolition of the ancient St. Nicholas oration:

> *O God, who hast adorned the blessed Bishop Nicholas*
> *with numberless miracles:*
> *grant, we beseech Thee,*
> *that by his merits and prayers*
> *we may be saved from the fires of hell.*

However, merits or the fires of hell could just as easily have been the culprits.

Why not "demythologize" the Queen of All Saints if the saints are? The oration for the Feast of Our Lady of Lourdes no longer references her apparition, but neither does the new oration for the Feast of Our Lady of the Rosary.

Finally, no oration recounting the miraculous in Our Lord's life was safe from the rationalists: God's voice no longer speaks from the cloud on the Feast of the Transfiguration, and Christ's miracle of resurrecting Lazarus has been permanently buried.

---

[21] Vincentian Father Carlo Braga was a modern-day architect of liturgical reform, both before and after Vatican II. Fr. Braga was a close collaborator of Annibale Bugnini in the creation of the post-Conciliar liturgy, in addition to numerous scholarly publications on the liturgy.

[22] Braga, Carlo, C. M. "Il «Proprium de Sanctis»." *Ephemerides Liturgicae*, translated by Matthew Hazell, vol. 84, no. 6, 1970, pp. 401–31. Roma: Edizioni Liturgiche. [Available in English at: *New Liturgical Movement*, newliturgicalmovement.org/2022/07/the-post-vatican-ii-reform-of-proper-of.html].

None of this should surprise anyone who has taken a scripture course in a seminary or a (nominally) Catholic university since Vatican II. Modernist scripture experts habitually dismiss the miracles reported in the Bible, including those accomplished by Our Lord, as impossible, unlikely, incomprehensible, myths, fables, ordinary natural phenomena, "faith reflections," and generally devoid of historical truth. While the modernists who designed Paul VI's Mass could not remove the supernatural from the scriptural readings, they could and did remove it from the orations, imposing their rationalist skepticism on the unknowing layman. Nevertheless, he retained his devotion to Our Lord, Our Lady, and the saints.

The Repercussions

When the texts of the new orations are compared to the texts of the old orations, a long list of Catholic doctrines that the revisers either obliterated or left to fade into the background emerges: hell, judgment, God's wrath, punishment for sin, the wickedness of sin as the greatest evil, detachment from the world, the souls of the departed, Christ's kingship on earth, the Church Militant, and the triumph of the Catholic faith.

The list reads like a curriculum of Catholic teachings and practices that modernists, Protestants, and rationalists reject. And as the Society of St. Pius X's study of liturgical reform pointed out, many of these beliefs are tied to the teaching that the Mass is a sacrifice of propitiation for sin, a doctrine that Protestants and modernists all reject.

To dismiss all of the differences in the orations as mere style or emphasis is to ignore the evidence. The revisers said unequivocally that they were changing "doctrinal realities."

This has serious repercussions. One of the Consilium's experts, Msgr. A.G. Martimort argued that the Missal's orations comprise the single most important liturgical *locus theologicus* (source for proving theological truths), since they "interpret the assembly's shared faith."

It is not unexpected, then, that theologians used the withdrawal of specific terms and concepts from the new Missal to criticize teachings that are part of the deposit of faith as early as the early 1970s." Armed with evidence of how Paul VI's Missal changed the doctrinal content of the orations, it becomes a simple matter for the modernist theologian to undercut further the Church's teaching on such minor matters as sin, hell, the true Church and the soul — all while claiming with a straight face that he, too, is loyal to the Magisterium.

Then there is the guy in the back row. According to Braga, the new Missal's contents "will have a transformational influence on catechesis." And it has, mainly because modernists, influenced by Jungmann's pastoral care theory, regard public worship as a classroom for invigorating the celebrating assembly.

In this setting, it is difficult for the layperson to understand why fasting, detachment, or the soul are essential to him because they are no longer part of his weekly devotion. And suppose he no longer believes (or is even aware of) these and other key elements of Church teaching. In that case, it largely stems from the mutilation of Catholic theology in Paul VI's Missal orations.

The Canceled Saints of 1969

The italic text following the saint's name is the official reason for their removal from the universal calendar.

These saints and commemorative feast days were deemed to either have not been of importance to the universal Church, or that not enough historical information exists to verify the accuracy of their hagiographies. Presented for the reader's own edification are popular accounts of the lives of these saints.

A number of these sanctoral hagiographies, including all of French language origin, are reprinted courtesy of: Monastère Magnificat, 290 7e Rang, Mont-Tremblant, QC J8E 1Y4, Canada. Please visit them at https://sanctoral.com.

Rev. Hugo Hoever's 1955 Preface to the *Lives of the Saints for Every Day of the Year: Illustrated*

The advantages Catholics derive from reading the Lives of the Saints are numerous because they are not only sources of knowledge but also handmaids of virtue and perennial fountains of progress in perfection.

In perusing the following biographical sketches of God's saints, among which may be found short historical accounts of the principal Feast Days of the Liturgical Year, we are unconsciously moved to imitate them. We are thus drawn nearer to men and women genuinely great and good. By admiring their actions, we learn to follow their examples.

The saints still live in their deeds and the edification they have given to the Church. Their light still shines before men. From the earliest ages, their examples have been innumerable Christians' inspiration, joy, hope, and consolation.

The reader will find in the Lives of the Saints numberless motives to console him in adversity, counsel him in doubt, support and strengthen him in temptation, caution him against impending dangers, and rebuke him in his transgressions. The lives of those men and women who have been martyrs to truth and justice are truly absorbing and inspiring records unmatched throughout the history of mankind.

To some degree, each saint is an imitation of all of the virtues and perfections of the God-Man, Jesus Christ. At the same time, each imitates more fully and vividly depicts one particular perfection of our Lord. Thus, the diligent and prayerful reader is confronted with an overall brilliant picture of the numberless perfections of Christ. He perceives in a Francis of Assisi our Lord's overwhelming love for the poor; in a Francis de Sales, His profound humility; in a Francis Xavier, His indefatigable labor for souls. He cannot help but arrive at a fuller, deeper, and, above all, more practical knowledge of Jesus—a knowledge of Him as He is, coupled with a desire to follow Him.

In turn, this knowledge of our Lord is also a knowledge of God the Father. "If you had known Me, you would also have known My Father" (John 14:7). And it is this knowledge of God the Father and the Son which is the fulfillment of the Christian's life — the beginning and the end of everlasting life. "Now this is everlasting life, that they may know Thee, the only true God, and Him whom Thou hast sent, Jesus Christ" (John 17:3).

Adapted from *Lives of the Saints for Every Day of the Year: Illustrated* (pp. 3-4), by Rev. Hugo H. Hoever, SOCist, Ph.D., 1955, New York, N.Y.: Catholic Book Publishing Co. Reprinted with permission.

JANUARY

Saint Telesphorus, Pope, and Martyr (†137) — January 5

The commemoration of Telesphorus, added to the Roman Calendar in 1602, is deleted. In the martyrology of Jerome, the reference on this day is not to Pope Telesphorus but to another martyr from Africa about whom nothing is known.

By the death of Saint Sixtus[23], the first of that name, Pope, and Martyr, succeeded in Saint Peter's Chair Saint Telesphorus, also Pope and Martyr. He was of Greece by birth and had been an anchorite[24], and for his great sanctity and high merits, two days after the death of Saint Sixtus, he was elected Chief Bishop with much applause. In his time arose many heretics and false prophets, which disturbed the Church of God, and by their wicked and dishonest lives, were a discredit to the Christian religion. As they lived lewdly, given to all vice and baseness, calling themselves Christians, the Gentiles believed that all Christians were like unto them. And that their religion gave license to live in that manner; did they despise all those who professed it, and persecuted them, judging them unworthy of living, and deserving any torment whatsoever. But our Lord was pleased that by the diligence and vigilance of Saint Telesphorus, Saint Justin, the philosopher and martyr, and other holy and learned persons, whom God raised in His good time for the protection of His Church, the truth was discovered. The heretics, with their followers, were known for wicked, and

---

[23] Pope Sixtus I, also known as Xystus, was a Roman of Greek descent who served as bishop of Rome from around 115 until his death in 126.
[24] An anchorite or anchoret is a Christian who withdraws from secular society for religious reasons in order to live an intensely prayer-oriented, ascetic, or Eucharist-focused life.

the Catholics for Good, as they were. Saint Telesphorus, in his life and conversation, was very like to those holy chief pastors, his predecessors, and as such he ought to be, who undertook so high a dignity.

He ordained before Easter that there should be a fast kept for seven weeks, and the clergy began to fast from Quinquagesima Sunday[25]: and from henceforth, some have believed Telesphorus instituted the fast of Lent. But the truth is, the institution is from the Apostles. Before this bishop's time, it was practiced in the Church of God, as gathered from Saint Ignatius and other holy and most ancient writers. He also commended that Mass should be celebrated on the night of the Nativity and that in the Mass should be said the Hymn of the Angels, Gloria in Excelsis Deo. He gave orders four times in December and then ordained twelve priests, eight deacons, and thirteen bishops. He was martyred during the time of Antonius Pius[26], Emperor, in the year of our Lord 154. He was buried in the Vatican, near the body of Saint Peter, Prince of the Apostles, having governed the Church eleven years nine months, wanting three days. The Holy Church celebrates his Commemoration on the fifth of January, the day of his martyrdom; Pope Clement VIII commanded it to be added to the reformed Breviary, which by his order was published in 1602.

[Ribadeneyra, Pedro de. "The Life of Saint Telesphorus, Pope and Martyr." *The Lives of Saints, With Other Feasts of the Year, according to the Roman Calendar. Written in Spanish by the Reverend Father Peter Ribadeneyra, Priest of the Society of Jesus. Translated Into English by W.P. (William Petre) Esq; The Second Edition Corrected and Amended*, vol.1, pp. 75-76. London. Printed by B.S., 1730. *HathiTrust Digital Library*, hdl.handle.net//2027/nyp.33433003053000.]

---

[25] Quinquagesima is the last Sunday of Shrovetide, the Sunday before Ash Wednesday, in the Western Christian Churches.

[26] Aelius Hadrianus Antoninus Pius, Roman emperor: 10 July 138 – 7 March 161.

Saint Hyginus, Pope, and Martyr (74–142) — January 11

The memorial of Hyginus, added to the Roman calendar in the twelfth century, is deleted. He cannot be counted among the martyrs since nothing is known about the circumstances of his death.

He was placed in the chair of Saint Peter after the martyrdom of Saint Telesphorus in the year 139. Eusebius informs us that he sat for four years. The church then enjoyed some calm under the mild reign of the emperor Antoninus Pius. Unfortunately, however, several martyrs suffered in his time by the fury of the populace or the cruelty of certain magistrates. The emperor himself never consented to such proceedings. On the contrary, when informed of them by the governors of Asia, Athens, Thessalonica, and Larissa, he wrote to them in favor of the Christians, as is recorded by Saint Justin and Eusebius.

But the devil had recourse to other arts to disturb the peace of God's church. Cerdo, a wolf in sheep's clothing, in the year 140, came from Syria to Rome and began to teach the false principles, which Marcion adopted afterward with more success. He impiously affirmed that there were two Gods; the one rigorous and severe, the author of the Old Testament; the other merciful and good, the author of the New, and the father of Christ, sent by him to redeem man from the tyranny of the former; and that Christ was not really born of the Virgin Mary or true man, but such in shadow only and appearance. Our holy pope, by his pastoral vigilance, detected that monster and cut him off from the communion of the church. The heresiarch[27], imposing upon him by a false repentance, was again received, but

---

[27] A heresiarch, also known as an arch-heretic in Christian theology, is the originator of heretical doctrine or the founder of a sect that upholds such doctrine.

the zealous pastor, having discovered that he secretly preached his old opinions, excommunicated him a second time.

Another minister of Satan was Valentine, who was a Platonic philosopher, puffed up with the vein opinion of his learning. So full of resentment for another is being preferred to him in an election to a certain bishopric in Egypt, as Tertullian relates, revived the errors of Simon Magus[28], and added to them many other absurd fictions, as of thirty eons or ages, a kind of inferior deities, with whimsical histories of their several pedigrees. Having broached these opinions at Alexandria, he left Egypt for Rome. At first, he dissembled his heresies, but his extravagant doctrines became known by degree. Hyginus, being the mildest of men, endeavored to reclaim him without proceeding to extremities; so that Valentine was not excommunicated before the first year of Saint Pius, his immediate successor.

Saint Hyginus did not sit for quite four years, dying in 142. We do not find that he ended his life by martyrdom, yet he is styled a martyr in some ancient calendars, as well as in the present Roman Martyrology; undoubtedly on account of the various persecutions which he suffered and to which his high station in the church exposed him in those difficult times.

[Butler, Alban. *The Lives of the Fathers, Martyrs, and Other Principal Saints. Compiled from Original Monuments and Authentic Records*, vol. 1. Dublin: James Duffy, 1866. *HathiTrust Digital Library*, catalog.hathitrust.org/Record/001941109.]

---

[28] Simon Magus, also known as Simon the Sorcerer or Simon the Magician, was a religious figure who clashed with Peter in Acts 8:9-24. The act of simony, or paying for position, was named after Simon, who attempted to buy his way into the Apostles' power.

Saint Felix of Nola, Priest, and Confessor (†January 14, 255 AD) — January 14

The ancient memorial of Felix, who lived at Nola and died there about 250, is left for the particular calendars. Felix was a confessor of the faith but not a martyr.

It is observed by the judicious Tillemont, regarding the life of this saint, that we might doubt its extraordinary circumstances were they not supported by the authority of a Paulinus; but those great miracles ought to be received with the greater reverence when authorized by incontestable vouchers.

Saint Felix was a native of Nola, a Roman colony in Campania, fourteen miles from Naples, where his father Hermias, who was by birth a Syrian and had served in the army, had purchased an estate and settled himself. He had two sons, Felix and Hermias, to whom he left his inheritance at his death. The younger sought advancement in the world among the lovers of vanity by following the profession of arms, which was the surest road to riches and honors at that time. But, to become what his name in Latin imported, that is happy, Felix resolved to follow no other standard than that of the King of kings, Jesus Christ. For this purpose, despising all earthly things, lest the love of them might entangle his soul, he distributed the better part of his substance among the poor and was ordained Reader Exorcist and, lastly, a priest by Maximus, the holy bishop of Nola; who, charmed with his sanctity and prudence, made him his principal support in those times of trouble, and designed him for his successor.

In the year 250, the emperor Decius[29] raised a bloody persecution against the church. Maximus, seeing

---

[29] Gaius Messius Quintus Traianus Decius, Roman emperor: September/October 249 – June 251.

himself principally aimed at, retired into the desert, not through the fear of death, which he desired, but rather not to tempt God by seeking it and to preserve himself for the service of his flock. The persecutors, not finding him, seized on Felix, who, in his absence, was very vigilant in discharging all his pastoral duties. The governor caused him to be scourged; then loaded with bolts and chains about his neck, hands, and legs and cast into a dungeon, in which, as Saint Prudentius informs us, the floor was spread all over with potsherds and pieces of broken glass, so that there was no place free from them, on which the saint could either stand or lie. One night an angel appeared in great glory, filled the prison with a bright light, and bade Saint Felix go and assist his bishop, who was in great distress. The confessor seeing his chains fall off and the doors open, followed his guide and was conducted by heaven to the place where Maximus lay, almost perished with hunger and cold, speechless, and without sense: for, through anxiety for his flock, and the hardships of his solitary retreat, he had suffered more than martyrdom. Not being able to bring him to himself, Felix had recourse to prayer; discovering a bunch of grapes within reach, he squeezed some of the juice into his mouth, which had the desired effect. The good bishop no sooner beheld his friend Felix, but he embraced him and begged to be conveyed back to his church. The saint taking him on his shoulders, carried him to his episcopal house in the city before day appeared, where a pious ancient woman took care of him.

With the blessing of his pastor, Felix repaired secretly to his lodgings and there kept himself concealed, praying for the church without ceasing, till peace was restored to it by the death of Decius in the year 251. He no sooner appeared again in public, but his zeal so exasperated the pagans that they came armed to apprehend him; but though they met him, they knew him not; they even asked him where Felix was, a question he did not think proper to give a direct answer! The persecutors going a little further perceived their mistake and returned, but in the meantime, the saint had stepped a little out of the way and crept through a hole in a ruinous old wall, instantly closed by spider webs. His enemies, never imagining anything could have lately passed where they saw so close a spiders' web after a fruitless search elsewhere, returned in the evening without their prey. Felix found among the ruins, between two houses, an old well half dry, hid in it for six months; and received money to exist through a devout Christian woman. Peace was restored to the church by the emperor's death, the saint quitted his retreat, and was received in the city as an angel sent from heaven.

Soon after, with Saint Maximus dying, all were unanimous on electing Felix as bishop. Still, he persuaded the people to choose Quintus because the older priest of the two had been ordained seven days before him. Quintus, when bishop, always respected Saint Felix as his father and followed his every advice. The remainder of the saint's estate having been confiscated in the persecution, he was advised to lay claim to it, as others had done, who thereby recovered what had been taken from them. He answered that he should be more secure in possessing Christ in poverty. He could not even be prevailed upon to accept what the rich offered him. He rented a little spot of barren land, not exceeding three acres, which he tilled with his own hands in such manner as to receive his subsistence from it and to have something left for alms. Whatever was bestowed on him, he gave immediately to the poor. If he had two coats, he was sure to provide them with the better; and often exchanged his only one for the rags of some beggar. He died in a good old age on the fourteenth of January, on which day the Martyrology, under the name of Saint Jerome, and all others of later date mention him. Five churches have been built at or near where he was first interred, without the precincts of the city of Nola. His precious remains are kept in the cathedral, but certain portions are in Rome, Benevento, and other places. Pope Damasus, in a pilgrimage which he made from Rome to Nola, to the shrine of this saint, professes, in a short poem which he composed in acknowledgment, that he was miraculously cured of a distemper through his intercession.

Saint Paulinus, a Roman senator in the fifth age, forty-six years after the death of Saint Damasus, came from Spain to Nola, desirous of being a porter in the church of Saint Felix. He testifies that crowds of pilgrims came from Rome, from all other parts of Italy, and more distant countries, to visit his sepulcher on his festival: he adds that all brought some present or different to his church, such as wax candles to burn at his tomb, precious ointments, costly ornaments, and such like; but that for his part, he offered to him the homage of his tongue, and himself, though an unworthy victim. He everywhere expresses his devotion to this saint in the warmest and strongest terms and believes that all the graces he received from heaven were conferred on him through the intercession of Saint Felix. To him, he addressed himself in all his necessities; by his prayers, he begged grace in this life and glory after death. He describes at large the holy pictures of the history of the Old Testament, which were hung up in the church of Saint Felix, inflamed all who beheld them and were as many books that instructed the ignorant. We may read with pleasure the pious sentiments each sight gave Saint Paulinus. He relates a significant number of miracles wrought at his tomb, as persons cured of various distempers and delivered from dangers by his intercession to several of which he was an eyewitness. He testifies that he had frequently experienced the most practical effects of his patronage and had been speedily succored by having recourse to him. Saint Augustine also gave an account of many miracles performed at his shrine. It was not formerly allowed to bury any corpse within the walls of cities.

The church of Saint Felix, out of the walls of Nola, not being comprised under this prohibition, many devout Christians sought to be buried in it, that their faith and devotion might recommend them after death to the patronage of this holy confessor upon which head Saint Paulinus consulted Saint Augustine. The holy doctor answered him by his book, *On the Care for the Dead*[30]: in which he shows that the faith and devotion of such persons would be available to them after death, as the suffrages and good works of the living on behalf of the faithful departed are profitable to the latter.

[Butler, Alban. *The Lives of the Fathers, Martyrs, and Other Principal Saints. Compiled from Original Monuments and Authentic Records*, vol. 1. Dublin: James Duffy, 1866. *HathiTrust Digital Library*, catalog.hathitrust.org/Record/001941109.]

Saint Paul the Hermit or Saint Paul of Thebes (227–342) — January 15

In the twelfth century, the memorial of Paul was assigned to the Roman calendar. Still, it may now be used only in particular calendars since many historical difficulties were found concerning Jerome's account of his life.

Saint Paul was born in Upper Egypt in about the year 229 and became an orphan at the age of fifteen. He was wealthy and highly educated. Fearing lest the tortures of terrible persecution might endanger his Christian perseverance, he retired to a remote village. But his pagan brother-in-law denounced him, and Saint Paul, rather

---

[30] Augustine, of Hippo Saint, *Saint Austins Care for the Dead, or His Bouke Intit'led De Cura Pro Mortuis, Translated, etc. (the Soules Supplication at the Houre of Deth. [in Verse.])*.

than remain where his faith was in danger, entered the barren desert, trusting that God would supply his wants. And his confidence was rewarded; on the spot to which Providence led him, he found the fruit of a palm-tree for food, its leaves for clothing, and the spring water for drink.

His first plan was to return to the world when the persecution was over, but tasting great delights in prayer and penance, he remained for the rest of his life, ninety years, in penance, prayer, and contemplation.

God revealed his existence to Saint Anthony, who sought him for three days. Seeing a thirsty she-wolf run through an opening in the rocks, Anthony followed her to look for water and found Paul. They knew each other at once and praised God together. While Saint Anthony was visiting him, a raven brought them a loaf of bread, and Saint Paul said, "*See how good God is! For sixty years, this bird has brought me half a loaf each day; now, Christ has doubled the provision for His servants at your coming.*"

The two religious passed the night in prayer, and then at dawn, Paul told Anthony that he was about to die and asked to be buried in the cloak given to Anthony by Saint Athanasius. He asked him this to show that he was dying in communion with Saint Athanasius, the invincible defender of the Faith against the Arian heresy. Anthony hastened back to fetch it, and when he returned to Paul, he saw his co-hermit rising to heaven in glory. He found his dead body kneeling as in prayer and saw two lions come and dig his grave. Saint Paul, The Patriarch of Hermits, died in his one hundred and thirteenth year.

[Shea, John G. *Little Pictorial Lives of the Saints, with Reflections for Every Day of the Year; Compiled from "Butler's Lives."* New York: Benziger, 1894. *HathiTrust Digital Library,* hdl.handle.net/2027/nyp.33433068232887.]

Saint Maurus (Maur), Abbot (510–584) — January 15

The memorial of Maur, added to the Roman Calendar in the twelfth century, is likewise left for particular calendars. Mentioned in the Dialogues of Gregory the Great as a disciple of Benedict, he is now distinguished from Maur of Glanfeuil (near Angers, France), mentioned in the Roman Martyrology.

Among the several noblemen who placed their sons under the care of Saint Benedict to be brought up in piety and learning, Equitius, one of that rank, left with him his son Maurus, then but twelve years old, in 522. The youth surpassed all his fellow monks in the discharge of monastic duties, and when he was grown up, Saint Benedict made him his coadjutor in the government of Subiaco. Maurus was a model of perfection to all brethren and favored by God with the gift of miracles by his singleness of heart and profound humility. Saint Placidus, a fellow monk, the son of the senator Tertullus, going one day to fetch water, fell into the lake and was carried the distance of a bow-shot from the bank. Saint Benedict saw this in the spirit in his cell and bid Maurus to run and draw him out. Maurus obeyed, walked upon the waters without perceiving it, and dragged out Placidus by the hair without sinking. He attributed the miracle to the prayers of Saint Benedict, the holy abbot, to the obedience of the disciple soon after that holy patriarch retired to Cassino, which he called Saint Maurus thither, in the year 528.

Saint Maurus came to France in 543, founded, by the liberality of king Theodebert, the great abbey of Glanfeuil, now called Saint-Maur-sur-Loire, which he governed for several years. In 581, he resigned the abbacy to Bertulf. He passed the remainder of his life in close solitude, in the uninterrupted contemplation of heavenly things, to prepare himself for his passage to eternity. After two years thus employed, he fell sick of a fever, with a pain in his side: he received the church's sacraments, lying on sackcloth before the altar of Saint Martin, and in the same posture expired on the 15th of January, in the year 584. He was buried on the right side of the altar in the same church, and on a roll of parchment laid in his tomb was inscribed this epitaph: "Maurus, a monk, and deacon, who came into France in the days of king Theodebert, and died the eighteenth day before February." Saint Maurus is named in the ancient French litany composed by Alcuin and in the Martyrologies of Florus, Usuard, and others. For fear of the Normans, in the ninth century, his body was translated to several places; lastly, in 868, to Saint Peter's des Fosses, then a Benedictine abbey, near Paris, where it was received with great solemnity by Æneas[31], bishop of Paris. A history of this translation, written by Eudo, at that time abbot of Saint Peter's des Fosses, is still extant. This *Abbaye des Fossés* (now Saint-Maur Abbey) was founded by Blidegisilus, deacon of the church of Paris, in the time of King Clovis II and Audebert, bishop of Paris: Saint Babolen was the first abbot. This monastery was reformed by Saint Mayeul, abbot of Cluny, in 988. In 1533, it was secularized by Clement VII at the request of Francis I. The deanery united to the bishopric of Paris, but the church and village have been born the name of Saint Maur for several ages. The abbey of Glanfeuil, now called Saint Maur–sur–Loire, was subjected to *Abbaye des Fossés* from the reign of Charles the Bald to the year 1096, in which Urban II, at the solicitation of the count of Anjou, re-established its primitive independence. Our ancestors revered Saint Maurus under the Norman kings: the noble family of

---

[31] From 858 to 870, Aeneas of Paris was the bishop of Paris. He is best known as the author of one of the contentious treatises against the Byzantines prompted by Photius' encyclical letters.

Seymour (from the French Saint Maur) borrowed its name from him, as Camden observes in his Remains. The church of Saint Peter's des Fosses, two leagues from Paris, now called Saint Maurus's, was secularized and made collegiate in 1533. The canons were removed to Saint Louis, formerly called Saint Thomas of Canterbury, at the Louvre in Paris, in 1750. The same year the relics of Saint Maurus were translated thence to the abbey of Saint-Germain-des-Prés[32], where they are preserved in a rich shrine. An arm of this saint was, with great devotion, translated to Mount Cassino in the eleventh century. By its touch, a demoniac was afterward delivered, as is related by Desiderius, at that time abbot of Mount Cassino, later pope, named Victor III.

[Butler, Alban. *The Lives of the Fathers, Martyrs, and Other Principal Saints. Compiled from Original Monuments and Authentic Records.* Dublin: James Duffy, 1866. *HathiTrust Digital Library,* catalog.hathitrust.org/Record/001941109.]

Saint Marcellus, Pope, and Martyr (†310) — January 16

Pope Marcellus died in Rome in 309. Since he is not a martyr nor a saint of universal significance, he is left for the particular calendars.

During the third century, paganism and Christianity vied for supremacy in the Roman Empire. Hoping to stifle the Church entirely, the emperor Diocletian in 303 began the last and fiercest of the persecutions. In time, Christian charity conquered pagan brutality. As the Church attracted increased members, the Roman government was compelled to recognize its

---

[32] Saint-Germain-des-Prés is a parish church in Paris's Saint-Germain-des-Prés district. It was originally the church of Childebert's Benedictine abbey, founded in the sixth century. I, the son of Clovis, King of the Franks, made it one of Paris's oldest churches.

existence. Still, after almost three hundred years, during which persecutions had forced Christian worship underground, the Church would finally come out into the open after the Edict of Nantes in 313. However, it was still young and disorganized, vulnerable to heresy and apostasy, and needed a strong leader to settle questions of doctrine and discipline.

Such a leader came to the Chair of Peter in 304, when Saint Marcellus was elected pope. Saint Marcellinus, his predecessor, while being taken to torture, had urged him not to cede to the decrees of Diocletian, and it became evident that Marcellus did not intend to temporize. Instead, he established new catacombs and saw that the divine mysteries were continually celebrated there. Then three years of relative peace were given to the church when Maxentius became emperor in 307, for he was too occupied with other difficulties to persecute the Christians.

After assessing the Church's problems, Saint Marcellus planned a robust reorganization program. Rome, then as now, was the seat of Catholicism, and his program was initiated there. First, he divided the territorial administration of the Church into twenty-five districts or parishes, placing a priest over each one, thus restoring an earlier division that the turmoil of the persecutions had disrupted. This arrangement permitted more efficient care in instructing the faithful, in preparing candidates for baptism and penitents for reconciliation. With these measures in force, the Church government took on a definite form.

Marcellus' most significant problem was dealing with the Christians who had apostatized during the persecution. Many of these were determined to be reconciled to the Church without performing the necessary penances. The Christians who had remained faithful demanded that the customary penitential discipline be maintained and enforced. Marcellus approached this problem with uncompromising justice; the apostates were in the wrong and, regardless of the consequences, were obliged to do penance. It was not long before the discord between the faithful and the apostates led to violence in the very streets of Rome.

An account of Marcellus' death, dating from the fifth century, relates that Maxentius, judging the pope responsible for the trouble between the Christian factions, condemned him to work as a slave on the public highway. After nine months of this hard labor, he was rescued by the clergy and taken to the home of a widow named Lucina; this woman welcomed him with every sign of respect and offered him her home for a church. However, when the emperor learned that Christian rites were being celebrated there, he profaned the church by turning it into a stable and forced the Holy Father to care for the animals quartered there. In these sad surroundings, Marcellus died on January 16, 310. First, he was buried in the catacombs of Priscilla, but later his remains were placed beneath the church's altar in Rome, which still bears his name.

[Guérin, Abbé (Paul), François Giry, and Simon Martin. *Les Petits Bollandistes: Vies Des Saints De L'Ancien et du Nouveau Testament.* Translated by the Monastère du Magnificat. Paris: Bloud et Barral, 1882. *HathiTrust Digital Library,* hdl.handle.net//2027/nnc1.0036694380]

Saint Prisca, Virgin, and Martyr (✝275) — January 18

Although the memorial of Prisca is very ancient, it is left to the calendar of her titular church on the Aventine. The Acts of Prisca are legendary and probably refer to someone else.

After many torments, she was a noble Roman lady and finished her triumph by the sword about the year 275. Her relics are preserved in the ancient church, which bears her name in Rome and gives her title to a cardinal. She is mentioned in the sacramentary of Saint Gregory and almost all western Martyrologies. The acts of her martyrdom deserve no regard: Saint Paul, in the last chapter of his epistle to the Romans, salutes Aquila, a person of Pontus, of Jewish extraction, and Priscilla, whom he and all churches thanked because they had exposed themselves for his sake. He mentions the church which assembled in their house, which he attributes to no other among the twenty-five Christians whom he saluted and were then at Rome. This agrees with the immemorial tradition in Rome that Saint Peter consecrated an altar and was baptized there in an urn of stone, which is now kept in the church of Saint Prisca. Aquila and Priscilla are still honored in this church as titular patrons of our saint, and a considerable part of their relics lies under the altar. Aquila and Priscilla were tent makers and lived at Corinth when they were banished from Rome under Claudius: she who is called Priscilla in the Acts of the Apostles, the Epistles to the Romans, and first to the Corinthians, is named Prisca in the second to Timothy.

[Butler, Alban. *The Lives of the Fathers, Martyrs, and Other Principal Saints. Compiled from Original Monuments and Authentic Records*. Dublin: James Duffy, 1866. *HathiTrust Digital Library,* catalog.hathitrust.org/Record/001941109.]

Saint Maris, Saint Martha, Saint Audifax, and Saint Abachum, Martyrs (†270) — January 19

The memorial of these martyrs, added to the calendar in the ninth century, is deleted. Therefore, besides their names, all that is known concerning them is the place and date of their burial in the cemetery on the Via Cornelia, January 19 or 20.

Maris, a nobleman of Persia, with his wife Martha, and two sons, Audifax and Abachum, being converted to the faith, distributed his fortune among the poor, as the primitive Christians did at Jerusalem and came to Rome to visit the tombs of the apostles. The emperor Aurelian then persecuted the church, and by his order, many Christians were shut up in the arena and shot to death with arrows, and their bodies burnt. Our saints gathered and buried their ashes with respect, for which they were apprehended. After many torments under the governor Marcianus, Maris and his two sons were beheaded, and Martha drowned thirteen miles from Rome at a place now called Santa Ninfa[33]. Their relics were found in Rome in 1590. They are mentioned with distinction in all the western Martyrologies from the sacramentary of Saint Gregory. Their relics are kept principally in Rome; part in the church of Saint Hadrian, part in that of Saint Charles, and Saint John Calybite. Eginhart, son-in-law and secretary of Charlemagne, deposited a portion of these relics which had been sent him from Rome in the abbey of Selghenstadt[34], of which he was the founder, in the diocese of Mentz.

The martyrs and confessors triumphed over the devil by prayer; by this, poor and weak as they were, they were rendered invincible; by engaging Omnipotence itself to be their comfort, strength, and protection. If the art of praying well be the art of living well, according to the received maxim of the fathers and masters of spiritual life, nothing is certainly of greater importance than for us to

---

[33] Santa Ninfa is a town and comune in Trapani, Sicily, in southern Italy.

[34] The Seligenstadt Monastery was a Benedictine monastery in Seligenstadt from the ninth to the nineteenth centuries. Seligenstadt is a town in the Offenbach district of the Darmstadt Regierungsbezirk in Hesse, Germany. Seligenstadt, one of Germany's oldest towns, was already significant in Carolingian times.

learn this sacred art of conversing with God in the manner we ought. We admire the beautiful effects this exercise produced in the saints, who were disengaged from earthly ties and made spiritual and heavenly; perfect angels on earth: but we experience nothing of this in ourselves. Prayer was in them the channel of all graces, the means of attaining all virtues, and all the treasures of heaven. In us, it is fruitless: the reason is plain, for the promises of Christ cannot fail: "we ask, and receive not, because we ask amiss."

[Butler, Alban. *The Lives of the Fathers, Martyrs, and Other Principal Saints. Compiled from Original Monuments and Authentic Records.* Dublin: James Duffy, 1866. *HathiTrust Digital Library,* catalog.hathitrust.org/Record/001941109.]

Saint Canutus (or Canute), King of Denmark, Martyr (†1086) — January 19

In 1670, the memorial of Canute, martyred in Denmark on July 10, 1086, was placed on the Roman calendar. Since the saint does not have universal significance, his memorial is left to the particular calendars.

Saint Canutus, King of Denmark, was endowed with excellent qualities of both mind and body. As a young prince, he cleared the seas of pirates and subdued several neighboring provinces harassing Denmark with their incursions. His courage rivaled in excellence with his ability in the conduct and skills of war, but his singular piety, when few of his land were Christian, eclipsed all his other endowments.

Saint Canutus succeeded his elder brother Harold on the throne of Denmark in 1080. He began his reign with a successful war against the troublesome, vicious enemies of the state and by planting faith in the conquered provinces. Then, amid the glory of his victories, he humbly prostrated himself at the foot of the crucifix, laying there his diadem and offering himself and his kingdom to the King of kings. Then, after having provided for the peace and safety of his country, he married Eltha, daughter of Robert, Earl of Flanders, who proved herself a spouse worthy of him. They are the parents of Blessed Charles, Count of Amiens and Flanders, a martyr for his faith, brutally slain like his father while in prayer.

The justice of Saint Canutus as sovereign became evident when he condemned to death a Danish lord whose vessel, to sustain the owner's luxury, had pillaged the ship of a neighboring country and massacred the crew. He applied himself to the reform of all internal abuses. For this purpose, he enacted severe but necessary laws for the strict administration of justice, the repression of violence, and tyranny by the powerful, without respect to persons. He favored and honored holy men and granted many privileges and immunities to the clergy. His charity and tenderness towards his subjects made him study all possible ways to make them happy people. He showed royal munificence in building and adorning churches and gave the crown he wore, of great value, to a church in his capital and residence, where the kings of Denmark are still buried.

To the virtues which constitute a great king, Canutus added those which prove the great Saint. A rebellion having sprung up in his kingdom, the king was surprised at the church by the rebels. Perceiving his danger, he confessed his sins at the foot of the altar and received Holy Communion. Then, stretching out his arms before the altar, the Saint fervently recommended his soul to his Creator; in this posture, he was struck down on his knees by the enemies of his Christian reign.

[Shea, John G. *Little Pictorial Lives of the Saints, with Reflections for Every Day of the Year; Compiled from "Butler's Lives."* New York: Benziger, 1894. *HathiTrust Digital Library,* hdl.handle.net/2027/nyp.33433068232887.]

Saint Anastasius, Martyr (†628) — January 22

The memorial of Anastasis, added to the Roman calendar in the twelfth century, is left for the particular calendars. The cult of Anastasius was introduced at Rome with the transfer of his body from Jerusalem, where he was martyred in 628, to the Basilica of Saint Vincent of the Saving Waters, on the Via Laurentina.

Saint Anastasius was a trophy of the holy cross of Christ when it was carried away into Persia by Chosros in the year 614 after he had taken and plundered Jerusalem. The martyr was a Persian, son of a Magian, instructed in the sciences of that sect, and a young soldier in the Persian troops. Upon hearing the news of the taking of the cross by his king, he became very inquisitive concerning the Christian religion: and its sublime truths made such an impression on his mind that is returned to Persia from an expedition into the Roman Empire, he left the army with his brother, who also served in it, and retired to Hierapolis. In that city, he lodged with a devout Persian Christian, a silversmith, with whom he often went to prayer. The holy pictures he saw moved him exceedingly and gave him the occasion to inquire daily more into our faith and to admire the courage of the martyrs whose glorious sufferings were painted in the churches. At length, desirous of baptism, he left Hierapolis, which city was subject to the Persians. He went to Jerusalem, where he received that sacrament at the hands of Modestus, who governed that church as vicar, during the absence of the patriarch Zachary, whom Chosros had led away captive into Persia. In baptism, he changed his Persian name Magundat into that of Anastasius, meaning, according to the signification of that Greek word, that he rose from death to a new and spiritual life. He had prepared himself with extraordinary devotion for that sacrament while a catechumen, and he spent in no less fervor the several days after it, which persons baptized passed in white garments, in prayer, and in receiving more perfect instructions in the faith. At the end of this term, Anastasius desired to become a monk in a monastery five miles distant from Jerusalem more efficiently and perfectly to keep his sacred baptismal vows and obligations. Justin, the abbot, made him first learn the Greek tongue and the psalter; then, cutting off his hair, gave him the monastic habit in the year 621.

Anastasius was always the first at all spiritual duties, especially in assisting with the celebration of the divine mysteries. His attention to pious discourse testified the intense thirst of his soul, nor was he less fervent in practice. He never read the triumphs of the martyrs without an abundance of tears and burned with an ardent desire for happiness. Being molested beyond measure with blasphemous thoughts of magic and superstitions, which his father had taught him, he was delivered from that troublesome temptation by discovering it to his director and by his advice and prayers. After seven years spent in great perfection in this monastery, his desire for martyrdom daily increasing, and having been assured by a revelation that his prayers for that grace were heard, he left that house and visited the places of devotion in Palestine, at Diospolis, Gerizim, and Our Lady's church at Cæsarea, where he stayed two days. This city, with the more significant part of Syria, was then subject to the Persians. The saint seeing certain Persian soothsayers of the garrison occupied in their abominable superstitions in the streets, boldly spoke to them, remonstrating against the blasphemy of such practices. The Persian magistrates apprehended him as a suspected spy. Still, he informed them that he once enjoyed the dignity of Magian with them and had renounced it to become a humble follower of Christ. Upon this confession, he was thrown into a dungeon, where he lay three days without eating or drinking till Marzabanes, the governor, returned to the city. Being interrogated by him, he confessed his conversion to the faith and equally despised his offers of great preferments and his threats of crucifying him. Marzabanes commanded him to be chained by the foot to another criminal, and his neck and one foot to be also linked together by a heavy chain, and condemned him in this condition to carry stones.

The Persians, especially those of his province of Rasech, and his former acquaintance, upbraided him as the disgrace of his country, kicked and beat him, plucked his beard, and loaded him with burdens above his strength. The governor sent for him a second time but could by no means prevail to pronounce the impious words used in their superstitions. The judge then threatened he would write immediately to the king against him if he did not comply. "Write what you please," said the saint, "I am a Christian: I repeat it again, I am a Christian." So Marzabanes commanded him to be immediately beaten with knotty clubs. The executioners were preparing to bind him fast on the ground. Still, the saint told him it was unnecessary, for he had courage enough to lie down under the punishment without moving, and he regarded it as his greatest happiness and pleasure to suffer for Christ. He only begged leave to put off his monk's habit, lest it should be treated with contempt, which only his body deserved. He, therefore, laid it aside respectfully, then stretched himself on the ground, and without being bound, he did not stir all the time of the cruel torment, bearing it without changing his posture. The governor again threatened him to acquaint the king of his obstinacy: "Whom ought we rather fear," said Anastasius, "a mortal man, or God, who made all things out of nothing?" The judge pressed him to sacrifice to fire and the sun and moon. The saint answered he could never acknowledge as gods, creatures which God had made only for our use; upon which he was remanded to prison.

After hearing of his sufferings, his old abbot sent two monks to assist him and ordered prayers for him. After carrying the stones all day, the confessor spent the more significant part of the night in prayer, to the surprise of his companions; one of whom, a Jew, saw and showed him to others at prayer in the night, shining in brightness and glory like a blessed spirit, and angels praying with him. As the confessor was chained to a man condemned for a public crime, he always prayed with his neck bowed downwards, keeping his chained foot near his companion not to disturb him. Marzabanes, in the meantime, having informed Chosros and received his orders, acquainted the martyr by a messenger, without seeing him, that the king would be satisfied on condition that he would only by word of mouth recant the Christian faith; after which he might choose whether he would be an officer in the king's service, or remain a Christian and a monk; adding, he might in his heart always adhere to Christ, provided he would but for once renounce him in words privately, in his presence, "in which there could be no harm, nor any great injury to his Christ," as he said. Anastasius answered firmly that he would never even seem to dissemble or deny his God. Then the governor told him he had orders to send him bound into Persia to the king. "There is no need of binding me," said the saint: "I go willingly and cheerfully to suffer for Christ." The governor put the mark on him and two other prisoners and ordered them to set out after five days. In the meantime, on the feast of the Exaltation of the Cross, the 14th of September, at the request of the Comerciarius, or tax-gatherer for the king, who was a Christian of distinction, Anastasius had left to go to the church and assist at the divine service. His presence and exhortations encouraged the faithful, excited the tepid, and moved all to tears. He dined that day with the Comerciarius and returned with joy to his prison. On the day appointed, the martyr left Cæsarea, in Palestine, with two other Christian prisoners, under a strict guard and was followed by one of the monks whom the abbot had sent to assist and encourage him. The acts of this martyrdom were written by this monk, or at least from what he related by word of mouth. The saint received great honors, much against his inclination, from the Christians wherever he came. This made him fear lest human applause should rob him of his crown by infecting his heart with pride. He wrote from Hierapolis and again from the river Tigris to his abbot, begging the prayers of his brethren.

Being arrived at Barsaloe in Assyria, six miles from Discartha or Dastagerde, near the Euphrates, where the king then was, the prisoners were thrown into a dungeon till his pleasure was known. An officer came from Chosros to interrogate the saint, who made an answer, regarding his magnificent promises, in these words: "My religious habit and poor clothes show that I despise from my heart the gaudy pomp of the world. The honors and riches of a king, who must shortly die himself are no temptation to me." The next day the officer returned to the prison and endeavored to intimidate him by blustering threats and reproaches. But the saint said calmly: "My lord judge, do not give yourself so much trouble about me. By the grace of Christ, I am not to be moved; so, execute your pleasure without more ado." The officer caused him to be unmercifully beaten with staves, after the Persian manner, insulting him all the time and often repeating that because he condemned the king's bounty, he should be treated in that manner every day he lived. This punishment was inflicted on him for three days; on the third, the judge commanded him to be laid on his back and a heavy beam pressed down by the weight of two men on his legs, crushing the flesh to the very bone. The martyr's tranquility and patience astonished the officer, who went again to acquaint the king with his behavior. In his absence, the jailer, being a Christian by profession, though too weak to resign his place rather than detain such a prisoner, gave everyone free access to the martyr. The Christians immediately filled the prison; everyone sought to kiss his feet or chains and kept whatever their touch had sanctified as relics: they also overlaid his fetters with wax to receive their impression. The saint strove to hinder them with confusion and indignation and expressed dissatisfaction with such actions. The officer returning from the king caused him to be beaten again, which the confessor bore instead as a statue than as flesh and blood. Then he was hung up for two hours by one hand, with a great weight at his feet, and tampered with by threats and promises. The judge, despairing of overcoming him, went back to the king for his last orders, that he and all the Christian captives should be put to death. He returned speedily to put them in execution. He caused Anastasius' two companions, with three score and six other Christians, to be strangled one after another, on the banks of the river, before his face, whom the judge, all the time, pressed to return to the Persian worship, and to escape so disgraceful a death, promising, in case of compliance, that he should be made one of the most extraordinary men in the court. Anastasius, with his eyes lifted to heaven, gave thanks to God for bringing his life to so happy a conclusion; and said he expected that he should have met with a crueler death in the torture of all his members: but seeing God granted him one so easy, he embraced with joy that end of a life which he otherwise must shortly have lost more painfully. He was accordingly strangled, and his head was cut off after his death. This was in the year 628, the seventeenth of the emperor Heraclius, on the 22nd of January, on which day both the Latins and Greeks keep his festival. His body, among the other dead, was exposed to be devoured by dogs, but it was the only one they left untouched. It was afterward redeemed by the Christians, who laid it in the monastery of Saint Sergius, a mile from the place of his triumph, in the city Barsaloe, called afterward from that monastery, Sergiopolis. The monk who attended him returned his Colobium or linen tunic without sleeves. The saint's body was later brought into Palestine. Some years later, it was removed to Constantinople and Rome.

The seventh general council proves the use of pious pictures from the head of this holy martyr, and his miraculous image was then kept in Rome with great reverence: where it is still preserved in the church belonging to the monastery of our Lady ad Aquas Sylvias, which now bears the name of Saints Vincent and Anastasius. The rest of his relics are deposited in the holy chapel at Scalas Sanctas[35], near Saint John Lateran. See the history of many miracles wrought by them in Bollandus. Saint Anastasius foretold the speedy fall of the tyrant Chosros: ten days after his martyrdom, the emperor Heraclius[36] entered Persia.

[Butler, Alban. *The Lives of the Fathers, Martyrs, and Other Principal Saints. Compiled from Original Monuments and Authentic Records.* Dublin: James Duffy, 1866. *HathiTrust Digital Library,* catalog.hathitrust.org/Record/001941109.]

---

[35] The Scala Sancta are 28 white marble steps that are Roman Catholic relics located in an edifice on the Holy See's extraterritorial property in Rome, Italy near the Archbasilica of Saint John in Laterano.

[36] Heraclius, also known as Heraclius I, was an Eastern Roman emperor who reigned from 610 to 641. His rise to power began in 608, when he and his father, the exarch of Africa, Heraclius the Elder, led a revolt against the unpopular usurper Phocas. Several military campaigns occurred during Heraclius' reign.

Saint Emerentia (or Emerentiana), Virgin and Martyr (†304) — January 23

The memorial of Emerentiana, celebrated since the ninth century, is now left to the particular calendars. Her name and her burial date, January 23 on the Via Nomentana, are the only facts known about her.

Emerentiana, the foster-sister of Saint Agnes, the famous Roman Virgin-Martyr, yet only a catechumen awaiting Baptism, was discovered by the Pagan Roman mob praying at the tomb of her mistress and was stoned to death.

[St. Augustine's Abbey (Ramsgate, England). *The Book of Saints: A Dictionary of Servants of God Canonized by the Catholic Church: Extracted from the Roman & Other Martyrologies.* London: A. & C. Black, 1921. *HathiTrust Digital Library,* hdl.handle.net/2027/njp.32101066153709]

Saint Peter Nolasco, Confessor (1189–1256) — January 28

The memorial of Peter, who died on December 25, 1256, was listed in the Roman calendar in 1664. Since he is not a saint of universal significance, it is now left to the particular calendars.

In the early thirteenth century, the Moors still held much of Spain, and in sudden raids from the sea, they carried off thousands of Christians, keeping them as slaves in Granada and their citadels along the African coast. Saint Peter Nolasco was a hero of these unfortunates, born about 1189 near Carcassonne in France. When he went to Barcelona to escape the heresy rampant in southern France, he consecrated the fortune he had inherited to redeem the captives taken on the seas by the

Saracens. He was obsessed with the thought of their suffering and desired to sell his person to deliver his brethren and take their chains upon himself. God made it known to him how agreeable that desire was to Him.

Because of these large sums of money he expended, Peter became penniless. He was without resources and powerless when the Blessed Virgin appeared to him and said to him: Find for Me other men like yourself, an army of brave, generous, unselfish men, and send them into the lands where the children of the Faith are suffering. Peter went to Saint Raymond of Peñafort, his confessor, who had had a similar revelation and used his influence with King James I of Aragon and Berengarius, Archbishop of Barcelona, to obtain approbation and support for the new community. On August 10, 1218, Peter and two companions were received as the first members of the Order of Our Lady of Ransom, dedicated to recovering Christian captives. To the three traditional vows of religion, its members joined a fourth, that of delivering their persons to the overlords, if necessary, to ransom Christians.

The Order spread rapidly. Peter and his comrades traveled throughout Christian Spain, recruiting new members and collecting funds to purchase the captives. Then they began negotiations with the slave-owners. Finally, they penetrated Andalusia[37], crossed the sea to Tunis and Morocco, and brought home cargo after cargo of Christians. Although Peter, as General of the Order, was occupied with its organization and administration, he made two trips to Africa where, besides liberating captives, he converted many Moors. He died after a long illness on Christmas night of 1256; Pope Urban VIII canonized him in 1628. His Order continues

---

[37] Andalusia is a largely autonomous region in southern Spain with hills, rivers, and farmland. From the eighth to the fifteenth centuries, it was ruled by the Moors.

its religious services, now devoted to preaching and hospital service.

[Shea, John G. *Little Pictorial Lives of the Saints, with Reflections for Every Day of the Year; Compiled from "Butler's Lives."* New York: Benziger, 1894. *HathiTrust Digital Library*, hdl.handle.net//2027/nyp.33433068232887; Guérin, Abbé (Paul), François Giry, and Simon Martin. *Les Petits Bollandistes: Vies Des Saints De L'Ancien et du Nouveau Testament.* Translated by the Monastère du Magnificat. Paris: Bloud et Barral, 1882. *HathiTrust Digital Library*, hdl.handle.net//2027/nnc1.0036694380.]

Saint Martina, Martyr (†226) — January 30

The memorial of Martina was added to the general calendar in 1635. It is now left to her titular church since nothing is known of St. Martina except Pope Donus (676-678) dedicated a church in the Roman Forum to a woman of this name.

Saint Martina, a Roman virgin, was the child of a noble Christian consul, of whom it was said that he was highly merciful towards the poor and very zealous for faith in the Most Holy Trinity. His daughter lost both her parents while she was still very young. For the love of Christ, she distributed all she inherited to the poor so that she might be freer to hasten towards martyrdom during the recently begun persecution.

Under the emperor Alexander Severus[38], she was discovered in a church one day by three officers of a search party and commanded to follow them to the temple of Apollo. She cheerfully agreed, saying she would do so after praying for a short time and taking leave of her bishop. The officers reported their important capture to the emperor, believing she would readily renounce her faith. But when he ordered her to speak, she replied that she would sacrifice to none other than the true God and

---

[38] Marcus Aurelius Severus Alexander, Roman emperor: 13 March 222 – 21 March 235

171

never to idols, the handiwork of men. Iron hooks tortured her, but her executioners were thrown to the ground amid a great light as she prayed and arose converted, like Saint Paul, to the Christian faith.

She was tormented the following day before the emperor, cruelly scourged while attached by her hands and feet to posts. When, one day later, she was taken to a temple of Diana, the demon left amid horrible screams. Fire from heaven fell and burnt the idol, which in tumbling crushed many of its priests and pagan worshipers. After suffering other tortures and being spared by an enraged lion and a fiery furnace, Saint Martina was finally beheaded. Her death occurred on January 1st during the fourth year of Alexander Severus.

Her relics were found in 1634, during the papacy of Urban VIII, near the Mamertine Prison, with those of several other martyrs. All were placed in a beautiful church dedicated to Saint Martina in the Roman Forum. Urban VIII spared no effort in promoting her veneration; through his solicitude, the Office was enhanced with hymns for Matins and Lauds. In these, we read that her soul rose to heaven, where she was seen afterward upon a royal throne while the Blessed sang praises to God.

[Guérin, Abbé (Paul), François Giry, and Simon Martin. *Les Petits Bollandistes: Vies Des Saints De L'Ancien et du Nouveau Testament.* Translated by the Monastère du Magnificat. Paris: Bloud et Barral, 1882. *HathiTrust Digital Library,* hdl.handle.net//2027/nnc1.0036694380.]

FEBRUARY

Saint Andrew Corsini, Bishop and Confessor (1302–1373) — February 4

The memorial of Andrew, who died at Florence, Italy, on January 6, 1374, was added to the Roman calendar in 1666. It is now left for the particular calendars since he is not a saint of universal significance.

Saint Andrew was born in Florence in 1301 to the illustrious Corsini family. A short time before the birth of Saint Andrew, his mother experienced a strange dream in which she had given birth to a wolf which became a lamb upon entering a Carmelite church. After a dissolute youthful life, Andrew repented when one day in 1318, his lonely mother told him of her dream. He rose and went to the altar in the church where his parents had offered to God the child they hoped to obtain from His mercy; there, he prayed to the Blessed Virgin with tears, then went to beg his admission to the Carmelite Order.

He began a life of great mortification. Ordained a priest in 1328, he studied in Paris and Avignon, and on his return, he became the Apostle of Florence and was the Prior of his convent there. In 1360 he was consecrated Bishop of Fiesole, near Florence, and gained an excellent reputation as a peacemaker between rival political factions and for his love of the poor. He was also named papal nuncio to Bologna, where he pacified dissenting factions and won the hearts of the nobility with whom he was associating. In addition, he wrought many miracles of healing and conversion during his lifetime.

At the age of 71, while he was celebrating the midnight Mass of Christmas, the Blessed Virgin appeared to him and told him he would leave this world on the feast of the Epiphany to meet the beloved Master he had

173

served so faithfully. In effect, he died on that day in 1373, in the thirteenth year of his episcopacy. So many miracles multiplied after Pope Eugenius IV immediately permitted a public cult. The city of Florence has always invoked him with confidence and happy results. He was canonized in 1629.

He is often represented holding his crosier, with a wolf and a lamb at his feet, or hovering over a battlefield on a cloud or a white steed — this in memory of his miraculous intervention in a battle the Florentine people won by his assistance.

[Guérin, Abbé (Paul), François Giry, and Simon Martin. *Les Petits Bollandistes: Vies Des Saints De L'Ancien et du Nouveau Testament.* Translated by the Monastère du Magnificat. Paris: Bloud et Barral, 1882. *HathiTrust Digital Library,* hdl.handle.net/2027/nnc1.0036694380; Shea, John G. *Little Pictorial Lives of the Saints, with Reflections for Every Day of the Year; Compiled from "Butler's Lives."* New York: Benziger, 1894. *HathiTrust Digital Library,* hdl.handle.net/2027/nyp.33433068232887.]

Saint Dorothy, Virgin, and Martyr († 304) — February 6

Since the thirteenth century, the memorial of Dorothy has been celebrated in the Roman calendar. Supposedly martyred at Caesarea in Cappadocia, her feast is abolished since the Acts of her life are entirely legendary.

Saint Dorothy was a young virgin celebrated already in Caesarea of Cappadocia[39], where she lived, for her angelic virtue. Her parents are believed to have been martyred before her in the Diocletian persecution; thus, when the Governor of Sapricius came to Caesarea and called her to appear before him, he sent this child of

---

[39] Since Greco-Roman times, the capital of Cappadocia has been Caesarea Mazaca (modern-day Kayseri, Turkey). Kayseri is a large industrialized city in Turkey's Central Anatolia region. It is the administrative center of Kayseri Province.

martyrs to the eternal home where they were waiting for her.

She explained that the God she adored was majestic — above all mortal emperors and their gods, none of whom created either heaven or earth. She was stretched upon the rack and offered honors if she would consent to sacrifice or death if she refused. And they waited. She asked why they delayed torturing her; they expected she might cede out of fright. She told them, *Do what you must do, that I may see the One for whose love I fear neither death nor torments, Jesus Christ*. She was asked, *Where is this Christ?* and she replied, *As Almighty, He is everywhere, but for the weak reason we say that the Son of God has ascended into heaven, to be seated at the right hand of the Almighty Father. He invites us to the garden of His delights, where the trees are always covered with fruits, the lilies are perpetually white, the roses ever in their freshness. If you believe me, you will also search for true liberty and labor to earn entry into the garden of God's delights. She was then placed in the custody of two women who had fallen away from the faith in the hope that they might pervert her, but the fire of her heart rekindled the flame in theirs, leading them back to Christ.*

When she was set once more on the rack, Sapricius himself was amazed at the heavenly expression on her face and asked her the cause of her joy. Because she said, I have brought back two souls to Christ, and I shall soon be in heaven rejoicing with the Angels. Her joy grew as she was buffeted in the face, and her sides were burned with red hot iron plates. *Blessed art Thou*, she cried when she was sentenced to be beheaded. *Blessed art Thou, O Lover of souls, who call me to paradise and invite me to Thy nuptial chamber!*

Saint Dorothy suffered in mid-winter, and on the road to her execution, a lawyer called Theophilus, who had grown accustomed to calumniating and persecuting the Christians, asked her, in mockery, to send him apples or roses from the garden of her Spouse. The Saint promised to grant his request. Just before she died, a little child stood by her side bearing three apples and three roses. She told him to take them to Theophilus and to say it was the present he sought from the garden of her Spouse. Saint Dorothy had gone to heaven, and Theophilus was still making merry over his challenge to her when the child entered his room. He recognized that the fruit and flowers were of no earthly growth and that the child was an Angel in disguise. He was converted to the faith and then shared in the martyrdom of Saint Dorothy.

[Shea, John G. *Little Pictorial Lives of the Saints, with Reflections for Every Day of the Year; Compiled from "Butler's Lives."* New York: Benziger, 1894. *HathiTrust Digital Library,* hdl.handle.net/2027/nyp.33433068232887; Guérin, Abbé (Paul), François Giry, and Simon Martin. *Les Petits Bollandistes: Vies Des Saints De L'Ancien et du Nouveau Testament.* Translated by the Monastère du Magnificat. Paris: Bloud et Barral, 1882. *HathiTrust Digital Library,* hdl.handle.net/2027/nnc1.0036694380.]

Saint John of Matha, Confessor (1160–1213) — February 8

In 1679, the Roman calendar recorded the memorial of John, who died at Rome on December 17, 1213. Since he is not a saint of universal significance, it is now left to the particular calendars.

The life of Saint John of Matha, born in southern France to an illustrious family, was consecrated to God by a vow at birth. His life from his youth was exemplary of his self-sacrifice for the glory of God and the good of his neighbor. As a child, his chief pleasure was serving the poor; he would say to them that he had come into the world for no other end but to care for them. Accordingly, he served every Friday in a hospital and obtained for the sick whatever they needed. Later he studied in Paris with such distinction that his professors advised him to become a priest so that his talents might render greater service to others. For this purpose, John gladly sacrificed his high rank and other worldly advantages.

At his first Mass, an Angel appeared, clad in white, with a red and blue cross on his breast, and his hands reposed on the heads of a Christian and a Moorish captive. To comprehend what this vision might signify, John went to Saint Felix of Valois, a holy hermit living near Meaux, under whose direction he led a life of extreme penance. Another sign was given to the two hermits by a stag they saw with a red and blue cross amid its antlers. The two Christians then set out together for Rome to learn the Will of God from the lips of the Sovereign Pontiff. Pope Innocent III consulted the Sacred College and had a Mass offered in the Lateran Basilica to understand what God was asking. At the moment of the Elevation, the Pope saw the same Angel in the same vision as had been given to Saint John. He told the two servants of God to devote themselves to the redemption of captives, and for this purpose, they founded the Order of the Holy Trinity, whose habit was first worn by the Angel.

The Order members fasted every day. Then, after preaching throughout Europe, winning associates for their Order, and gathering alms to buy back captives, they went to northern Africa to redeem the Christian slaves taken prisoner during the Crusades or while traveling on the seas. They also devoted themselves to the many sick, aged, and infirm captives they found in northern Africa and Spain, who could not travel and thus return home. Saint John, on one occasion, was assaulted in Morocco and left, in his blood, for dead. However, he was preserved by a miracle and again took up his charitable services.

The charity of Saint John of Matha in devoting his life to the redemption of captives was visibly blessed by God. Accordingly, the Pope approved the Constitution of the Order, and in 1198 it was canonically instituted with an establishment in Rome, where the liberated captives were taken from Ostia to give thanks to God and rest for a time.

On his second return from Tunis, he brought back one hundred and twenty liberated slaves. But when he was about to undertake another voyage, the Moors attacked the ship and disabled it before it could sail, removing the rudder and sails. Saint John told the passengers to take the oars and set out just the same, and then he prayed on his knees to the Star of the Sea, prayers the sailors and passengers repeated after him. Finally, he tied his cloak to the mast, saying, "*Let God arise, and let His enemies be scattered! O Lord, Thou wilt save the humble, and wilt bring down the eyes of the proud*". Suddenly wind filled the small sail, and a few days later brought the ship safely to Ostia, the port of Rome, three hundred leagues from Tunis.

Worn out by his heroic labors, John died in 1213, at the age of fifty-three.

[Guérin, Abbé (Paul), François Giry, and Simon Martin. *Les Petits Bollandistes: Vies Des Saints De L'Ancien et du Nouveau Testament.* Translated by the Monastère du Magnificat. Paris: Bloud et Barral, 1882. *HathiTrust Digital Library,* hdl.handle.net/2027/nnc1.0036694380; Shea, John G. *Little Pictorial Lives of the Saints, with Reflections for Every Day of the Year; Compiled from "Butler's Lives."* New York: Benziger, 1894. *HathiTrust Digital Library,* hdl.handle.net/2027/nyp.33433068232887.]

Saint Apollonia, Virgin, and the Martyrs of Alexandria († 249) — February 9

The memorial of Apollonia, a virgin and martyr from Alexandria, was listed in the Roman calendar during the thirteenth century. Although there is proof of her martyrdom during the persecutions of Decius (249-251), there is no observance of this saint in the Eastern calendars, and her memorial is left for the particular calendars.

At Alexandria, in 249, a mob rose in savage fury against the Christians during the persecution that the pagans of Alexandria instigated at the urging of a magician of that city. Metras, an old man, perished first. His eyes were pierced with reeds, and he was stoned to death. A woman named Quinta was the next victim. She was led to a heathen temple and told to worship; she replied by cursing the false god many times and was stoned to death. After this, the houses of the Christians were sacked and plundered, and they accepted the despoiling of their possessions with joy.

Saint Apollonia, an aged virgin, was the most famous among the martyrs, honored for her virtue and modesty. Her teeth were beaten out, and she was led outside the city, where a massive fire was kindled. She was told she must deny Christ or else be burned alive. She was silent for a moment, and then, moved by a unique inspiration of the Holy Ghost, she walked into the fire and died in its flames.

The same courage showed itself the following year when Decius became emperor, and the persecution grew until it seemed as if the very elect must fall away. The story of the witness to Christianity given by a fifteen-year-old boy named Dioscorus illustrates both the courage of the Alexandrian Christians and the esteem they had for the grace of martyrdom. This young man returned wise answers to the judge's arguments and proved invincible under torture. His older companions were executed, but Dioscorus was spared because of his tender years. The Christians could not suppose that he had been deprived of the martyr's crown unless to receive it afterward more gloriously. Dioscorus writes Dionysius, Bishop of Alexandria at this time, still is with us, reserved for some longer and greater combat.

There were indeed many Christians who came, pale and trembling, to offer the heathen sacrifices. But the judges were amazed at the multitudes who came spontaneously to receive the crown of martyrdom. Again, women triumphed over torture until, finally, the judges were glad to execute them at once and end the ignominy of their defeat.

[Shea, John G. *Little Pictorial Lives of the Saints, with Reflections for Every Day of the Year; Compiled from "Butler's Lives."* New York: Benziger, 1894. *HathiTrust Digital Library,* hdl.handle.net/2027/nyp.33433068232887.]

Saint Valentine, Priest, and Martyr († 268) — February 14

Although very ancient, the memorial of this saint is left to the particular calendars since little is known concerning him except his name and the fact that he was buried on the Via Flaminia on February 14.

Valentine was a holy priest in Rome who assisted the martyrs during the persecution under Claudius II[40]. His great virtue and influence became known, and he was apprehended and brought before the emperor's tribunal. *Why, Valentine, do you want to be the friend of our enemies and reject our friendship?* The Christian priest replied, *My Lord, if you knew the gift of God, you would be happy, and your empire with you; you would reject the cult of your idols and would adore the true God and His Son Jesus Christ.* One of the judges interrupted, asking

---

[40] Marcus Aurelius Claudius (Claudius II "Gothicus"), Roman emperor: c. September 268 – c. April 270.

the martyr what he thought of Jupiter and Mercury: *they were miserable and spent all their lives in debauchery and crime!* The judge, furious, cried, *He has blasphemed against the gods and the empire!* The emperor nonetheless continued his questioning with curiosity, pleased to have this opportunity to know what Christians thought. Valentine dared to provoke him to do penance for the blood of Christians he had shed. *Believe in Jesus Christ, be baptized, and you will be saved, and already in this life, you will ensure your empire's glory and the triumph of your arms.* Claudius began to be convinced and said to those in attendance, *Hear the beautiful doctrine this man is teaching us!* But the prefect of Rome, dissatisfied, cried out, *See how this Christian is seducing our prince! Claudius, weakening, abandoned the holy priest to another judge.*

This man, named Asterius, had a little girl who had been blind for two years. Hearing of Jesus Christ, the Light of the world, he asked Valentine if he could convey that light to his child. Saint Valentine placed his hand on her eyes and prayed: *Lord Jesus Christ, true Light, illuminate this blind child!* The child saw, and the Judge with all his family confessed Christ and received Baptism. The emperor, hearing of this, would have turned his gaze away from these conversions, but fear caused him to betray his sense of justice. Along with several other Christians, Saint Valentine was tortured and martyred in the year 268. This illustrious martyr has always been held in great honor in Rome, where a catacomb still exists for him.

[Shea, John G. *Little Pictorial Lives of the Saints, with Reflections for Every Day of the Year; Compiled from "Butler's Lives."* New York: Benziger, 1894. *HathiTrust Digital Library,* hdl.handle.net/2027/nyp.33433068232887.]

Saints Faustinus and Jovita, Martyrs († 122) — February 15

The memorial of Faustinus and Jovita, which was entered into the Roman Calendar in the thirteenth century, is abolished. In the Acts of the lives of these martyrs of Brescia, Jovita, a woman, appears as a deacon. The acts are considered legendary.

Saints Faustinus and Jovita, invincible martyrs of Christ, were brothers, notably born, but much more than noble because they were Christians, and shed their blood for Christ by a painful and prolonged martyrdom, which they endured, being put to most exquisite and cruel torments in diverse cities in Italy. These happy soldiers of Christ were born in Brescia, the chief city of Lombardy. From their childhood, they were piously inclined, modest, courteous, and straightly linked together with the band of fraternal charity.

Faustinus, the elder, was ordained a priest by Apollonius, bishop of that city, and Jovita was a deacon. The holy brothers began to exercise their function to the great profit and edification of the faithful, and by their preaching, many Gentiles were converted to our holy faith. Christian religion began to increase and flourish, and the fame of the two brothers was spread throughout all those parts and noised abroad through several towns of no small distance. The devil, envying this happy progress and resolved to disturb it, stirred up one Italicus, a minister of his and a deadly enemy of Christ and his Church. This man persuaded Emperor Hadrian [Adrian] to advance and continue the persecution which Trajan, his predecessor, had begun against the Christians and, in the first place, to put to death Faustinus and Jovita, who were principal preachers of that superstition, if he would have the gods to be favorable to him, and secure his empire.

The emperor gave the said Italicus ample commission to proceed against the brothers. The rest of the Christians, which he presently made use of, for coming to Brescia, he apprehended Faustinus and Jovita and, seeing before them the emperor's orders, urged them to be obedient and made them great and large promises if they would comply. But, on the contrary, he threatened them with all kinds of torments if they were stubborn and refractory. But finding them constant in confessing the faith, he thought it was not fit to proceed further until the emperor, who was going to France, should come to Brescia, where he was expected, that he might know his will concerning the brothers, that were considered persons for their nobility.

The emperor came and, acquainted with all that passed, strived to bring them to adore his gods. So he caused them to be led to the Temple of the Sun, where an Idol of the Sun stood, most richly adorned with innumerable rays of the finest gold, which cast forth such a radiant light. So the saints addressed themselves by prayer to the God of Heaven, and in a moment, that glorious statue was covered in soot, and the brightest shining beams became as black as coal.

The emperor stood amazed at this strange change and commanded the priests and ministers of the temple to clean the statue and rub off the soot. But as they offered to touch it, it fell to the ground and crumbled into ashes. At which point the emperor being much incensed, condemned the saints to be devoured by wild beasts. Four lions were let loose upon them that made such a fearful roaring that the Gentiles there did tremble. But as the lions drew on the holy brothers, they fawned upon them and licked their feet. After the lions were let out, Leopards, Bears, and other most savage beasts, and more to provoke them, were applied to burning torches. For all this, towards the saint, they were gentle as lambs but fell so fiercely and furiously upon the executioners that they tore them all into pieces. And whereas the idolatrous priests ascribing this miraculous preservation of the saints to the god Saturn would have them acknowledge as much, and therefore brought unto them his statue to be adored, the beasts also worried them, as likewise Italicus that accompanied them, and had been their principal author of this persecution. The Gentiles, strangely perplexed and frightened by this accident, cried out, "O god Saturn, help thy ministers." But their miserable god lay on the ground, trampled upon by the beasts and imbrued in the blood of the unfortunate ministers.

The wife of Italicus, whose name was Asra, as soon as she heard what was become of her husband, like a poor, desperate woman, came running to the amphitheater, where the emperor was sitting and cried out with a lamentable voice, "*What gods are these, Caesar, which you do adore? Gods that cannot defend their ministers, nor help themselves, and yet for their sake am I this day a widow*". And so, renouncing the false gods, she became a Christian with many others present. Among them was Calocerus[41], a principal man of the court, whose example was followed by a great train of servants and officers under him. And that all might see that these wonders were wrought by the power of God, who made the beasts so quiet and gentle to the saints, and permitted them to be most fierce and cruel to his enemies, the saints commanded them to go to the city quietly, without harming any creature, as they did, and went into the desert.

After this, the emperor's order laid the holy martyrs upon a fiery-hot iron bed. And they, as if they had been a bed of roses, with great joy gave thanks to God and

---

[41] Saint Calocerus was a Christian martyr who lived in the second century. He was most likely an officer in the Roman army under Hadrian, stationed in Brescia, Lombardy, Italy. His life and legend are linked to Saints Faustinus and Jovita, and according to legend, all three saints were Brescian soldiers.

sang psalms and hymns amid the flames. From thence, they were carried to prison, and strict order given that none should go to see or speak with them, nor that anything should be given to them to eat or drink, so that they may perish with hunger and thirst. But who can contend with God? There came angels from heaven to comfort and encourage those stout warriors of our Lord. They brought a heavenly light into the dark dungeon and gave new comfort and joy to the holy brothers, that were already abundantly content and satisfied with suffering for Christ.

The emperor, considering the constancy of the martyrs, the significant number of those who, by their example, were becoming Christians, and the authority and vogue which they had in the city, fearing some sedition, commended that all the multitude which had been converted by example of Calocerus should be put to death. Still, Calocerus, with the brothers Faustinus and Jovita, should be led in chains to Milan, whither the emperor was going. There they have tormented afresh. They tied them all three upon the ground, with their faces up, and with tunnels poured melted lead into their mouths to rid them of breath and life, but the lead (as if it had been endowed with reason and discretion) burned the tormentors, without doing any harm to the martyrs.

Then they put them up on the rack and clipped burning plates to their sides. Calocerus felt excessive pain caused by the fire, which penetrated his entrails. So they said to his companions, "*Faustinus and Jovita, pray to God for me, O holy martyrs, for this fire pains me exceedingly.*" And they answered, "*Be of good courage, Calocerus, this will soon pass, and Jesus Christ will assist and help you.*" And so it fell out, for presently Calocerus was refreshed and found such great ease and comfort that he told them he felt no more pain.

And notwithstanding, they threw towe, rosin, and oil into a great fire about the saints. Then, finally, the fire lost all its force. So the martyrs replenished with great content, praised our Lord, which had caused many of the spectators, who admired what they saw and could not conceive those things to be the work of our frail nature, to acknowledge the Author of such great wonders, and embrace our holy faith.

The emperor, not knowing what to do, and esteeming it an intolerable disgrace to be overcome by the martyrs, delivered Calocerus over to Antiochus, one of his prime officers, to put him to death, and returning to Rome, commanded Faustinus and Jovita to be led after him, were when they arrived, they were then again cruelly tormented, but visited and comforted by the chief bishop and pastor, the pope. From Rome, they were carried to Naples, where their torments were again renewed, and afterward, being cast into the sea, they were taken out thence by an angel, and by the power of him, who was fighting in them, they got the victory in all their combats. And from their torments came purer and shining than gold out of the crucible. Lastly, they were led back to Brescia, to the end that all those who had been converted to Christ by their exemplary life and constancy might be dismayed by their death.

This was the intention of the tyrants, but God had a different meaning, which was to honor, illustrate and defend that city wherein they had been born, with their blood, intercession, and merits, that they were headed out of the gate that leadeth to Cremona, while upon their knees, they were recommending their souls to God, who had armed them with strength and constancy to fight valiantly, and sustain such horrible batteries, and now made them worthy of his glory, rewarding them with a crown of martyrdom, upon the 15th of February, in the year 202, according to Baronius. The Roman Martyrology saith that Emperor Hadrian martyred them, and the Roman Breviary faith, that it was in the persecution of Trajan. The torments which these holy martyrs were put unto were so many, and of such different kinds, that Trajan might have begun them, and Hadrian ended them. However, it is more probable that all passed under Hadrian, who started no new persecution but carried on that which his predecessor Trajan had set on foot, and so from its author, it may well be called the Persecution of Trajan.

[Ribadeneyra, Pedro de. "The Life of St. Faustinus and St. Jovita, Martyrs." *The Lives of Saints, With Other Feasts of the Year, according to the Roman Calendar. Written in Spanish by the Reverend Father Peter Ribadeneyra, Priest of the Society of Jesus. Translated Into English by W.P. (William Petre) Esq; The Second Edition Corrected and Amended*, vol. 1, pp. 186-188. London. Printed by B.S., 1730. *HathiTrust Digital Library*, hdl.handle.net/2027/nyp.33433003052994.]

Saint Simeon, Bishop of Jerusalem, Martyr († 116) — February 18

The memorial of Simeon appeared in the general calendar in the twelfth century. Since this martyr of Jerusalem, whom the Byzantine rite honors on April 27, does not have universal significance, the memorial is left for the particular calendars.

Saint Simeon was the son of Cleophas, or Alpheus, brother to Saint Joseph, and Mary, sister of the Blessed Virgin. He was nephew to Saint Joseph, the Blessed Virgin, and cousin-german (a first cousin) to Christ. Simeon and Simon are the same names, and this saint is, according to the best interpreters of the holy scripture, the Simon mentioned, who was brother to Saint James the Lesser, and Saint Jude, apostles, and Joseph (called in the original text José). He was eight or nine years older than our Savior. We cannot doubt that he was an early follower of Christ, as his father, mother, and three brothers were, and an exception to that of Saint John, that our Lord's relations did not believe in him. Nor does Saint Luke leave any room to doubt that he received the Holy Ghost on the day of Pentecost with the Blessed Virgin and the apostles, for he mentions present Saint James and Saint Jude, and the brothers of our Lord. Saint Epiphanius relates that when the Jews massacred Saint James the Lesser, his brother Simeon reproached them for their atrocious cruelty. Saint James, bishop of Jerusalem, was put to death in the year 62, twenty-nine years after our Savior's resurrection. The apostles and disciples met at Jerusalem to appoint him a successor. They unanimously chose Saint Simeon, who had probably before assisted his brother in the government of that church.

In the year 66, in which Saints Peter and Paul suffered martyrdom in Rome, the civil war began in Judea with the seditions of the Jews against the Romans. God warned the Christians in Jerusalem of the impending destruction of that city and, by a divine revelation, commanded them to leave it, as Lot was rescued from Sodom. They, therefore, departed out of it the same year before Vespasian[42], Nero's general and afterward emperor, entered Judea, and retired beyond the Jordan to a small city called Pella[43], having Saint Simeon at their head. After the taking and burning of Jerusalem, they returned and settled themselves amidst its ruins till Hadrian entirely razed it. Saint Epiphanius and Eusebius assure us that the church here flourished significantly and that multitudes of Jews were converted by the great number of prodigies and miracles wrought in it.

[42] Caesar Vespasianus Augustus (Vespasian), Roman emperor: 1 July 69 – 23 June 79.
[43] Pella was an ancient Jordanian city in the northwest. It is situated in the eastern foothills of the Jordan Valley, close to the modern village of Abqat Fal, some 27 kilometers (17 miles) south of the Sea of Galilee (Lake Tiberias).

Saint Simeon, amidst the consolations of the Holy Ghost and the remarkable progress of the church, had the affliction to see two heresies arise within its bosom, namely, those of the Nazarenes and the Ebionites; the first seeds of which, according to Saint Epiphanius, appeared at Pella. The Nazoreans were a sect of men between Jews and Christians but despised by both. They allowed Christ to be the greatest of the prophets but said he was a mere man whose natural parents were Joseph and Mary: they joined all the ceremonies of the old law with the new and observed both the Jewish Sabbath and the Sunday. Ebion added other errors to these, which Cerinthus had also espoused, taught many superstitions, permitted divorces, and allowed the most infamous abominations. He began preaching at Cocabe, a village beyond the Jordan, where he dwelt, but he later traveled into Asia, thence to Rome. The authority of Saint Simeon kept the heretics in some awe during his life, which was the longest upon earth of any of our Lord's disciples. But, as Eusebius says, he was no sooner dead than a deluge of execrable heresies broke out of hell upon the church, which does not openly appear during his life.

Vespasian and Domitian[44] had commanded all to be put to death who were of the race of David. Saint Simeon had escaped their searches, but Trajan, having given the same order, certain heretics and Jews accused him, of being both of the race of David and a Christian, to Atticus, the Roman governor in Palestine. So the holy bishop was condemned by him to be crucified: who, after having undergone the usual tortures during several days, which, though one hundred and twenty years old, he suffered with so much patience that he drew on him a universal admiration, and that of Atticus in particular, he died in 107, according to Eusebius in his chronicle, but in

---

[44] Caesar Domitianus Augustus (Domitian), Roman emperor: 14 September 81 – 18 September 96.

116, according to Dodwell, Bishop Loyde, and F. Pagi. He must have governed the church of Jerusalem for about forty-three years.

The eminent saints among the primitive disciples of Jesus Christ were entirely animated by his spirit, and being dead to the world and themselves, they appeared like angels among men. Free from the secret mixture of the sinister views of all passions to a degree which was a miracle of grace, they had in all things only God, his will and honor before their eyes, equally aspiring to him through honor and infamy. During human applause, they remained perfectly humbled in the center of their nothingness: when loaded with reproaches and contempt and persecuted with all the rage that malice could inspire, they were raised above all these things to stand fearless amidst racks and executioners, inflexibly constant in their fidelity to God, before tyrants, invincible under torments, and superior to them almost as if they had been impassible. Their resolution never failed them; their fervor seemed never slackened. Such incredible men wrought continual miracles in converting souls to God. We bear the name of Christians and wear the habit of saints but are full of the spirit of worldlings, and our actions are infected with its poison. We secretly seek ourselves, even when we flatter ourselves that God is our only aim, and while we undertake to convert the world, we suffer it to pervert us. When shall we begin to study to crucify our passions and die to ourselves so we may lay a solid foundation of true virtue and establish its reign in our hearts?

[Butler, Alban. *The Lives of the Fathers, Martyrs, and Other Principal Saints. Compiled from Original Monuments and Authentic Records*. Dublin: James Duffy, 1866. *HathiTrust Digital Library,* catalog.hathitrust.org/Record/001941109.]

Saint Gabriel of Our Lady of Sorrows (or Saint Gabriel of the Sorrowful Virgin), Confessor (1838–1862) — February 27

The memorial of Gabriel Possenti, who died in the Abruzzi Mountains in 1862, entered the Roman calendar in 1932. Since he is not a saint of universal significance, his feast is now left to the particular calendars.

Saint Gabriel of Our Lady of Sorrows was born on January 3, 1838, in Assisi. His father, Sante Possenti, was an outstanding lawyer, grand assessor, or registrar of Spoleto. He and his wife had thirteen children, of whom Francis, the baptismal name of Gabriel, was the eleventh. When Francis was only four years old, his mother died, and judging from subsequent events of his life, Our Lady took him under her maternal care. As a child, Francis was very ordinary and among his faults were a temper, which was not always controlled, and a certain fastidiousness about his dress and personal appearance. However, in his teen years, he was popular with the boys and girls his age and loved social affairs, especially the theater.

Mr. Possenti, realizing that his son had scholastic ability, sent him to the Jesuit school in Spoleto. While there, he became dangerously ill. This sickness was most likely the turning point in his spiritual life, for he promised Our Lady that if he recovered, he would enter the religious life. His prayer was granted, but Francis did not take any steps to enter the novitiate. About two years later, another sickness attack brought Francis to death's door, and again he promised Our Lady that he would become religious if only she would cure him. Our Lady graciously heard and answered his prayer again. This time Francis sought admittance to the Jesuit novitiate and was accepted, but strangely enough, he procrastinated regarding his entrance. Of course, he was only seventeen and perhaps unsure about which congregation he should join. While he was making up his mind, another great sorrow struck the family. Francis' favorite sister died of cholera. Her death seems to have broken for him the last cord of attachment to the things of this world. He experienced a great desire to dedicate himself to Our Lady of Sorrows and the Passion of her Divine Son. The grace to embrace the austere order of the Passionists came to him on a procession in Spoleto as a miraculous picture of Our Lady was carried in front of him. Francis admitted later that he felt the fire of divine love rising in his heart and a yearning to give himself to a life of contemplation on the sufferings of the Savior.

Francis lost no time in entering the Passionist novitiate at Morrovalle. The words in the tract[45] of today's Mass express his sentiments during the remaining years of his life. In religion, he was known as Brother Gabriel. He advanced rapidly in perfection, as may be proved by a letter he wrote with great sincerity and confidence to one of his friends in the world, a boy by the name of Philip. The letter reads, "*If you truly love your soul, shun bad companions, shun the theatre. I know by experience how very difficult it is to enter such places in the state of grace to come away without losing it or at least exposing it to great danger. Avoid pleasure—parties and avoid evil books. I assure you that if I had remained in the world, it seems certain to me that I should not have saved my soul. Tell me, could anyone have indulged in more amusements than I? Well, what is the result? — nothing but bitterness and fear. Dear Philip, do not despise me, for I speak from my heart. I ask your pardon for all the scandal I may have given you, and I protest that whatever evil I may have spoken about*

---

[45] Ps. 83[84]:11, "For better is one day in thy courts above thousands. I have chosen to be an abject in the house of my God, rather than to dwell in the tabernacles of sinners."

anyone, I now retract it and beg of you to forget it all and to pray for me that God may forgive me likewise."

This letter, and the testimony of his novice master, which is more important, give us some idea of the great purity of heart and the burning love for God that characterized his spiritual life. This love made him beg for public penances and corporal austerities, which had to be refused at times because they were beyond the strength of his delicate physical nature. Gabriel tried very hard to hide the secrets of his Lord. During recreation with his companions, he was cheerful and often provoked laughter.

The happy religious life of Brother Gabriel was cut short when tuberculous disease forced his superior to send him to the infirmary. During the long hours of his forced inactivity, Gabriel penetrated ever more deeply into the sufferings of Christ and the sorrows of Mary. Finally, after only four years of religious life, on February 27, 1862, at the age of twenty-four, this Lily of the Passion was culled from the garden of the cloister to give its fragrance among the saints of heaven and to be an inspiration to youth still combating the temptations of life on earth.

It has been said that God raised up Saint Gabriel to be an inspiration to the youth of the nineteenth century, but until the end of time, many young people, and older people, too, will wonder at his sanctity and give glory to God. The Cause of Gabriel of Our Lady of Sorrows made significant progress once it was introduced, as many miracles bore witness to his holiness. He was canonized as a saint by Pope Benedict XV on Ascension Day, 1920, and Pius XI extended his office and Mass to the universal Church.

[Sisters of Charity of Saint Elizabeth (Convent Station, N.J.). "Saint Gabriel of Our Lady of Sorrows, Confessor." *Daily Missal Meditations: Meditations for Every Day of the Year Based on the Liturgy of the Mass, pp. 493-497.* New York: Benziger Bros, 1959. HathiTrust Digital Library, hdl.handle.net/2027/uva.x030120586.]

MARCH

Saint Lucius, Pope, and Martyr († 253) — March 4

The memorial of Lucius, who died in Rome in 254, was placed in the general calendar in 1602. Since he is mentioned in the Depositio Episcoporum (354), there is no reason to denote him as a martyr, and the feast is now abolished.

Saint Lucius was a Roman by birth and one of the clergy of that church under Saints Fabian and Cornelius. This latter being crowned with martyrdom, in 252, Saint Lucius succeeded him in the pontificate. The emperor Gallus[46] having renewed the persecution of his predecessor Decius, at least in Rome, this holy pope was no sooner placed in the chair of Saint Peter but was banished with several others, though to what place is uncertain. "*Thus,*" says Saint Dionysius of Alexandria, "*did Gallus deprive himself of the succor of heaven by expelling those who every day prayed to God for his peace and prosperity.*" Saint Cyprian wrote to Saint Lucius to congratulate him on his promotion and for the grace of suffering banishment for Christ. Our saint had been but a short time in exile when he was recalled with his companions to the incredible joy of the people who went out of Rome in crowds to meet him. Saint Cyprian wrote to him a second letter of congratulation on this occasion. He says, "*He had not lost the dignity of martyrdom because he had the will, as the three children in the*

---

[46] Gaius Vibius Trebonianus Gallus, Roman emperor: June 251 – c. August 253.

194

furnace, though preserved by God from death: this glory added a new dignity to his priesthood, that a bishop assisted at God's altar, who encouraged his flock to martyrdom by his example as well as by his words. By giving such graces to his pastors, God showed where his true church was: for he denied the like glory of suffering to the Novation heretics. The enemy of Christ only attacks the soldiers of Christ: heretics he knows to be already his own and passes them by. He seeks to throw down those who stand against him." He adds in his name and that of his colleagues: "*We do not cease in our sacrifices and prayers* (in sacrificiis et orationibus nostris) *to God the Father, and Christ his Son, our Lord, giving thanks and praying together, that he who perfects all may consummate in you the glorious crown of your confession, who perhaps has only recalled you that your glory might not be hidden; for the victim, which owes his brethren an example of virtue and faith, ought to be sacrificed in their presence.*"

In his letter to Pope Stephen, Saint Cyprian avails himself of the authority of Saint Lucius against the Novation heretics, as having decreed against them that those who were fallen were not to be denied reconciliation and communion but to be absolved when they had done penance for their sin. But, Eusebius says, he did not sit in the pontifical chair above eight months; and he seems, from the chronology of Saint Cyprian's letters, to have sat only five or six and to have died on the 4th of March, in 253, under Gallus, though we know not in what manner. The most ancient calendars mention him on the 5th of March. Others, with the Roman, on the 4th, which seems to have been the day of his death, as the 5th that of his burial. His body was found in the Catacombs and laid in the church of Saint Cecily in Rome, where it is now exposed to public veneration by order of Clement VIII.

[Butler, Alban. *The Lives of the Fathers, Martyrs, and Other Principal Saints. Compiled from Original Monuments and Authentic Records.* Dublin: James Duffy, 1866. *HathiTrust Digital Library,* catalog.hathitrust.org/Record/001941109.]

The Forty Martyrs of Sebaste, Martyrs († 320) — March 10

In the twelfth century, the memorial of these martyrs was placed in the Roman calendar. Since there are many doubts concerning the truth of the Acts of their lives, the feast is now suppressed.

The Forty Martyrs were soldiers quartered at Sebaste in Armenia, about the year 320. When their legion was ordered to offer sacrifice to idols, they refused to betray the faith of their baptism and replied to all persuasive efforts, "*We are Christians!*" When neither cajolings nor threats could change them, they were chained together after several days of imprisonment and taken to the execution site. It was a cruel winter, and they were condemned to lie without clothing on the icy surface of a pond in the open air until they froze to death.

The forty, not merely undismayed but filled with joy at the prospect of suffering for Jesus Christ, said: *No doubt it is difficult to support so acute a cold, but it will be agreeable to go to paradise by this route; the torment is of short duration, and the glory will be eternal. This cruel night will win us an eternity of delights. Lord, forty of us are entering combat; grant that we may be forty to receive the crown!*

There were warm baths close by, ready for any among them who would deny Christ. One of the confessors lost heart, renounced his faith, and cast himself into the basin of warm water prepared for that intention. But the sudden temperature change suffocated him, and he expired, losing both temporal and eternal life. The still living martyrs were fortified in their resolution, beholding this scene.

Then the ice was suddenly flooded with a bright light; one of the soldiers guarding the men, nearly blinded by the light, raised his eyes, and saw Angels descend with forty crowns which they held in the air over the martyrs' heads. Still, the fortieth one remained without a destination. The sentry was inspired to confess Christ, saying: That crown will be for me! He abandoned his coat and clothing and went to replace the unfortunate apostate on the ice, crying out: I am a Christian! And the number of forty was again complete. They remained steadfast while their limbs grew stiff and frozen and died.

Among the forty, there was a young soldier named Meliton who held out longest against the cold, and when the officers came to cart away the dead bodies, they found him still breathing. They were moved with pity and wanted to leave him alive, hoping he would still change his mind. But his mother stood by, and this brave woman could not bear to see her son separated from the band of martyrs. So she encouraged him to persevere and lifted his frozen body into the cart. Finally, he was just able to make a sign of recognition and was borne away, to be thrown into the flames with the dead bodies of his brethren. Their bones were cast into the river, but they floated and were gathered up by the faithful.

[Shea, John G. *Little Pictorial Lives of the Saints, with Reflections for Every Day of the Year; Compiled from "Butler's Lives."* New York: Benziger, 1894. *HathiTrust Digital Library,* hdl.handle.net/2027/nyp.33433068232887; Jaud, Leon. *Vie Des Saints Pour Tous Les Jours De L'annee: Avec Une Pratique De Piete Pour Chaque Jour.* Translated by the Monastère du Magnificat. Tours: A. Mame, 1950. Print.]

APRIL

Saint Hermenegild, Martyr († 586) — April 13

The memorial of Hermenegild, who died at Seville in 586, was placed in the Roman calendar in 1632. Since this saint is not of universal significance, his memorial is left to the particular calendars.

Leovigild, Arian King of the Visigoths, had two sons, Hermenegild and Recared, who were reigning conjointly with him. All were Arians, but Hermenegild married a zealous Catholic, the daughter of Sigebert, King of France, and by her holy example was converted to the faith. On hearing the news, his father denounced him as a traitor and marched to seize his person. Hermenegild tried to rally the Catholics of Spain in his defense, but they were too weak to make any stand, and after a two years fruitless struggle, Hermenegild surrendered on the assurance of a free pardon. Once he was safely in the royal camp, the king had him loaded with fetters and cast into a foul dungeon at Seville.

Tortures and bribes were employed to shake his faith, but Hermenegild wrote to his father that he regarded the crown as nothing and preferred to lose his scepter and life rather than betray the truth of God. At length, on Easter night, an Arian bishop entered his cell and promised him his father's pardon if he would receive Communion from his hands. Hermenegild indignantly rejected the offer and knelt with joy for his death-stroke, praying for his persecutors. The same night a light streaming from his cell told the Christians keeping vigil nearby that the martyr had won his crown and was celebrating the Resurrection of the Lord with the Saints in glory.

King Leovigild, on his death-bed, was changed interiorly. He had witnessed the miracles after his son's cruel death, and he told his son and successor, Recared, to seek out Saint Leander, whom he had persecuted. Recared should follow Hermenegild's example, said the king, and be received by the bishop into the Church. Recared did so, and although his father himself had not dared to renounce the false faith publicly, after his father's death, the new king labored so earnestly for the extirpation of Arianism that he brought over the whole nation of the Visigoths to the Church. Nor is it to be wondered, says Saint Gregory, that he came thus to be a preacher of the true faith since he was the brother of a martyr, whose merits helped him to bring so many into the haven of God's Church.

[Shea, John G. *Little Pictorial Lives of the Saints, with Reflections for Every Day of the Year; Compiled from "Butler's Lives."* New York: Benziger, 1894. *HathiTrust Digital Library,* hdl.handle.net/2027/nyp.33433068232887.]

Saints Tiburtius, Valerian, and Maximus, Martyrs († 229) — April 14

Although the exact date of the death of Justin is not known, his feast is changed to June 1, which is the custom of the Byzantine rite. Since little is known about Tiburtius, Valerian, and Maximus except for their names and the date of their burial on the Via Appia on April 14. this memorial is now left to the particular calendars.

These holy martyrs have always been held in singular veneration in the church, as appears from the ancient calendar of Fronto, the sacramentary of Saint Gregory, Saint Jerome's Martyrology, that of Thomasius, etc. Valerian was espoused to Saint Cecily and converted by her to the faith. With her, he became the instrument of the conversion of his brother Tiburtius. Maximus, the officer appointed to attend their execution, was brought to the faith by the example of their piety and received with them the crown of martyrdom in the year 229. The theatre of their triumph seems to have been Rome, though some have imagined they suffered in Sicily. They were interred in the burying place of Prætextatus, which, from them, took the name of Tiburtius. It was contiguous to that of Calixtus. In that place, Pope Gregory III. repaired their monument in 740, and Hadrian I. built a church under their patronage. But Pope Paschal translated the remains of these martyrs, of Saint Cecily and the popes' Saints Urban and Lucius, into the city, where the celebrated church of Saint Cecily stands. These relics were found in it in 1599, visited by order of Clement VIII., and approved genuine by the Cardinals Baronius and Sfondrate. The Greeks vie with the Latins in their devotion to these martyrs.

Most agreeable to the holy angels was this pious family, converted to God by the zeal and example of Saint Cecily, who frequently assembled to sing together the divine praises with heavenly purity and fervor. We shall also draw upon ourselves the protection, constant favor, and tender attention of the heavenly spirits if we faithfully imitate the same angelical exercise. Mortification, temperance, humility, meekness, purity of mind and body, continual sighs toward heaven, prayer, accompanied with tears and vehement heavenly desires, disengagement of the heart from the world, pure and diligent attention to God and his holy will, and a perfect union by the sincerest fraternal charity, are virtues and exercises infinitely pleasing to them. The angels of peace are infinitely delighted to see the same perfect intelligence and union, which make an essential part of their bliss in heaven, reign among us on earth, and we have all but one heart and one soul. Happy are those holy souls who have renounced the world in order more perfectly to form in their hearts the spirit of these virtues, in which they cease not, day and night, to attend to the divine praises, and consecrate themselves to Jesus Christ by employing their whole life in this divine exercise. Their profession is a prelude to, or rather a kind of anticipation of, the bliss of heaven. The state of the blessed surpasses it in certain high privileges and advantages. First, they praise God with greater love and esteem because they see and know him more clearly, as he is in himself. Secondly, they praise him with more joy because they possess him fully. Thirdly, their praises have neither end nor interruption. Yet our present state also has its advantages. First, if our praises are mingled with tears, compunction, watchfulness, and conflicts, they merit an immense increase of grace, love, and bliss for eternity. Secondly, our praises cost labor, difficulty, and pain: they are a purgatory of love; those of the blessed the reward and the sovereign bliss. Thirdly, we praise God in a place where he is little loved and little known: we celebrate his glory in an enemy's country amidst the contradiction of sinners. This obliges us to acquit ourselves of this duty with the utmost fidelity and fervor. A second motive to excite us to assiduity in this exercise is that it associates us already with the angels and saints and makes the earth a paradise: it is also, next to the sacraments, the most powerful means of our sanctification and salvation. With what delight do the holy angels attend and join us in it! With what awe and fervor, purity of heart, ardent love, and profound sentiments of humility, adoration, and all virtues, ought we in such holy invisible company to perform this most sacred action! We should go to it penetrated with fear and respect, as if we were admitted into heaven's sanctuary and mingled in its glorious choirs. We ought to behave at it as if we were in paradise, with the utmost modesty, in silence, annihilating ourselves in profound adoration with the seraphim and pronouncing every word with interior sentiment and relish. From prayer, we must come as if we were just descended from heaven, with an earnest desire of speedily returning thither, bearing God in our souls, all animated and inflamed by him, and preserving that spirit of devotion with which his presence filled us at prayer.

[Butler, Alban. *The Lives of the Fathers, Martyrs, and Other Principal Saints. Compiled from Original Monuments and Authentic Records.* Dublin: James Duffy, 1866. *HathiTrust Digital Library,* catalog.hathitrust.org/Record/001941109.]

Saint Anicetus, Pope, Martyr († 161) — April 17

The memorial of Anicetus, listed in the Roman calendar from the twelfth century, is now suppressed. His death date is unknown, and there is no reason to consider him a martyr.

Saint Anicetus, the eleventh successor of Saint Peter, succeeded Saint Pius I and reigned for eleven years. During that time, he had to combat the dangerous errors of Gnosticism, Christ's ancient enemy, already rampant in the days when Saint John the Apostle wrote his letters to the churches of Asia. Saint Anicetus was visited in Rome by Saint Polycarp, bishop of Smyrna, who desired to consult with him. Whom he, in turn, asked to celebrate the feast of Easter in the Church of Rome, as Saint Irenaeus, Polycarp's disciple, relates. They had not been able to find a solution to the question of a difference in the date of Easter in the Orient and the Occident, which Pope Saint Victor would later settle, but remained close friends. Saint Anicetus' vigilance protected his flock from the wiles of the false preachers, Valentine, and Marcion, attempting to corrupt the faith in the empire's capital.

Saint Anicetus established the tonsure for the clergy as a practice of ecclesiastical discipline; a letter to this purpose, which he wrote to the bishops of the churches of Gaul, is still extant.

The Roman Breviary tells us that he received the palm of martyrdom for the Christian faith one month after the death of Emperor Antoninus the Pious. Of the first fifty-four bishops of Rome, as they are seen portrayed in the Basilica of Saint Paul in Rome, fifty-three are honored among the Saints; and of two hundred and forty-eight popes, from Saint Peter to Clement XII († 1740), seventy-eight are named in the Roman martyrology. In the primitive ages, the spirit of fervor and perfect sanctity was conspicuous in most of the faithful, especially in their pastors. The tenor of their lives breathed it, so wise as to render them living miracles, angels on earth, breathing copies of their Divine Redeemer, the odor of whose virtues, holy law, and religion they spread on every side.

[Guérin, Abbé (Paul), François Giry, and Simon Martin. *Les Petits Bollandistes: Vies Des Saints De L'Ancien et du Nouveau Testament.* Translated by the Monastère du Magnificat. Paris: Bloud et Barral, 1882. *HathiTrust Digital Library,* hdl.handle.net/2027/nnc1.0036694380; Shea, John Dawson Gilmary, 1824-1894. *Pictorial Lives of the Saints: With Reflections for Every Day of the Year.* New York: Benziger Brothers, 1889. *HathiTrust Digital Library,* hdl.handle.net/2027/uva.x000393042.]

Saint Soter and Saint Caius, Popes, Martyrs (†175 and †296) — April 22

The memorial of Soter, who died around 175, and of Caius, who died on April 22, 296, entered the Roman calendar in the thirteenth century. The feast is now suppressed since there is no reason to consider them martyrs. Moreover, Caius is included in the Depositio Episcoporum of 354, and nothing is known concerning the day of Soter's death.

Saint Soter was raised to the papacy upon the death of Saint Anicetus in 161. By the sweetness of his discourses, he comforted all afflicted persons with the tenderness of a father. He assisted the indigent with liberal alms, especially those who suffered for the Faith. He liberally extended his charities, according to the custom of his predecessors, to remote churches. He aided that of Corinth, to which he addressed an excellent letter. In his letter of thanks to Saint Soter, Saint Dionysius of Corinth adds that the Pontifical letter and the letter of Saint Clement, Pope, were read for the edification of the faithful on Sundays during their assemblies to celebrate the divine mysteries.

One of Saint Soter's ordinances required all Christians except those in public penance to receive Communion on Holy Thursday. Saint Soter vigorously opposed the heresy of Montanus and governed the Church up to the year 175. He was martyred on April 22, 175, under the emperor Marcus Aurelius and buried on the Via Appia in the cemetery of Callixtus[47].

Pope Saint Caius, born in Dalmatia, was a relative of the emperor Diocletian. For that reason, the cruel emperor did not spare him or his family during the bloody persecution of the years 283 to 296, during which the Christians of Rome were obliged to conceal themselves in caverns and cemeteries.

Saint Caius counseled a patrician named Chromatius to receive the tracked disciples of Christ in his country residence. He visited them on a Sunday and said to the faithful assembled there that Our Lord Jesus Christ, knowing the fragility of human nature, established two degrees in the practice of Christianity, confession and

---

[47] The Catacomb(s) of Callixtus (also known as the Callixtus Cemetery) is one of Rome's Catacombs on the Via Appia (Appian Way), most notable for housing the Crypt of the Popes, which once housed the tombs of several popes from the second to fourth centuries.

martyrdom. *Our Savior did so,* he said, *so that those who do not believe they could stand up under torment may conserve the faith's grace by their confession. Our Lord had indeed specified, when you are persecuted in one city, flee to another...* Then he said, *those who wish to stay in the house of Chromatius, remain with Tiburtius, while those who prefer to return with me to the city, come.* So several followed him back to Rome; the martyrs of the same persecution were the brothers, Saints Marcus and Marcellinus and Saint Sebastian.

Saint Caius received the crown of martyrdom in the final year of the persecution, 296, and was buried in the cemetery of Callixtus, where his body was found in 1622, with an inscription identifying him as Vicar of Christ.

[*Pictorial Lives of the Saints: With Reflections for Every Day of the Year.* New York: Benziger Brothers, 1889. *HathiTrust Digital Library,* hdl.handle.net/2027/uva.x000393042; Guérin, Abbé (Paul), François Giry, and Simon Martin. *Les Petits Bollandistes: Vies Des Saints De L'Ancien et du Nouveau Testament.* Translated by the Monastère du Magnificat. Paris: Bloud et Barral, 1882. *HathiTrust Digital Library,* hdl.handle.net/2027/nnc1.0036694380; Shea, John Dawson Gilmary, 1824-1894.]

The Greater Litany — 25 April

The greater litany is abolished since it duplicates the lesser litany on the rogation days.

April 25 is honored in the Liturgy by what is sometimes called Saint Mark's Procession. The term, however, is incorrect since the Procession was a privilege peculiar to April 25 previously to the institution of the Evangelist's Feast, which, even as late as the 6th century, had no fixed day in the Roman Church. The real name of this Procession is The Greater Litanies. The word Litany means Supplication and is applied to the religious rite of singing specific chants while proceeding from place to place to propitiate Heaven. The two Greek words *Kyrie Eleison* (Lord, have mercy on us) were also called Litany, as likewise were the invocations that were afterward added to that cry for mercy and now form a liturgical prayer used by the Church on certain solemn occasions.

The Greater Litanies (or processions) are so called to distinguish them from the Minor Litanies, that is, processions of less importance as far as the solemnity and concourse of the faithful were concerned. We gather from an expression of Saint Gregory the Great that it was an ancient custom in the Roman Church to celebrate, once a year, a Greater Litany, at which all the clergy and people assisted. Accordingly, this holy Pontiff chose April 25 as the fixed day for this Procession and appointed the Basilica of Saint Peter as the Station.

The question naturally presents itself — why did Pope Saint Gregory choose April 25 for a Procession and Station in which everything reminds us of compunction and penance and which would seem so out of keeping with the joyous season of Easter? Liturgists have shown that in the 5th and probably even in the 4th century, April 25 was observed in Rome as a day of great solemnity. The faithful went, on that day, to the Basilica of Saint Peter to celebrate the anniversary of the first entrance of the Prince of the Apostles into Rome, upon which he thus conferred the inalienable privilege of being the capital of Christendom. From that day, we count the twenty-five years, two months, and some days Saint Peter reigned as Bishop of Rome. The Sacramentary of Saint Leo gives us the Mass of this solemnity, which ceased to be kept afterward. Saint Gregory, to whom we are mainly indebted for the arrangement of the Roman Liturgy, was anxious to perpetuate the memory of a day that gave Rome her grandest glory. He, therefore, ordained that the Church of Saint Peter should be the Station of the Great

Litany, which was always to be celebrated on that auspicious day. April 25 comes so frequently during the Octave of Easter that it could not be kept as a feast, properly so called, in honor of Saint Peter's entrance into Rome; Saint Gregory, therefore, adopted the only means left of commemorating the great event.

But there was a striking contrast resulting from this institution, of which the holy Pontiff was fully aware but which he could not avoid: it was the contrast between the joys of Paschal Time and the penitential sentiments and Station of the Great Litany. Laden as we are with the manifold graces of this holy Season and elated with our Paschal joys, we must sober our gladness by reflecting on the motives which led the Church to cast this hour of shadow over our Easter sunshine. After all, we are sinners, with much to regret and much to fear; we have to avert those scourges which are due to the crimes of mankind; we must, by humbling ourselves and invoking the intercession of the Mother of God and the Saints, obtain the health of our bodies and preservation of the fruits of the earth; we have to offer atonement to Divine Justice for our own and the world's pride, sinful indulgences, and insubordination. Therefore, let us enter into ourselves and humbly confess that our share in exciting God's indignation is great. Our poor prayers, united with those of our Holy Mother the Church, will obtain mercy for the guilty and ourselves who are of their number.

[Guéranger, Prosper, and Lucien Fromage. *The Liturgical Year.* Translated by Laurence Shepherd. Dublin: J. Duffy, 1867–1890. catalog.hathitrust.org/Record/012192952.]

Saints Cletus and Marcellinus, Popes and Martyrs (†89 and †304) — April 26

It appears that Cletus was not a martyr, and the day of his burial is unknown. Likewise, there is some doubt about the burial day of Marcellinus, who died in 304 while the savage persecution of Diocletian was raging. Their memorial dates from the thirteenth century in the Roman calendar and is now suppressed.

Saint Cletus was the third bishop of Rome and succeeded Saint Linus, which circumstance alone shows his eminent virtue among the first disciples of Saint Peter in the West. He sat twelve years, from 76 to 89. In the canon of the Roman Mass (which Bossuet and all others agree to be of primitive antiquity), Bede, and other Martyrologists, style him a martyr. He was buried near Saint Linus in the Vatican, and his relics remain in that church.

Saint Marcellinus succeeded Saint Caius in the bishopric of Rome, in 296, about the time that Dioclesian set himself up for a deity and impiously claimed divine honors. Theodoret says that in those stormy times of persecution, Marcellinus acquired great glory. He sat in Saint Peter's chair for eight years, three months, and twenty-five days, dying in 304, a year after the cruel persecution broke out, in which he gained much honor. He has been styled a martyr, though his blood was not shed in the cause of religion, as appears from the Liberian Calendar, which places him among those popes that were not put to death for the faith.

It is a fundamental maxim of the Christian morality and truth that Christ has established in the most explicit terms and in innumerable passages of the gospel that the cross, or sufferings and mortification, are the road to eternal bliss. They, therefore, who lead not here a crucified and mortified life, are unworthy ever to possess the unspeakable joys of his kingdom. Our Lord himself, our model and our head, walked in this path, and his great apostle puts us in mind that he entered bliss only by his blood and by the cross. Nevertheless, this is a truth that the world can never understand, how so ever it is preached by Christ and recommended by his powerful example and that of his martyrs and all the saints. Yet, nevertheless, Christians still pretend, by the joys and pleasures of this world, to attain the bliss of heaven, and shudder at the very mention of mortification, penance, or sufferings. So prevalent is this fatal error, which self-love and the example and false maxims of the world strongly fortify in the minds of many, that those who have given themselves to God with the greatest fervor, are always bound to stand upon their guard against it, and daily to renew their fervor in the love and practice of penance, and to arm themselves with patience against sufferings, lest the weight of the corruption of our nature, the pleasures of sense, and flattering blandishments of the world, draw them aside, and make them leave the path of mortification, or lose courage under its labors, and under the afflictions with which God is pleased to purify them, and afford them means of sanctifying themselves.

[Butler, Alban. *The Lives of the Fathers, Martyrs, and Other Principal Saints. Compiled from Original Monuments and Authentic Records.* Dublin: James Duffy, 1866. *HathiTrust Digital Library,* catalog.hathitrust.org/Record/001941109.]

Saint Peter of Verona, Dominican Priest, and Martyr (1206–1252) — April 29

The memorial of Peter, who died near Milan on April 6, 1252, appeared in the Roman calendar in 1586. It is left to the particular calendars since he is not of universal significance.

In 1205, the glorious martyr Peter was born at Verona to Manichean[48] parents; there, he nonetheless attended a Catholic school. One day his Manichean uncle asked what he learned there. Naturally, the Creed answered Peter: *I believe in God, Creator of heaven and earth.* No arguments could shake his faith, and at age sixteen, he received the habit from Saint Dominic himself at Bologna.

After his ordination, he preached to the heretics of Lombardy and converted multitudes. Saint Peter was constantly obliged to dispute with heretics, and although he could confound them, the devil still tempted him one day against faith. Instantly he had recourse to prayer before an image of Our Lady and heard a voice saying to him the words of Jesus Christ in the Gospel, *I have prayed for thee, that thy faith may not fail; and do thou, when once thou hast turned again, strengthen thy brethren* (Luke 22:32).

He often conversed with the Saints, and one day the martyred virgins Catherine, Agnes, and Cecilia appeared to him and conferred with him. A passing religious, hearing their feminine voices, accused him to their Superior, who, without hesitation or questions, exiled him to a convent where no preaching was being done. Saint Peter submitted humbly but complained in prayer to Jesus crucified that He was abandoning him to his bad reputation. The crucifix spoke: *And I, Peter, was I too not innocent? Learn from Me to suffer the greatest sorrows with joy. Eventually, his innocence was brought to light; for his part, he had learned to love humiliation and confusion in his solitude.*

Again, engaged in preaching, miracles accompanied his exhortations. He traveled all over Italy

---

[48] Manichaeism is a former major religion founded in the Sasanian Empire in the third century by the Parthian prophet Mani. Manichaeism teaches a complex dualistic cosmology that describes the conflict between a good, spiritual world of light and an evil, material world of darkness.

and became famous. Once when preaching to a vast crowd under the burning sun, the heretics defied him to procure shade. He prayed, and a cloud overshadowed the audience.

Every day at the elevation of the Mass, he prayed, *Grant, Lord, that I may die for Thee, who for me didst die.* His prayer was answered. His enemies, confounded by him, sought his life. Two of them attacked him in 1252 on the road to Milan and struck his head with an ax. Saint Peter fell, commended himself to God, dipped his finger in his blood, and wrote on the ground, I believe in God, Creator of heaven and earth. He was then stabbed to death. The religious brother accompanying him also suffered death. The details of the crime were made known by Saint Peter's murderer, named Carino, who confessed his crime after fleeing from justice, asking for penance from the Dominican Fathers. He took the habit and, according to their testimony, lived the life of a saint and persevered to the end. Miracles at Saint Peter's tomb and elsewhere converted a great many heretics.

[Shea, John G. *Little Pictorial Lives of the Saints, with Reflections for Every Day of the Year; Compiled from "Butler's Lives."* New York: Benziger, 1894. *HathiTrust Digital Library,* hdl.handle.net/2027/nyp.33433068232887; Guérin, Abbé (Paul), François Giry, and Simon Martin. *Les Petits Bollandistes: Vies Des Saints De L'Ancien et du Nouveau Testament.* Translated by the Monastère du Magnificat. Paris: Bloud et Barral, 1882. *HathiTrust Digital Library,* hdl.handle.net/2027/nnc1.0036694380.]

MAY

Saints Alexander, Pope; Eventius and Theodulus, Priests and Martyrs; and Saint Juvenal, Bishop, and Confessor (✝ second century) — May 3

Little is known about Alexander, Eventius, and Theodulus, but their names and burial place on the Via Nomentana on May 3, and their memorial is left to the particular calendars. The memorial of Juvenal, Bishop of Narni but not a martyr, is likewise left to the particular calendars.

On the same day as the invention of the Holy Cross, the Catholic Church celebrates the martyrdom of Saint Alexander, pope, and martyr, who was born in Rome, and the son of a citizen there, called by the same name. He succeeded in Saint Peter's Chair Saint Evaristus, pope and martyr, and was the seventh pope after Saint Peter if we include Saints Linus and Cletus. They immediately succeeded the Apostle one after the other. Saint Alexander was admirable for his sanctity and most eminent for his faith and constancy in his martyrdom.

He was thirty years old when he was promoted to the government of the Church, but his life and doctrine did abundantly supply his want of years. Through his preaching and heavenly conversation, he converted many senators and a significant part of the Roman nobility to our holy faith, and among them, a principal magistrate named Hermes, with all his family who was twelve hundred and fifty persons, for which very reason he was apprehended by the governor of the city, Aurelianus, and cast into prison, where he wrought many miracles, of which this one was very great and most remarkable.

For being loaded with iron bolts, there came one night to him a child with a lighted taper in his hand that said to him, "*Alexander, follow me.*" The saint made his prayers first to God and then, understanding him to be an angel of our Lord, followed him, and neither walls, doors, nor guards could stop or hinder him. The child led him to the house of Quirinus[49] tribune, where Hermes was in the hold, who had a great desire to speak with Saint Alexander, and the saint had promised him, notwithstanding his imprisonment, would come to him. When they met, they embraced each other. They shed tears of joy and devotion and animated themselves to suffer courageously for our Lord Jesus Christ. This did much astonish Quirinus, the tribune, after discussing with Hermes, who told him the manner of his conversion to the holy faith. When he also saw his daughter Balbina, much afflicted with the king's evil, cured by Saint Alexander, with only touching her with his chains, he became a Christian, with his daughter and all those he kept as prisoners. And Saint Alexander commanded Saint Eventius and Saint Theodulus, priests from the eastern parts of Rome, to baptize them all.

When this was told to Aurelianus, he was exceedingly furious and angry and first tormented Quirinus and put him to death, then cut off the head of Hermes and commanded all those that had been baptized in prison, together with Balbina, Quirinus' daughter, to be drowned in the sea. Then he sent for Alexander with the two priests, Eventius and Theodulus. Then, when they had interchanged some discourse for a while, Aurelianus said, "*Let us leave off wording it, and fall to works*," and commanded the hangman to strip Saint Alexander naked,

---

49 Saint Quirinus, Roman tribune, and martyr († 30 March 116).

and stretch him on the [rack], and with iron hooks to tear off his flesh, and to burn his sides with lighted torches.

In this torment, the saint was most quiet and still and spoke not a word. When Aurelianus wondered and asked him, "*Why he held his peace and complained not,*" he answered, "*When a Christian prays, he speaks to God.*" Eventius and Theodulus were put to the same torments, and Eventius was eighty-one years old, had been baptized at eleven, and received holy orders at twenty. The greatness and sharpness of the sufferings served only to make the holy martyrs firmer and more constant in the faith and love of our Lord Jesus Christ.

And Aurelianus, unable to make them relent, and condescend to his will, commanded an oven to be heated and Alexander and Eventius to be cast into it. Still, Theodulus was made to stand at the mouth of it, seeing them consumed with the burning flames and fearing the like punishments, he might move to sacrifice to the gods. But, Theodulus, not only with undaunted courage, beheld his companions in the fire but also inflamed with a tremendous fire of divine love, leaped in among them because they called him and told him that they felt no pain but instead found great ease and refreshment. And so it was, the flames did not hurt them, and they came all three out of the oven bright and shining and the same color as gold that had been refined in the crucible.

The hardened and rebellious heart of the tyrant was nothing softened by the miracle, for he commanded Eventius and Theodulus to be beheaded. And, as for Alexander, that he might die a crueler death, all members and parts of his body were priced and stabbed by keen and sharp-pointed awls of steel. In which torment he gave up his most blessed soul to God (though the Book of Roman Bishops records he was also beheaded after he had been so horribly misused) on the third day of May, in the year of our Lord 132, according to Cardinal Baronius, in the reign of Emperor Hadrian[50], who Trajan has adopted[51], called himself Trajan Hadrian. Where arises the mistake of some authors who write Saint Alexander suffered under Trajan.

Aurelianus was overjoyed for putting these holy martyrs to death as if he got some famous victory. Still, his joy was soon turned to lamentations, for he heard a voice that said, "*Aurelian, for those whom thou has deprived of life, the gates of heaven are opened, and the gates of hell are for the.*" This voice put Aurelianus beside himself, and falling to the ground, he ate his own tongue and, so dying, yielded his wicked soul to be eternally tormented in the flames of hell.

The bodies of Saint Alexander and his companions were buried out of the city on the Via Nomentana[52], seven miles from Rome, and afterward translated to the church of Saint Sabina in the city, which is a convent of the Dominican Friars. Baronius said According to Baronius, Saint Alexander was a pope for ten years, five months, and twenty days Yet Eusebius only gives him ten years, but the Book of Roman Bishops adds to the ten years, seven months, and two days. Saint Alexander was most zealous for his divine service. He ordained that at Holy Mass, priests should consecrate unleavened bread to signify the purity of the Blessed Sacrament and to imitate our blessed Savior, who, instituting this sacred mystery, did the same at the Last Supper. He also decreed that in the consecration of the chalice, they should mingle a little water with the wine,

---

[50] Hadrian reigned as Emperor of Rome from 117 to 138. He was born into a Roman family that had moved to Spain from the Italian city of Atri in Picenum some 250 years before. His father was a senator and Emperor Trajan's first cousin.

[51] Trajan reigned as Emperor of Rome from 98 to 117. Trajan is remembered as a successful soldier-emperor who presided over one of the greatest military expansions in Roman history and led the empire to the greatest territorial extent in history by the time of his death, as officially declared by the senate *Optimus Princeps* (the greatest of emperors).

[52] Via Nomentana is an ancient Italian road that runs 23 kilometers northeast from Rome to Nomentum.

thereby signifying the union of Christ with His Church and representing the blood and water that issued forth of His precious side. But when we say that Saint Alexander did institute these holy ceremonies, it is not to be understood or inferred that he was the first to form them, for the Apostles used them before. What they learned of Christ and taught the Church, this holy bishop did approve and establish by his holy Canons.

The holy Church commemorates Saint Juvenal, Bishop of Narni, a city in Umbria, forty miles from Rome, joining him with the Holy Martyrs, Saint Alexander, and His Companions. The Roman Breviary and the martyrologies of Bede, Ado, and Usuardus say of him, "*That he was a man of a most holy life, and renowned for his miracles, and that he converted almost the entire city of Narni to the faith of Christ.*" Saint Gregory also spoke of another Juvenal, buried in Narni and died a martyr, mentioned in the Roman Martyrology on the seventh of May.

[Ribadeneyra, Pedro de. "The Lives of St. Alexander Pope, St. Eventius and St. Theodulus Priests, and Martyrs; and also of St. Juvenal Bishop, and Confessor." *The Lives of Saints, With Other Feasts of the Year, according to the Roman Calendar. Written in Spanish by the Reverend Father Peter Ribadeneyra, Priest of the Society of Jesus. Translated Into English by W.P. (William Petre) Esq; The Second Edition Corrected and Amended, vol. 1, pp. 322-323.* London. Printed by B.S., 1730. *HathiTrust Digital Library,* hdl.handle.net/2027/nyp.33433003052994.]

Saint Antoninus, Bishop, and Confessor (1389–1459) — May 10

Antoninus died at Florence on May 2, 1459, and entered the Roman calendar in 1683. Since he is not of universal significance, his feast is now left to the particular calendars.

Saint Antoninus, or Little Antony, as he was called from his small stature, was born in Florence in 1389. After a childhood of singular holiness, he begged to be admitted very young into the Dominican house at Fiesole. Still, to test his sincerity and perseverance, the Superior told him he must first learn by heart the book of the Decretals, or Canon Law, containing several hundred pages. This impossible task was accomplished within twelve months, and Antoninus received the coveted habit in his sixteenth year.

While still young, he filled several important posts of his Order and was consulted on questions of difficulty by the most learned men of his day, known because of his remarkable prudence as the Counselor. He wrote several works on theology and history and served as Papal Theologian at the Council of Florence. In 1446 he was compelled to accept the archbishopric of that city. In this dignity, he earned himself the title of the Father of the Poor, for all he had was at their disposal. Saint Antoninus never refused alms, which were asked in the name of God. He gave his clothes, shoes, or furniture when he had no money.

One day, being sent by the Florentines to the Pope, as he approached Rome, a beggar came up to him almost naked and asked him for alms, for Christ's sake. Outdoing Saint Martin, Antoninus gave him his whole cloak. When he entered the city, another one was given him; by whom, he knew not. His household consisted of only six persons; his palace contained no plate or costly furniture and was often nearly destitute of the necessities of life. His one mule was frequently sold for the relief of the poor but was ordinarily repurchased for him again by some wealthy citizen.

Saint Antoninus died on May 2, 1459, kissing the crucifix, and repeating the words, *To serve God is to reign.*

[Shea, John G. *Little Pictorial Lives of the Saints, with Reflections for Every Day of the Year; Compiled from "Butler's Lives."* New York: Benziger, 1894. *HathiTrust Digital Library,* hdl.handle.net/2027/nyp.33433068232887.]

Saints Gordian and Epimachus, Martyrs († 362 and † 250) — May 10

Little is known about Gordian and Epimachus except for their names and the date of their burial on the Via Latina on June 10. Their memorial is now left for particular calendars.

After the most ungodly and wicked Julian the Apostate[53] had been proclaimed emperor by his army in France, and by the death of Constantius II, his cousin-german[54] was made absolute lord and sovereign, and he began to pluck off the mask of piety, with which had previously deceived and deluded the Christians by seeming to favor them. For now, he was wholly bent upon their utter ruin and destruction and upon the setting up again and increasing the worship and veneration of the false gods. But because he affected still the name and reputation of a clement and merciful prince, and envied the Christians that lost their lives for the true faith and religion, the glory and title of martyrs, also fearing, because Christian religion was much spread, and did greatly flourish in the world, that open persecution might occasion some stirs and troubles in the empire, he endeavored, for the reason of state, to undermine them secretly, and to go cunningly and craftily about the execution of his cursed and abominable intentions. Therefore, he put such men in office and authority,

---

[53] From 361 to 363, Julian (Flavius Claudius Julianus) was a Roman emperor as well as a well-known Greek philosopher and author. In the Christian tradition, Julian the Apostate is remembered for his rejection of Christianity and promotion of Neoplatonic Hellenism in its place.

[54] A cousin-german is a first cousin (the child of someone's aunt or uncle).

making them governors of cities and provinces, whom he knew to be cruel and vicious men, and to bear spleen and spite against the holy religion, so to fling the stone, as they say, and to hide the arm, and utilizing our ministers to bring that to pass, which he thought not fit to appear in himself.

Among the officers chosen by Julian to execute his wicked design was Gordian, whom he made governor of Rome, and, as it were, his viceroy[55]. And Gordian conducted his commission with cruelty and shed much innocent Christian blood. Among many that he apprehended for their piety and religion was a venerable old priest, Januarius, with whom Gordian had long and different discourses. At last, when it pleased the Almighty God to move his heart, he opened his eyes to a ray of heavenly light that shone upon him and resolved to become a Christian and soon after was baptized by Saint Januarius. He, and his wife Marina, with three hundred fifty of his family. He delivered up to Januarius an idol of Jupiter, which he had kept and worshipped in his house, which was cast into the fire and broken into pieces and the pieces thrown upon a dunghill.

Julian came to know of this, which put him into a great rage, that his prime officers, whom he had chiefly instructed with the charge of extinguishing the Christian religion, and maintaining his profane superstition, should fall off from him and become Christians.

Then, discarding Gordian out of all office and honor, he gave orders to Clementianus, a tribune, to apprehend and punish him, which he set about, commanding Gordian to be brought before him, loaded with many chains as he was able to bear, then taxing him of ingratitude to the emperor, threatening him with many torments if he refused to sacrifice to the gods. But

---

[55] A viceroy is someone who rules a country or province on behalf of his sovereign or king and has the authority to act in the sovereign's name.

Gordian, standing firm and constant in his confession of Jesus Christ, scoffed at Julian and his foolish gods. Wherefore, Clementianus made him be tormented and most cruelly scourged, and to have his bones bruised and broken with whips armed with lead, while the blessed man gave our Lord thanks for giving him the grace to suffer for him, and for placing him in the rank of martyrs. The tribune, at length, seeing he lost his labor, commanded he should be beheaded before the temple of the goddess Tellus[56], which signifies the earth, and that no one should offer to bury him but that the dogs should devour his body. But our Lord, to show his goodness and power, ordained those hungry dogs coming to the place should not touch the body but keep and defend it with their barking.

After it had laid there for five days, one that had been Gordian's servant, and some other Christians, carried it away in the night and buried it a mile from Rome on the Via Latina[57] in a grotto, into which Saint Epimachus' body had been translated not long before, whose martyrdom the Church also celebrates upon this day, who having been taken at Alexandria for the faith of Christ, after a long and hard imprisonment, and several grievous torments, which for many days he endured with admirable patience and constancy, at length was burned. His bones and ashes were brought to Rome by Christians and put into this grotto.

The Church keeps them both on the tenth of May, on which Saint Gordian was martyred in the year of our Lord 362, in the reign of Julian the Apostate. The relics of these most blessed martyrs were translated into

---

[56] Tellus Mater or Terra Mater ("Mother Earth") is a goddess of the Earth in ancient Roman religion and myth. Although Tellus and Terra are nearly indistinguishable during the Imperial era, Tellus was the name of the original earth goddess in Republic or earlier religious practices.
[57] The Via Latina was a Roman road in Italy, running southeast from Rome for about 200 kilometers.

Germany in 770, as written by Hermannus Contractus[58] in his *Chronicle.* Those that have written of Saint Gordian, and Saint Epimachus, besides the *Roman Martyrology,* are venerable Bede, Usuardus, Ado, and Surius in his third tome, and Baronius, in his annotations upon the *Roman Martyrology,* and the fourth tome of his Annals.

[Ribadeneyra, Pedro de. "The Lives of St. Gordian, St. Epimachus, Martyrs." *The Lives of Saints, With Other Feasts of the Year, according to the Roman Calendar. Written in Spanish by the Reverend Father Peter Ribadeneyra, Priest of the Society of Jesus. Translated Into English by W.P. (William Petre) Esq; The Second Edition Corrected and Amended, vol. 1, pp. 340-341.* London. Printed by B.S., 1730. *HathiTrust Digital Library,* hdl.handle.net/2027/nyp.33433003052994.]

Saint Flavia Domitilla, Virgin, and Martyr († 1st century) — May 12

(Previously celebrated with the memorials of Nereus and Achilles and Pancras; now celebrated separately with their proper Masses according to the ancient Roman custom.) Since the veneration of Domitilla has no foundation in tradition, her memorial, which dates from the Roman calendar in 1595, is now abolished.

She was niece to the consul and martyr Saint Flavius Clemens, his sister's daughter, as Eusebius testifies; consequently, she was the little niece of Emperor Domitian, who, having put to death her illustrious uncle, banished her for her faith into Pontia. There she lived with her holy eunuchs, Nereus and Achilleus, in devotion exercises, dwelling in separate cells that remained standing three hundred years later. Saint Jerome tells us that Saint Paula, going from Rome to Jerusalem, took this island on her way, visited them with respect and devotion,

---

[58] Blessed Hermann of Reichenau, also known as *Hermann the Lame* or *Hermannus Contractus,* was a Benedictine monk and scholar of the 11th century. He wrote many hymns as well as works on history, music theory, mathematics, and astronomy.

and was animated with zeal by their sight. So that father calls her banishment a long martyrdom. Nerva and Trajan were, perhaps, unwilling to restore the relations of Domitian with the other exiles whom they recalled. The acts of Saints Nereus and Achilleus say that she returned to Terracina and was there burnt under Trajan because she refused to sacrifice to idols. Her relics are kept together with those of Saints Nereus and Achilleus, who, though her servants here on earth, enjoy an equal honor and condition with her in glory.

This royal virgin found true happiness and joy in suffering for virtue, while worldly pomp and honors are only masks that often cover the basest slavery and much inward bitterness. Sinners who seem the most fortunate in the eyes of the world feel in their breasts frequent returns of fear, anxiety, and remorse. They are only enemies to solitude, retirement, and all serious and calm reflection because they cannot bear to look into themselves and tremble at the very sight of their frightful wounds. To turn their eyes on themselves, they study to drown their faculties in a hurry for dissipation, business, or diversion. Nay, though nauseous and tired with a dull and tasteless repetition of follies, they choose to repeat them still for fear of being left alone, at liberty to think of themselves. But what becomes of them when sickness, disasters, or a wakeful hour force them to view their miserable state and the dangers which hang over them? Their gaudy show of happiness is merely exterior and only imposed upon others: but their pangs and agonies are interior: these they feel. So the servant of God, who in his sweet love enjoys an inward peace and comfort which the whole world cannot rob him of, carries his paradise within his breast, whatever storms hover about him.

[Butler, Alban. *The Lives of the Fathers, Martyrs, and Other Principal Saints. Compiled from Original Monuments and Authentic Records.* Dublin: James Duffy, 1866. *HathiTrust Digital Library,* catalog.hathitrust.org/Record/001941109.]

Saint Boniface, Martyr († 307) — May 14

The <u>Suffering of Boniface of Tarsus</u> is entirely legendary, and his memorial, which dates from the twelfth-century Roman calendar, is abolished.

There lived at Rome, about the beginning of the fourth century, a certain lady called Aglaë, young, beautiful, well-born, and so rich and fond of making a figure in the world that she had entertained the city three several times with public shows at her charge. Her chief steward was one Boniface, with whom she entertained criminal commerce. Though addicted to wine and all kinds of debauchery, this man was remarkable for three good qualities: hospitality, liberality, and compassion. Whenever he saw a stranger or traveler, he would assist him cordially. He used to go about the streets and into public places at night. He relieved the poor according to their necessities. After several years' commerce in the cruel way already mentioned, Aglaë, touched with a motion of divine grace, and feeling some compunction within herself, called Boniface to her, and thus opened her mind to him: "You are sensible how deep we are plunged in vice, without reflecting that we must appear before God to give an account of all our actions. I have heard some say that they who honor those who suffer for the sake of Jesus Christ shall have a share in their glory. In the East, the servants of Jesus Christ every day suffer torments and lay down their lives for his sake. Go thither then, and bring me the relics of some of those conquerors, that we may honor their memories and be saved by their assistance." Boniface came into the proposal and raised a considerable sum of money to purchase the bodies of the martyrs from their executioners and to distribute them among the poor. He said to Aglaë on his departure, "I will not fail to bring back with me the relics of martyrs if I find any, but what if my own body should be brought to you for that of a martyr?" She reproved him for jesting in a matter so serious. The steward set out but was now entirely a new man. Penetrated with sentiments of compunction, in all that long journey from Rome into the East, he neither ate meat nor drank wine; his fasts were accompanied with prayers, tears, and penitential works. The church, at that time, enjoyed peace in the West, but in the East, the persecution, which Dioclesian had begun, was carried on with great cruelty by Galerius Maximianus[59]. It raged most fiercely in Cilicia under an inhuman governor named Simplicius. Therefore, Boniface directed his journey to Tarsus, that country's capital. He no sooner arrived at the city, but descending, he sent away all his servants with the horses to an inn and went himself straight to the court of the governor, whom he found seated on his tribunal, and many holy martyrs suffering under their tortures; one hanged up by the feet, with his head over a fire: another stretched almost to the tearing of his limbs on four planks or stakes: a third sawn asunder: a fourth had his hands cut off: a fifth was fixed to the ground by a stake run through his neck: a sixth having his hands and feet tied behind him, the executioners were beating him with clubs. There were no less than twenty tortured after this cruel manner. The sight shocked the beholders, while their courage and resolution filled them with amazement. Boniface went boldly up to these champions of Christ and, having saluted them, cried out: "Great is the God of the Christians, great is the God of the holy martyrs! I beseech you, the servants of Jesus Christ, to pray for me, that I may join with you in fighting against the devil." The governor thought himself insulted by so bold an action in his presence and asked him in great wrath who he was. The martyr answered that he was a Christian and that having Jesus Christ as his master, he

---

[59] Gaius Galerius Valerius Maximianus, Roman emperor: 1 May 305 – May 311.

feared nothing the governor could inflict to make him renounce that sacred name. Simplicius, in a rage, ordered some reeds to be sharpened and thrust under his nails; this being done, he commanded boiling lead to be poured into his mouth. After calling upon Jesus Christ for his assistance, Boniface begged the prayers of the other expiring martyrs, who all joined in putting up their petitions to God for him. The people, disgusted with so much cruelty, began to raise a tumult and cried out: "Great is the God of the Christians." Simplicius was alarmed and withdrew. But the next day, seated on his tribunal, he ordered Boniface to be brought before him a second time. The martyr appeared constant and undaunted. The judge commanded him to be cast into a cauldron of boiling pitch, but he came out without receiving any hurt. Lastly, he was condemned to lose his head; after a short prayer for the pardon of his sins and the conversion of his persecutors, he cheerfully presented his peck to the executioner. His companions, in the meantime not finding his return to the inn, searched for him in those parts of the city where they thought him most likely to be found. Being at last informed by the jailer's brother that a stranger had been beheaded the day before for his faith in Christ, and being shown the dead body and the head, they assured him that it was the very person they were in search of, and besought him to bestow the martyr's relics upon them; this he refused to do without a reward: so they paid down five hundred pieces of gold, and having embalmed it, carried it home with them, praising God for the happy end of the blessed martyr. Aglaë, upon information of the affair, gave God thanks for his victory and, taking some priests with her, met the corpse with tapers and perfumes half a mile out of Rome, on the Via Latina; and in that very place raised a monument in which she laid them, and some years after built a chapel. She from that time led a penitential retired life and, dying fifteen years after, was buried near his relics. They were found in Rome in 1603, together with those of Saint Alexius, in the church in Rome formerly called Saint Boniface, but now of Saint Alexius. The bodies of Saint Boniface and Saint Alexius lie under the stately high altar in two rich marble tombs. The martyrdom of Saint Boniface happened about the year 307.

While we praise the divine mercy, who of sinners maketh saints, we ought earnestly to pray that he changes our hearts from vessels of corruption into vessels of grace and his divine charity. Regret and sorrow for sin have many degrees. Still, until it has entirely subdued the corruptions, changed the affections, and purified the heart, it is not saving repentance or that charity and love which animates or impregnates the new creature. A sure proof of regeneration or a genuine conversion is victory. *He that is born of God overcometh the world.* But, nevertheless, the maxims of the gospel, the rules of the church, and reason itself forbid us to look upon him as a sincere convert whose life is very uneven, inconstant, and contradictory to itself; if he is today a saint, and tomorrow a sinner; if he follows today the impulses of the Holy Ghost, and yield tomorrow to the temptations of the enemy; or if he has not the courage to fly the dangers and renounce the occasions which are fatal to him.

[Butler, Alban. *The Lives of the Fathers, Martyrs, and Other Principal Saints. Compiled from Original Monuments and Authentic Records.* Dublin: James Duffy, 1866. *HathiTrust Digital Library,* catalog.hathitrust.org/Record/001941109.]

Saint Ubaldus, Bishop, and Confessor (1085–1160) — May 16

The memorial of Ubaldus, who died at Gubbio in 1160 and was added to the Roman calendar in 1605, is now left to the particular calendars since this saint is not of universal significance.

Saint Ubaldus was born of a noble family at Gubbio, a city of the Ecclesiastical State, near the marquisate of Ancona. He had his education in the seminary of Saints Marian and James and made significant progress in his profane and sacred studies, but the Holy Scriptures, those springs of living waters, were his chief delight. Many honorable matches were proposed to him by his friends, but he rejected all such offers and made a vow of celibacy. His ardor in the perfect practice of virtue strengthened him against the bad example of many tepid companions. However, not approving certain irregularities he saw tolerated among them, he exchanged this house for the seminary of Saint Secundus, where he finished his studies. The bishop of Gubbio made him before his cathedral that he might reform several abuses in the behavior of the canons. Ubaldus prepared himself for this important work by fasting, prayers, and tears, by which he hoped to engage the divine assistance. He easily prevailed on three of his canons who were the best disposed to join him in his exercises and life rules; their example soon began to work upon the rest. The saint visited a community of regular canons, esteemed for their regularity and sanctity, which had been established by Peter de Honestis, a person of singular piety, in the territory of Ravenna. He stayed there three months to take a clear view of the discipline of the house, and he carried its rule back with him to Gubbio and, in a short time, got it received by the whole chapter to render their reformation complete. After some years of their house and cloister being burnt down, Ubaldus saw this as a favorable opportunity to leave his post and retire to some desert. In this view, he made his way to that of Font-Avellano, where he found Peter of Rimini, to whom he communicated his design of quitting the world. That great servant of God opposed the motion as a dangerous temptation and encouraged him to return to his former vocation, in which God had fixed him for the good of others. The saint, therefore, returned to Gubbio, rebuilt the cloisters, and rendered his chapter more flourishing than it had ever been to the great edification of the whole country. In 1126, Saint Ubaldus was unanimously chosen bishop of Perugia[60]; but he hid in the country so that the deputies of that city were not able to find him; and when they departed, he went to Rome, threw himself at the feet of Pope Honorius II and with many tears begged that he might be excused; employing all the interest he had in the world to obtain the favor he desired. Honorius granted his request; but the see of Gubbio becoming vacant two years after, the pope directed the clergy of that city to proceed to his election according to the forms prescribed by the canons: in consequence of which his holiness consecrated him with his own hands at the beginning of the year 1129. The new bishop made it his whole business to adorn the dignity of his station with all the virtues of a true successor of the apostles. He practiced a perpetual mortification of all his senses and lived dead to all the enjoyments of the world: he was indefatigable both in the exercise of penance and in the labors of his ministry; frugal, humble, sincere, and full of compassion for all the world. But mildness and patience, by which he appeared insensible to injuries and insults, was one of the brightest parts of his character. Once, it happened that the workers encroached upon his vineyard to repair the wall of the city. The bishop

---

[60] Perugia is the capital of the Umbria region in Italy.

mildly put them in mind of it and desired them to forbear. The overseer of the work moved with savage fury and scornfully pushed him into a great heap of mortar. The good bishop got up all covered with lime and dirt without making the least expostulation. The people demanded that the overseer, in punishment for the offense, should be banished and his goods confiscated. The saint endeavored to make it pass for an accident; but when that could not satisfy the people, who knew how it happened, he being desirous to deliver the man out of the hands of the magistrates, maintained that the cognizance of the misdemeanor belonging to his court, he would take care to do himself justice. The workman stung remorse and proffered to accept any punishment the bishop should think proper to inflict on him, even though his life was to pay for the offense. The holy prelate, rising from his chair, went up to him and told him with a smiling countenance that by way of satisfaction for the injury received, he insisted on his giving him a kiss of peace, as a token of perfect reconciliation, and that he begged of God to pardon him that and all other offenses. After which, he saluted him.

The saint often defended his flock from public dangers. Hearing one day that a sedition was raised in one of the streets, wherein some were wounded, others killed, he ran out and, venturing himself between the combatants, fell amidst their naked swords. The mutineers thinking him dead, all threw away their weapons, running to take him up, and everyone condemned him as the murderer of their holy bishop. Then the saint, thanking God that the tumult was appeased, dispelled their fears by assuring them that he had received no hurt. Emperor Frederick Barbarossa, having taken and plundered Spoleto in his cruel wars in Italy, threatened to do the like Gubbio. Ubaldus, moved by a more than fatherly tenderness for his flock, met the emperor on the road and, in his first interview, softened the heart of that tyrant to compassion and obtained of him the safety of his people. In the two last years of his life, he labored under a complication of painful distempers, which he bore with the patience of a saint. On Easter day, in 1160, his devotion to the glorious mystery of that festival made him forget his infirm condition, get up, say mass, and give the people discourse on eternal life. From the cathedral, he would be carried to the church of Saint Laurence, near which he had an apartment. He continued there until the feast of the Ascension in retirement to prepare himself for death. After that, he was removed into his own house, where he repeated his last instructions to his clergy and people, who came to visit him and beg his last blessing. Having received the rites of the church, he expired on the 16th of May, 1160. The people from all the neighboring provinces attended his funeral in crowds and were eyewitnesses of the many miracles God performed at his tomb. So tender was the devotion which this spectacle excited everyone that animosities and disputes over the whole country were extinguished, and a most beautiful spirit of charity was infused into all hearts. Injuries were forgotten, and cities that had been long at variance renewed the sincerest league of friendship. Saint Ubaldus had been favored with the miraculous gift of curing diseases in his lifetime, which he performed by the sign of the cross and prayer; yet, when a certain blind man addressed himself to him to be cured, the bishop told him that his corporal sight would be prejudicial to his soul and that his temporal blindness would be repaid with the clear vision of God in heaven for all eternity: at which the good man was so well satisfied, that he no longer desired to be cured. Pope Celestine III canonized Saint Ubaldus in 1192.

[Butler, Alban. *The Lives of the Fathers, Martyrs, and Other Principal Saints. Compiled from Original Monuments and Authentic Records.* Dublin: James Duffy, 1866. *HathiTrust Digital Library,* catalog.hathitrust.org/Record/001941109.]

Saint Paschal Baylon, Confessor (1540–1592) — May 17

Paschal Baylon died at Villareal, Spain, in 1592, and his feast was added to the Roman calendar in 1784. Since he is not of universal significance, his memorial is left for particular calendars.

From his childhood, Saint Paschal seems to have been marked out for the service of God. Amid his daily labors as a shepherd, he found time to instruct and evangelize the rude herders who kept their flocks on the hills of Aragon. Then, at twenty-four, he entered the reformed Franciscan Order near the town of Monforte del Cid, Spain, where he remained, out of humility, a simple lay brother, occupying himself by preference with the roughest and most servile tasks.

He was distinguished by his ardent devotion and love for the Blessed Sacrament. He would spend hours on his knees before the tabernacle, often raised from the ground in the fervor of his prayer. And there, from the authentic and eternal Truth, he drew such stores of wisdom that, unlettered as he was, he was considered by all a master in theology and spiritual science.

Shortly after his profession, he was sent to Paris on business connected with his Order. The journey was full of perils, owing to the hostility of the Huguenots, who were numerous at the time in the south of France, and on four separate occasions, Paschal was in imminent danger of death at their hands. Twice he was taken for a spy, but it was not God's will that His servant should obtain the crown of martyrdom which he so earnestly desired, though he regarded himself as unworthy of it. So he returned in safety to his convent, where he would later die in the odor of sanctity in 1592.

Multitudes witnessed the miracles during the three days his body was exposed for veneration. As a result, he was canonized in 1690 and, in 1897, declared patron of all Eucharistic congresses and confraternities.

[Shea, John G. *Little Pictorial Lives of the Saints, with Reflections for Every Day of the Year; Compiled from "Butler's Lives."* New York: Benziger, 1894. *HathiTrust Digital Library,* hdl.handle.net/2027/nyp.33433068232887; Levy, Rosalie. *Heavenly Friends, a Saint for Each Day.* Boston: Saint Paul Editions, 1958. Print.]

Saint Venantius of Camerino, Martyr († 250) — May 18

There are many difficulties concerning the truth of the Acts of the life of this martyr. His memorial, which was added to the general calendar in 1670, is now left to local calendars.

Saint Venantius, born at Camerino in Italy during the persecution of Decius, was taken into custody at fifteen years old as a Christian preaching Christ to others. His history is one of the most miraculous in the annals of the early martyrs.

Having learned that he was about to be arrested, he presented himself to the governor of Camerino, Antiochus, at the city gates. He said to him that the lives of the gods were filled with every kind of crime, that there was only one God, whose unique Son had become a man to deliver his fellow humans from the tyranny of sin. When it was impossible to shake his constancy either by threats or promises, he was condemned to be scourged but miraculously saved by an Angel. He was then burnt with torches and suspended over a low fire so the smoke might suffocate him. The judge's secretary, while admiring the steadfastness of the Saint, saw an Angel robed in white, who stamped out the fire and again set free the youthful martyr. This man proclaimed his faith in Christ and was baptized with his whole family. Shortly afterward, he won the martyr's crown.

Venantius was summoned to appear before Antiochus. Unable to make him renounce his faith, the governor cast him into prison with an apostate soldier, who strove vainly to tempt him. Antiochus, furious, ordered his teeth and jaws to be broken and had him thrown into a furnace, from which the Angel once more delivered him. Finally, the Saint was sent to a city magistrate to be condemned, but this judge, after hearing his defense of Christianity, fell headlong from his seat and expired, saying, The God of Venantius is the true God; let us destroy our idols.

When this circumstance was told to Antiochus, he ordered Venantius to be thrown to the lions. These brutes, however, forgetting their natural ferocity, crouched at the feet of the Saint. Then, by order of the tyrant, the young martyr was dragged through a heap of brambles and thorns and retired half-dead, but the next day he was cured; God had manifested the glory of His servant once more. Then, on behalf of soldiers who had dragged him outside the city over stones and rocks and were suffering from thirst, the Saint knelt on a rock and signed it with a cross; immediately, a jet of clear, cool water welled up from the spot. This miracle converted many of those who beheld it. The rock remained imprinted by his knees and was placed in a church in Camerino, where it remains.

The governor finally had Venantius and his converts beheaded on the same day, in the year 250. The bodies of these martyrs are kept in the same church at

Camerino[61]. The Church has carefully studied the Acts of Saint Venantius' martyrdom and declared them authentic.

[Guérin, Abbé (Paul), François Giry, and Simon Martin. *Les Petits Bollandistes: Vies Des Saints De L'Ancien et du Nouveau Testament.* Translated by the Monastère du Magnificat. Paris: Bloud et Barral, 1882. *HathiTrust Digital Library,* hdl.handle.net/2027/nnc1.0036694380; Shea, John G. *Little Pictorial Lives of the Saints, with Reflections for Every Day of the Year; Compiled from "Butler's Lives."* New York: Benziger, 1894. *HathiTrust Digital Library,* hdl.handle.net/2027/nyp.33433068232887.]

Saint Peter Celestine, Pope (1221–1296) — May 19

Peter Morrone, who died near Anagni in 1296, was canonized in 1313 but honored more as a hermit than a pope, as the fourteenth-century calendar of the papal chapel attests. His memorial was placed on the universal calendar in 1668 and is now left to the particular calendars because he is not a saint of universal significance.

Saint Peter Celestine was the eleventh of the twelve children of a poor Italian farmer. Peter had visions of our Blessed Lady, Angels, and Saints as a child. His heavenly visitors encouraged him in his prayers and scolded him when he fell into any fault. Nevertheless, his mother, though only a poor widow, sent him to school, feeling sure that he would one day be a Saint.

At age twenty, he left his home in Apulia to live in mountain solitude. Here he passed three years, assaulted by the evil spirits, and beset with temptations of the flesh but consoled by the visits of Angels. After this, his seclusion was invaded by disciples who refused to be sent away; the rule of life he gave them formed the foundation of the Celestines, a branch of the Order of Saint Benedict.

---

[61] Camerino is a town in the Marche province of central-eastern Italy. It is about 40 miles from Ancona in the Apennines, between the valleys of the rivers Potenza and Chienti.

Angels assisted in the church Peter built; unseen bells rang peals of surpassing sweetness, and heavenly music filled the sanctuary when he offered the Holy Sacrifice; he had consented to be ordained, to find in the Holy Eucharist assistance against temptation.

Suddenly the poor anchorite found himself torn from his loved solitude, having been named by acclamation to the Papal throne, which had remained vacant for twenty-seven months. Resistance was of no avail. He took the name of Celestine to remind him of the heaven he was leaving, for which he sighed. He was seventy-two years old. After five months, Peter judged himself unfit for the office, summoning the cardinals to his presence. He solemnly resigned his trust.

He worked many great miracles during the remaining three years of his life. On the day after his abdication, his blessing after Mass healed a lame man. Saint Peter left the palace, desiring seclusion, but was brought back by the papal guards, for his successor feared a schism; crowds had followed Saint Peter. Lest he is prevailed upon to take back his office, he was put under surveillance at Anagni. Content, he remarked: I desired nothing but a cell, and a cell they have given me. And there, he enjoyed his former loving intimacy with the Saints and Angels and sang the Divine praises almost continually.

At length, on Pentecost Sunday, he told his guards he would die within the week and immediately fell ill. Nevertheless, he received the Last Sacraments, and the following Saturday, as he finished the concluding verse of Lauds, *Let every spirit bless the Lord! he closed his eyes to this world and opened them to the vision of God.*

[Guérin, Abbé (Paul), François Giry, and Simon Martin. *Les Petits Bollandistes: Vies Des Saints De L'Ancien et du Nouveau Testament.* Translated by the Monastère du Magnificat. Paris: Bloud et Barral, 1882. *HathiTrust Digital Library,* hdl.handle.net/2027/nnc1.0036694380; Shea, John G. *Little Pictorial Lives of the Saints, with Reflections for Every Day of the Year; Compiled from "Butler's Lives."*

New York: Benziger, 1894. *HathiTrust Digital Library,* hdl.handle.net/2027/nyp.33433068232887; Jaud, Leon. *Vie Des Saints Pour Tous Les Jours De L'annee: Avec Une Pratique De Piete Pour Chaque Jour.* Translated by the Monastère du Magnificat. Tours: A. Mame, 1950. Print.]

Saint Pudentiana, Virgin († 174) — May 19

The memorial of Pudentiana, which was placed in the Roman calendar in the eighth century, is left to her titular church for observance. The Acts of Pudentiana and Praxedes offer no historical explanation for the origin of the titular church of Pudens and Praxedes.

When the glorious apostle, and prince of the apostles, Saint Peter, came to Rome, it is a common and certain tradition that he lodged in the house of a grave and principal senator, whose name was Pudens and had for a wife a most worthy and honorable lady, Priscilla, by whom he had two sons, Novatus and Timothy, and as many daughters, Potentiana, or rather Pudentiana, and Praxedes.

All of them, as well as parents as children, became Christians and were great servants of God, receiving many blessings from his liberal and bountiful hand. Pudens had besides for his master, the holy apostle, Saint Paul, who maketh an honorable mention of him in his second epistle to Timothy. These saints deserved to have their house turned into a church, which was called the Title, or Church of Pudens, from the master and owner of it, or pastor, because when Hermes, a priest, was to consecrate it, there appeared to him an angel in the habit and shape of a pastor, or shepherd, and was the first title that was ever erected in Rome and is at present called the Church of Saint Pudentiana, whose feast (to omit at this time to speak of her the saints, her brothers) the Church celebrates this day, as a most holy virgin, who after the death of her parents, sold her estate, which was very significant, and gave the price to the poor, and retired herself into a little house with her sister Praxedes.

The two virtuous sisters attended day and night to prayer, fasting, and penance. They busied themselves in gathering the blood of martyrs, burying their holy bodies, and maintaining and encouraging all Christians. Saint Pudentiana, by her most exemplary life and wholesome counsel and admonitions, converted all those of her family, ninety-six in all, to the faith of Christ. They were all baptized by Pope Pius I. Because the emperor Antonius had commanded that the Christians should have no churches publicly to resort to celebrate divine service, the holy pope repaired to the house of Saint Pudentiana, where he said Mass. Many Christians came to hear it secretly and to receive the most sacred body of our Lord.

And the holy virgin entertained them with most sincere affection and relived their necessities. And while she was wholly taken up in their laudable exercises of devotion and charity, it pleased our Lord to call her to himself, to give her the reward of her holy labors, and to change her mortal and temporal life into eternal happiness and bliss.

Her body was buried on the nineteenth of May, in her parents' sepulcher, in the churchyard of Priscilla, on the Via Salaria. She died in the year of our Lord, 174, in the reign of Antonius Pius. On the same day, the Roman Martyrology makes mention of her father, Saint Pudens. Besides the Roman Martyrology, venerable Bede, Usuardus, and Saint Ado speak of Saint Pudentiana, as also Baronius in his notes upon the Martyrology and in the second tome of his Annals.

[Ribadeneyra, Pedro de. "The Life of St. Pudentiana, Virgin." *The Lives of Saints, With Other Feasts of the Year, according to the Roman Calendar. Written in Spanish by the Reverend Father Peter Ribadeneyra, Priest of the Society of Jesus. Translated Into English by W.P. (William Petre) Esq; The Second Edition Corrected and*

Amended, vol. 1, p. 350. London. Printed by B.S., 1730. *HathiTrust Digital Library*, hdl.handle.net//2027/nyp.33433003053000.]

Saint Urban, Pope, and Martyr (abt. 175–230 AD) — May 25

Although the memorial of Urban is ancient, it is deleted since the ancient liturgical books do not honor Pope Urban I but an unknown bishop-martyr from a city outside of Rome.

Reigned 222-30, date of birth unknown; died 23 May, 230. According to the *Liber Pontificalis*, Urban was a Roman, and his father's name was Pontianus. After the death of Callistus I (14 October, 222), Urban was elected Bishop of Rome, of which Church he was the head for eight years, according to Eusebius (Church History VI.23). The document called the Liberian catalog of popes puts the beginning of his pontificate in the year 223, and it's close in the year 230. The dissension produced in the Roman Church by Hippolytus continued to exist during Urban's pontificate. Hippolytus and his adherents persisted in schism; it was probably during the reign of Urban that Hippolytus wrote his *Philosophumena*[62], in which he attacked Pope Callistus severely. Urban maintained the same attitude towards the schismatical party and its leader that his predecessor had adopted. The historical authorities say nothing of any other factious troubles in the life of the Roman Church during this era. In 222, Alexander Severus became the Roman emperor. He favored religious eclecticism and protected

---

[62] The *Refutation of All Heresies*, also known as the *Elenchus* or *Philosophumena*, is a comprehensive Christian polemical work from the early third century, whose authorship is debated between Hippolytus of Rome and an unknown Pseudo-Hippolytus. It catalogs both pagan beliefs and thirty-three gnostic Christian systems that Hippolytus deemed heretical, making it a valuable source of information on contemporary opponents of Christian orthodoxy as it is understood today.

Christianity. His mother, Julia Mamaea, was a friend of the Alexandrine teacher Origen, whom she summoned to Antioch. Hippolytus dedicated his work on the Resurrection to her. The favorable opinion of Christianity held by the emperor and his mother was that Christians enjoyed complete peace in essential, although their legal status was not changed. The historian Lampridius (Alex. Sever., c. 22 A.D.) says emphatically that Alexander Severus made no trouble for the Christians: "*Christianos esse passus est*" (Christians have suffered). Undoubtedly the Roman Church experienced the happy results of these kindly intentions and was unmolested during this emperor's reign (222–235). The emperor even protected Roman Christians in a legal dispute over a piece of land ownership. When they wished to build a church on a piece of land in Rome, which was also claimed by tavern-keepers, the matter was brought before the imperial court. Severus decided in favor of the Christians, declaring it was better that God should be worshipped on that spot (Lampridius, "Alex. Sever.", c. 49 A.D.).

Nothing is known concerning the personal labors of Pope Urban. The increase in the extent of various Roman Catacombs in the first half of the third century proves that Christians grew primarily in numbers during this period. The legendary Acts of Saint Cecilia connect the saint, as well as her husband and brother-in-law, with Urban, who is said to have baptized her husband and her brother-in-law. This narrative, however, is purely legendary and has no historical value; the same is true of the Acts of the martyrdom of Urban himself, which are of still later date than the legend of Saint Cecilia. The statement of the *Liber Pontificalis* that Urban converted many by his sermons rests on the Acts of Saint Cecilia. Another statement on the same authority that Urban had ordered the making of silver liturgical vessels is only an invention of the later editor of the biography early in the sixth century, who arbitrarily attributed to Urban the making of certain vessels, including the patens for twenty-five titular churches of his own time. The particulars of the death of Urban are unknown, but, judging from the peace of his era, he must have died a natural death. The *Liber Pontificalis* (The Pontifical Book) states that he became a confessor in the reign of Diocletian; the date added is without authority. His name does not appear in the *Depositio Episcoporum* (Deposition of Bishops) of the fourth century in the *Kalendarium Philocalianum* (Calendar of the Philocalians).

Two different statements are made in the early authorities regarding the grave of Urban; however, only one refers to the pope of this name. In the Acts of Saint Cecilia and the *Liber Pontificalis,* it is said that Pope Urban was buried in the Catacomb of Praetextatus on the Via Appia. The Itineraries of the seventh century to the graves of the Roman martyrs all mention the grave of an Urban in connection with the graves of several martyrs buried in the Catacomb of Praetextatus. One of the Itineraries gives this Urban the title "Bishop and Confessor." Consequently, from the fourth century, all Roman tradition has venerated the pope of this name in the Urban of the Catacomb of Praetextatus. In excavating a double chamber of the Catacomb of Saint Callistus, De Rossi found, however, a fragment of the lid of a sarcophagus that bore the inscription *OUPBANOCE (piskopos)* [URBAN (bishop)]. He also proved that in the list of martyrs and confessors buried in the Catacomb of Saint Callistus, drawn up by Sixtus III[63], the name of an Urban is to be found. Therefore, the great archaeologist De Rossi concluded that the Urban buried in Saint Callistus was the pope.

---

[63] Pope Sixtus III was the bishop of Rome from July 31, 432 to August 18, 440. His election to the papacy coincided with a period of increased construction in Rome.

In contrast, the saint of the same name buried in Saint Praetextatus was the bishop of another see who died in Rome and was buried in this catacomb. Most historians agree with this opinion, which is chiefly founded on the Acts of Saint Cecilia. The lettering of the above-mentioned epitaph of an Urban in Saint Callistus indicates a later period, as a comparison with the lettering of the papal epitaphs in the papal crypt proves. In the list prepared by Sixtus III and mentioned above, Urban is not given in the succession of popes but appears among the foreign bishops who died in Rome and were buried in Saint Callistus.

Thus, it seems necessary to accept the testimony that Pope Urban was buried in the Catacomb of Praetextatus, while the Urban lying in Saint Callistus is a bishop of a later date from some other city. This view best reconciles the statements of the *Martyrologium Hieronymianum* (The Martyrology of Jerome). Under the date of 25 May (VIII kal. Jun.) is to be found the notice: *Via nomentana miliario VIII natale Urbani episcopi in cimiterio Praetextati* (Eight miles from the name of the road, the birthplace of Pope Urban in the churchyard of Praetextatus), *Martyr. Hieronym., ed. De Rossi-Duchesne*, 66). The catacomb on the Via Nomentana, however, is that which contains the grave of Pope Alexander, while the Catacomb of Praetextatus is on the Via Appia. Duchesne has proved (Lib. Pontif., I, XLVI–XLVII) that in the list of graves of the popes from which this notice is taken, a line dropped out and that it originally stated that the grave of Pope Alexander was on the Via Nomentana and the grave of Pope Urban on the Via Appia in the Catacomb of Praetextatus. Consequently, 25 May is the day of the burial of Urban in this catacomb. As the same martyrology contains under the date of 19 May (*XIV kal. Jun.*) a long list of martyrs headed by the two Roman martyrs Calocerus and

Partenius, who are buried in the Catacomb of Saint Callistus, and including an Urban, this Urban is the foreign bishop of that name who lies buried in the same catacomb.

[Herbermann, Charles G, Edward A. Pace, Condé Bénoist Pallen, Thomas J. Shahan, John J. Wynne, and Andrew A. MacErlean. *The Catholic Encyclopedia: An International Work of Reference on the Constitution, Doctrine, Discipline, and History of the Catholic Church: in Fifteen Volumes.* New York: Robert Appleton Co., 1907. archive.org/details/07470918.1.emory.edu.]

Saint Eleutherius (Eleutheros), Pope and Martyr (c. 174–189) — May 26

There is no longer any memorial of Eleutherius, initially placed in the Roman calendar in the twelfth century. Therefore, Pope Eleutherius was not martyred, and his death date is unknown.

Pope (c. 174-189). The *Liber Pontificalis* says that he was a native of Nicopolis, Greece. From his contemporary Hegesippus, we learn that he was a deacon of the Roman Church under Pope Anicetus (c. 154-164), and remained so under Saint Soter, the following pope, whom he succeeded about 174. While the condition of Christians under Marcus Aurelius was distressing in various parts of the empire, the persecution in Rome itself does not seem to have been violent. De Rossi, it is true, dates the martyrdom of Saint Cecilia towards the end of this emperor's reign; this date, however, is by no means certain. During the reign of Commodus (180-192), the Christians enjoyed a practically unbroken peace, although the martyrdom of Saint Apollonius at Rome took place at the time (180-185). The Montanist movement, which originated in Asia Minor, made its way to Rome and Gaul in the second half of the second century, particularly during the reign of Eleutherius; its peculiar nature made it difficult to take from the outset a decisive stand against it. During the violent persecution at Lyons in 177, local confessors wrote from prison concerning the new movement to the Asiatic and Phrygian brethren and Pope Eleutherius. The bearer of their letter to the pope was the presbyter Irenæus, soon afterward Bishop of Lyons. It appears from statements of Eusebius concerning these letters that the faithful of Lyons, though opposed to the Montanist movement, advocated forbearance and pleaded for the preservation of ecclesiastical unity.

Just when the Roman Church took its definite stand against Montanism is not certainly known. It would seem from Tertullian's account, *Treatise against Praxeas*, that a Roman bishop did some conciliatory letters at the one-time address to the Montanists. Still, these letters, says Tertullian, were recalled. He probably refers to Pope Eleutherius, who long hesitated, but, after a conscientious and thorough study of the situation, is supposed to have declared against the Montanists. In Rome, heretical Gnostics and Marcionites continued to propagate their false teachings. The *Liber Pontificalis* ascribes to Pope Eleutherius a decree that Christians should despise no kind of food, *Et hoc iterum firmavit ut nulla esca a Christianis repudiaretur, maxime fidelibus, quod Deus creavit, quæ tamen rationalis et humana est* (And again he confirmed this, that no food should be rejected by Christians, especially the faithful, which God created, which, however, is rational and human). Possibly he did issue such an edict against the Gnostics and Montanists; it is also possible that on his responsibility, the writer of the *Liber Pontificalis* attributed to this pope a similar decree current about the year 500. The same writer is responsible for a curious and interesting assertion concerning the early missionary activity of the Roman Church; indeed, the *Liber Pontificalis* contains no other statement equally remarkable. Pope Eleutherius, says this writer, received from Lucius, a British king, a letter in which the latter declared that by his behest, he wishes to become a Christian, *Hic accepit epistula a Lucio Brittanio rege, ut Christianus efficerentur per ejus mandatum* (This man received a letter from King Lucius Britannia to become a Christian by his command). Whence, the author of the first part of the Liber Pontificalis, drew this information, it is now impossible to say. But, historically speaking, the fact is quite improbable and has been rejected by all recent critics.

At the end of the second century, the Roman administration was so securely established in Britain that there could no longer have been on the island any native kings. That some tribal chief, known as king, should have applied to the Roman bishop for instruction in the Christian faith seems improbable enough at that period. The unsupported assertion of the *Liber Pontificalis*, a compilation of papal biographies that in its earliest form cannot antedate the first quarter of the sixth century, is not a sufficient basis for accepting this statement. Some consider it a story intended to demonstrate the Roman origin of the British Church and, consequently, the latter's natural subjection to Rome. To make this clearer, they locate the origin of the legend in the seventh century, during the dissensions between the primitive British Church and the Anglo-Saxon Church recently established in Rome. But for this hypothesis, all proof is lacking. It falls before the simple fact that the first part of the *Liber Pontificalis* was compiled long before these dissensions, most probably (Duchesne) by a Roman cleric in the reign of Pope Boniface II (530-532) or (Waitz and Mommsen) early in the seventh century. Moreover, during the entire conflict centered around the peculiar customs of the Early British Church, no reference is ever made to this alleged King Lucius. Saint Bede is the first English writer (673-735) to mention the story repeatedly

(Hist. Eccl., I, V; V, 24, *De temporum ratione*[64], ad an. 161), and he took it, not from native sources, but the *Liber Pontificalis*. Harnack suggests a more plausible theory (Sitzungsberichte der Berliner Akademie[65], 1904, I, 906-916). In the document he holds, from which the compiler of the *Liber Pontificalis*[66] drew his information, the name found was not Britanio, but Britio. Now, this is the name (Birtha-Britium) of the fortress of Edessa. The king in question is, therefore, Lucius Ælius Septimus Megas Abgar IX, of Edessa, a Christian king, as is well known. In this hypothesis, the original statement of the Liber Pontificalis had nothing to do with Britain. The reference was to Abgar IX of Edessa. But the compiler of the *Liber Pontificalis* changed Britio to Brittanio and made a British king of the Syrian Lucius.

The ninth-century *Historia Brittonum*[67] sees in Lucius a translation of the Celtic name *Llever Maur*[68], says that the envoys of Lucius were Fagan and Wervan, and tells us that with this king, all the other island kings (*reguli Britanniæ*) were baptized (Hist. *Brittonum*, xviii). Thirteenth-century chronicles add additional details. The *Liber Landavensis*[69], for example (ed. Rees, 26, 65), makes known the names of Elfan and Medwy, the envoys sent by Lucius to the pope, and transfers the king's dominions to Wales. An echo of this legend penetrated even Switzerland. In a sermon preached at Chur and preserved in eighth- or ninth-century manuscript, Saint Timothy is represented as an apostle of Gaul, whence he came to Britain and baptized there a king named Lucius, who became a missionary, went to Gaul, and finally settled at Chur, where he preached the gospel with great success.

---

[64] On the nature of the times.
[65] Meeting reports of the Berlin Academy.
[66] Pontifical Book.
[67] History of the Britons.
[68] Great light.
[69] The Book of Landavensis.

In this way, Lucius, the early missionary of the Swiss district of Chur, became identified with the alleged British king of the *Liber Pontificalis*. The latter work is authority for the statement that Eleutherius died on 24 May and was buried on Vatican Hill (*in Vaticano*) near the body of Saint Peter.

[Herbermann, Charles G, Edward A. Pace, Condé Bénoist Pallen, Thomas J. Shahan, John J. Wynne, and Andrew A. MacErlean. *The Catholic Encyclopedia: An International Work of Reference on the Constitution, Doctrine, Discipline, and History of the Catholic Church: in Fifteen Volumes.* New York: Robert Appleton Co., 1907. archive.org/details/07470918.1.emory.edu.]

Saint Felix I, Pope († 274) — May 30

This memorial, which entered the Roman calendar in the thirteenth century, is now suppressed. The ancient liturgical books do not refer to Pope Felix, whose burial on December 30, 274, is listed in the Depositio Episcoporum, but to Felix, a martyr buried on the Via Aurelia.

He was a Roman by birth and succeeded Saint Dionysius in the government of the church in 269. Paul of Samosata, the proud bishop of Antioch, to the guilt of many enormous crimes, added that of heresy, teaching that Christ was no more than a mere man, in whom the Divine Word dwelt by its operation, and as in its temple, with many other gross errors concerning the capital mysteries of the Trinity and Incarnation. Two councils were held at Antioch to examine his cause, but he escaped condemnation by various arts and subterfuges. However, in a third, assembled at the same place in 269 and convicted of heresy, pride, and many scandalous crimes, he was excommunicated and deposed. Domnus was substituted in his room. Paul still maintained himself in possession of the episcopal house. The bishop, therefore, had recourse to the emperor Aurelian, who, though a pagan, gave an order that the house should belong to him to whom the bishops of Rome and Italy adjudged it, as Eusebius writes. Saint Felix had declared himself against that heresiarch, for the council had sent the synodal letter to Saint Dionysius, who is dead. It had been delivered to Saint Felix. It must have been on that occasion that our holy pope wrote to Maximus, bishop of Alexandria, a learned epistle, quoted by the council of Ephesus, Saint Cyril of Alexandria, and Saint Vincent of Lerins; in which he clearly explained the Catholic doctrine of the whole mystery of the Incarnation. Saint Cyril has preserved us a fragment of it. The persecution of Aurelian breaking out, Saint Felix, fearless of dangers, strengthened the weak, encouraged all, baptized the catechumens, and continued to exert himself in converting infidels to the faith. He obtained the glory of martyrdom, which title is given to him by the council of Ephesus, Saint Cyril, and Saint Vincent of Lerins. He governed the church for five years and passed to a glorious eternity in 274. The western Martyrologies name him on the 30th of May.

The example of Christ and all his saints should encourage us to suffer with patience and joy under all trials. We shall soon begin to feel that it is sweet to tread in the steps of a God-man and find that if we courageously take up our crosses, he will make them light by bearing them with us. The soul will find it sweet to be abandoned by creatures so that she may more perfectly feel their emptiness and learn that men are false and treacherous. Then will she place her complete confidence in God alone and cleave to him with her whole heart. Forsaken and forgotten by creatures, she finds no relish but in God who enters her more powerfully and fills her with his consolations the more sweetly, as she is the more weaned and separated from all earthly things and more purely adheres to him who never forsakes those who sincerely seek Him. *O, happy exchange!* cries out Saint Francis of Sales, *the soul thus abandoned in the eyes of men now possesses God instead of creatures.*

[Butler, Alban. *The Lives of the Fathers, Martyrs, and Other Principal Saints. Compiled from Original Monuments and Authentic Records.* Dublin: James Duffy, 1866. *HathiTrust Digital Library,* catalog.hathitrust.org/Record/001941109.]

Saint Petronilla, Virgin († First century) — May 31

The memorial of Petronilla, dating from the eighth century, is left for particular calendars. Nothing is known about this virgin martyr apart from her name and burial in Domitilla's cemetery on the Via Ardeatina on May 31.

Among the disciples of the apostles in the primitive age of saints, this holy virgin shone as a bright star in the church. She lived when Christians were more solicitous to live well than to write much: they knew how to die for Christ; but did not compile long books or disputations, in which vanity often has a greater share than charity. Hence no account of her actions hath been transmitted down to us. But we may judge how eminent her sanctity was from the luster by which it was distinguished among the apostles, prophets, and martyrs. Her name is the feminine and diminutive of Peter, and she is said to have been a daughter of the apostle Saint Peter, which tradition is confirmed by certain writings quoted by the Manichees in the time of Saint Augustine, which affirm that Saint Peter had a daughter whom he cured of a palsy. We learn from the gospel that Saint Peter was married before his vocation to the apostleship. However, Saint Jerome and other ancient fathers testify that he lived in continency after his call. Saint Clement of Alexandria assures us that his wife attained the glory of martyrdom, at which that apostle himself encouraged her, bidding her to remember our Lord. But it seems not certain whether Saint Petronilla was more than the spiritual daughter of that apostle. She flourished at Rome and was buried on the way to Ardea, where anciently a cemetery and a church bore her name; so famous that in it, a station or place for the city's assembly in public prayer was established by Gregory III. She is commemorated in the true Martyrology of Bede, in those which bear the name of Saint Jerome, etc.

The saints, whether in sickness or health, in public or private life, devoted all their thoughts and actions to God and thus sanctified all their employments. The great end they lived was always present in their minds, and they thought every moment lost in which they did not make some advances toward eternal bliss. How will their example condemn at the last day the trifling fooleries and the more significant part of the conversation and employments of the world, which aim at nothing but present amusements, as if it were the business of a rational creature to divert his mind from thought and reflection, and forget the only affair—the business of eternity.

[Butler, Alban. *The Lives of the Fathers, Martyrs, and Other Principal Saints. Compiled from Original Monuments and Authentic Records*. Dublin: James Duffy, 1866. *HathiTrust Digital Library*, catalog.hathitrust.org/Record/001941109.]

JUNE

Saint Erasmus of Formia (or Saint Elmo), Bishop and Martyr († 303) — June 2

The memorial of Erasmus, who died at Formia as a martyr, was added to the Roman calendar in the eleventh or twelfth century. It is now left to local calendars.

The holy church joins Saint Marcellinus and Saint Peter in the same solemnity. Saint Erasmus, bishop, and martyr, who in the time of the emperors Dioclesian and Maximian, fought valiantly for the faith of Jesus Christ: and was often put to most bitter and cruel torments. First, Dioclesian stripped him naked and severely scourged him with leather thongs, armed with pellets of lead; after this, he had his bones broken with knotty cudgels. And finding that all these horrible pains could not bring him to relent in his constancy and forsake the law of Christ, he caused a great cauldron to be set upon the fire, full of pitch, rosin, wax, and brimstone. When all this was melted together and exceedingly hot, the saint was cast into it: but by the will and special protection of our Lord, it caused no harm or damage to him. Many people, being much moved, renounced their false gods and were made Christians by this miracle.

The emperor commanded he should be carried back into the prison; and that upon pain of death, nobody should give him anything to eat or drink. But before midnight, while the blessed martyr was praying, all the prison shined with an incomparable light. A sweetest and delightful savor proceeded from it: and presently, an angel appearing to him shook off his bolts and chains and said, Erasmus, rise and follow me: for you are to convert many souls to our Lord. So the angel carried him to Lucrinum, a town of Apulia in the Kingdom of Naples. Where God wrought by this his Saint many and very great miracles; through which, and by his heavenly life and doctrine, innumerable infidels, detesting their dark ignorance, embraced the light of the Gospel and were brought into the fold of our Lord Jesus Christ.

The fame of Saint Erasmus was spread through all the country, and the emperor Maximian coming thither, hearing the report of his admirable miracles and rare virtues, desired to see him and sent some to bring him.

When he arrived, he asked him to what religion he belonged. The saint lifted his eyes to heaven to implore God's grace and assistance to answer well. The tyrant, being incensed, commanded the officers to strike him on the face and said to him, look where you should look, and sacrifice to the gods. Not long after, he put upon his bare body a coat of red-hot iron; and seeing it did not burn or anyway molest him, he fretted, swelled with indignation and rage; and by and by cast him into a vessel full of pitch, rosin, and oil, boiling and seething on the fire, hoping that therein he would be soon consumed. But what force has fire against the will and appointment of God? So the saint remained in the cauldron a long while and received no harm at all, which did incredibly vex and torment the tyrant, who commended him for being taken thence and kept in prison until he could invent some way to afflict him.

But that very night, an angel appeared to him and, breaking his chains, took him to the seaside where a little bark was prepared for him. So entering, and with the angel guiding it, he arrived in Formia or Nola, in the province of Campania, not far from Cajeta. There he did what he used to do, and by his example, preaching and miracles, he enlightened the blind nation and communicated to it the sovereign light of the holy Gospel.

One day, as he was praying, he heard a voice from heaven that said to him, Erasmus, my faithful servant, seeing thou hast fought like a good soldier for me, come and receive your crown. And at the same instant, he saw the richest and most glorious crown brought him down from heaven and, bowing his head, answered: Lord, receive my soul in peace. And when he had spoken this, his soul was seen in the form of a white dove to fly up to heaven, accompanied by the angels, to be received by him, and given to him the strength to fight so bravely, and had so often delivered him from torments and death, as we have here related. But, according to Baronius, he died on the second of June, in the year of our Lord 303. Pope Saint Gregory saith that his body was placed in the cathedral church of Formia and later translated to Cajeta, where it is present; and is reverenced and honored with great devotion. The glorious patriarch, Saint Benedict, was a great client of Saint Erasmus and built two stately churches in his honor, one in Rome, and one in Vercelli, as is observed by Cardinal Baronius. This life is taken out of Saint Ado and is set down much more at large by Saint Antonius, Archbishop of Florence, and Vincentius of Beauvais. Pope Gelasius II, having been a monk at Mont-Cassin, wrote the Life of Saint Erasmus, Bishop and Martyr, and some other saints, as Petrus Diaconus assures us in his book of the famous men of the monastery. And all other martyrologies mention Saint Erasmus.

[Ribadeneyra, Pedro de. "The Life of Saint Erasmus, Bishop and Martyr." *The Lives of Saints, With Other Feasts of the Year, according to the Roman Calendar. Written in Spanish by the Reverend Father Peter Ribadeneyra, Priest of the Society of Jesus. Translated Into English by W.P. (William Petre) Esq; The Second Edition Corrected and Amended,* vol. 1, pp. 381-382. London. Printed by B.S., 1730. *HathiTrust Digital Library,* hdl.handle.net//2027/nyp.33433003053000.]

Saint Francis Caracciolo, Confessor (1563–1608) — June 4

The memorial of Francis, who died at Agnone, Italy, in 1608, was placed on the general calendar in 1807. It is left to the particular calendars since he does not have universal significance.

Saint Francis was born in the kingdom of Naples in 1563 to the princely family of Caracciolo. In childhood, he shunned all amusements, recited the Rosary regularly, and loved to visit the Blessed Sacrament and distribute his food to the poor. To avoid idleness, however, he engaged in hunting, which pastime was not pleasing to God; and Our Lord, to detach him from the world, sent him a terrible trial. When he was twenty-two years old, he developed leprosy and soon was on the brink of death. Seeing his body in this deplorable condition taught him contempt for the world's vanity and youth's physical strength, and he promised God to serve Him alone if he were cured. However, the illness disappeared almost at once. He, therefore, left his parents, sold his portion of the inheritance for the benefit of the poor, and went to study for the priesthood at Naples. He dedicated himself to visiting prisoners and galley slaves and preparing criminals for death; he spent his leisure hours visiting the Blessed Sacrament in unfrequented churches.

God called him, when only twenty-five, to found the Order of Regular Minor Clerics with two other priests with similar aspirations. The Rule they drew up prescribed that each day one of the members fast on bread and water, another takes the discipline, a third wear a hair shirt, and each succeeds another for perpetual adoration before the Blessed Sacrament. Thus, they hoped to appease the anger of God unceasingly and draw down His blessings by their penance. In addition, they took the usual vows, adding a fourth — not to accept dignities unless required by their sovereign.

These very humble priests resolved to arrive in extreme poverty in Rome to seek approbation for their Order, and they mingled with the poor who were asking for alms at the door of the Capuchin Fathers. But, when recognized by relatives, they asked for no favor except that of being taken to the presence of the Holy Father, Sixtus V[70]. The Pope approved the new Congregation. He gave

---

[70] Pope Sixtus V, born Felice Piergentile, was the leader of the Catholic Church from April 24, 1585 until his death in 1596. As a young man, he joined the Franciscan order, where he demonstrated his talents as a scholar and preacher, earning him the patronage of Pius V, who elevated him to the rank of cardinal. Cardinal Montalto was his title as a cardinal.

them a church in Naples, which became the first center of the Order.

To establish the new Order, Francis, with John Augustine Adorno[71], his co-founder, undertook journeys throughout Italy and Spain, on foot and without money, content with the shelter and crusts given out of charity. A saintly pilgrim exiled from England predicted to Francis that he would be the new Order's first General. A Dominican in Spain, before he had heard them talk of their intentions, received the two of them and gave them food, saying, *You are the founders of a new Order which will soon spread, for the glory of God and the salvation of souls, and will be especially flourishing in this kingdom.* Asked when that would occur, he replied, *Not for three years.* In Spain, Adorno again heard the same prophecy from Saint Louis Bertrand, who insisted on kissing his feet.

The prediction was realized. When Saint Francis returned to Valencia, he found that the twelve religious who had remained there had multiplied in number to the point that the house could no longer contain them. In 1591 he was elected the first General of his Order while still prey to the sorrow recently caused by the premature death of Adorno at the age of forty. He redoubled his austerities and devoted seven hours daily to meditation on the Passion, besides passing most of the night praying before the Blessed Sacrament. He was commonly called the Preacher of Divine Love, and in Spain, the Order did indeed flourish.

It was always before the Blessed Sacrament that his ardent devotion was most clearly visible. In the presence of his divine Lord, his face emitted brilliant rays of light, and he often bathed the ground with his tears as he prayed, according to his custom, prostrate before the

---

[71] Venerable In Genoa, Italy, John Augustine Adorno was born to a noble family in 1551. He is a co-founder of the Minor Clerks Regular Congregation.

tabernacle, constantly repeating with the royal psalmist, *The zeal of Thy house has consumed me!* At Ancona in Italy, he had gone to prepare another foundation that his holy soul, on the eve of Corpus Christi 1608, went to join his Savior in Heaven. He was forty-four years old when he fell ill with a severe fever. He died exclaiming, *Let us go, and let us go to heaven!* When his body was opened after death, his heart was found seemingly burnt, with these words imprinted around it: *Zelus domus tuae comedit me — The zeal of Thy house has consumed me.*

[Guérin, Abbé (Paul), François Giry, and Simon Martin. *Les Petits Bollandistes: Vies Des Saints De L'Ancien et du Nouveau Testament.* Translated by the Monastère du Magnificat. Paris: Bloud et Barral, 1882. *HathiTrust Digital Library,* hdl.handle.net/2027/nnc1.0036694380; Shea, John G. *Little Pictorial Lives of the Saints, with Reflections for Every Day of the Year; Compiled from "Butler's Lives."* New York: Benziger, 1894. *HathiTrust Digital Library,* hdl.handle.net/2027/nyp.33433068232887.]

Saints Primus and Felicianus, Martyrs († 286) — June 9

The memorial of these martyrs from Praeneste, whose relics were brought to Rome in 648, is left to the particular calendars.

These two martyrs were brothers who lived in Rome, heirs of a family of great wealth, toward the latter part of the third century. It was through the assiduous love of Pope Felix I that they had the happiness, in their mature years, of being converted to the Christian faith; afterward, they encouraged each other for many years in the practice of all good works. They seemed to possess nothing but for the poor, and often, during the persecutions, they spent both nights and days with the confessors in their dungeons or at the places of their torments and execution. Some they exhorted to persevere; others who had fallen, they raised again. They made themselves the servants of all in Christ so that all might attain salvation through Him.

Though their zeal was remarkable, they had escaped the dangers of many bloody persecutions; they had grown old in the heroic exercises of their virtue when it pleased God to crown their labors with a glorious martyrdom. Primus was about ninety years old when the pagans raised so great an outcry against the brothers that they were apprehended and put in chains. They were inhumanly scourged and tortured and then sent to a town twelve miles from Rome to be chastised again, as avowed enemies to the gods, by a prefect who detested the Christians. There they were cruelly tortured to make them renounce their faith, both together and then separately, but the grace of God strengthened each of them. Felicianus was nailed by his hands and feet to a post and left without food or water for three days; Primus was beaten with clubs and burnt with torches. God spared them amidst these tortures, and wild beasts in an arena imitated their God's mercy. Finally, they were beheaded on June 9, 286.

[Shea, John G. *Little Pictorial Lives of the Saints, with Reflections for Every Day of the Year; Compiled from "Butler's Lives."* New York: Benziger, 1894. *HathiTrust Digital Library,* hdl.handle.net/2027/nyp.33433068232887.]

Saint John of Sahagún, Confessor, Augustinian (1430–1479) — June 12

The memorial of John, who died at Sahagún, Spain, on June 11, 1479, entered the Roman calendar in 1729. It is now left for the particular calendars since this saint does not have universal significance.

Saint John, one of the greatest preachers Spain has ever known, was born at Saint Fagondez and gave signs of his future sanctity from his early youth. He was the fruit of the ardent prayers of his parents after sixteen years of sterility; God blessed them afterward with several children. He was entrusted to the Benedictines of the monastery of Saint Fagondez for his education. He distributed virtually all the wealth accruing to the poor from several benefits. At the same time, he lived in great poverty, but soon he renounced all of these and obtained from his bishop permission to study theology in Salamanca. As a young priest, he was already regarded as a Saint, so ardent was his devotion at Holy Mass. He entered the Order of Saint Augustine soon after he had bestowed on a poor man half of his clothing and the following night experienced so significant an increase in the love of God that he referred to this as his conversion.

He was a model religious and soon was entrusted with important offices in his Order — master of novices, definitor for the province, and prior of the convent of the city of Salamanca. He commanded well because he knew so well how to obey. When he observed in himself a slight defect in his obedience, he repaired it with extraordinary penances. Often while offering the adorable Sacrifice with tender piety, he enjoyed the sight of Jesus in glory and held sweet colloquies with Him. The ineffable bliss of these moments caused him to spend much more time than the other priests celebrating Holy Mass, and everyone was complaining. Only when his Superior forbid him to delay in this way was he obliged to acknowledge the favors he enjoyed.

The power of his holiness was seen in his preaching, which produced a complete reformation of morals in Salamanca. He had a special gift for reconciling differences and putting an end to the quarrels and feuds among noblemen, which at that period were very

257

common and fatal. The boldness shown by Saint John in reproving vice endangered his life. Having been corrected by the Saint for oppressing his vassals, a powerful nobleman sent two assassins to slay him. Still, the remarkable holiness of the Saint's aspect, the result of the peace constantly reigning in his soul, struck such awe into their minds that they could not execute their purpose and humbly begged his forgiveness. The falling sick nobleman was brought to repentance and recovered his health by the prayers of the Saint whom he had endeavored to murder.

Saint John was also very zealous in denouncing the vices of impurity, and it was in defense of holy purity that he met his death. A lady of noble birth but sinful life, whose companion in sin he had converted, contrived to administer a fatal poison to the Saint. After several months of terrible suffering, borne with unvarying patience, Saint John went to his reward on June 11, 1479. This painful death and the cause for which he suffered it have caused several of his historians and panegyrists to say that he won a martyr's crown. Many striking miracles followed at his tomb and elsewhere, even by the simple invocation of his name. He was canonized in 1690 by Pope Alexander VIII.

[Guérin, Abbé (Paul), François Giry, and Simon Martin. *Les Petits Bollandistes: Vies Des Saints De L'Ancien et du Nouveau Testament.* Translated by the Monastère du Magnificat. Paris: Bloud et Barral, 1882. *HathiTrust Digital Library,* hdl.handle.net/2027/nnc1.0036694380; Shea, John G. *Little Pictorial Lives of the Saints, with Reflections for Every Day of the Year; Compiled from "Butler's Lives."* New York: Benziger, 1894. *HathiTrust Digital Library,* hdl.handle.net/2027/nyp.33433068232887.]

Saint Basilides and Companions, Martyrs (✝ 303) — June 12

The memorial of Basilides, Cyrinus, Nabor, and Nazarius, placed initially in the Roman calendar in the eighth century, is now abolished. The story of the passion of these saints is entirely legendary. It concerns three commemorations occurring on the same day: the burial of Basilides, a Roman martyr, on the Via Aurelia; the transfer of the body of Cyrinus, bishop of Siscia; and the dedication of the Basilica of Nabor and Nazarius, martyred at Milan.

Beside John of Sahagún, the Apostle of peace, are grouped four warriors of our Lord's army. Thus, to this day, peace and war go hand in hand, but one in the kingdom of the Son of God. The three-fold peace preached by Christ, namely, man's peace with his God, with himself, and with his brethren, all fellow citizens in the Holy City—is to be won only at the cost of combat with Satan, the flesh, and the world, which is the "accursed city." Therefore, together with the Church, let us blend in one united homage our praises of the glorious Confessor of these later ages and the stern veterans of persecuting times.

Basilides, Cyrinus, Nabor, and Nazarius were Roman soldiers of illustrious birth and valor. Having embraced the Christian religion and being found publishing that Christ is the Son of God, they were arrested by Aurelius, Prefect of Rome, under Diocletian. They were imprisoned as they despised his orders to sacrifice to the gods. While they were at prayer, a brilliant light broke forth before the eyes of all present and shone in all the prison. Marcellinus, the jailer, and many others were moved by this heavenly glory to believe in the Lord Christ. Having gone forth from the prison, they were afterward thrown in again by Emperor Maximian, who caused them, first, to be beaten with scorpions for having, despite his orders, continued to have ever in their mouth that there is but one Christ, one God, one Lord, and so they were laden with chains. Thence, on the seventh day,

259

they were brought out and set before the emperor, and there persisting in mocking the foolish idols and declaring Jesus Christ to be God, they were accordingly condemned to death and beheaded. Their bodies were given to wild beasts to be devoured, but as they refused to touch them, the Christians took and buried them honorably.

From you, we learn, O soldiers of Jesus Christ, the nature of that *peace* He brought *upon earth to men of goodwill*. Its reward is no other than God himself, who by it and together with it, communicates himself to such as are worthy. Its invigorating sweetness overpowers every sensitive feeling. Even tortures such as Christians, after your example, must be ready to undergo to preserve this priceless treasure intact. Amidst torments and beneath the death-stroke, this peace upheld you, keeping your mind and heart free, fixed alone on heaven: this peace now forms your eternal beatitude forever, in the presence of the undivided and ever tranquil Trinity. Whatsoever be the varied condition of our life here below, lead us, O holy Martyrs, by the path of this perfect peace, fraught as it necessarily is with valor and love, unto the repose of endless bliss.

[Guéranger, Prosper, and Lucien Fromage. *The Liturgical Year.* Translated by Laurence Shepherd. Dublin: J. Duffy, 1867-1890. catalog.hathitrust.org/Record/012192952.]

Saints Vitus, Modestus, and Crescentia, Martyrs (✝ 303) — June 15

The memorial of Vitus, the martyr, who died in Lucania[72], is left to the particular calendars. Although their names were added to the Roman calendar in the eleventh

---

[72] Lucania was a historically significant region of Southern Italy. It belonged to the Lucani, an Oscan people. It reached all the way from the Tyrrhenian Sea to the Gulf of Taranto.

century, Modestus and Crescentia are considered fictitious.

Saint Vitus, sometimes called Guy, was a child who was nobly born and had the happiness to be instructed in the Faith under the tutelage of his Christian nurse, Crescentia, and Modestus, his preceptor. His father was not aware of his baptism. The boy received the gift of miracles. Before he reached the age of twelve, Valerian came to Sicily representing Diocletian, less to be governor of that island than persecutor of Christians. Vitus was denounced to him as one of them, and Valerian sent for his father, telling him to use his paternal authority to bring his son into line and have him practice the religion of the empire. Hylas promised to do so.

Finding Vitus unmoved by his tears and embraces, his warnings of what he would lose if he did not acquiesce to the emperor's wishes, and every persuasion based on the grief his son would cause him by continuing to adore a man who died on a shameful cross, Hylas delivered Vitus up to Valerian. The governor, in turn, could not change this child's mind; when Valerian asked him why he resisted his father's will and did not submit to the emperor's laws, Vitus answered, I only disobey the emperors and my father to obey God, my sovereign Lord, and first Father. He did not fear chastisement, he said, or death and would gladly endure all things rather than adore demons, the sworn enemies of men.

Valerian ordered that he be scourged, but the arms of the executioners grew limp, and even the hand of Valerian, which he had raised to give the command, withered. They accused him of being a magician, but Saint Vitus cured them to show them that the spirit of Jesus Christ is one of gentleness and that His true disciples have only love for all their enemies. Hylas, his father, furious at his son's refusal to comply with all efforts to change him, resolved to put him to death. But Modestus, his tutor, was told by an Angel to flee with him and his nurse, Crescentia, to Italy.

There all three would win the crown of martyrdom. Diocletian, hearing of the miracles of Saint Vitus, sent for him but imprisoned him after Vitus delivered the emperor's son from a demon but refused to deny Jesus Christ. A furious lion would not harm the young Christian but lay down at his feet and licked them. When he and his two Christian preceptors were attached to racks and tortured, their protecting Angel released them, but not until after lightning had struck the idol temples and caused them to fall amidst a terrible storm. Many idolaters among the spectators were converted on this occasion. They were set free after this incident, but Saint Vitus prayed that their souls might finally be released, and his prayer was answered. They were buried at the place to which they had first come in Italy, in the kingdom of Naples.

[Guérin, Abbé (Paul), François Giry, and Simon Martin. *Les Petits Bollandistes: Vies Des Saints De L'Ancien et du Nouveau Testament.* Translated by the Monastère du Magnificat. Paris: Bloud et Barral, 1882. *HathiTrust Digital Library,* hdl.handle.net/2027/nnc1.0036694380.]

Saint Gregory Barbarigo, Bishop and Confessor (1625–1697) — June 17

The memorial of Gregory, who died at Padua on June 18, 1697, was added to the Roman calendar in 1960. It is left now for particular calendars because it lacks universal significance.

One of the greatest bishops of the seventeenth century was Gregory Barbarigo. He was born in Venice in 1625 to the noble family of Gregory Luigi Barbarigo.

Educated in his native city, he gave evidence of a successful career in the world. But Gregory intended to dedicate his life entirely to God, and with this in mind, he began his studies for the priesthood.

As a seminarian, Gregory was an example to his fellow students. He was faithful to his prayer life and diligent in his studies. He seemed aware that success in the apostolate depends entirely upon a deep interior life.

Gregory was chosen to accompany Luigi Contarini, the Venetian Ambassador to Minster for the Bishop of Bergamo. In 1660, Gregory was made a Cardinal, and four years later, he was transferred to the bishopric of Padua.

Of the thousands under his care, he was particularly concerned for the poor. Those who served him in the diocese of Padua claim that he gave away at least eight hundred thousand crowns. There were many other secret contributions. The liberality with which the holy Bishop treated all in need proves that he was completely detached from this world's goods.

Bishop Gregory Barbarigo was not only solicitous in nourishing hungry bodies. He established one of the best colleges of his day and a seminary, which contained one of the most excellent libraries in Italy. A great lover of the Scriptures and the Fathers of the Church, the bishop managed to have the best source material for the young students. Saint Gregory has been called a second Charles Borromeo.

One of the undertakings dear to the heart of Saint Gregory was the establishment of harmony and sympathetic understanding among the churches of the Oriental Rites in schism. While no lasting or widespread union was affected, nevertheless, the tireless efforts made by the Saint have shown some favorable results in our day.

Saint Gregory was like the servant in the Gospel who received the five talents, traded wisely with them, and gained five more. As the master was well pleased with his servant, so must the Lord have been pleased with his faithful servant, Gregory. He was indeed "a great priest, who in his days pleased God, and was found just; and in the time of wrath was made a reconciliation. There was not found like to him, who kept the law of the Most High" (Sir. 44:16–20[73]).

The great priest died on June 15, 1697, at seventy-two. Sixty-four years later, he was beatified by the Venetian Pope Clement XIII, and in 1960, under Pope John XXIII, former Patriarch of Venice, he was canonized.

To work up to the maximum of one's talents, to be constant and faithful in the discharge of the duties of one's vocation-this is the lesson to be learned from Saint Gregory Barbarigo.

[Sisters of Charity of Saint Elizabeth (Convent Station, N.J.). "Saint Gregory Barbarigo, Bishop, and Confessor." *Daily Missal Meditations: Meditations for Every Day of the Year Based on the Liturgy of the Mass.* New York: Benziger Bros, 1959. HathiTrust Digital Library, hdl.handle.net//2027/uva.x030120584.]

Saint Marcus and Saint Marcellinus, Martyrs († 286) — June 18

The memorial of Marcus and Marcellian is left for the particular calendars. Little is known about these martyrs besides their names and burial in the Balbina cemetery on the Via Ardeatina on June 18.

Saint Marcus and Saint Marcellinus were twin brothers of an illustrious family in Rome who had been

---

[73] *Ecce sacerdos magnus* is an antiphon and responsory used by confessor bishops in the Liturgy of the Hours and the Graduale Romanum, as well as the Epistle in their proper Mass.

converted to the Faith in their youth and were honorably married.

When Diocletian ascended the imperial throne in 284, the pagans raised persecutions; the brothers were then thrown into prison and condemned to be beheaded. Their friends obtained a delay of the execution for thirty days so that they might prevail on them to worship the false gods. Tranquillinus and Martia, their afflicted pagan parents, accompanied by their sons' wives and little babes, endeavored to move them with the most tender entreaties and tears. But Saint Sebastian, an officer of the emperor's household, arriving in Rome soon after their confinement, visited and encouraged them daily.

The issue of the conferences was the happy conversion of the father, mother, and wives, Nicostratus, the public stenographer, and soon afterward Chromatius, the judge, who set the Saints at liberty abdicating the magistracy, retired into the country. Marcus and Marcellinus were concealed by a Christian officer of the imperial household in his apartments in the palace, but they were betrayed by an apostate and reimprisoned. Fabian, a judge who had succeeded Chromatius, condemned them to be bound to two pillars, their feet nailed to them. In this posture, they remained a day and a night and, on the following day, were stabbed with lances. Their martyrdom occurred in the year 286. Their tomb and that of their father, Saint Tranquillinus, was found in Rome, in 1782, in the church of Saint Cosmas and Saint Damian, adjoining that of the martyred pope, Saint Felix II. They are honored particularly in Spain, where the city of Badajoz escaped destruction by their intercession.

[Shea, John G. *Little Pictorial Lives of the Saints, with Reflections for Every Day of the Year; Compiled from "Butler's Lives."* New York: Benziger, 1894. *HathiTrust Digital Library,* hdl.handle.net/2027/nyp.33433068232887.]

Saint Juliana Falconieri, Virgin (1270–1341) — June 19

The memorial of Juliana, who died at Florence in 1341, entered the Roman calendar in 1738. However, because of a lack of universal significance, it is now left to the particular calendars.

Saint Juliana Falconieri was born in 1270 in answer to prayer. Her father was the builder of the splendid church of the Annunziata in Florence, while her uncle, Saint Alexis Falconieri, became one of the seven Founders of the Servite Order. Under his surveillance, Juliana grew up more like an angel than a human being, as he said. Her great modesty was remarkable; never during her entire life did she look at her reflection in a mirror. But, on the other hand, the mere mention of sin made her shudder and tremble, and once, on hearing of a scandal, she fainted.

Her devotion to the sorrows of Our Lady drew her to the Servants of Mary or Servite Order. At the age of fourteen, after refusing an offer of marriage, she received the habit from Saint Philip Benizi, General of the Order. Her sanctity attracted many novices, for whose direction she was bidden to draw up a rule, and thus she became the foundress of the *Mantellate Sisters*.

She was the servant of her Sisters rather than their mistress, while outside her convent, she led a life of apostolic charity, converting sinners, reconciling enemies, and healing the sick. She was sometimes rapt for whole days in ecstasy, and her prayers saved the Servite Order when it was in danger of being suppressed.

Saint Juliana, in her old age, suffered various painful illnesses. She was wasting away through a stomach disease that prevented her from taking food and bore her silent agony with constant cheerfulness, grieving only for the deprivation of Holy Communion. At last, when in her seventieth year she was at the point of death, she begged to be allowed once more to see and adore the Blessed Sacrament. It was brought to her cell and reverently laid on a corporal placed over her heart. At this moment, she expired, and the Sacred Host disappeared. After her death, the form of the Host was found stamped upon her heart at the exact spot over which the Blessed Sacrament had been placed. Saint Juliana died in her convent in Florence in 1341. Miracles have been frequently affected through her intercession.

[Shea, John G. *Little Pictorial Lives of the Saints, with Reflections for Every Day of the Year; Compiled from "Butler's Lives."* New York: Benziger, 1894. *HathiTrust Digital Library,* hdl.handle.net/2027/nyp.33433068232887.]

Saints Gervasius and Protasius, Martyrs (✝ 2nd Century) — June 19

Nothing is known about Gervase and Protasius apart from the finding of their relics by Ambrose at Milan in 386. Their memorial is left to the particular calendars.

Saint Ambrose calls these saints the protomartyrs of Milan. They seem to have suffered in the first persecution under Nero or, at the latest, under Domitian. They are said to have been the sons of Saints Vitalis and Valeria, both martyrs, the first at Ravenna, the second at Milan. This latter city was where Saints Gervasius and Protasius were rendered illustrious by their glorious martyrdom and miracles. Saint Ambrose assures us that the divine grace prepared them a long time for their crown by the excellent example they gave and by the constancy with which they withstood the world's corruption. He adds they were beheaded for the faith. They are said to have been twin brothers.

In the fourth age, the faithful at Milan had lost the remembrance of these saints. Yet the martyrs had not ceased to assist that church in its necessities, and the discovery of their relics rescued it from the utmost danger. Empress Justina, widow of Valentinian I. and mother of Valentinian the Younger, who then reigned, and resided at Milan, was a violent abettor of Arianism and used her utmost endeavors to expel Saint Ambrose. The Arians did not hesitate to have recourse to the most horrible villainies and forgeries to compass that point. In so critical a conjuncture, our martyrs declared themselves the visible protectors of that distressed church. In his twenty-second book of The City of God and his Confessions, Saint Augustine says that God revealed to Saint Ambrose by a vision in a dream the place where their relics lay. In his life of Saint Ambrose, Paulinus says an apparition of the martyrs themselves did this. The bishop was going to dedicate a new church, which was afterward called the Ambrosian basilic, and now Saint Ambrose the Great. The people desired him to do it with the same solemnity as he had already consecrated another church in the quarter near the gate that led to Rome in honor of the holy apostles, in which he had laid a portion of their relics. He was at a loss to find relics for this second church. The bodies of Saints Gervasius and Protasius lay unknown before the rails which enclosed the tomb of Saints Nabor and Felix. Saint Ambrose caused this place to be dug up, and there found the bodies of two large men, with their bones entire and in their natural position, but the heads separated from their bodies, with a large quantity of blood, and all the marks which could be desired to ascertain the relics.

A possessed person brought to receive the imposition of hands before he began to be exorcised was seized and, in horrible convulsions, thrown down by the evil spirit upon the tomb. The sacred relics were taken up whole and laid on litters in their natural situation, covered with ornaments, and conveyed to the basilic of Faustus, now called Saints Vitalis and Agricola, near Saint Nabor, which at present bears the name of Saint Francis. They were exposed here for two days, and a great concourse of people watched the two nights in prayer. On the third day, the 18th of June, they were translated into the Ambrosian basilic with the honor due to martyrs and the public rejoicings of the whole city. In the way happened the famous cure of a blind man named Severus, a citizen of Milan, well known to the entire town. He had been a butcher but was obliged to lay aside his profession by the loss of his sight. Hearing of the discovery of the relics, he desired to be conducted to the place where they were passing by. Upon touching the fringe of the ornaments with which they were covered, he perfectly recovered his sight in the presence of an infinite multitude. This miracle is related to Saint Ambrose, Saint Augustine, and Paulinus, who were all three then at Milan. Severus made a vow to be a servant in the church of the saints; that is, the Ambrosian basilic, where their relics lay. When he went from Milan in 387, Saint Augustine left him in that service, and he continued in it when Paulinus wrote the life of Saint Ambrose in 411. Many other lame and sick persons were cured of various distempers by touching the shrouds covering the relics or linen cloths thrown upon them. Devils also, in possessed persons, confessed the glory of the martyrs and declared they could not bear the torments they suffered in the presence of the bodies of the saints. Saint Ambrose attests to all this in his letter to his sister, in which he inserted the sermon he preached in the Ambrosian basilic when the relics arrived there. Two days after, he deposited them in the vault under the altar on the right hand. Saint Ambrose adds that the blood found in their tomb was likewise an instrument of many miracles. We find the relics of these saints afterward dispersed in several churches, chiefly this blood, which was gathered and mixed with a paste, as Saint Gaudentius says. Also, linen cloths dipped in this blood were distributed in many places, as Saint Gregory of Tours relates. Saint Augustine mentions a church in their honor in his diocese of Hippo, where many miracles were wrought, and describes a remarkable one. He preached his two hundred and eighty-sixth sermon on their festival in Africa, where we find it marked in the old African Calendar on the 19th of June, on which day it was observed over all the West; and with great solemnity at Milan and in many dioceses and parish churches, of which these martyrs are the titular saints. Saint Ambrose observes that the Arians at Milan, by denying the miracles of these martyrs, showed they had a different faith from that of the martyrs; otherwise, they would not have been jealous of their miracles: but this faith, as he says, is confirmed by the tradition of our ancestors, which the devils are forced to confess, but which the heretics deny.

[Butler, Alban. *The Lives of the Fathers, Martyrs, and Other Principal Saints. Compiled from Original Monuments and Authentic Records*. Dublin: James Duffy, 1866. *HathiTrust Digital Library,* catalog.hathitrust.org/Record/001941109.]

Saint Silverius, Pope, and Martyr († 537 or 538) — June 20

The memorial of Silverius, who died in exile on the island of Palmaria in 537, entered the Roman calendar in the twelfth century. It is left to the particular calendars because he is not a saint of universal significance.

Silverius was a son of Pope Hormisdas, who had been married before he entered the ministry. Upon the death of Saint Agapetus, and after a vacancy of forty-seven days, Silverius, then subdeacon, was elected Pope and consecrated on the 8th of June, 536, despite maneuvers on the part of heretics opposed to the Council of Chalcedon.

The heretical Empress Theodora, resolved to win Silverius over to her interests, wrote to him, ordering that he should either acknowledge as lawful bishop the Eutychian heretic Anthimos, who had been deposed as the patriarch of Constantinople, or come in person to Constantinople and reexamine his cause. Without the slightest hesitation or delay, Silverius returned her a short answer, by which he gave her to understand that he neither could nor would obey her unjust demands, which would be to revoke his predecessor's decision and betray the cause of the Catholic faith.

Finding that she could expect nothing from him, the empress resolved to have him deposed. Vigilius, the archdeacon of the Roman Church, a man of diplomacy, was then at Constantinople. To this ambitious ecclesiastic, the empress exposed her wishes. She promised to make him pope and bestow on him seven hundred pieces of gold if he would engage himself to condemn the Council of Chalcedon and receive the three deposed Eutychian patriarchs into Communion. Vigilius assented to these conditions, and the empress sent him to Rome, charged with a letter to the Roman general Belisarius, commanding him to drive out Silverius and contrive the election of Vigilius to the pontificate.

Vigilius urged the general to execute this project. To implement it, the Pope was accused of corresponding with the enemy, and a forged letter was supposedly written by him to the king of the Goths, inviting him to the city and promising to open the gates to him. These dealings succeeded; Vigilius was made Pope, and Silverius was banished to Patara in Lycia.

The bishop of Patara received the illustrious exile with all possible marks of honor and respect and, thinking himself bound to undertake his defense, journeyed to Constantinople and spoke boldly to the emperor Justinian. He terrified him with threats of divine judgments for the expulsion of a bishop of so great a see, telling him, *There are many kings in the world, but there is only one Pope over the Church of the whole world.* Justinian appeared startled at the atrocity of the proceedings and gave orders that Silverius be sent back to Rome. The enemies of the Pope contrived to prevent this, however, and he was intercepted on his road toward Rome and transported to the deserted island of Palmaria, where he died of hunger a year later, on the 20th of June, 538, and was buried.

It was perhaps in response to the martyred pope's prayers that after his death, the usurper of the pontifical throne, Vigilius, though he had wished to step down, was forced to remain in function and then transformed, like Saul of Tarsus, into another man. Nevertheless, he exercised the pastoral duties with as much courage, piety, zeal, and faith, as he formerly had used violence, avarice, and cruelty during his predecessor's lifetime. The traitor Belisarius was accused of conspiracy against the emperor, stripped of all he had, and his eyes put out; he was obliged to beg for alms in Constantinople. But he, too, repented and built a church with an inscription over the door, which was a public reparation for his fault.

[Guérin, Abbé (Paul), François Giry, and Simon Martin. *Les Petits Bollandistes: Vies Des Saints De L'Ancien et du Nouveau Testament.* Translated by the Monastère du Magnificat. Paris: Bloud et Barral, 1882. *HathiTrust Digital Library,* hdl.handle.net/2027/nnc1.0036694380; Shea, John G. *Little Pictorial Lives of the Saints, with Reflections for Every Day of the Year; Compiled from "Butler's Lives."* New York: Benziger, 1894. *HathiTrust Digital Library,* hdl.handle.net/2027/nyp.33433068232887.]

Saint William of Vercelli, Abbot († 1142) — June 25

The memorial of William, who died at Guglietti in 1142, was added to the general calendar in 1785. Because it does not have universal significance, it is now left for particular calendars.

Saint William of Monte Vergine, born in Vercelli, a city of Lombardy, lost his father and mother in his infancy and was brought up by a relative in great sentiments of piety. At fifteen years of age, having an earnest desire to lead a penitential life, he left his native region and made a long and austere pilgrimage to the shrine of the Virgin founded by Saint James at Saragossa. He would have made the pilgrimage to Jerusalem, but God told him that he was calling him to a solitary life, and he retired into the kingdom of Naples. There he chose for his abode an uninhabited mountain and lived in perpetual contemplation and the exercises of rigorous penitential austerities.

After a miracle of healing wrought by his prayers, he was discovered, and his contemplation was interrupted, so he decided to move to another mountain, where he built a magnificent church in honor of Our Lady. With several former secular priests who joined him there, in 1119, he began the establishment of the *Congregation of Monte Vergine*, or Mount of the Virgin. This site is between Nola and Benevento in the same kingdom of Naples. These sons of Our Lady lived in great austerity. Seeing the progress in holiness of the good religious being formed there, the devil sowed division and criticism. Still, God drew good from evil when Saint William went elsewhere and founded several more monasteries, both for men and women, in various places in the kingdom of Naples. Moreover, he assisted

273

the king of Naples, who greatly revered him, in practice, all the Christian virtues of a worthy sovereign. In gratitude, the king had a house of the Order built at Salerno opposite his palace to have him near him more often.

When Saint William died on the 25th of June, 1142, he had not yet written a Rule for his religious; his second successor, Robert, fearing the dissolution of a community without constitutions, placed them under that of Saint Benedict and is regarded as the first abbot of the Benedictine Congregation of Monte-Vergine. A portrait of the Virgin venerated there has been an unfailing source of holy compunction; pilgrims continue to visit it.

[Guérin, Abbé (Paul), François Giry, and Simon Martin. *Les Petits Bollandistes: Vies Des Saints De L'Ancien et du Nouveau Testament.* Translated by the Monastère du Magnificat. Paris: Bloud et Barral, 1882. *HathiTrust Digital Library,* hdl.handle.net/2027/nnc1.0036694380; Shea, John G. *Little Pictorial Lives of the Saints, with Reflections for Every Day of the Year; Compiled from "Butler's Lives."* New York: Benziger, 1894. *HathiTrust Digital Library,* hdl.handle.net/2027/nyp.33433068232887.]

Saints John and Paul, Martyrs († 362) — June 26

There are many historical difficulties concerning the deaths of John and Paul, and their memorial is left to their titular church.

These two Saints were brothers and were officers of the Roman army in the days of Constantine the Great. They served in the house of Constance, daughter of Constantine, who was consecrated to God; their virtues and services to her father rendered them very dear to her. They would soon glorify God by a great moral victory; after despising the world's honors, they triumphed by martyrdom over its threats and torments.

With the aid of the liberality of the Christian princess, they practiced many works of charity and mercy until the deaths of both Constantine and Constance. Then, they resigned from their position in the palace at the accession of Julian the Apostate to the imperial throne. But unfortunately, Julian had returned to the cult of idols and attempted to re-establish it in the empire. The Christian brothers saw many wicked men prosper in their impiety but were not dazzled by their example. On the contrary, they considered worldly prosperity accompanied by impunity in sin the most dreadful of all judgments, indicating reprobation. And history reveals how false and short-lived glittering prosperity of Julian was.

While still in power, the apostate attempted to win back these influential officers into active service. When he was refused, he gave them ten days to reconsider. The officer Terentianus, who at the end of that time brought a little idol of Jupiter for their adoration to their house, found them in prayer. In the middle of that night, they were decapitated secretly in their garden since the emperor feared their execution might cause sedition in Rome. He instigated a rumor that they had been exiled, but the demons took hold of possessed persons in Rome and published the fact of their martyrdom everywhere.

The son of the officer who had slain them also became possessed, and it was only after their father, Terentianus, had prayed at the martyrs' tomb that the child was liberated. This so impressed him that he became a Christian, with all his family, and wrote the history we have reported.

By renouncing favors and their heroic resistance, the martyrs purchased an immense weight of never-fading glory and were a spectacle worthy of God. Their house became a magnificent Christian Basilica at the end of the fourth century.

[Shea, John G. *Little Pictorial Lives of the Saints, with Reflections for Every Day of the Year; Compiled from "Butler's Lives."* New York: Benziger, 1894. *HathiTrust Digital Library,* hdl.handle.net/2027/nyp.33433068232887; Guérin, Abbé (Paul), François Giry, and Simon Martin. *Les Petits Bollandistes: Vies Des Saints De L'Ancien et du Nouveau Testament.* Translated by the Monastère du Magnificat. Paris: Bloud et Barral, 1882. *HathiTrust Digital Library,* hdl.handle.net/2027/nnc1.0036694380.]

JULY

Saints Processus and Martinian, Martyrs († 67) — July 2

All that is known about Processus and Martinian are their names and the fact that they were buried on the Via Aurelia in the cemetery of Damasus on July 2. For this reason, their memorial, though of ancient origin, is left for the particular calendars.

Among the soldiers that guarded the glorious apostles, Saint Peter and Saint Paul, while by Nero's[74] command, they were detained in the prison *Mamertinus*[75], who considered the miracles that the holy Apostles wrought in the prison, by curing diseases and driving out devils from possessed persons, and withal hearing their admirable and heavenly doctrine, being enlightened in soul with rays of the eternal light, and strengthened by the powerful assistance of divine grace, resolving to become Christians, and casting themselves at the feet of the Apostles, opened to them their mind, and besought them to admit them by holy baptism into the number of the

---

[74] Nero Claudius Caesar Augustus Germanicus was the fifth and final Roman Emperor of the Julio-Claudian dynasty, reigning from AD 54 to AD 68. At the age of 13, he was adopted by the Roman Emperor Claudius, and succeeded him on the throne.

[75] The Mamertine Prison, also known as the Tullianum in antiquity, was a prison with a dungeon in ancient Rome's Comitium. It was built in the seventh century BC on the northeastern slope of Capitoline Hill, facing the Curia and the imperial fora of Nerva, Vespasian, and Augustus.

faithful. They also desired the Apostles to leave prison, for they were content to stay in their place and undergo whatever penalty they should be judged fit to be imposed upon them for their escape from the hands of justice.

Saint Peter received them with charity and confirmed them in their holy resolution. And because there was no water at hand to baptize them, he made the sign of the cross upon the rock whereon the prison was built. He there sprung a fountain of clear water, so plentiful and so durable, that it is running to this day, and neither can the long continuance of time dry it up, nor the multitude of people that resort to the drinking of it does not diminish or make it scarcer. With the water of this fountain, Processus and Martinian were baptized, and of soldiers of Nero, they became soldiers of Jesus Christ. Many more converted and baptized with them, forty-seven men and women.

But Paulinus the judge, understanding that Processus and Martinian had professed themselves as Christians, caused them to be apprehended and brought before him and endeavored with kindness and smooth language to persuade them *to leave this folly* (as he termed it) and to return to the worship of the Roman gods that conserved the empire, and to that religion which they were born and brought up in, for by this means they might expect great preferments and not lose the honor or dignity they now enjoyed, and their life to boot. But finding these persuasions availed nothing with them, he took another course and commanded their mouths to be bruised and their teeth to be dashed out with great stones, in which torment the holy martyrs, all imbued in blood, lifting their eyes to heaven, gave thanks, and said, "Glory be in the highest to God."

Then, Paulinus called for an idol of Jupiter, set it up on an altar, and would have the martyrs adore it. But, still, instead of adoring, they spit in the face of it, which

277

put Paulinus into an intolerable chase and fury, who took revenge upon himself, stripped them naked, and stretched them upon the [rack], where they were racked most cruelly. Their sides, moreover, were burned with red-hot plates of iron. But, this notwithstanding, they sang with much spiritual joy and jubilee of heart, "*Your name, O Lord, let it be forever blessed and hallowed; Let your angels praise you, and all your creatures give you everlasting glory and benediction.*"

Their bodies were also torn and rented with scorpions, besides other torments to which they were put. And while these holy martyrs endured all with incredible joy and constancy, suddenly Paulinus was stuck blind, for one of his eyes fell out of his head, and withal the devil seizing upon his body, he began even in this world to feel the pains and dolors which expected him in hell, and after three days, died most miserably.

Pomponius, his son, to avenge his father's death, acquainted Emperor Nero with all that happened. He added that Processus and Martinian were magicians and conjurers and that their enchantments had killed his father. At this point, the Emperor gave an order to Cæfarius, the governor of the city, to put them to death, and the governor sentenced them to have their heads cut off, which was executed outside the city on the Via Aurelia[76]. Their bodies were left in the fields to be devoured by the dogs. Still, a virtuous and great lady, Lucina, who had heartened and encouraged the martyrs in the torments, took them up, embalmed them with due reverence and adoration, and buried them in a manner of her own. Later they were translated into a church dedicated to their honor, but when that church fell into ruin, they were taken up again and carried to the prince of the Apostles, Saint Peter's Church. They were

---

[76] The Via Aurelia (Latin for *Aurelian Way*) is a Roman road in Italy that was built around 241 BC.

martyred on the second of July in the year of our Lord 69 and the thirteenth year of the reign of Nero.

Saint Gregory, in his thirty-second sermon, which he made in the church where the bodies of these holy martyrs rest, says, "*The sick come to the bodies of these saints, and return back found; those who have forgotten themselves, come, and are tormented by the devils; the possessed come, and are freed. How do we think these saints live in heaven, where they are truly living, seeing that even upon the earth, where they are dead, they live notwithstanding such a multitude of miracles?*" And there, among other things, he tells of a holy and pious woman that often visited their bodies; how these saints once appeared to her and promised *to requite well at the day of judgment the devotion she had visited them.* All *Martyrologies* make mention of Saints Processus and Martinian, the *Roman*, those of Bede, Usuardus, and Ado. Surius writes of them in his fourth tome of the *Lives of the Saints*, and Baronius in the fifth of his *Annals.*

[Ribadeneyra, Pedro de. "The Lives of St. Processus and St. Martinian, Martyrs." *The Lives of Saints, With Other Feasts of the Year, according to the Roman Calendar. Written in Spanish by the Reverend Father Peter Ribadeneyra, Priest of the Society of Jesus. Translated Into English by W.P. (William Petre) Esq; The Second Edition Corrected and Amended, vol. 2, pp. 8-9.* London. Printed by B.S., 1730. *HathiTrust Digital Library,* hdl.handle.net/2027/nyp.33433003053000.]

Seven Holy Brothers, Martyrs († 150) — July 10

Although of ancient origin, the memorial of the Seven Brothers is deleted from the calendar. The account of their passion is fictitious. It combines the accounts of four different events commemorated on the same day. These include the burial of Felix and Philip in the cemetery of Priscilla, that of Vitalis, Martial, and Alexander in the cemetery of the Jordans, and that of Silenus in the cemetery of Maximus. While all these burials took place on the Via Salaria, the final event commemorated was the burial of Januarius in the cemetery of Praetextatus on the Via Appia.

In the reign of Marcus Aurelius, Emperor there lived in Rome a noble and venerable matron and widow, Felicitas, who had seven sons she had brought up from their infancy in the holy Christian faith, and in all laudable and pious exercises becoming their condition and age. This devout widow made a vow to live continent and chaste and employed herself wholly in prayer, fasting, and works of charity. And by her example, many Gentiles were moved to become Christians, and all Christians were stirred up to live virtuously according to their profession. This did so much to raise the spleen and move the gall of the idolatrous priests, the deadly enemies of all goodness and piety, that they persuaded the emperor to command Felicitas and her children to be apprehended *because the immortal gods,* they said*, were highly offended and angry. There were no other means to appease their wrath but by compelling these Christians to offer sacrifice to them.*

Saint Felicitas and her sons were all taken. The arraignment was remitted to Publius, prefect or governor of the city. Taking Felicitas aside, he used all the persuasions and inducements he could to bring her *freely to sacrifice to the gods that he might not be obliged to come to rigor and severity towards her and her sons.* But Saint Felicitas answered him, *Do not think, O Publius, to win me with thy fair and flattering language or to terrify me with threats for I have the spirit of God within me that will not suffer me to be overcome with Satan, and therefore sure I am I shall be too hard for thee who art his minister.* Publius replied, *O unhappy and miserable woman, is it possible thou should not be so weary of life and so desirous to die that thou wilt not permit even thy children to live but will force me to destroy them by most bitter and cruel torments? My children*, says Felicitas, *if they offered sacrifice to the gods, would die an everlasting death. But now, seeing they acknowledge and worship Jesus Christ, they are now to live eternally with them.*

The next day, the judge sitting in the Temple of Mars sent for Felicitas, and her sons, who were brought before him. Addressing his speech to the mother said, *take pity of thy children, O Felicitas, who are now in the flourishing prime of youth, and by their good parts and abilities, may aspire to the greatest honors and preferments.* Saint Felicitas answered, *Thy pity is impiety and thy counsel cruel and deceitful.* And then, turning towards her children, she exhorted them to constancy in this manner, *My sons, look up to heaven, where Christ expects you with all his saints. Fight manfully for the good of your souls and show yourselves faithful and constant in the love of the true God, Christ Jesus.* Which words were heard by the judge, who was highly exasperated, taking it for an intolerable afront that she gave her children such counsel before him and commanded she should be cruelly buffeted.

Then, sending for the eldest of the sons named Januarius and urging all his art and skill, he mingled fair promises with threats and sweetness with rigor to induce the young man to adore the gods. But he answered him most constantly, *Thou goes about to persuade me to do a foolish thing, contrary to all reason, but I confide in my Lord Jesus Christ that He will preserve me from so great an impiety.* The judge ordered that he be stripped and beaten most cruelly, so he was sent back to prison. Then he called for the rest of the brothers in order and used his art and force to subdue their minds and bring them to adore his gods and obey the emperor. Bur finding his plots and endeavors were to no purpose and that all seven brothers (the Holy Ghost speaking by their mouths) made him the same answer in different words after they had been most barbarously whipped, he informed the emperor of the whole state of the business. The emperor sent word that they should all be put to death by different torments.

Which cruel sentence was executed in this manner: Januarius, the eldest, had first his flesh torn off with whips and after was beaten so long with thick cords, at the end of which were plummets of lead, until he gave up the ghost. Felix and Philip were all bruised and broken with cudgels. Silvanus was thrown down from a high rock. Alexander, Vitalis, and Martialis were beheaded. And at length, their virtuous mother, Saint Felicitas, was also martyred four months after them, and the Church commemorates her feast on the twenty-third of November. The Church keeps the feast of these seven brothers on the day of their martyrdom, on the tenth of July, in the year of our Lord 175, in the days of Marcus Aurelius, emperor.

[Ribadeneyra, Pedro de. "The Lives of Seven Brothers, Martyrs, Sons of Saint Felicitas." *The Lives of Saints, With Other Feasts of the Year, according to the Roman Calendar. Written in Spanish by the Reverend Father Peter Ribadeneyra, Priest of the Society of Jesus. Translated Into English by W.P. (William Petre) Esq; The Second Edition Corrected and Amended*, vol. 2, pp. 14-15. London. Printed by B.S., 1730. *HathiTrust Digital Library*, hdl.handle.net//2027/nyp.33433003053000.]

Saints Rufina and Secunda, Virgins, Martyrs († 257) — July 10

The memorial of Rufina and Secunda entered the Roman calendar in the twelfth century to mark the transfer of their relics to the Lateran Church. However, it is now left to the particular calendars because all that is known about them, aside from their names, is that they were buried on the Via Cornelia.

They were sisters and the daughters of one Asterius, a man of a senatorial family in Rome. Their father promised them in marriage, the first to Armentarius and the second to Verinus, who were then both Christians, but afterward apostatized from the faith when Valerian and Gallien raised the storm in 257 fell upon the church. The two virgins resisted their solicitations to imitate their impiety and fled out of Rome; but were overtaken, brought back, and after other torments, condemned by Junius Donatus, prefect of Rome, to lose their heads. They were conducted twelve miles out of Rome, executed in a forest on the Via Aurelia, and buried in the same place. It was then called the Black Forest, Sylva Nigra, but from these martyrs, this name was changed into that of Sylva Candida or the White Forest. A chapel was built over their tomb, which Pope Damasus demolished, erecting a large church in its room. A town rose in the same place, called Sylva Candida, and made an episcopal see. But the city was destroyed by barbarians in the twelfth century. Calixtus II united the bishopric to that of Porto, and the relics of the saints were translated at the same time, in the year 1120, to the Lateran basilic, where they are kept near the baptistery of Constantine.

[Butler, Alban. *The Lives of the Fathers, Martyrs, and Other Principal Saints. Compiled from Original Monuments and Authentic Records.* Dublin: James Duffy, 1866. *HathiTrust Digital Library,* catalog.hathitrust.org/Record/001941109.]

Saint Pius I, Pope, and Martyr (✝ 157) — July 11

There is no reason to consider Pius a martyr, and even the date of his death is unknown. Therefore, his memorial, dating from the eleventh century in the Roman calendar, is abolished.

Saint Pius, pope, and martyr, was the son of Rufinus and was born at Aquileia. He succeeded Saint Hyginius[77] on Saint Peter's Chair, who had also been martyred in the year of Christ [138 or 139] in the reign of Emperor Antoninus[78]. Saint Pius made the most profitable ordinations for the Church. He imposed significant penalties upon priests who behaved negligently about the sacrifice and administration of the sacrament of the altar, those who did maliciously forswear, and even those who did not reprove them when they heard of them.

He commanded that all goods and possessions of the Church, which were dedicated to serving God and maintaining ecclesiastical persons, should be inviolably conserved. He ordained that virgins should not be consecrated before age twenty-five. He made a decree wherein he commanded that the Holy Feast of Easter should always be kept on a Sunday, seeing that our Lord rose from death to life on a Sunday. And this had been instituted before by the Apostles. Still, Saint Pius established and confirmed it again to remove the abuse that had crept into some churches, that imitated Jesus in keeping Easter, and was moved to make this ordination by a little book which a brother of his Saint Hermes, a holy man, dedicated unto him. By dialog, an angel in the habit of a shepherd warns all Christians to solemnize our Lord's resurrection on a Sunday.

He consecrated at Rome the place called *Thermæ Novatianæ*[79] in honor of Saint Pudentiana at the request

---

[77] Pope Hyginus was the bishop of Rome from around the year 138 until his death in the year 142. According to tradition, during his pontificate, he established the various prerogatives of the clergy and defined the grades of the ecclesiastical hierarchy. Hyginus established godparents at baptism to help the baptized throughout their Christian lives.

[78] Antoninus Pius reigned as Emperor of Rome from 138 to 161. He was one of the Nerva-Antonine dynasty's Five Good Emperors. Antoninus was born into a senatorial family and held various positions during Emperor Hadrian's reign.

[79] During Antoninus Pius' reign, the Thermae Novatianae, also known as the Baths of Timothy (*Thermae Novatianae Sive Timotheanae*), were built. The site's history is complicated and contested, but some facts are clear. The remains can still be seen about 20 feet below street level on Via Balbo.

of her sister Praxedes and enriched it with gifts, and often said Mass there. He blessed a font in it in which he baptized diverse [persons] with his own hands. He wrote several yet extant epistles with his Decretals[80] in the *Book of Councils.*

Besides this, he wrote two others to Justus, Bishop of Vienna; in one, he writes, "*Have great care of the bodies of martyrs as of the members of Jesus Christ, for the Apostles were very careful of the body of Saint Stephen. Visit the saints in prison that none grow cold or relent in the faith. Encourage and animate them all to persevere. Let priests and deacons respect and reverence you, not as greater, but as ministers of Christ. Let all the people find rest, protection, and security in your sanctity. I would have you know, most dear brother and companion, that God hath revealed to me that I am soon to end the course of my pilgrimage. I only request that you remain firm and constant in the union of the Church and not forget me. All the senate and the poor company of priests and ministers of Christ that are in Rome salute you, and I salute all the College of our brethren in our Lord that are with you*".

This is contained in the epistle of Saint Pius, wherein he discovers her fervent zeal and the abundance of that heavenly spirit that possessed him and the excellent care and solicitude he had for the good and the advancement of the Church. In fine, having with great holiness of life governed the Church of God for nine years, six months, wanting three days, according to Baronius, he was crowned with martyrdom. However, there was a great variety of opinions concerning the time of his popedom.

---

[80] Decretals are letters from the Pope that formulate decisions in Catholic Church ecclesiastical law. They are usually given in response to consultations, but they are sometimes given on the pope's own initiative.

He gave Holy Orders five times during December and consecrated twelve bishops, eighteen priests, and twenty-one deacons. He was buried in the Vatican. The Church solemnizes his memory on the eleventh of July, the day of his martyrdom in the year 167, in the days of Marcus Aurelius[81] and Lucius Verus[82], emperors.

[Ribadeneyra, Pedro de. "The Life of St. Pius Pope, the first of that Name and Martyr." *The Lives of Saints, With Other Feasts of the Year, according to the Roman Calendar. Written in Spanish by the Reverend Father Peter Ribadeneyra, Priest of the Society of Jesus. Translated Into English by W.P. (William Petre) Esq; The Second Edition Corrected and Amended, vol. 2, p. 17.* London. Printed by B.S., 1730. *HathiTrust Digital Library,* hdl.handle.net/2027/nyp.33433003053000.]

Saint John Gualbert, Confessor (999-1073) — July 12

The memorial of John, who died near Florence on July 12, 1073, entered the general calendar in 1595. It is now left for the particular calendars since he is not of universal significance.

Saint John Gualbert was born in Florence in the year 999. He was raised with care in piety and the study of the humanities, but no sooner had he entered adult life than he acquired a taste for pleasures. God, desiring to save and sanctify him, found a means to open his eyes. He followed the profession of arms during that troubled period when on Good Friday, as he rode into Florence accompanied by armed men, he encountered his brother's murderer in a place where neither could avoid the other. John would have slain him, according to the customary vengeance of those times; but his adversary,

---

[81] Marcus Aurelius Antoninus was a Stoic philosopher and Roman Emperor from 161 to 180. He was the final of the Five Good Emperors and the last emperor of the Pax Romana, a period of relative peace and stability for the Roman Empire that lasted from 27 BC to 180 AD.

[82] Lucius Aurelius Verus reigned as Emperor of Rome alongside his adoptive brother Marcus Aurelius from 161 to 169. He belonged to the Nerva-Antonine dynasty.

who was unprepared to fight, fell upon his knees with his arms outstretched in the form of a cross and implored him, for the sake of Our Lord's holy Passion, to spare his life. Saint John said to his enemy. I cannot refuse what you ask in Christ's name. I grant you not only your life but my friendship. Pray that God may forgive me my sin! They embraced and parted; grace had triumphed.

A humble and changed man, he went to a nearby abbatial church. While he prayed with fervor for forgiveness, the figure of our crucified Lord, before which he was kneeling, bowed its head toward him as if to confirm His pardon and manifest His gratitude for the generous pardon John himself had granted. Abandoning the world then, Saint John devoted himself to prayer and penance in the Benedictine Order. His virtue and austerity were so great that when his abbot died, he was unanimously chosen to replace him, but he could not be prevailed upon to accept that honor. He retired to Vallombrosa, which became the cradle of a new Order which followed the Rule of Saint Benedict in all its austerity. It was from this shady valley, a few miles from Florence, that the Order spread over Italy.

Once during a time of famine, he went to the nearly empty storeroom, and at his prayer, the provisions multiplied to the point that he could distribute grain to all his houses and to all the poor who presented themselves. Again, when he found one of the monasteries too rich, he prayed a stream flowing past it to take on the violence of a torrent and overturn the building. This was done without delay. Another time, the enemies of the Saint came to his convent of Saint Salvi, plundered it, set fire to it, and, after treating the monks with ignominy, beat them and injured them. Saint John rejoiced. Now, he said, you are true monks. Oh, how I envy your lot!

Saint John Gualbert fought vigorously against simony and, in many ways, promoted the interests of the

Faith in Italy. After a life of great austerity, he died while Angels sang near his bed on July 12, 1073.

[Jaud, Leon. *Vie Des Saints Pour Tous Les Jours De L'annee: Avec Une Pratique De Piete Pour Chaque Jour.* Translated by the Monastère du Magnificat. Tours: A. Mame, 1950. Print.; Shea, John G. *Little Pictorial Lives of the Saints, with Reflections for Every Day of the Year; Compiled from "Butler's Lives."* New York: Benziger, 1894. *HathiTrust Digital Library,* hdl.handle.net/2027/nyp.33433068232887.]

Saints Nabor and Felix, Martyrs († 303) — July 12

The memorial of Nabor and Felix, martyrs from Milan, added to the Roman calendar in the twelfth century, is left for the particular calendars.

The holy martyrs Nabor and Felix were taken at Milan by the command of Emperor Maximian[83]. He, together with Dioclesian[84], was a most bloody persecutor of Christians and resolved to be so during life, committed them to prison and gave the strictest order that nothing should be given them to eat. So the saints remained some time in prison, enduring with much patience the nastiness of the place, hunger, and other incommodities. But, when the tyrant despaired by keeping them in this brutal confinement, to make them alter their resolution, he made them brought again before him and commanded Nabor in the presence of Felix should be a long while beaten with cudgels[85] and then brought upon the rack

---

[83] Maximian, also known as Herculius, was the Emperor of Rome from 286 to 305. From 285 to 286, he was Caesar, and from 286 to 305, he was Augustus. He shared the latter title with his co-emperor and superior, Diocletian, whose political acumen supplemented Maximian's military ferocity.

[84] Diocletian, also known as Iovius, was the Emperor of Rome from 284 to 305. Diocletian rose through the ranks of the military early in his career, eventually becoming a cavalry commander for Emperor Carus' army, despite being born into a low-status family in the Roman Province of Dalmatia.

[85] A short, thick stick used as a weapon.

where his sides were most cruelly burned with fiery torches. All his body was torn and rent with iron claws.

But, perceiving that neither Nabor relented for all these torments, nor was Felix anything moved of his case if he should be put to the like, both were invincible and inflexible. So he cast them into a great fire which did nothing to damage them nor consume as much as one hair of their head. Which notwithstanding, could not bring the tyrant to acknowledge God's power or give over his cruelty and wicked designs. On the contrary, he became more rigid and obstinate and miscalled God's virtue and strength, enchantments, and witchcraft. And so, he sent them back to prison. And some days after made them be taken thence again and gave orders they should be beheaded near the Célere River. So a noble Lady called Sabina buried their Bodies. The Church solemnizes them on the day of their martyrdom on the twelfth of July in the year of our Lord 303, in the reign of Dioclesian and Maximian. Saint Ambrose mentions them, and Paulinus writes in the *Life of Saint Ambrose* that the Christians most frequented the church where their holy bodies are buried.

[Ribadeneyra, Pedro de. "The Lives of St. Nabor and St. Felix, Martyrs." *The Lives of Saints, With Other Feasts of the Year, according to the Roman Calendar. Written in Spanish by the Reverend Father Peter Ribadeneyra, Priest of the Society of Jesus. Translated Into English by W.P. (William Petre) Esq; The Second Edition Corrected and Amended, vol. 2, p. 18.* London. Printed by B.S., 1730. *HathiTrust Digital Library,* hdl.handle.net/2027/nyp.33433003053000.]

Saint Alexius of Rome, Confessor († 404) — July 17

The memorial of Alexius was added to the Roman calendar in the twelfth century. The account of his life is entirely fictitious, and the feast is abolished.

Saint Alexius, born in Rome in the fourth century, was the only son of parents pre-eminent among the Roman nobles for their virtue and great wealth. They were particularly noted for their almsgiving; three tables were prepared daily for all who came for assistance — pilgrims, the poor, and the sick. Their son, the fruit of their prayers, was married with sumptuous feasting to a noble young lady of the imperial family. Still, on his wedding night, by God's extraordinary inspiration, he secretly left Rome, longing for solitude where he could serve God alone. So he went to Edessa in the far East, gave away all that he had brought with him, content after that to live by alms at the gate of Our Lady's church in that city. In the most profound grief, his family could not fathom the mystery of his disappearance and would have been consoled if God had taken him instead through death.

The servants of Saint Alexius, whom his father had sent in search of him, arrived in Edessa and, seeing him among the poor at the gate of Our Lady's church, gave him alms, not recognizing him. After which the man of God, rejoicing, said, I thank You, Lord, who has called me and granted that I should receive alms for Your Name's sake from my slaves. Therefore, deign to fulfill in me the work You have begun.

After seventeen years spent at the portico of the church, when his sanctity was miraculously confirmed by the Blessed Virgin, speaking through Her image to an officer of the church, Saint Alexius once more sought obscurity by flight. On his way to Tarsus, contrary winds drove his ship to Rome. No one recognized, in this pale and tattered mendicant, the heir of Rome's noblest house, not even his sorrowing parents, who had vainly sent throughout the world in search of him. So saint Alexius begged a miserable shelter in his palace under a staircase from his father's charity, with the leavings of his table as food. There he spent another seventeen years, bearing the mockery and ill-usage of his servants patiently and witnessing daily the still inconsolable grief of his spouse and parents.

At last, when death had ended this cruel martyrdom, they learned too late, in the year 404, who it was that they had unknowingly sheltered. All heard a voice in attendance at the Pope's Mass: *Seek the man of God, he will pray for Rome, and the Lord will be favorable to it; he will die Friday.* All the city undertook in vain to find this unknown Saint. But God had commanded Alexius himself to write down his life story and sign it. In this way, He confirmed His servant's sanctity when he was found lifeless in his retreat, holding that document in his hand. The Pope read aloud what was written on the parchment of the Saint, and everywhere in Rome, there was a single cry of admiration impossible to describe. The house of Alexius' father, Euphemian, was later transformed into a church dedicated to Saint Alexius.

[Shea, John G. *Little Pictorial Lives of the Saints, with Reflections for Every Day of the Year; Compiled from "Butler's Lives."* New York: Benziger, 1894. *HathiTrust Digital Library,* hdl.handle.net/2027/nyp.33433068232887.; Guérin, Abbé (Paul), François Giry, and Simon Martin. *Les Petits Bollandistes: Vies Des Saints De L'Ancien et du Nouveau Testament.* Translated by the Monastère du Magnificat. Paris: Bloud et Barral, 1882. *HathiTrust Digital Library,* hdl.handle.net/2027/nnc1.0036694380.]

Saint Symphorosa and Her Seven Sons, Martyrs († 120) — July 18

The memorial of Symphorosa and her children, added to the Roman calendar in the twelfth century, is abolished since the account of their lives is not worthy of belief. It appears to be an imitation of the martyrdom of Felicity and her seven children.

Trajan's persecution to some degree continued during the first year of Hadrian's reign, whence Sulpicius

Severus[86] placed the fourth general persecution under this emperor. However, he stopped it about the year 124, probably both by the apologies of Quadratus and Aristides and by a letter that Serenius Granianus, proconsul of Asia, had written to him in favor of the Christians. Nay, he had Christ in veneration, not as the Savior of the world, but as a wonder or novelty, and kept his image together with that of Apollonius of Tyana[87]. This God was pleased to permit that his afflicted Church might enjoy some respite. It was, however, again involved in the disgrace which the Jews (with whom the Pagans at these times in some degree confounded the Christians) drew upon themselves by their rebellion, which gave occasion to the last entire destruction of Jerusalem in 134. Then, as Saint Paulinus informs us, Hadrian caused a statue of Jupiter to be erected on the place where Christ rose from the dead, and a marble Venus on the site of his crucifixion; and at Bethlehem, a grotto consecrated in honor of Adonis or Thammuz, to whom he also dedicated the cave where Christ was born. But, towards the end of his reign, this prince abandoned himself more than ever to acts of cruelty, and awakened by a fit of superstition, he again drew his sword against the innocent flock of Christ. He built a magnificent country palace at Tibur, now Tivoli, sixteen miles from Rome, upon the most agreeable banks of the Anio River, now called Aniene River, also formerly known as the Teverone River. Here he placed whatever could be procured most curious out of all the provinces. Having finished the building, he intended to dedicate it by heathenish ceremonies, which he began by offering sacrifices to

---

[86] Sulpicius Severus was a Christian writer from Aquitania in modern-day France who lived from around 363 to 425. He is best known for his sacred history chronicle and biography of Saint Martin of Tours.

[87] Apollonius of Tyana (c. 15 – c. 97) was a Greek Neopythagorean philosopher from Tyana in the Roman province of Cappadocia in Anatolia. He is the subject of Philostratus' *Life of Apollonius of Tyana*, which was written over a century after his death.

induce the idols to deliver their oracles. The demons answered: "The widow Symphorosa and her seven sons daily torment us by invoking their God; if they sacrifice, we promise to be favorable to your vows."

This lady lived with her seven sons upon a plentiful estate they enjoyed at Tivoli. She liberally expended her treasures in assisting the poor, especially in relieving the Christians who suffered for the faith. She was the widow of Saint Getulius or Zoticus, who had been crowned with martyrdom with his brother Amantius. They were both tribunes of legions or colonels in the army and were honored among the martyrs on the 10th of June. Symphorosa had buried their bodies in her farm, and sighing to see her sons and herself united in immortal bliss, she prepared herself to follow them by the most vigorous exercise of all good works.

Hadrian, whose superstition was alarmed at this answer of his gods or their priests, ordered her and her sons to be seized and brought before him. She came with joy in her countenance, praying for herself and her children that God would grant them the grace to confess his holy name with constancy. The emperor urged them, at first on favorable terms, to sacrifice. Symphorosa answered: "My husband Getulius and his brother Amantius, being your tribunes, have suffered diverse torments for the name of Jesus Christ rather than sacrifice to idols; and they have conquered your demons by their death, choosing to be beheaded rather than to be overcome. The death they suffered drew upon them disgrace among men, but glory among the angels, and they now enjoy eternal life in heaven." The emperor changing his voice, said to her angrily: "*Either sacrifice to the most powerful gods, with thy sons, or thou thyself shalt be offered up as a sacrifice together with them.*" Symphorosa answered: "*Your gods cannot receive me as a sacrifice; but if I am burnt for the name of Jesus Christ, my death will increase the torment your devils endure in their flames. But can I hope for so great a happiness as to be offered a sacrifice to the true and living God with my children?"* Hadrian said: *"Either sacrifice to my gods, or you shall all miserably perish."* Symphorosa said: *"Do not imagine that fear will make me change; I am desirous to be at rest with my husband whom you put to death for the name of Jesus Christ."* The emperor then ordered her to be carried to the temple of Hercules, where she was first buffeted on the cheeks and afterward hung up by the hair of her head. When no torments could shake her invincible soul, the emperor gave orders that she should be thrown into the river with a great stone fastened about her neck. Her brother Eugenius, one of the chiefs of the council of Tibur, took up her body and buried it on the road near that town.

The next day the emperor sent for her seven sons altogether and encouraged them to sacrifice and not imitate their mother's stubbornness. He added the severest threats but found all to be in vain. He ordered seven stakes with engines and pullies to be planted around the temple of Hercules and the pious youths to be bound upon them; their limbs were in this posture tortured and stretched in such a manner that the bones were disjointed in all parts of their bodies. The young noblemen, far from yielding under the violence of their tortures, were encouraged by each other's example and seemed more eager to suffer than the executioners were to torment. At length, the emperor commanded them to be put to death, in the same place where they were, in different ways. The eldest, called Crescens had his throat cut; the second, named Julian, was stabbed in the breast; Nemesius, the third, was pierced with a lance in his heart; Primativus received his wound in the belly, Justin in the back, Stacteus on his sides, and Eugenius the youngest died by his body being cleft asunder into two parts across his breast from the head downwards. The emperor came the next day to the temple of Hercules and gave orders for a deep hole to be dug and for all the bodies of these martyrs to be thrown into it. The heathen priest called the place, *The Seven Biothanati*[88], signified in Greek and in the style of art magic, such as die by a violent death, mainly as were put to torture. After this, a stop was put to the persecution for about eighteen months. During which interval of peace, the Christians took up the remains of these martyrs and interred them with honor on the *Via Tiburtina*, the midway between Tivoli and Rome, where still are seen some remains of a church erected in memory of them in a place called to this day *Sette Fratelli* (Seven Brothers). Their bodies were translated by a pope called Stephen into the church of the Holy Angel in the fish market in Rome, where they were found in the pontificate of Pius IV[89]. with an inscription on a plate that mentioned this translation.

Saint Symphorosa set not before the eyes of her children the advantages of their riches and birth or their father's honorable employments and great exploits but those of his piety and the triumph of his martyrdom. She continually entertained them on the glory of heaven and the happiness of treading in our Divine Redeemer's steps by practicing humility, patience, resignation, and charity, which virtues are best learned in the path of humiliations and sufferings. In these, a Christian finds his solid treasure and unalterable peace and joy both in life and death. The honors, riches, applause, and pleasures with which the worldly sinner is sometimes surrounded can never satiate his desires; often, they do not even reach his heart, which

---

[88] Suicides were called βιοθάνατοι (biothanati) in the early Church because they offered violence to themselves. Because suicide was a crime that could not be punished, the Church denied the suicide the honor and solemnity of Christian burial, allowing him to die excommunicated and devoid of all memorials in her prayers.

[89] From 25 December 1559 to his death in 1565, Pope Pius IV, born Giovanni Angelo Medici, was the head of the Catholic Church and ruler of the Papal States.

under this gorgeous show bleeds as it were inwardly, while silent grief, like a worm at the core, preys upon his vitals. Death at last always draws aside the curtain and shows them to have been no better than mere dreams and shadows which passed in a moment but have left a cruel sting behind them, which fills the mind with horror, dread, remorse, and despair, and racks the whole soul with confusion, perplexities, and alarms.

[Butler, Alban. *The Lives of the Fathers, Martyrs, and Other Principal Saints. Compiled from Original Monuments and Authentic Records.* Dublin: James Duffy, 1866. *HathiTrust Digital Library,* catalog.hathitrust.org/Record/001941109.]

Saint Margaret of Antioch, Virgin, and Martyr († 275) — July 20

Because the Acts of the life of Margaret, or Marina, are legendary, her memorial, which was added to the Roman calendar in the thirteenth century, is abolished.

Saint Margaret was born in the third century at Antioch of Pisidia[90] in southern Asia Minor. Her mother died while she was an infant, and was instructed in the Christian faith by a virtuous nurse. When her father, a pagan priest named Aedesius, learned she was a Christian, he drove her out of the house. She became a shepherdess to earn her living.

When a Roman prefect arrived in the region to persecute the Christians, Margaret was imprisoned. The prefect, fascinated by her beauty, desired to save her life and add her to many of his wives and concubines. He attempted to overcome her resistance by questioning her

---

[90] *Antioch in Pisidia*, also known as *Antiochia in Pisidia* or *Pisidian Antioch*, and in the Roman Empire, Latin: Antiochia Caesareia or Antiochia Colonia Caesarea, was a city in the Turkish Lakes Region, at the crossroads of the Mediterranean, Aegean, and Central Anatolian regions, and formerly on the border of Pisidia and Phrygia, hence also known as *Antiochia in Phrygia*. The location is about 1 km northeast of Yalvaç, Isparta, Turkey.

before an assembly of virtually the entire city. Her reply to his ultimatum, offering her a choice between joy and torments, was recorded and became renowned. She said: The true life and true joy, and thanks be to God, I have already found, and have placed them in the stronghold of my heart that they may never be removed. I adore and glorify the Lord Jesus Christ, venerate Him with confidence, and will never cease to honor Him with my whole soul. Know that no human power, no torture will be able to extract so great a treasure from my heart. When the prefect replied that someone had undoubtedly put such ideas into her very young and inexperienced head, an extended dialogue ensued, Margaret, striving to make him understand the reason for her confidence and that God Himself gives replies to those who believe in Him when they are questioned, according to His promise.

Hearing her say that her Lord was not merely a man but very genuinely God and Man at one same time, whose power was far above that of emperors, he became furious and sent her to be scourged, suspended in the air by her hands. Many spectators wept and begged her to pity herself. She replied: *Illustrious gentlemen and noble ladies, do not weaken my courage, for as the Apostle said, bad conversation corrupts good habits. But I forgive you because you act this way out of sympathy and do not possess the true light...* Cast into prison still alive, she was visited by a demon whom she put to flight by a sign of the cross; there followed a vision of the cross of salvation, accompanied by a voice urging her to persevere. On the following day, she was subjected to the torment of burning torches and felt no pain. She continued under other ineffectual tortures to encourage the spectators to understand who it was she adored and finally was beheaded with many of those whom her words had caused to believe as she did.

[Guérin, Abbé (Paul), François Giry, and Simon Martin. *Les Petits Bollandistes: Vies Des Saints De L'Ancien et du Nouveau Testament.* Translated by the Monastère du Magnificat. Paris: Bloud et Barral, 1882. *HathiTrust Digital Library,* hdl.handle.net/2027/nnc1.0036694380.]

Saint Praxedes, Virgin († 165) — July 21

The memorial of Praxedes, founder of the titular church on the Esquiline, is left to that church. The accounts of this saint are legendary.

The holy virgin Praxedes was a Roman, daughter of Pudens, a senator, and sister of Novatus, Timothy, and Pudentiana, who are all honored as saints in the Church. The life of Saint Praxedes was a continual occupation and exercise in prayer, fasting, watching, and penance. She spent much of her means and revenues, wherewith she was most richly stored, in succoring and relieving the poor and needy, particularly in serving and comforting those who suffered and were afflicted for the faith of Jesus Christ, of whom there was an infinite multitude. For she provided for their necessities, visited, and comforted them in prison, dressed their wounds, urged them to be patient in their pains, gathered up their blood, buried their bodies, commended herself most earnestly and affectionately to their prayers, rejoiced for their conquests and victories, and desired exceedingly to imitate their sufferings and death for our Lord Jesus Christ, that she might take part with them in their rewards and crowns.

She harbored the saints in her house, entertained and cherished them with all love and kindness. And they used to meet and assemble in her home as in a secure harbor and place of refuge, to pray together, to hear Mass, and to receive the most precious body of our Lord. But as the persecution of Emperor Marcus Aurelius[91] endured a long while, and an infinite quantity of Christian blood was daily spilled, the virgin's tender heart was wonderfully wounded with compassion. After which she prayed to our Lord *that if it were according to His holy will and pleasure, he would vouchsafe to deliver and take her away from the miseries of the present life and bring her to a place where she might forever enjoy his holy presence and where the tears would be dried up and washed away, where the cruel and heartless murdering of such an infinity of his servants was continually drawing from her eyes.* Our merciful Lord heard her devout prayer and took her out of this world on the twenty-first of July in 164, in Marcus Aurelius's and Lucius Verus's reign. Her body was buried with her father and those of her family by a priest named Pastor, who wrote her *Life*. All Martyrologies make mention of her.

[Ribadeneyra, Pedro de. "The Life of St. Praxedes, Virgin." *The Lives of Saints, With Other Feasts of the Year, according to the Roman Calendar. Written in Spanish by the Reverend Father Peter Ribadeneyra, Priest of the Society of Jesus. Translated Into English by W.P. (William Petre) Esq; The Second Edition Corrected and Amended, vol. 2, pp. 41-42.* London. Printed by B.S., 1730. *HathiTrust Digital Library,* hdl.handle.net/2027/nyp.33433003053000.]

Saint Apollinaris of Ravenna, First Bishop of Ravenna, and Martyr († 79) — July 23

Since Apollinaris of Ravenna does not have universal significance, his memorial is left to the particular calendars.

When Saint Peter, setting out for Rome, left Antioch after seven years as its spiritual head, he took several of the faithful of that city, among them Apollinaris,

---

[91] Marcus Aurelius Antoninus was a Stoic philosopher and Roman Emperor from 161 to 180. He was the final of the Five Good Emperors and the last emperor of the Pax Romana, a period of relative peace and stability for the Roman Empire that lasted from 27 BC to 180 AD.

a disciple of Jesus Christ. He consecrated him as bishop a few years later and sent him to Ravenna as its first bishop.

His first miracle was on behalf of the blind son of a soldier who gave him hospitality when he arrived in Ravenna. When the apostle told him of the God he had come to preach and invited him to abandon the cult of idols, the soldier replied: Stranger, if the God you preach is as powerful as you say, beg Him to give sight to my son, and I will believe in Him. So the Saint had the child brought and made the sign of the cross on his eyes as he prayed. The miracle was instantaneous, to the great amazement of all, and news of it spread rapidly. A day or so later, a military tribune sent for him to cure his wife from a long illness, which again he did. The tribune's house became a center of apostolic action, and several persons sent their children to the Saint to instruct them there. Little by little, a flourishing Christian assembly was formed, and priests and deacons were ordained. The Saint lived in a community with two priests and two deacons.

The idolatrous priests aroused the people against him, as we see the enemies of Saint Paul do in the *Acts of the Apostles*. He was left half-dead on the seashore after being severely beaten but was cared for by the Christians and recovered rapidly. A young girl whom he cured after having her father promise to allow her full liberty to follow Christ consecrated her virginity to God. It was after this that, in the time of Vespasian, he was arrested and interrogated and again flogged, stretched on the rack, and plunged into boiling oil. Finally, alive still, he was exiled to Illyria, east of the Adriatic Sea.

He remained three years in that country, having survived a shipwreck with only a few persons whom he converted. Then he evangelized the various districts with the aid of his converts. When an idol ceased to speak during his sojourn in one of these regions, the pagans again beat him and threw him and his companions on a ship that took them back to Italy. Soon imprisoned, he escaped but was seized again and subjected to flogging for the last time. He died on July 23rd of the year 79. His body lay first at Classis, four miles from Ravenna, and a church was built over his tomb; later, the relics were returned to Ravenna. Pope Honorius had a church built to honor the name of Apollinaris in Rome in about the year 630. From the beginning, the Church has held his memory in high reverence.

[Guérin, Abbé (Paul), François Giry, and Simon Martin. *Les Petits Bollandistes: Vies Des Saints De L'Ancien et du Nouveau Testament.* Translated by the Monastère du Magnificat. Paris: Bloud et Barral, 1882. *HathiTrust Digital Library,* hdl.handle.net/2027/nnc1.0036694380.]

Saint Liborius, Bishop of Le Mans, Confessor († 397) — July 23

The memorial of Liborius, bishop of Le Mans in the fourth century, was inscribed in the Roman calendar in 1702. It is now left to the particular calendars because it does not have universal significance.

Saint Liborius was born of an illustrious family of Gaul (a region in the Roman Empire which extended to the area on the west bank of the Rhine River of present-day Germany) and became Bishop of Le Mans, France. He was a trusty companion to Saint Marinus (Martin of Tours). They were both bishops, neighbors in office. Saint Liborius was bishop for about 49 years and ordained 217 priests, 186 deacons and 93 subdeacons, and other churchmen. He is said to have died on July 23, 397 A.D., with Bishop Martin at his side. He was buried in the

Apostle Basilica of Le Mans, beside his predecessor, Julian, the founder of the bishopric.

Much of the religious life of Bishop Liborius covered the second half of the 4th century. By this time, the Roman Empire ended its persecution of Christianity with Emperor Constantine the Great's Edict of Milan in 313. Freed from persecution, the Christian faith was now free to grow. However, during this time, foreign tribes roamed the land. As a result, there was chaos and misery. Bishop Liborius' Episcopal area had been Christian for some time, but heathen Druids were still active and could influence the people through their mysterious pagan rites. So, Bishop Liborius built many churches and celebrated the Eucharist with piety and dignity. The well-trained priests in his diocese finally triumphed over the Druids. Nowadays, we would call the works of Bishop Liborius and his clergy at the time primary evangelization.

He is said to have healed sufferers from "gravel and allied complaints," and for this reason, his feast was introduced by Pope Clement XI, himself a victim who was cured by the saint's intercession.

Miracles are said to have occurred at his tomb. In 835, Bishop Aldrich placed some relics of his body on an altar in the cathedral, and in the following year, on the instructions of Emperor Louis the Pious[92], sent the body to Bishop Badurad of Paderborn, a diocese founded in 799 by Pope Leo III and Emperor Charlemagne[93] that had no saint of its own.

In the year 836 A.D. (9th century), the relics of Saint Liborius were brought from Le Mans, France, to Paderborn, Germany. At this time, relics of the saints

---

[92] From 813, Louis the Pious, also known as the Fair and the Debonaire, was King of the Franks and co-emperor with his father, Charlemagne. From 781, he was also King of Aquitaine.

[93] Charlemagne, also known as Charles the Great, was a Carolingian dynasty member who reigned as King of the Franks from 768, King of the Lombards from 774, and the first Holy Roman Emperor from 800.

were well guarded and venerated in churches and dioceses with them. The willingness of the diocese of Le Mans to hand over the relics of Saint Liborius to the diocese of Paderborn was a true act of charity. The event forged a long-lasting friendship between the sister cities of Le Mans and Paderborn; it has existed for over 1,000 years.

From this arose a "love bond of lasting brotherhood" that has survived all the hostilities of the succeeding centuries and is the oldest contract still in force. Both churches bound themselves to help each other by prayer and material assistance, as they have done on more than one occasion.

["Life of St. Liborius." *Saint Liborius Parish, Archdiocese of Joliet*, 2014, stliboriuscatholicparish.wordpress.com/the-parish/st-liborius.]

Saint Christina, Virgin, and Martyr († 300) — July 24

Nothing is known about Christina except her name and place of burial at Saint-Trond, and her memorial, added to the Roman calendar in the twelfth century, is left for the particular calendars.

Saint Christina was the daughter of a rich and powerful magistrate named Urban. Her father, who was deep in the practices of paganism, had several golden idols. His young daughter broke them, then distributed the pieces among the poor. Infuriated by this act, Urban became the persecutor of his daughter. He had her whipped with rods and thrown into a dungeon.

Nevertheless, Christina remained unshaken in her faith. Her tormentor brought her forth to have her body torn by iron hooks, then fastened to a rack beneath which a fire was kindled. But God watched over His servant and turned the flames back toward the onlookers, several of whom perished.

The torments this young girl was subjected to would seem as challenging to devise as to imagine, but God was always beside her. After a heavy stone was attached to her neck, Saint Christina was thrown into the lake of Bolsena but was rescued by an Angel and seen wearing a stole and walking on water, accompanied by several Angels. Hearing she was still alive, her father died suddenly amid atrocious suffering. A new judge succeeded him; a cruel pagan experienced in persecuting the Christians. He tried to win her by reminding her of her nobility, suggesting she was in serious error. Her reply infuriated him: Christ, whom you despise, will tear me out of your hands! Then Saint Christina suffered the most inhuman torments. The second judge also was struck down by divine justice. A third one named Julian succeeded him. Magician! he cried; adore the gods, or I will put you to death! She survived a raging furnace after remaining in it for five days. Serpents and vipers thrown into her prison did not touch her but killed the magician who had brought them there. She sent them away in the name of Christ after restoring the unfortunate magician to life; he was converted and thanked the God of Christina and the Saint. Then her tongue was cut out.

The Saint prayed to be allowed to finish her course. When she was pierced with arrows, she gained the martyr's crown at Tyro, a city that formerly stood on an island in Lake Bolsena (*Lago di Bolsena*) in Italy but has since been swallowed up by the waters. Her relics are now at Palermo in Sicily. Her tomb was discovered in the 19th century at Bolsena, marked with an inscription dating from the 10th century.

[Guérin, Abbé (Paul), François Giry, and Simon Martin. *Les Petits Bollandistes: Vies Des Saints De L'Ancien et du Nouveau Testament.* Translated by the Monastère du

Magnificat. Paris: Bloud et Barral, 1882. *HathiTrust Digital Library,* hdl.handle.net/2027/nnc1.0036694380.]

Saint Christopher, Martyr († 251) — July 25

The memorial of Christopher, which entered the Roman calendar in 1550, is not a part of the ancient Roman tradition. It is now left to the particular calendars. Although the Acts of Christopher's life are legendary, his cult's existence is ancient.

The valiant and glorious martyr, Saint Christopher, was by nation a Cananean; being moved by a particular inspiration of God, he came into the province of Lycia to preach and announce the name of Christ to those who were ignorant of him. But first, he armed himself with continual prayer against all encounters and difficulties he was to meet in this holy enterprise. He was a proper and big man, comely, and of an excellent disposition. Whereby he drew his eyes upon him and gained all men's affections. He carried a wand in his hand; upon a time, he pitched in the ground; it suddenly became green and budded. Which miracle caused the conversion of divers to the holy faith of Christ. And as well as Saint Christopher's prayers, his preaching, and beautiful signs that our Lord wrought by him, Christian religion in a short time was wonderfully propagated, and the church made the most prosperous progress until Decius came to the empire, Saint Christopher was taken in Samos, which is a city of the province of Lycia.

The judge, who exceedingly desired to draw him to his superstition, and persuade him to worship his idols, left nothing un-attempted which he thought might be of power to work upon his mind. But, on the contrary, he spoke to him fair and promised him great rewards if he would yield. Then again threatened him with all manner of torments if he refused to do what he was urged to do. But finding his courage to be of steel, and that it was to speak to a rock, to go about to entice or intimidate him, he found out a diabolical device and sent two lewd and wanton women to him, to solicit him to sin; thinking that if he could bereave him of virtue, it would be no complicated matter to dispossess him of the faith and love of Jesus Christ, whom Saint Christopher defended and maintained to be God. So these impudent creatures entered the prison where the saint was but presently were seized upon by so dreadful a fear and horror that they were made to acknowledge and detest their wickedness and to cast themselves at Saint Christopher's feet; whom they besought with many tears *to obtain the pardon and mercy for them of Almighty God.* And he did well to instruct and confirm them in the faith of our Lord Jesus Christ, that they came soon to lay down their lives for the same, together with others, whom the holy man had gained and converted by his preaching. And besides these, diverse others, that were people of good quality, did with great zeal suffer death and shed their blood for our Lord's sake.

But the most inhuman and barbaric judge, despairing ever to conquer the invincible courage and constancy of Saint Christopher, resolved at least to satisfy his rage and cruelty in revenging himself upon him. And to make him die by some unusual and exquisite torments, he would first have him be most unmercifully whipped. Then he puts on an extremely hot iron helmet that it seemed like fiery coal, glowing and sparking upon his head. Afterward, having commanded a form or bench of iron to be made, in length and breadth proportional to his body, he stretches him upon it, kindles under it a fire, and continually pours upon him seething oil to consume him with a flow fire, and most painful; yet withal long and lingering death.

But the noble martyr was so favored and assisted by the Almighty God that he said to the judge, with a pleasant and smiling countenance, *Through the power of Jesus Christ, I feel not thy torments.* And so, without being hurt or singed, he rose from that fiery bed. At this point, many of those present believed in Christ.

The judge made him be tied to a post and stand on a mark for all the soldiers to shoot at. But not an arrow could hit him. But, on the contrary, one of the shafts recoiling back fastened itself in the eye of an officer and put it out. But he, taking up some of the sacred blood which had fallen from the martyr while he was scourged and applying it to his eye, recovered sight both of body and soul.

In fine, this glorious saint had his head cut off. But when he was under the sword of the executioner, before the final blow was given, he made a humble prayer to Almighty God and begged of Him, *That neither hail, nor fire, nor storm, nor famine, nor plague might annoy the place where his body should be buried.* Then, after prayer, he rendered his soul into the hands of his Creator, who had made him victorious over death and torment.

Saint Christopher converted to God by his preaching to 48,000 persons. Saint Ambrose speaks of this glorious saint and martyr, and in the Preface of the Mass, which he puts for his feast, has these words, for they are as it were an abridgment of his life. *Lord,* sayeth he, *thou didst so furnish and adorn Saint Christopher with virtue, grace, and science, that by his divine doctrine and miracles be converted 48,000 persons, dispersing the darkness of gentility and discovering to them the light of faith. He reduced to the glory of chastity Niceta and Aquilina, lewd courtesans that had long weltered in the ordure of sin, teaching them to confess their faith, die for it, and receive the crown of martyrdom. Moreover, when he lay in the fire upon an iron bed, he feared not the raging heat; he could not be pierced by a million arrows, which the soldiers were shooting at him for a whole day. One of the arrows struck out the eye of an executioner, but the blood of the blessed martyr soaked into the ground restored his vision and cured his corporal blindness, giving him sight to his soul. He obtained pardon for sinners and grace that diseases and infirmities might be cured at his intercession.* Thus writes Saint Ambrose.

The martyrdom of Saint Christopher was on that day, in which the holy Church celebrates it, to wit, the 25th of July, in the year of our Lord 254, in the reign of Decius emperor, according to the Roman Martyrology and Cardinal Baronius. Saint Christopher is usually pictured with the infant Jesus on his shoulders, passing over a river. No other ground than that Saint Christopher passed through many waters of afflictions, pains, and torments, with strength and virtue which our Lord Jesus gave him. His picture is ordinarily put in some high place because of the grace God gave him to defend us from storms and tempests, according to what he begged God.

[Ribadeneyra, Pedro de. "The Life of Saint Christopher, Martyr." *The Lives of Saints, With Other Feasts of the Year, according to the Roman Calendar. Written in Spanish by the Reverend Father Peter Ribadeneyra, Priest of the Society of Jesus. Translated Into English by W.P. (William Petre) Esq; The Second Edition Corrected and Amended*, vol. 2. London. Printed by B.S., 1730, pp. 57-58. *HathiTrust Digital Library*, hdl.handle.net//2027/nyp.33433003052994.]

Saint Pantaleon of Nicomedia, Physician, and Martyr (✝ 303) — July 27

Almost nothing is known about the Eastern martyr, Pantaleon, whose Acts are legendary. His memorial was added to the Roman calendar in the twelfth century and is now left to the particular calendars.

Saint Pantaleon was born in Nicomedia to a pagan father and a Christian mother, who died while her son was still a child. He was among the court physicians of Emperor Galerius Maximianus (Gaius Galerius Valerius Maximianus, 250–311). Deceived by hearing the false maxims of the world applauded, he was without religion when God decided to rescue his soul from its unhappy darkness. A zealous and prudent Christian named Hermolaus took particular notice of him and awakened his conscience, telling him that although the famous physicians of ancient times had possessed the science which cures bodies, Jesus Christ was a far more excellent Physician, able to heal not only bodies but souls, by His divine doctrine. Hermolaus succeeded in bringing him into the fold of the Church.

The young Christian strove to procure for his father the same grace he had received, and his words had already begun to separate him from his idols, when one day, a blind man, led by friends, came to the door and begged Pantaleon to cure him. His father was present and heard the promise his son made to this man to do so if he would give to the poor the money he was offering him. The father was amazed and feared that the promise could not be fulfilled. But the young Saint prayed and touched the eyes of the blind man, invoking the name of Jesus Christ, and his eyes were opened. Pantaleon's father and the blind man were baptized because of this miracle. When Eustorgus, his father, died, Saint Pantaleon liberated all his slaves and, having sold most of his possessions, gave the liberated ones and others the assistance their poverty required. He cured other illnesses and soon became renowned in Nicomedia.

Saint Pantaleon, a very sincere penitent, ardently wished to expiate his former idolatry by the martyrdom he could foresee. When bloody persecution broke out at Nicomedia in 303, the blind man he had cured was beheaded upon refusing to admit that it was the gods who had healed him. Saint Pantaleon distributed all he had left among the poor to prepare himself for the imminent combat. Not long after this act of charity, he was arrested and subjected to various tortures, during which he was preserved from death. Three other Christians, of whom one was Hermolaus, were apprehended. After suffering many torments, the four confessors were all sentenced to be beheaded.

The relics of Saint Pantaleon were translated to Constantinople, and there received a great honor. His blood, conserved in a small vial, is said to liquefy on his feast day and become oxygenated. Charlemagne brought a part of his relics into France, where they are presently divided again, a portion being in the abbey of Saint Denys near Paris and the head at Lyons. Saint Pantaleon, whose name means the all-compassionate one, is the patron of physicians.

[Guérin, Abbé (Paul), François Giry, and Simon Martin. *Les Petits Bollandistes: Vies Des Saints De L'Ancien et du Nouveau Testament.* Translated by the Monastère du Magnificat. Paris: Bloud et Barral, 1882. *HathiTrust Digital Library,* hdl.handle.net/2027/nnc1.0036694380.]

Saints Nazarius and Celsus, Martyrs (✝ First century) — July 28

Except for the finding of their relics by Ambrose in 395, nothing is known about Nazarius and Celsus, martyrs from Milan. Their memorial, placed on the Roman calendar in the twelfth century, is now left to the particular calendars.

Saint Nazarius, born in Rome, was the son of a pagan military man who held an important post in the Roman army. His mother, honored by the Church as

Saint Perpetua, was a zealous Christian, instructed by Saint Peter or his disciples in the perfect maxims of Christianity. Nazarius, at the age of nine, embraced the Faith with so much ardor that he copied in his own young life all the great virtues he saw in his teachers. He was baptized by Saint Linus, who would later become Pope. His pagan father was touched by his son's virtue and seconded his project to go elsewhere to preach the Gospel. Out of zeal for the salvation of others, Nazarius, therefore, left Rome, his native city, and preached the Faith in many places with fervor and disinterestedness fitting for a disciple of the Apostles.

Ten years later, he is known to have been in Milan. He was driven from the city by the prefect after being whipped, leaving Italy to go to eastern Gaul or France. A young boy named Celsus was brought to him; his mother asked him to teach and baptize her son and to take him for his disciple. The child was docile, Nazarius did so, and they were never separated. However, when conversions multiplied, the local governor was alarmed, and the apostle was again arrested, beaten, and tortured. The wife of this governor was a Christian, however, and succeeded in obtaining liberty for the two young innocents. They were freed on the condition that they would no longer preach at this place.

The two fervent Christians went to the Alpine villages where only a few solitary settlers braved the rigors of the climate and the altitude. However, they were not rebuffed and went as far as Embrun. There they built a chapel to the true God and continued to Geneva, Treves, where Saint Nazarius was arrested and imprisoned. Celsus followed him in tears, longing to share his captivity. When after a few days, the prefect ordered them brought before him, they were treated cruelly but appeared before the magistrate, their faces shining with glory. The prodigies that followed caused fear in the pagans, and they were released and told to leave the region.

They returned to Milan but were soon arrested there also. When they would not sacrifice to the gods of the empire, after several tortures in which God again preserved them, they were sentenced to be beheaded. They embraced one another in transports of joy and praise to God for this grace. During the reign of Nero, in about the year 56, these generous Martyrs added their blood to the treasure of the Christians.

Their bodies were buried separately in a garden outside the city, where they were discovered and taken up by Saint Ambrose in 395. In the tomb of Saint Nazarius, whose decapitated body and head were perfectly conserved, a vial of the Saint's blood was found as fresh and red as if it had been spilled that same day. Saint Ambrose conveyed the bodies of the two martyrs into the new Apostles church he had just built. An evil spirit delivered a woman in their presence. Saint Ambrose sent some of these relics to Saint Paulinus of Nola, who received them with great respect as a most valuable gift, as he testifies, and placed them in honor at Nola.

[Shea, John G. *Little Pictorial Lives of the Saints, with Reflections for Every Day of the Year; Compiled from "Butler's Lives."* New York: Benziger, 1894. *HathiTrust Digital Library,* hdl.handle.net/2027/nyp.33433068232887; Guérin, Abbé (Paul), François Giry, and Simon Martin. *Les Petits Bollandistes: Vies Des Saints De L'Ancien et du Nouveau Testament.* Translated by the Monastère du Magnificat. Paris: Bloud et Barral, 1882. *HathiTrust Digital Library,* hdl.handle.net/2027/nnc1.0036694380.]

Saint Innocent I, Pope, and Confessor (✝ 417) — July 28

The memorial of Innocent I, who died on March 12, 417, dates from the thirteenth century in the Roman calendar. Since it honors another saint, it is now abolished.

Saint Innocent, the pope, the first of that name, succeeded Anastasius in Saint Peter's Chair, on the 17th of May, in the year of our Lord 402. He was born in Alba, a city near Rome, and his father's name was Innocent. The bloody persecutions of tyrants were now at an end. The Church flourished with a sense of sweet and delightful peace, by the goodness and piety of Theodosius emperor and two of his sons, Arcadius and Honorius, where the former succeeded him in the empire of the east; and the other in Italy and western parts. But, this notwithstanding, Saint Innocent wanted not persecutions, for he had great combats and very troublesome afflictions. He governed the Church for a while; Alaric, king of the Goths, with a powerful army falling upon Italy, besieged Rome, stormed it, and exercised barbarous hostilities and lamentable desolations upon it the city and people of Rome. However, he used much respect for the churches, especially that of the glorious prince of the apostles, Saint Peter. This sacking of Rome was the beginning of the fall and ruin of the Roman empire.

Almighty God ordained that Saint Innocent should be then at Ravenna; whither he went some while before, to treat with the emperor Honorius about some good agreement to be made with Alaricus, and the applying of some timely remedy for preventing this great calamity, which was then feared. Paulus Orosius writes, *That God withdrew this holy pope from Rome, as he hath taken a lot out of Sodom, that he might not see the affliction and desolation of his people.*

Saint Innocent also had a great debate and contest with emperor Alaricus and his lady, the empress Eudoxia; because upon false accusations and malicious slanders, they had driven into banishment the holiest and most eloquent patriarch, Saint John Chrysostom; in which banishment that blessed and worthy saint was deprived of life, to the great offense of God, and incomparable loss of the Church. For this wicked act, Saint Innocent excommunicated Arcadius and Eudoxia; condemned all those that had given unjust sentences against Saint John Chrysostom; and, during his persecution, took him under his protection, comforted him with many excellent letters, and finally, after his death, solemnized his memory with tremendous honor.

Saint Innocent behaved himself with great zeal and vigor against certain heretics that troubled the peace of the Church in his time, to wit, Pelagius, Celestius, and Julian; against whom Saint Augustine and Saint Jerome, that were of the same age, writ ever learnedly, with whom Saint Innocent contracted a straight league of friendship. He appointed, or instead, he gave the reason for the fast of Saturday and ordained that the *Pax* should be given to the people at Mass after consecration, before the priest's communion.

He declared *the bishop to be the minister of the sacrament of Confirmation and the priest of Extreme Unction.* Then, at the request of Vestina, a Roman matron, he consecrated a church in honor of the holy martyrs Gervasius and Protafius and called it by the title of Vestina; for that, she bestowed upon it all her wealth. But now, this church bears the name of Saint Vitalis and the tile of Cardinal.

He gave Holy Orders four times in December and ordained fifty-four bishops and thirteen deacons. According to Cardinal Baronius, although others assigned him a long time, he governed the Church of God for fifteen years, one month, and ten days. This blessed man wrote many learned and grave epistles; among which one is to the Second Council of Toledo, wherein he reprehends certain abuses that were then in Spain in the consecration of priests; and some to the Councils at Carthage and Milevum, held there in his time. In which epistles appear his holy zeal and vigilance in his pastoral function.

Saint Jerome highly extols this pope's sanctity; writing to Demetriades bids her *embrace the faith and doctrine that Saint Innocent taught.* Many other doctors say as much and enlarge themselves upon the praises of his singular integrity and goodness. He passed out of this life to the eternal on the day the Church keeps his feast, jointly with the festival memory of the holy martyrs, Nazarius, Celsius, and Victor, pope; to wit upon the twenty-first of July, in the year of our Lord 417.

[Ribadeneyra, Pedro de. "The Life of Saint Innocent, Pope and Confessor." *The Lives of Saints, With Other Feasts of the Year, according to the Roman Calendar. Written in Spanish by the Reverend Father Peter Ribadeneyra, Priest of the Society of Jesus. Translated Into English by W.P. (William Petre) Esq; The Second Edition Corrected and Amended,* vol. 2, pp. 63-64. London. Printed by B.S., 1730. *HathiTrust Digital Library,* hdl.handle.net//2027/nyp.33433003053000.]

Saint Victor I, Pope, and Martyr († 201) — July 28

Since there is no reason to consider him a martyr, the memorial of Victor I, placed in the Roman calendar in the thirteenth century, is deleted. The date of his death is unknown.

He was a native of Africa and succeeded Saint Eleutherius in the pontificate in 192, the nineteenth of Commodus. The practice of those virtues which had prepared him for that dignity rendered him a true successor of the apostles. He vigorously opposed the rising heresies of that age. Theodotus of Byzantium, a tanner, having apostatized from the faith to save his life in late persecution, afterward, to extenuate his guilt, pretended that he had denied only a man, not God; teaching that Christ was nothing more than a mere man, as the Socinians teach at this day; whereas the Arians allowed him to have been before the world, though himself a creature Theodotus, going to Rome, there drew many into his blasphemous error; for he was well versed in polite literature; but Victor checked his progress by excommunicating him, with Ebion, Artemon, and another Theodotus, who had taught the same blasphemy. This other Theodotus, called Trapezita, or the banker, was the author of the Melchizedekian heresy, pretending that Melchizedek was greater than Christ.

Montanus, a new convert in Mysia, near Phrygia, out of an unbounded desire to invade the first dignities of the church, and filled with rage to see himself disappointed, began to preach against the church; and, having pride and ambition given entrance to the devil, commenced false prophet, and sometimes losing his senses, began in an enthusiastic strain to utter unique expressions. Prisca, or Priscilla, and Maximillia, two women of quality, but debauched lives, left their husbands and, being filled with the same spirit, spoke like Montanus, void of sense, and after an elegant and unusual manner, pretending they succeeded the prophets among the disciples of the apostles. Montanus placed himself above the apostles, saying he had received the Paraclete, or the Holy Ghost promised by Christ, to perfect his law. He denied that the church had the power to forgive the sins of idolatry, murder, and impurity and hardly received any sinners on repentance. Saint Paul had allowed second marriages, but Montanus forbade them as inconsistent with the perfect law of chastity and forbade Christians to flee during persecution. The Montanists were called from their country, Cataphryges, and Pepuzeni, from Pepuzium, a little town in Phrygia, their capital, and called Jerusalem. They boasted of their martyrs, as the Marcionites did, which other heretics seldom pretend to, as Saint Irenæus and Origen take notice; nor could these have any significant number. Apollonius, a Catholic writer, quoted by Eusebius, confounding the hypocrisy of the Montanists, reproached their pretended prophetesses with infamous debaucheries and with receiving presents, saying: "*Does a prophet color his hair, paint his eyebrows, play at dice, or lend out money on usury? I will demonstrate that they are guilty of these things.*" The Catholics met to examine their pretended new prophecies and convicted them of falsehood because the true prophets were not beside themselves when they spoke; also, the Montanists had lied in their predictions and opposed the church's doctrine. Asterius Urbanus, a learned priest (for he calls Saint Zoticus fellow-priest), confounded them by these arguments in a great conference held at Ancyra about 188. Their prophecies and errors were condemned as impious, and the followers of Montanus were driven out of the church and excommunicated. It was reported that Montanus and Maximillia, led away by the spirit that possessed them, afterward hanged themselves. Eusebius relates these particulars.

Tertullian, who fell into this heresy about the time of the death of Pope Victor, says that this pope at first admitted to the communion of the church these pretended prophets. And it was easy to be deceived, a matter of fact, concerning persons at such a distance and who appeared under the garb of hypocrisy. But he had no sooner answered their letters, in which he acknowledged them brethren, but Praxeas coming from the East, brought him an ample account of their tenets and practice: Victor immediately recalled his letters of communion and condemned these innovators. This Praxeas was a Phrygian[94] and, puffed up because he had suffered imprisonment for the faith, began to sow a new

---

[94] Phrygia was a kingdom in Anatolia's west central region, in what is now Asian Turkey, centered on the Sangarios River in classical antiquity.

heresy at Rome, maintaining but one person in God and attributing crucifixion to the Father as well as the Son; whence his followers were called Patripassians. His errors being brought to light, he was also cut off from the communion of the church.

At about the same time, Tatian fell from the church. He was a Syrian, a Platonic philosopher, and a disciple of Saint Justin, a martyr, after whose death he taught for some time in Rome. Afterward, returning to Syria in 171, he broached his errors, which he did not advance to Rome. He borrowed several of them from Marcion, Valentinus, and Saturninus, teaching two principles: the Creator is God's evil principle. He added several new errors, as that Adam was damned. He condemned marriage as no less criminal than adultery, whence his followers were called Encratitæ, or the continent. They were likewise called Hydroparastatæ, or Aquarii, because, in consecrating the Eucharist, they used only water, for they condemned all use of wine and flesh-meat. The ancients observed that Tatian's fall was owing to pride, which often attends an opinion of knowledge. Of this, there cannot be a more dangerous symptom in a scholar than a fondness for novelty and singularity, especially if joined with obstinacy and opiniativeness.

Saint Victor was watchful to cut off these scandals at their root and everywhere to maintain the purity of the faith with unity. Upon this motive, he exerted his zeal in the dispute about the time of celebrating Easter. The churches of Lesser Asia kept it with the Jews on the fourteenth day of the first moon after the vernal equinox, on whatever day of the week it fell. The Roman church, and all the rest of the world, kept Easter always on Sunday immediately following that fourteenth day. Pope Anicetus permitted these Asiatics to keep their custom, even in Rome, but Pope Soter, his successor, obliged them to conform to the tradition of places where they should be.

Several councils held in Rome, Palestine, Pontus, Gaul, Corinth, and other places, unanimously determined the point according to Roman custom. Yet Polycrates, bishop of Ephesus, wrote strenuously in defense of the Asiatic custom, which he said was derived from Saint Philip who died at Hierapolis, from Saint John the Evangelist, Saint Polycarp, bishop, and martyr, Sagarus, bishop and martyr, who died at Laodicea, and others. Victor seeing the Asiatics fixed in their resolution, threatened to cut them off from the communion of the church; from the words of Eusebius, some moderns infer with Baronius, Coustant, and De Marca, that he excommunicated them in a letter, but immediately suspended or recalled the sentence: others with Thomassin, Natalis Alexander, and Graveson, think that he only threatened it; which opinion best agrees with the sequel. To reconcile the different passages of authors, F. John Philip Monti thinks Pope Victor, upon receiving the refractory answer of Polycrates, drew up a sentence of ex-communication, but never sent or published the same, being overcome by the advice of Saint Irenæus. The schism which Blastus, a priest, had lately formed at Rome, upon the difference of this rite, for which Pope Eleutherius had degraded him, probably made Saint Victor more severe in extirpating a practice that became daily more dangerous to the unity of the church. Still, prudence and charity recommended toleration some time longer, which he was prevailed upon to grant by a letter of Saint Irenæus, who wrote to him on that subject in his name and in that of his brethren in Gaul. Saint Victor died soon after this, in the year 201, the ninth of Severus, after he had sat ten years. He is styled a martyr by some writers of the fifth age and in an ancient pontifical written in 530. Though Severus only published the edicts for his persecution in 202, several Christians had suffered in his reign before that time, as Tillemont remarks. F. Pagi thinks Saint Victor did not die by the sword because he is called only confessor in some Martyrologies. However, his dignity and zeal exposed him to continual persecutions, for which alone he might deserve the title of martyr.

[Butler, Alban. *The Lives of the Fathers, Martyrs, and Other Principal Saints. Compiled from Original Monuments and Authentic Records.* Dublin: James Duffy, 1866. *HathiTrust Digital Library,* catalog.hathitrust.org/Record/001941109.]

Saint Felix II, Pope, and Martyr († 360) — July 29

Since nothing is known about Felix except his name and the date of his burial on the Via Portuense on July 29, his memorial is left to the particular calendars.

On the feast of Saint Martha, the holy Church commemorates Saint Felix, pope, the second of that name, and martyr, who was Roman born, son of Anastasius, and held Saint Peter's chair one year and three months, as Damasus writes. He assembled a council at Rome and in it condemned the Arian emperor Constantius, showing himself a professed enemy of heretics and armed with fortitude and constancy as he became the sovereign prelate and pastor of God's Church. This courage of his so incensed the Arians against him that they put him to death, and the Church honors him as a martyr. His holy body was found in Rome on the 28th of July, the eve of his martyrdom, in a chapel of the Saints Cosmas and Damien, in a marble chest with this inscription: *This is the Body of St. Felix, Pope, and Martyr, who condemned Constantius.* This was of happy memory in the year 1582, in the time of Pope Gregory XIII.

He administered Holy Orders once in December, where he ordained twenty-one priests, five deacons, and nineteen bishops. And because in the story of Saint Felix, there are many great difficulties, and different opinions of authors, concerning his being true and lawful pope; as also about the manner and time of his government and martyrdom; what has been related here of him, is held, and received generally for certain. Those that desire to be more fully informed of what concerns him and his predecessor, Saint Liberius, may read the third tome of controversies of Cardinal Bellarmine, who has written of him very certainly and grounded.

[Ribadeneyra, Pedro de. "The Life of Saint Felix II, Pope and Martyr." *The Lives of Saints, With Other Feasts of the Year, according to the Roman Calendar. Written in Spanish by the Reverend Father Peter Ribadeneyra, Priest of the Society of Jesus. Translated Into English by W.P. (William Petre) Esq; The Second Edition Corrected and Amended*, vol. 2, p. 66. London. Printed by B.S., 1730. *HathiTrust Digital Library*, hdl.handle.net//2027/nyp.33433003053000.]

Saints Simplicius and Faustinus, Brothers, and Beatrice, Their Sister, Martyrs († 303) — July 29

The memorial of Simplicius, Faustinus, and Beatrice is also left to the particular calendars. Therefore, all that is known about them is their names and the fact that they were buried on the Via Portuense in the cemetery of Generosa (Catacombe di Generosa) on July 29.

With Saint Felix, the holy Church joins the holy martyrs, Saint Simplicius and Saint Faustinus, brothers, and Saint Beatrice, their sister. The latter died in Rome for the faith of Jesus Christ in the persecution of the emperors Dioclesian and Maximian. Saint Simplicius and Saint Faustinus were apprehended. When there was no means to make them relent in the constant profession of the faith and law of Jesus Christ, one of the emperor's officers commanded *they should be most cruelly tormented and beheaded after that. As for their bodies, they should be thrown into the Tiber River.* But their holy sister Beatrice took them out of the water, buried them, and then retired into the house of a virtuous and godly widow named Lucina. The last night and day attended only to prayer, penance, and works of piety and devotion.

These two blessed souls kept each other company for seven months. Then our Lord permitted that a certain powerful and wealthy man named Lucretius, blinded with avarice[95], should pretend to a farm which Beatrice had, to join it to another belonging to himself. And the better to bring this design about without putting himself to the trouble of going to the law for it, knowing well that Beatrice was a Christian, he summoned her to appear before him, and when she came, bid her offer sacrifice to the gods.

But, when she most resolutely acknowledged herself as a Christian, he protested that she would never adore gods of wood and stone. So he sent her to prison and gave her an order to have her strangled at night. In this manner, Beatrice's glorious virgin and martyr passed from mortal to eternal life. Her dear companion Saint Lucina buried her body near her brothers Simplicius and Faustinus. But afterward, Pope Leo II built a goodly church in Rome, into which he translated the bodies of these blessed martyrs.

But, to an end, we may learn what disasters avarice usually causes and see that God finally discovers and severely chastises all wicked and deceitful plots. It is good to notice what occurred in Lucretius after Saint Beatrice. For as soon as she was dead, he seized up that farm (which indeed was the only cause that she was condemned to die, though he made use of the pretext and color of religion), and the day he took possession of it, he made a great feast and invited his friends. With whom as he was very merry

---

[95] Insatiable desire for riches; excessive, miserly desire to acquire and hoard wealth.

and jovial, and scoffed at the holy martyrs, and could not contain himself for joy to see that he was made now lord of their land and goods, presently a little child that was in the arms of its nurse being of sudden inspired and moved by the spirit of God, cries out with a loud, clear, and intelligible voice, *"Hear Lucretius, thou hast killed, and has taken possession, and thou art has fallen into the hands of the enemy."* With which words, Lucretius was struck as with a thunderclap. For his color left him, and his blood was as if it were frozen in his veins, and immediately the devil, seizing upon his body, tormented him in a most lamentable manner for three hours. After which he cast forth his unhappy soul to his eternal woe and misery, but to the great benefit of many, who by this example understood, *that there is a reward for the good, and punishment for the wicked, and that God at length takes off the mask of the fraudulent and crafty, and that goods ill-gotten are the poison and destruction of those who purchase them.* The Church keeps the feast of these holy martyrs on the twenty-ninth of July, the day on which they suffered, in the year of our Lord 302, under Dioclesian and Maximian. All Martyrologies mention them, the Roman and those of Bede, Usuardus, and Ado. Their martyrdom is briefly set down in the Acts of Saint Anthimus[96], Martyr.

[Ribadeneyra, Pedro de. "The Life of St. Simplicius, St. Faustinus Brothers, and St. Beatrice their Sister, Martyrs." *The Lives of Saints, With Other Feasts of the Year, according to the Roman Calendar. Written in Spanish by the Reverend Father Peter Ribadeneyra, Priest of the Society of Jesus. Translated Into English by W.P. (William Petre) Esq; The Second Edition Corrected and Amended,* vol. 2, pp. 66-67. London. Printed by B.S., 1730. *HathiTrust Digital Library,* hdl.handle.net/2027/nyp.33433003053000.]

---

[96] Anthimus of Rome, also known as Sant'Antimo in Italian, is a Christian saint. His life is largely made up of legend. He was said to be born in Bithynia. He was a Christian priest who was imprisoned for his beliefs during the reigns of Emperors Diocletian and Maximian.

Saints Abdon and Sennen, Persian Martyrs at Rome († 254) — July 30

The memorial of Abdon and Sennen is left for particular calendars. Only their names are known, and the date of July 30 for their burial on the Via Portuense in the cemetery of Pontian (Catacombe di Pontina).

The emperor Decius, the enemy of Christians, had defeated the king of Persia and became the master of several countries over which he reigned. He had already condemned to torture and death Saint Polychrome with five members of his clergy. Saint Abdon and Saint Sennen, illustrious Persian dignitaries of the third century whom the king of Persia had highly honored, were secretly Christian; it was they who had taken up the body of the martyred bishop, which had been cast contemptuously before a temple of Saturn, to bury it at night, with honor. The two royal officials, now fallen under the domination of Rome, were grieved to witness the emperor's cruelty towards the faithful and believed it their duty to make known their love for Jesus Christ; thus, without fear of their new sovereign, they undertook by all possible means to spread and fortify the faith, to encourage the confessors and bury the martyrs.

Decius, learning of their dedication, was highly irritated. He sent for the two brothers to appear before his tribunal and attempted to win them over to sacrifice to the gods by appealing to his recent victory as a sign of their favor. The Saints replied, however, that this victory was not proof of such power since the unique true God, Creator of heaven and earth with His Son, Jesus Christ, gives victory to some and defeat to others for reasons hidden in the designs of His providence. They said they could never adore any but Him, and Decius imprisoned them. Soon afterward, when he learned of the death of the viceroy he had left to govern in his place in Rome, he returned to Rome and took his two captives with him to serve as splendid trophies of his Persian victory. These magistrates were wearing jewels and rich fabrics under their chains.

He arraigned them before the Senate, in whose presence they again testified to the divinity of Christ, saying they could adore no other. The next day they were flogged in the amphitheater; then, two lions and four bears were released to devour them. But the beasts lay down at their feet and became their guardians, and no one dared approach for a time. Finally, the prefect sent out gladiators to slay them with the sword, which God's permission was done. Their bodies remained three days without burial, but a subdeacon, who afterward wrote their history, took them up and buried them on his terrain.

Under Constantine the Great, their tombs were discovered by divine revelation, and their relics were reburied in the Pontian cemetery, which afterward was called by their names. Finally, we see them in a picture of the catacombs crowned by Our Lord Himself. Their glorious martyrdom occurred in the year 254.

[Guérin, Abbé (Paul), François Giry, and Simon Martin. *Les Petits Bollandistes: Vies Des Saints De L'Ancien et du Nouveau Testament.* Translated by the Monastère du Magnificat. Paris: Bloud et Barral, 1882. *HathiTrust Digital Library,* hdl.handle.net/2027/nnc1.0036694380.]

AUGUST

The Seven Maccabees, Brothers, with Their Mother (or Holy Maccabees), Martyrs († 164 BC) — August 1

Left to the particular calendars: until 1960, they were merely commemorated in the celebration of Saint Peter in Chains; under the revised rules, the memorial of Saint Alphonsus Liguori, now on 1 August, does not admit commemorations.

The Seven Brothers, called Maccabees, are holy Jewish martyrs who suffered death in the persecution of Antiochus Epiphanes, the impious king of Syria. The Jews returned from the Babylonish captivity in the first year of the reign of Cyrus. They were allowed to form a republic, be governed by their laws, and live according to their religion. Artaxerxes Longimanus extended their privileges, but their liberty was limited and dependent. They lived in a certain degree of subjection to the Persian kings and shared the fate of that empire under Alexander the Great and after his death under the Seleucidæ, kings of Syria. Antiochus III (the sixth of these kings) was complimented with the surname of The Great on account of his conquests in Asia Minor and his reduction of Media and Persia. However, these two latter provinces submitted themselves again to the Parthians. But this prince met afterward with great disgraces, especially in his war with the Romans, who curtailed his empire, taking from him all his dominions which lay west of Mount Taurus, a good part of which they bestowed on Eumenes. He was likewise obliged to give up to them all his armed galleys and all his elephants, to pay to them for twelve years the annual tribute of one thousand talents (or two hundred and fifty-eight thousand three hundred- and thirty-three-pounds sterling) and one hundred and forty thousand *modii* of the best wheat (or thirty-five thousand English bushels), and to send to Rome twenty hostages, of which his son Antiochus was to be one. In Elymais, a province of Persia between Media and the Persian Gulf, which, from the death of Alexander, was governed by its kings, there stood two famous rich temples, the one of Diana, the other of Jupiter Belus. Antiochus, after his fall, being in extreme want of money, marched to Elymais and, in the night, plundered this temple of Belus. Still, the inhabitants pursued and slew him and recovered the treasure. The Jews had often done essential services to this king, and several of his predecessors, particularly in the reign of his father, Seleucus II. When a numerous army of Gauls or Galatians had invaded Babylonia, and the Syrians and Macedonians did not dare to meet them in the field, six thousand Jews boldly attacked and, by divine assistance, defeated and repulsed them, having slain a hundred and twenty thousand of them.

Seleucus III, the eldest son of Antiochus, succeeded him on the throne and continued for some time to favor the Jews as his father had done. The Jews were then in such high esteem that sovereign princes courted their friendship and made magnificent presents to the temple; Seleucus furnished all of his treasury's expenses. As a result, Judea enjoyed a profound peace; and their laws were observed with a religious strictness under their worthy high-priest Onias III, until a misunderstanding that happened between him and Simon, a powerful man of the tribe of Benjamin, and governor of the temple, brought a series of evils on the whole nation. This contest grew to such a height that Simon, finding he could not carry his iniquitous design into execution or get the better of the zealous high-priest, who had then held that dignity about sixteen years, went away to Apollonius, governor of Cœlesyria and Palestine under Seleucus, and acquainted him, that there were immense treasures deposited in the temple of Jerusalem, which might be seized upon for the king's use. So the governor sent to inform Seleucus of the matter, who, being in distress for money to pay the Roman tribute, was taken with the bait and dispatched Heliodorus to fetch the treasure away to Antioch.

When this officer arrived at Jerusalem and had disclosed his commission to the high-priest, the pontiff made the strongest remonstrances against the sacrilegious attempt, urging that the sacred treasure consisted of things consecrated to God or the deposits of orphans and widows. Heliodorus, still intent upon executing the king's orders, entered the place with a body of armed men; and, as he was about to seize upon the treasure, there appeared a man on horseback in shining armor, who flew upon him with the utmost fury, and whose horse struck him with his forefeet. At the same time, they saw two other strong, beautiful, and glorious young men standing by him, one on each side, scourging him severely. Heliodorus fell to the ground half dead, and all who presumed to accompany him were struck with fear and trembling. Being carried out in a litter almost dead, he continued in this condition till some of his friends entreated Onias to call upon God to grant him his life; having offered a sacrifice for the man's recovery, he was restored to health. He thereupon went back to Antioch and made a faithful relation to the king of all that had befallen him; adding that if he had any enemy whom he desired to get rid of, he needed but sent him to rifle that sacred place, and he would see him come back in such a condition, as would convince him, that the Jewish temple was under the protection of some divine and irresistible power. Heaven did not long defer punishing this king for his sacrilegious attempt by that very hand which he had employed in it. Seleucus had agreed with the Romans to send his son

Demetrius, then ten years old, to remain a hostage in Rome in the place of his brother Antiochus, who should be allowed to return to Syria. During the absence of the two heirs to the crown, Heliodorus cut off Seleucus by poison and placed himself on the throne. Antiochus, who was then at Athens on his return, obtained by great promises the assistance of Eumenes, king of Pergamus, and Attalus, that king's brother, who led him into Syria with a powerful army, and driven out the usurper, left him in quiet possession of the kingdom. Antiochus took the title of Epiphanes, or The Illustrious, though, by the whole series of his life, he better deserved that of Vile or Despicable, which was given him long before his birth by the prophet Daniel, and which is confirmed by Polybius and Philarchus, his contemporaries, quoted by Athenæus. Livy and Diodorus Siculus say that he would frequently ramble about the streets of Antioch with two or three lewd companions, drink and carouse with the dregs of the people, intrude himself into the parties of the vilest rakes, and be their ringleader in wanton frolics, public lewdness, and a thousand ridiculous follies, without any regard to virtue, law, decency, or his royal character: above all other vices, he was addicted to drunkenness and lust, and most profuse and extravagant in squandering away his revenues. Upon the death of Ptolemy Epiphanes in Egypt and his widow Cleopatra, a war was lighted up between the Syrians and the two Ptolemies, the elder brother surnamed Philometor, and the younger Physcon or Big-bellied, who sometimes reigned jointly, and sometimes the one, sometimes the other alone, as their parties prevailed. However, the latter survived and was the most profligate and barbarous tyrant ever reigned in Egypt.

Joshua or Jesus, the wicked brother of Onias, the good high-priest, blinded by ambition, changed his name into that of Jason, which he thought more conformable and pleasing to the Greeks, and repairing to Antiochus

Epiphanes, as soon as he was settled on the throne, for the price of four hundred and forty talents of silver, procured from him the high-priesthood, and an order that Onias should not only be deposed, but sent to Antioch, and confined to dwell there. Jason, apostatizing in many articles from the Jewish religion, gave Antiochus another sum of a hundred and fifty talents of silver for the liberty of erecting at Jerusalem a gymnasium, or place of public exercises, such as were practiced in Greece, with an academy for training up youth in the fashion and manners of the heathen; and for the liberty of making such as he thought fit free of the city of Antioch. By this bait, he drew many into his apostasy, whom commerce with the heathens and vanity or interest had already disposed to prefer worldly advantages to those to come. Jason had not enjoyed his ill-gotten dignity three years when another Jew, brother of the treacherous Simon above-mentioned, changed his name Onias into that of Menelaus, bought the high-priesthood of Antiochus for three hundred talents more, and outdid Jason in his apostasy, endeavoring to engage the Jews to forsake their religion, and wholly to conform to that of the heathens. He procured Onias, the true high-priest, to be put to death at Antioch.

Ominous signs in the heavens prognosticated the evils that would befall the city of Jerusalem. They were begun by the seditions raised by Jason and Menelaus. Upon a false report that Antiochus was slain in the Egyptian war, Jason came out of the land of the Ammonites and, at the head of a thousand men, possessed himself of the city and temple of Jerusalem. But he was obliged to retire upon the approach of Antiochus, who led his army from Egypt to Jerusalem; in three days, he killed four score thousand Jews in that city, sold forty thousand to neighboring nations for slaves, and made as many more prisoners. His fury did not stop here. He caused the traitor Menelaus, who had recovered his good graces, to lead him into the holiest recesses of the temple, and he laid his impious hands upon all that was most sacred. He seized the golden altar of incense, the golden table of the shew-bread, the golden candlestick, the censors, vessels, and other holy utensils, and the crowns, golden shields, and other ornaments which had been dedicated to the temple, besides one thousand eight hundred talents of gold and silver, which he forcibly took out of the treasury. He took away the gold plating that covered the gates, the veil of the innermost sanctuary, and all that was valuable, whether for its metal or quality. After this, leaving Philip, a most brutish Phrygian, governor of Judea, and the impious Menelaus in possession of the high priesthood, he returned to Antioch in triumph, "*thinking through pride, that he might now make the land navigable, and the sea passable on foot; such was the haughtiness of his mind.*" He thence set out at the head of a numerous army on another expedition into Egypt, having nothing less in view than the entire conquest of that prosperous kingdom. He reduced the country as far as Memphis and received the submission of most other cities and provinces. Thence he marched towards Alexandria, but at Eleusina, a village four miles from that city, was met by Gaius Popillius Laenas, Gaius Decimius Flavus, and Gaius Hostilius Mancinus, three ambassadors sent by the Roman senate, with an order that he should suspend all hostilities, and put an end to the war; which, if he refused to do, the Roman people would no longer look upon him as their friend and ally. Popillius delivered to him this decree at the head of his army. When the king desired to leave to advise his council about an answer, the ambassador drew a circle around him in the sand with the staff he held in his hand and, raising his voice, said: "*You shall not go out of this circle till you either accept or reject the proposal which is made you.*" Hereupon the king answered: "*I will do what your republic requires of me.*"

Antiochus, exceedingly mortified at this check, led back his army; but being resolved to vent his rage upon the Jews, in his return detached Apollonius with twenty-two thousand men to plunder Jerusalem. Apollonius came to that city dissembling his design under an outward show of a peaceable intention. But on the next Sabbath day, when all things were in profound quiet, he commanded his soldiers to go through the streets and massacre all persons they should meet; which they did without the least resistance from the Jews, who suffered themselves to be butchered for fear of violating the Sabbath. About ten thousand persons who escaped the slaughter were carried away captives, and others fled. Apollonius then ordered the city to be plundered and afterward set on fire. The walls were demolished, the service of the temple entirely abandoned, and the holy place everywhere polluted. The temple itself was dedicated to Jupiter Olympius, and his statue was erected on the altar of burnt offerings, which Daniel foretold. Sacrifices were begun to be offered to this abominable idol on the king's birthday, the 25th day of the month Casleu, which answers to part of our November and December.

About the same time, the temple of the Samaritans on Mount Gerizim was dedicated to Jupiter Hospitalis, or the Protector of Strangers, which implied that the Samaritans were not originally natives of that country, but a colony of strangers settled there. They later strove to prevent the king's orders, so ready were they to offer sacrifice to their abominable idol. Many also among the Jews, who professed the true religion, apostatized under this persecution; but others courageously sealed their fidelity to the law of God with their blood. Altars and statues were set up in every town of Judea, and groves were in every part consecrated to idolatrous mysteries; and the Jews were compelled, under pain of death, to offer sacrifice to idols; so that the whole land became a scene of idolatry, debaucheries, and the most horrid butcheries. It was made immediate death to be caught observing the Sabbath, the rite of circumcision, or any other part of the Mosaic law. Two women, having been discovered to have circumcised their children, were led, with their infants hung about their necks, through the streets of Jerusalem and thrown headlong from the walls at length. Great multitudes fled into the deserts and hid in holes and caverns among craggy rocks. Philip, the governor, being informed that a considerable number of Jews were assembled in caves to keep the Sabbath, marched against them with sufficient force; and, after having in vain offered them a general amnesty if they would forsake their religion, caused them all, men, women, and children, to be burnt. The persecutors committed to the flames the books of the law of God and put to death everyone with whom those books were found and whoever observed the law of the Lord. Still, many determined that they would not eat unclean things and would rather die than be defiled with forbidden meats or break the holy law of God.

Among the glorious martyrs who preferred torments and death to the slightest violation of the divine law, one of the most eminent was Eleazer. He was one of the chiefs among the scribes or expounders of the law, a man ninety years old and, notwithstanding his great age, of a comely aspect. His countenance breathing a mixture of majesty and sweetness inspired all who approached him with reverence for his person and confidence in his virtue. The persecutors flattered themselves that they should gain all the rest if they could succeed in perverting this holy man, whose example held many others steadfast. Him, therefore, they brought upon the butchering stage;

and as it was their design not so much to torment as to seduce him, they employed threats and promises successively. Finding these weapons too feeble against so stout a soldier, they had recourse to a ridiculous act of violence, opening his mouth by force that they might at least thrust into it some swine's flesh; not considering that an action in which the heart has no share, can never be construed a criminal transgression of the law; but this free consent was what they could never extort from the martyr. To purchase life by such infidelity he justly regarded as the basest infamy and crime; and, out of a holy eagerness rather than suffer the most dreadful torments and death, he courageously walked of his own accord towards the place of execution. Certain Gentiles or apostates who were his friends, being moved with a false and wicked pity, taking him aside, desired that flesh might be brought which it was lawful for him to eat, that the people might believe that he had eaten swine's flesh. The king was satisfied by such a pretended obedience. Still, the holy old man rejected with horror the impious suggestion. He answered that by such a dissimulation, the young men would be tempted to transgress the law, thinking that Eleazer, at the age of four score and ten years, had gone over to the rites of the heathens; adding that if he should be guilty of such a crime, he could not escape the hand of the Almighty, either alive or dead. Having spoken thus, he was immediately carried to execution; and they that led him were, by his resolute answer, exceedingly exasperated against him. When he was ready to expire under the stripes, he groaned and said: "*O Lord, whose holy light pierces the most secret recesses of our hearts, thou seest the miseries I endure; but my soul feeleth a real joy in suffering these things for the sake of thy law, because I fear thee.*" With these words, the holy man gave up the ghost, leaving, by his death, an example of noble courage and a memorial of virtue to his whole nation.

The glorious conflict of this venerable old man was followed by the martyrdom of seven brothers, who suffered the most exquisite torments with invincible courage and constancy. At the same time, their heroic mother, divested of all the weakness of her sex, stood by, encouraging, and strengthening them, in the Hebrew tongue, and last of all died herself with the same cheerfulness and courage. Their victory was the more glorious because they triumphed over the king in person, who seems to have taken a journey to Jerusalem on purpose to endeavor, by the weight of his authority and by the most brutal inventions of cruelty, to overcome the inflexible constancy of men who were proof against all the deceptions and most barbarous racks of his ministers. Some moderns think they instead suffered at Antioch than at Jerusalem: but this latter city seems to be the theatre of this and the other transactions related by the sacred writer. By order of Antiochus, these seven brothers were apprehended with their mother and tormented with whips and scourges to compel them to eat swine's flesh against their divine law. The eldest said to the tyrant: "*We are ready to die rather than to transgress the laws of God.*" The king, being provoked at this resolute answer, commanded the frying pans and brazen caldrons to be made hot; then the tongue of him who had spoken thus to be cut out, and the skin of his head to be drawn off, and afterward the extremities of his hands and feet to be chopped off, his mother and the rest of his brothers looking on.

When he was maimed in all his parts, the tyrant commanded him, yet alive, to be brought to the fire, and to be fried in a pan. While he was suffering therein a long time, the other brothers and the mother encouraged one another to die manfully because God, who is glorified by the fidelity of his servants, takes pleasure in beholding them suffering for his truth. The first, having thus ended his painful life, the guards advanced with his second brother. The executioner, having flayed off all the hair and skin of his beard, face, and head, inquired whether he would eat the meats the king commanded before they proceeded further and tormented him. Finding, by his answer, that he was in the exact noble resolution with his brother, they inflicted on him the same torment. When he was at the last gasp, he said to the king, with courage and strength which God alone can inspire in those moments: "You indeed destroy our mortal life; but the king of the world for whose laws we suffer will raise us in the resurrection of eternal life." After him, the third was made a laughing stock; and when he was commanded, he quickly put forth his tongue and courageously stretched out his hands, saying with confidence: "These have I received from heaven, and with pleasure resign them, to bear testimony to the laws of God; and I trust that I shall one day receive them again from the omnipotent hand of Him who gave them." The king and his courtiers stood amazed at his courage, not understanding how religion could inspire such an excess of the greatness of soul by which a tender youth despised the most frightful torment in such an age. Still, the tyrant seeing his power set at naught and foiled, grew more enraged than ever. After this martyr was dead, without giving himself time to breathe or to put any questions to the fourth, he commanded him to be flayed, his hands and feet maimed, and his body at length thrown into the burning pan. Still, looking upon the king, he said: "*Death is our advantage, who meet it with an assured hope in God that He will raise us again. As for thee, thou wilt have no share in the resurrection to eternal life.*" No sooner had his brother finished his course, but the fifth was brought forth to be butchered after the like manner unless he chose to accept the conditions of escape. Still, the executioners finding him resolute, inflicted on him the same torments as those already mentioned. Near his end, he told the king that he ought not to imagine God had entirely forsaken his people and that he had reason to tremble for himself, for he should very soon find himself and his family overtaken by the divine vengeance. When he died, the sixth youth was brought forward and put into the hands of the bloody executioners. On his refusal to comply with the king's orders, they immediately fell to work, cutting, slashing, and burning him without being able to shake his constancy. Addressing himself also to the vicious king in his last moments, he said: "*Deceive not thyself; for though we suffer these things because we have offended God, do not flatter thyself that thou wilt escape unpunished: who hast attempted to fight against God.*"

The admirable mother, animated by a lively faith, saw her seven sons slain by the most brutal torments in the space of one day. Filled with heavenly wisdom and more than heroic courage, she overcame the weakness of her sex and, giving nothing to nature, did not let drop one dangerous tear, which might have discouraged her children; all this time, she thought of nothing but of securing their victory to which she animated them by the most vigorous and most inflamed exhortations. She bravely encouraged everyone in her language: "*I know not how you were formed in my womb,*" said she to them, "*you received not a soul or life from me; nor did I frame your limbs. God, the Creator of the world, gave you all this; it is easy for him to repair his work, and he will again restore to you, in His mercy, that breath and life which you now despise for the sake of his laws.*" All this while, the tyrant was intent only on the insult he thought was put upon him by the courageous martyrs, who seemed to outbrave his power, to which he desired to make everything bend. His mind was wholly taken up in carrying his impotent revenge to the utmost extremities. Still, his rage was turned into despair when he saw himself already so often defeated and that of these heroic brothers, there now remained only one tender child alive. He earnestly desired at least to overcome him. For this purpose, he had recourse to that feigned compassion which tyrants often make so dangerous a use of and by a thousand engaging caresses endeavored to seduce him. He called himself his master, his king, and his father. He promised him upon his oath that if he would comply with his desire and turn to his religion, he would make him prosperous, happy, and powerful; would treat him as his friend, and consistently rank him among his principal favorites; in a word, that his obedience should be recompensed beyond his utmost desires.

The youth not being yet moved, the king addressed himself also to the mother with seeming compassion for her loss and implored her to prevail upon her only surviving child; in pity to herself, at least to spare this small remnant of the family, and not give herself the affliction of having her whole offspring torn away from her at once. She joyfully undertook to provide him with counsel, but of a very different kind from that intended by the king; for, bearing towards her son and leaning to his ear, she said in her language: "*My dear child, now my only one, have pity on me thy mother, who bore thee nine months in my womb, and gave thee suck three years, and nourished thee, and brought thee up unto this age. Afflict me not by any base infidelity and cowardice. Look up to the heavens, behold the earth and the vast variety of creatures in both; and consider, I conjure thee, my son, that God made them all out of nothing, by His almighty power. This is the God whom thou adores. Have him before thy eyes, and thou wilt not fear this bloody executioner. Show thyself worthy of thy brothers, and receive death with constancy; that I may have the comfort to see you all joined in martyrdom and meet you in the place of eternal mercy and repose.*"

The young martyr had the patience scarcely to hear his mother finish these words but, desiring to complete his sacrifice and follow his brothers, cried out to his executioners: "*For whom do you wait? I do not obey the king's command but the divine law's precept.*" Then, addressing himself to the king, he said: "*You, who glory in the invention of so much malice and evil against the Hebrews, shall not escape the hand of God. We suffer thus for our sins, yet God will be again reconciled to his servants. My brothers, having undergone a short pain, are under the covenant of eternal life. Like them, I offer up my life and my body for the holy laws of our fathers, begging God to be speedily merciful to our people. In my brothers and me, the wrath of the Almighty shall cease, which has been justly brought upon our nation.*" The king hearing him speak to this purpose, was no longer master of himself but, condemning himself for having had this little spark of patience, resolved to wreak his vengeance on this tender child with greater excess and cruelty than he had done on all his brothers. This last therefore stood the utmost shock of the executioners' rage and exhausted their invention and strength. Persevering faithful to his last breath, he deserved to receive the most glorious crown. Standing alone amidst the mangled limbs of her seven sons, the mother triumphed with joy and embraced their dead bodies with greater tenderness than she had ever embraced them living. She sighed to arrive at the like crown of martyrdom and prayed that God would give her a share in the glory of her sons to survive, whom one day would have been her grief. Antiochus, always the same tyrant, ashamed to yield and incapable of relenting or forgiving, gave orders that the mother should likewise be tormented and put to death. She, therefore, was cut off last of all. These martyrs suffered in the year of the world 3837, of the era of the Seleucidæ 145, before Christ 164.

Antiochus, covered with confusion and shame to see himself defeated by a weak woman and her children, retired; giving everywhere the strictest orders for the destruction of the Jewish religion, but God turned his rage and vain projects to his disgrace and ruin and raised his people again to a flourishing condition. This was affected by the glorious achievements chiefly of the sons of Mattathias, who had left Jerusalem and retired into the mountains near Modin, his native place, when the temple was profaned. He was an eminent priest of the family of Joarib, the first of the twenty-four classes appointed by David to officiate in the temple. He was descended from Aaron by his eldest son and successor, Eleazar. He was the son of John, the son of Simon, the son of Asmoneus, from whom the princes of this family, who afterward reigned in Judea, were called Asmoneans. Mattathias was then very old and had with him his five sons, John surnamed Gaddis, Simon surnamed Thasi, Judas called Machabeus, Eleazar, and Jonathan. When the officers of King Antiochus arrived at Modin, to compel all the Jews to forsake the true religion, he went to the town; and, to encourage others to remain steadfast, declared to those officers that he would continue faithful to God and, imitating the zeal of Phineas, he slew an apostate who was going to offer sacrifice to an idol. After which, he fled into the wilderness and was followed by others. Dying soon after, in the hundred and sixty-sixth year before Christ, he appointed Judas Machabeus general.

With six thousand men, this valiant captain defeated and slew Apollonius, the governor of Samaria and a great persecutor of the Jews, who had marched against him with numerous armies. Seron, deputy-governor of Cœlesyria, under Ptolemy Macron, the chief governor, advanced with a new body of forces but was overthrown and killed. Philip the Phrygian, governor of Jerusalem, was sent to Antioch for succor. Antiochus, being absent beyond the Euphrates, Lysias, whom he had left regent, dispatched forty thousand feet to Ptolemy Macron, governor of Cœlesyria and Phenicia, with Nicanor and Gorgias, two experienced commanders. Still, Judas discomfited Nicanor and burned Gorgias's camp. When Timotheus, governor of the country beyond the Jordan, with Bacchides, another famous general, came up, he met and overthrew them in a set battle, killing twenty thousand of their men. Upon this news, Lysias, the regent, came in person into Judea with sixty thousand feet and five thousand horses. Judas, by divine assistance, gave him an entire overthrow and obliged him to fly to Antioch. After the enemy's retreat, Judas purified the temple, celebrated the dedication for eight days, and restored the sacrifices to the true God. This dedication was performed on the twenty-fifth of the month Casleu, in the hundred and the sixtieth year before Christ, the second of Judas's government, on the very day on which the abomination of desolation had polluted the temple, or the statue of Jupiter Olympius set up in it three years before. Judas prospered exceedingly and performed exploits of velour against three Syrian kings and other enemies of the people of God, far more wonderful and glorious than those of the most famous heroes recorded in profane history. He was no less eminent for virtue and religion. He died in battle with great honor in the hundred and fifty-seventh year before Christ, having been general six years, and executed the office of high-priest three years, as Josephus says.

Menelaus, the apostate high-priest, having been condemned to death by the young King Antiochus IV., or Eupator, son of Epiphanes, and smothered in ashes, Alcimus, an apostate of the race of Aaron, obtained of King Demetrius Soter (who by the murder of Antiochus Eupator, and his regent Lysias, had stepped into the throne) the title of high-priest, and fought against Judas, and his religion and country. Onias, son of Onias III, to whom the high priesthood belonged, retired to Alexandria upon the intrusion of Alcimus and, with leave of Ptolemy Philometer, built a temple at Heliopolis in Egypt for the Hellenistical Jews in the year 169 before Christ. Alcimus being struck with a palsy, and carried off by a miserable death, Jonathan, the worthy brother of Judas Machabeus, who after his death had been chosen general of the people of God, was appointed lawful high-priest in the hundred and fifty-third year before Christ and was succeeded in both those dignities by his virtuous and valiant brother Simon. The posterity of this last enjoyed the same and are called the Asmonean princes. His son and immediate successor, John Hyrcanus, discharged the functions of that double office with virtue, wisdom, and velour; and added to his dominions Idumæa, Samaria, and Galilee. His sons Aristobulus (during a short reign of one year) and Alexander Jannæus, about one hundred and seven years before Christ, assumed the regal diadem and title but degenerated from the virtue of their ancestors. From their time, pride, hypocrisy, and luxury began to overrun the Jewish state and nation and pave the way to the most grievous of all crimes, the crucifixion of the Son of God, by which that ungrateful people completed the measure of their iniquities.

The servants of God equally triumphed by a glorious death or temporal victories in the cause of virtue. The miserable conflict the persecutor sustained with himself in the terrible agonies of his unfortunate death was infinitely different. Antiochus being much distressed for money, his treasury being constantly drained by his perpetual follies and extravagant expenses, he marched with fifty thousand men beyond the Euphrates in quest of spoils; but attempting to plunder a rich temple in Persepolis, and afterward another at Elymais, he was in both places repulsed by the inhabitants. He fled with great grief and shame towards Babylonia. He met an express on the road about Ecbatana with news that Judas had defeated Lysias, taken his fortresses in Judea, and exterminated the idol he had set up. Swelling angrily, he said he would march straight to Jerusalem, making it a sepulcher of the Jews. In this fit of rage, he commanded his chariot to be driven with the utmost speed and without stopping. He had no sooner done speaking than God struck him with an incurable disease, and dreadful pain in his bowels came upon him, and bitter torments of the inner parts. Still breathing revenge in his rage against the Jews and traveling in great haste, he fell from his chariot, and his body was grievously bruised. Then he, who seemed to command the waves of the sea and to be raised above the condition of man, being cast down to the ground, was carried in a litter, worms swarmed out of his body, and his flesh fell off. The man, who, a little before, thought he could reach to the stars, no man could endure carrying because of the intolerable stench of his body, which was noisome to the whole army; and when he was not able to bear the smell of his flesh, and great grief came upon him, he called for all his friends, and said to them: "Sleep is gone from my eyes. *I am fallen away, and my heart is cast down through anxiety. And I said in my heart: Into what tribulation am I come, and into what floods of sorrow, wherein I now am? I who was pleasant and beloved in my power; now I remember the evils I did in Jerusalem. I know that for this cause these evils have found me: and behold I perish with great grief in a strange land.* He promised to make Jerusalem a free city and to favor it with the most honorable privileges, equal to those which the commonwealth of Athens enjoyed; to adorn the temple with lavish gifts, increase the holy vessels, and allow out of his revenues the charges belonging to the sacrifices; also, that he would become a Jew, and go through every place of the earth, and declare the power of God; but his repentance was only founded on temporal motives. Wherefore the Holy Ghost says of him: *This wicked man prayed to the Lord, whom he did not like, to obtain mercy.* He died one hundred and sixty years before the Christian era. The feast of the Seven Maccabees and their mother was celebrated on the 1st of August in the first ages of the church, as may be seen by very ancient Calendars, especially that of Carthage. Also, by those of the Syrians, Arabians, and other Orientals. We have panegyrics in honor of these Martyrs by Saints Gregory of Nazianzus Chrysostom, Augustine, Gaudent, and Leo the Great.

[Butler, Alban. *The Lives of the Fathers, Martyrs, and Other Principal Saints. Compiled from Original Monuments and Authentic Records.* Dublin: James Duffy, 1866. *HathiTrust Digital Library,* catalog.hathitrust.org/Record/001941109.]

Saint Stephen I, Pope and Martyr († 257) — August 2

Since this pope is not a saint of universal significance, his memorial is left for particular calendars. The Depositio Episcoporum (354) lists the death of Stephen not by martyrdom, for the year 267.

Saint Stephen was a Roman by birth. After being promoted to Holy Orders, he was made Archdeacon of Rome under the holy Popes Saint Cornelius and Saint Lucius. When these had both suffered martyrdom, Saint Stephen was elected Head of the Church in 254.

Controversy concerning the rebaptizing of heretics gave Saint Stephen much trouble. The heretics were rebaptizing Catholics who left the orthodox faith to join them; certain oriental bishops decided to rebaptize those who returned to it from their errors, and some African bishops joined them in this practice. It is the teaching of the Catholic Church; however, that baptism given with natural water and in the name of the Three Persons of the Blessed Trinity is valid, even if conferred by those in error. Saint Stephen suffered patiently when accused of favoring heresy by ratifying such baptisms; he did not doubt that the great men in whom a mistaken zeal seemed to obscure the truth would, when the heat of the dispute had subsided, calmly open their eyes to the truth. Thus, by his zeal, he preserved the integrity of the Faith and, by his toleration and forbearance, saved many souls.

When the persecutions grew violent, he assembled the faithful in the underground tombs of the martyrs, going from one catacomb to another to baptize neophytes, celebrate Mass and encourage them to remain faithful to Christ. After twelve members of his clergy were martyred, he was arrested; but he was set free when a violent storm so frightened the soldiers and executioners sent to put him to death that they fled. Nonetheless, he was followed to a catacomb by the emperor's satellites, and on August 2, 257, he was beheaded while seated in his pontifical chair. The chair, stained with his blood, was placed with his relics in the Church he had built and is still shown in the same church, today Saint Sylvester *in capite.*

[Guérin, Abbé (Paul), François Giry, and Simon Martin. *Les Petits Bollandistes: Vies Des Saints De L'Ancien et du Nouveau Testament.* Translated by the Monastère du Magnificat. Paris: Bloud et Barral, 1882. *HathiTrust Digital Library,* hdl.handle.net/2027/nnc1.0036694380; Shea, John G. *Little Pictorial Lives of the Saints, with Reflections for Every Day of the Year; Compiled from "Butler's Lives."* New York: Benziger, 1894. *HathiTrust Digital Library,* hdl.handle.net/2027/nyp.33433068232887.]

Dedication of Our Lady of Snows (435) — August 5

The title of this memorial is changed to the Dedication of the Chapel of St. Mary Major, without any reference to the legendary account of its foundation on Esquiline Hill.

There are in Rome three patriarchal churches in which the Pope officiates on different feast days. These are the Basilicas of Saint Peter on the Vatican Hill, Saint John Lateran, and Saint Mary Major on the Esquiline Hill. The last-named, the Liberian Basilica, was founded in the time of Pope Liberius in the fourth century; it was consecrated to the Virgin Mary by Sixtus III in the year 435, under the title of Saint Mary *ad Nives,* or *at the snow,* because the Mother of God Herself chose, and indicated by a miracle, its site to be that of Her first church in Rome.

In the fourth century, a patrician by the name of John and his pious spouse had no children; already advanced in age and without heirs, they resolved to consecrate their wealth to the Most Blessed Virgin. They prayed to know how the Queen of Heaven would like them to use their fortune. On August 5, 366, She appeared to each of them in a dream and told them that Her Divine Son's and Her own will was that their wealth is employed in the construction of a church on Mount Esquiline, at a place which in the morning they would find covered with snow. They consulted together when the dawn broke and went to the Pope to tell him what God had made known to them. He had had a similar dream and could not doubt that this was a celestial prodigy. He assembled the clergy and people, and all went in procession towards the indicated place to verify the reality of the marvel. When they arrived on the hilltop, they saw an area covered with snow, extending over a space sufficient to build a vast church. It was built at the expense of the noble couple with great magnificence and given the name of Saint Mary of the Snows.

The same Basilica is called Saint Mary *ad Praesepe, of the Manger,* from Bethlehem's holy crib or manger, where the Infant Jesus was laid at His birth. It was transported to Rome and kept in a great underground chapel of the church. Today, this Basilica bears the name of Saint Mary Major because it is the first of the numerous Roman churches dedicated to Mary both by its beauty and antiquity.

[Shea, John G. *Little Pictorial Lives of the Saints, with Reflections for Every Day of the Year; Compiled from "Butler's Lives."* New York: Benziger, 1894. *HathiTrust Digital Library,* hdl.handle.net/2027/nyp.33433068232887.]

Saints Donatus, Bishop of Arezzo in Tuscany, and Hilarinus, Martyrs († 361) — August 7

Donatus was a bishop but not a martyr, as the martyrology of Jerome and the Act of his life are legendary. His memorial, which was added to the Roman calendar in the twelfth century, is now left to the particular calendars. [The feast for Saint Hilarinus (or Hilary) was moved to 16 July.]

Saint Donatus, bishop of Arezzo, a city in Italy in the province of Tuscany, was the son of noble and wealthy parents and very holy and virtuous; for they suffered martyrdom as appears, under Dioclesian and Maximian, leaving Donatus, their son, very young; who, to avoid the fury of the persecution, went to Arezzo; and there became a disciple of a good religious man, Hilarinus, a great servant of God, and one that did diverse miracles. Saint Donatus became a mirror of virtue and sanctity and well-versed in all kinds of good learning. He was thought worthy to be promoted to Holy Orders and was made deacon by Saturus, bishop of that city. After his death, he was chosen by the general consent and congratulation of all the faithful inhabitants, his successor, and the bishop of Arezzo.

God did many incredible miracles by Saint Donatus; amongst which Pope Saint Gregory recounts this: the pagans, having broken a chalice of glass, with which at those times, they used to say Holy Mass; Saint Donatus commanded that all the pieces of it should be gathered up and put together; and then made his prayer to Almighty God, and the chalice was presently entire and whole as if it had never been broken. After which seventy-nine persons that were infidels embraced our holy faith and became Christians, as written by Saint Ado, bishop of Vienna.

He cured divers sick of several diseases; freed many possessed with wicked spirits; in a great drought, he obtained rain from heaven by his prayers; and himself being then out of the city, and returning home in the rain, were not wet.

Eustachtius, one of the emperor's treasurers, had received significant sums of money for the emperor and gave it to his wife to keep, whose name was Euphrosyne. In her husband's absence, who advertised that soldiers were coming to Arezzo, for fear of being plundered by them, hid the money in the ground and died before her husband returned. When Eustachtius came home, he found his wife was dead and knew not what was become of the money. Yet he was called upon to pay it out of hand; and not having the money to discharge so vast a sum, he was exceedingly troubled and perplexed; and at length had recourse to Saint Donatus for counsel and help; who were going with him to the woman's grave, after he prayed some while to our Lord, spoke this: *Euphrosyne, I do conjure and command thee in the name of God, to tell us where thou did hide the money your husband left you.* Presently a voice from the grave was heard, which answered Saint Donatus and told him where the money was hidden, bidding him *dig in such place, for there he found it.* So they went to the assigned location, opened the ground, and found the money; Eustachtius was freed from further pain and trouble.

Saint Antoninus recounts that an honest and good man, having borrowed of his neighbor ten pounds, and had given him underhand a bill of payment of it, at the time appointed, paid it but forgot to take an acquaintance of him or call for his account, and not long after, he died. Still, the deceitful creditor, being a man of no conscience, would not permit the corpse to be buried until he was satisfied, and the money, for which he had the man's hand to show, was paid him. The poor sad widow of the deceased party goes to Saint Donatus. She assures him that her husband had paid the money before his death but had forgotten to take in his bill, and therefore she was *unjustly troubled and her husband deprived of the last rites and obsequies.* Saint Donatus went to the body that lay exposed upon the bier; and said to him: *rise speedily and answer for yourself, for this man prohibits you from being buried.* The dead man immediately arose and, sitting straight on the bier; convinced his creditor of fraud in denying the receipt of the money and making him deliver up his bill, tore it in the presence of all, and then begged Saint Donatus *to let him return to his rest*; which the saint granted him.

Through these and other miracles, he converted many idolaters and waged a terrible war against the devils. When Quadrancianus, a prime officer of Julian the Apostate, had intelligence, he caused both Donatus and Hilarinus to be taken; and compelled to sacrifice to the gods; and when the blessed saints laughed at his menaces and threats, he made Saint Hilarinus so long and so often beaten with cudgels, that he died in the torment.

But Saint Donatus had his mouth cruelly bruised with stones and was kept close for a while in a dark prison and, at last, beheaded. Their bodies were buried near the city. This martyrdom happened on the seventh of August in the year 662, and the second of the reign of Julian. And although Saint Donatus and Saint Hilarinus consummated their martyrdom on the same day, the holy church solemnizes the memory of Saint Donatus on the day of his death and of Saint Hilarinus on the sixteenth of July, when his body was translated to Ostia.

The Martyrologies make mention of Saint Donatus; to wit, the Roman, and those of Saint Bede, Saint Ado, and Saint Usitardus. Saint Antoninus, bishop of Florence, writes of him: *Baronius, in his annotations upon the martyrology, observes the acts of Saint Donatus as confused, as he may see, that will read them in that author. We have taken out what seems to be most accurate and agree with what ecclesiastical, and other authors have written of the reign of Julian.*

At the same time and place, Saint Hilarinus, a monk, received the like crown, being beaten to death with clubs. His relics were afterward translated to Ostia.

[Ribadeneyra, Pedro de. "The Life of Saint Donatus, Bishop and Martyr." *The Lives of Saints, With Other Feasts of the Year, according to the Roman Calendar. Written in Spanish by the Reverend Father Peter Ribadeneyra, Priest of the Society of Jesus. Translated Into English by W.P. (William Petre) Esq; The Second Edition Corrected and Amended*, vol. 2, pp. 146-147. London. Printed by B.S., 1730. *HathiTrust Digital Library*, hdl.handle.net//2027/nyp.33433003053000.; Butler, Alban. *The Lives of the Fathers, Martyrs, and Other Principal Saints. Compiled from Original Monuments and Authentic Records*. Dublin: James Duffy, 1866. *HathiTrust Digital Library*, catalog.hathitrust.org/Record/001941109.]

Saint Cyriacus and his Companions, Martyrs († 303) — August 8

Since only their names and the date of their burial on the Via Ostiensis on August 8 are known, the memorial of Cyriacus, Largus, and Smaragdus is left for the particular calendars, despite its antiquity.

Saint Cyriacus, born of a noble patrician family, embraced the Christian religion and gave all his wealth to the poor. He was ordained a deacon at Rome under Pope Marcellinus. Diocletian was emperor at that time, assisted by Maximian, his favorite. The latter decided to build a beautiful palace for the emperor, with magnificent baths, and to make the Christians work at the construction. Among the new slaves were elderly gentlemen and persons of the highest rank, clerics, and priests. The labor was hard and the food scanty. A Roman nobleman desired to relieve the sufferings of these laborers and sent four Christians with alms and encouragement; these were Saint Cyriacus, Saint Sisinius, Saint Largus, and Saint Smaragdus. They pursued their charities at the risk of their lives and worked vigorously alongside those growing very weak. When Maximian heard of it, he had Saint Sisinius and an old gentleman whom he had helped decapitated.

Saint Cyriacus was well known to Diocletian, who was fond of him. Suddenly Diocletian's daughter became possessed by a furious demon, and she announced that only Cyriacus could deliver her. Diocletian sent for him, and he cured her. She became a Christian like her mother, who is today, Saint Serena. A short time later, the daughter of the king of Persia also became possessed and cried out like Diocletian's daughter that she could be delivered only by Cyriacus, who was in Rome. A message was sent to Diocletian, who asked his wife to persuade the deacon to go to Persia for this purpose. He did so with his two remaining Christian companions and again cast out the demon, thus bringing about the conversion of the king, his family, and the four hundred persons he baptized. The three confessors returned to Rome, having refused all compensation for their services, saying that they had received the gifts of God gratuitously and wished to share them gratuitously, not deriving profit from them.

The barbarous Maximian, hearing of their return in 303, had them seized, imprisoned, tortured, and finally decapitated with twenty other courageous Christians. Their bodies were first buried near the place of their execution on the Via Salaria but were later removed to the city. An abbey in France, at Altorf in Alsace, possesses relics of Saint Cyriacus and bears his name. [The Altdorf Monastery was a Benedictine monastery in Altorf in Alsace, not far from Strasbourg in France. During the French Revolution in 1791, the revolutionaries dissolved the abbey, and the thirteen Benedictine monks were forced to leave.]

[Guérin, Abbé (Paul), François Giry, and Simon Martin. *Les Petits Bollandistes: Vies Des Saints De L'Ancien et du Nouveau Testament.* Translated by the Monastère du Magnificat. Paris: Bloud et Barral, 1882. *HathiTrust Digital Library,* hdl.handle.net/2027/nnc1.0036694380; Shea, John G. *Little Pictorial Lives of the Saints, with Reflections for Every Day of the Year; Compiled from "Butler's Lives."* New York: Benziger, 1894. *HathiTrust Digital Library,* hdl.handle.net/2027/nyp.33433068232887.]

Saint Romanus, Martyr († 258) — August 9

The Acts of Romanus's life are legendary, and his veneration is unknown to the ancient Roman tradition. His memorial, a twelfth-century addition to the Roman calendar, is left for the particular calendars.

Saint Romanus was a soldier in the legion of emperor Valerian in Rome at the time of the arraignment and interrogation of Saint Lawrence. Seeing the joy and constancy and the absolute silence of that holy martyr during his first torments, he could not understand how a creature of flesh and blood could be thus tormented without opening his mouth to complain. He was moved to embrace the Faith, and at that very moment, he beheld beside the Saint a young man of incomparable grace and beauty, who was wiping away the perspiration of the martyr's face and the blood of his wounds. Addressing himself to Saint Lawrence, still on the rack, he asked to become a Christian. The Saint was untied and imprisoned and later was able to respond to the pressing request of the soldier, who brought him in prison the water for his baptism.

Saint Romanus was summoned before the tribunal, for everyone soon learned of his conversion. He said fearlessly and joyfully, there as he had said elsewhere, *I am a Christian!* He was condemned and beheaded immediately, the day before the martyrdom of Saint Lawrence, on August 9, 258. A priest buried the body of Saint Romanus in a cavern on the road to Tibur, but his remains were translated to Lucca, where they are kept under the high altar of a beautiful church that bears his name.

[Guérin, Abbé (Paul), François Giry, and Simon Martin. *Les Petits Bollandistes: Vies Des Saints De L'Ancien et du Nouveau Testament.* Translated by the Monastère du Magnificat. Paris: Bloud et Barral, 1882. *HathiTrust Digital Library,* hdl.handle.net/2027/nnc1.0036694380; Shea, John G. *Little Pictorial Lives of the Saints, with Reflections for Every Day of the Year; Compiled from "Butler's Lives."* New York: Benziger, 1894. *HathiTrust Digital Library,* hdl.handle.net/2027/nyp.33433068232887.]

Saint Tiburtius, Martyr († 286) — August 11

In addition to his name, all that is known of Tiburtius is the date of his burial on the Via Labicana on August 11. His memorial is left for particular calendars.

A certain pagan prefect of Rome, Agrestius Chromatius, saw a holy man named Tranquillinus arrive before his tribunal. The prefect condemned many Christians to martyrdom, including the twin brothers, Marcus and Marcellinus. Still, when Saint Tranquillinus, their father, told him how he had recovered from gout through his baptism, Chromatius listened to him. Unfortunately, he had the same disorder. He sent for a priest and was freed from his infirmity when baptized. He then liberated 400 slaves and retired to a country home, sheltering many Christians who feared they could not resist torture during the persecutions.

Saint Tiburtius, whom the Church honors today, was the son of Chromatius and was baptized with him. He was later ordained a subdeacon and one day raised to life a man whom he found on the ground, his body broken by a fall from the upper story of a residence. Under Diocletian, Tiburtius was betrayed to the persecutors by an unfaithful Christian. He courageously confessed his ardent faith, saying, I sacrifice only to one God, the Creator of the world, who reigns over heaven and earth. My greatest desire is to be immolated and sacrifice myself for this confession. After being condemned to walk on hot coals, which he did without suffering, he was beheaded at a site three miles from Rome. A church was afterward built at this site and named for him.

[Guérin, Abbé (Paul), François Giry, and Simon Martin. *Les Petits Bollandistes: Vies Des Saints De L'Ancien et du Nouveau Testament.* Translated by the Monastère du Magnificat. Paris: Bloud et Barral, 1882. *HathiTrust Digital Library,* hdl.handle.net/2027/nnc1.0036694380; Shea, John G. *Little Pictorial Lives of the Saints, with Reflections for Every Day of the Year; Compiled from "Butler's Lives."* New York: Benziger, 1894. *HathiTrust Digital Library,* hdl.handle.net/2027/nyp.33433068232887.]

Saint Susanna, Virgin, and Martyr († 286) — August 11

The thirteenth-century addition to the Roman calendar of the memorial of Susanna is left to her titular church. The Acts of her life were written to explain the origin of her titular church and are fictitious. Her memorial is left for the particular calendars.

Saint Susanna was nobly born in Rome, the daughter of a certain Gabinius, who, after his conversion, became a priest; she was also the niece of Pope Saint Caius, her father's brother. This family was also related to the emperor Diocletian. Susanna's father had raised her with great care in fear of God and the love of Jesus Christ, and she had made a private vow of virginity. Diocletian, wishing to obtain the consent of this lovely maiden to marry his favorite, Maximian, sent a certain Claudius, another member of her family, to propose the espousals. She refused to consent, making known to her father and Saint Caius her vow and saying that even if she had not resolved to conserve her chastity, she would not wish to marry a man responsible for the massacre of an infinite number of Christians. The emperor's messenger was converted by her confession of faith and became a fervent penitent.

When Diocletian received no answer from his messenger concerning the commission's results and then learned of the conversion of Claudius, he was very irritated. With Claudius, he arrested Suzanne, Gabinius, her father, and several other Christians. He had Suzanne beaten in her residence, then decapitated secretly. The emperor's wife, Prisca, who was also a Christian secret, buried her body clandestinely and prayed to her as a holy martyr. Later the house of Gabinius was transformed by Pope Saint Caius into a church; it eventually became a convent for Cistercian nuns. Saint Susanna suffered towards the beginning of Diocletian's reign, about the year 295.

[Guérin, Abbé (Paul), François Giry, and Simon Martin. *Les Petits Bollandistes: Vies Des Saints De L'Ancien et du Nouveau Testament.* Translated by the Monastère du Magnificat. Paris: Bloud et Barral, 1882. *HathiTrust Digital Library,* hdl.handle.net/2027/nnc1.0036694380; Shea, John G. *Little Pictorial Lives of the*

Saints, with Reflections for Every Day of the Year; Compiled from "Butler's Lives." New York: Benziger, 1894. *HathiTrust Digital Library,* hdl.handle.net/2027/nyp.33433068232887.]

Saint Cassian (of Imola), Martyr (✝ 303) — August 13

Cassian was martyred in the Cornelian Forum, but his cult was not a part of the Roman tradition. The memorial of Cassian was added to the Roman calendar in the fourteenth century and is now left for particular calendars.

He was a Christian schoolmaster and taught children to read and write at Imola, a city twenty-seven miles from Ravenna in Italy. Violent persecution being raised against the church, probably that of Decius or Valerian, or according to some, that of Julian, he was taken up and interrogated by the province's governor. As he constantly refused to sacrifice to the gods, the atrocious judge, having informed himself of what profession he was, commanded that his scholars should stab him to death with their iron writing pencils, called styles; for at that time, it was the custom for scholars to write upon wax laid on a board of boxen wood, in which they formed the letters with an iron style or pencil, sharp at one end, but blunt and smooth at the other, to erase what was to be effaced or corrected. They also often wrote on boxen wood itself, as Saint Ambrose mentions. The smaller the instruments were, and the weaker the executioners, the more lingering and crueler this martyr's death. He was exposed naked to two hundred boys; among whom some threw their tablets, pencils, and penknives at his face and head and often broke them upon his body; others cut his flesh or stabbed him with their penknives, and others pierced him with their pencils, sometimes only tearing the skin and flesh, and sometimes raking in his very bowels. Some made it

356

their brutal sport to cut part of their writing task in his tender skin. Thus, covered with his blood and wounded in every part of his body, he cheerfully bade his little executioners not to be afraid; and to strike him with greater force; not meant to encourage them in their sin but to express the ardent desire he had to die for Christ. The Christians interred him at Imola, where afterward, his relics were honored with a rich mausoleum. Prudentius tells us that on his journey to Rome, he visited this holy martyr's tomb and prostrated before it implored the divine mercy for the pardon of his sins with many tears. He mentions a moving picture of the saint's martyrdom hanging over the altar, representing his cruel death in the manner he has recorded it in verse. He encourages all others with him to commend their petitions to this holy martyr's patronage, who fails not to hear pious supplications. His sacred remains are venerated in a rich shrine at Imola in the cathedral.

[Butler, Alban. *The Lives of the Fathers, Martyrs, and Other Principal Saints. Compiled from Original Monuments and Authentic Records.* Dublin: James Duffy, 1866. *HathiTrust Digital Library,* catalog.hathitrust.org/Record/001941109.]

Saint Eusebius, Priest, and Martyr (✝ end of the Third Century) — August 14

The ancient memorial of Eusebius is left to the calendar of his titular church on the Esquiline. The martyrology of Jerome mentions Eusebius as the founder of the church that bears his name.

The Church celebrates on this day the memory of Saint Eusebius, who distinguished himself among the Christians of his time by his spirit of prayer and apostolic virtues. When he was arraigned, Maxentius, the governor of the province, interrogated him and was furious at the

Saint's constancy while he was placed on the rack, and his sides were torn with iron hooks. He sentenced him to die by fire at the stake. Still, his unusual serenity when going to the place of execution caused him to be summoned back to the tribunal, obviously by a particular disposition of Providence.

The emperor himself being in the region, the governor went to him and told him the prisoner asked to be taken before him. The reason for this request was that there had not been any recent edicts published against the Christians. Saint Eusebius was advanced in age, and the emperor Maximian said, after questioning him, "*What harm is there that this man should adore the God he talks of as superior to all the others?*" But the brutal Maxentius would not listen, and, like Pilate facing Christ, the Emperor told the persecutors of the accused man to judge the affair themselves. Maxentius, therefore, sentenced him to be decapitated. Eusebius, hearing the sentence, said aloud, "*I thank Your goodness and praise Your power, O Lord Jesus Christ, because in calling me to prove my fidelity, You have treated me as one of Yours.*" His martyrdom occurred towards the end of the third century.

[Shea, John G. *Little Pictorial Lives of the Saints, with Reflections for Every Day of the Year; Compiled from "Butler's Lives."* New York: Benziger, 1894. *HathiTrust Digital Library,* hdl.handle.net/2027/nyp.33433068232887; Guérin, Abbé (Paul), François Giry, and Simon Martin. *Les Petits Bollandistes: Vies Des Saints De L'Ancien et du Nouveau Testament.* Translated by the Monastère du Magnificat. Paris: Bloud et Barral, 1882. *HathiTrust Digital Library,* hdl.handle.net/2027/nnc1.0036694380.]

Saint Hyacinth (of Poland), Missionary Preacher and Thaumaturge († 1257)

The memorial of Hyacinth, who died at Kraków on August 15, 1257. entered the Roman calendar in 1625.

Since he is not of universal significance, his memorial is left to the particular calendars.

Saint Hyacinth, named the glorious Apostle of the North, was born to noble parents in Poland in about 1185. In 1218, as a Canon of Kraków, he accompanied the bishop of that region to Rome. There he met Saint Dominic and soon afterward was one of the first to receive the habit of the Friar Preachers, in a group clothed by the patriarch himself. He became a living copy of his dear master. The church was his only chamber, and the ground his only bed. So remarkable was his progress in virtue that Dominic sent him with a small group to preach and plant the Order in Poland, where he founded two houses within a year.

His apostolic journeys extended over numerous and vast regions. Austria, Bohemia, Livonia, the shores of the Black Sea, Tartary, Northern China in the east, Sweden, Norway, and Denmark to the west, were evangelized by him, and he is said to have visited Scotland. Everywhere he traveled unarmed, without a horse, with no money, no interpreters, no furs in the severe winters, and often without a guide, abandoning to Divine Providence his mission in its entirety. Everywhere multitudes were converted, churches and convents were built; one hundred and twenty thousand pagans and infidels were baptized by his hands. He worked many miracles; at Kraków, he raised a dead youth to life. He had inherited from Saint Dominic perfect filial confidence in the Mother of God; to Her, he ascribed his success, and to Her aid, he looked for his salvation. At the request of this indefatigable missionary, Saint Thomas Aquinas wrote his famous philosophical *Summa contra Gentiles*, proving the reasonableness of the Faith on behalf of those unfamiliar with doctrine.

While Saint Hyacinth was in Kyiv, the Tartars sacked the town, but it was only as he finished Mass that the Saint heard of the danger. Without waiting to un-vest, he took the ciborium in his hands and left the church. Then occurred the most famous of his countless prodigies. As he passed by a statue of Mary, a voice said: "*Hyacinth, My son, why do you leave Me behind? Take Me with you....*" The figure was heavy alabaster, but when Hyacinth took it in his arms, it was light as a reed. With the Blessed Sacrament and the statue, he walked to the Dnieper River and crossed dry-shod over the surface of the waters to the far bank.

On the eve of the Assumption, 1257, he was advised of his coming death. Despite an unrelenting fever, he celebrated Mass on the feast day and communicated as a dying man. He was anointed at the foot of the altar and died on the great Feast of Our Lady.

[Shea, John G. *Little Pictorial Lives of the Saints, with Reflections for Every Day of the Year; Compiled from "Butler's Lives."* New York: Benziger, 1894. *HathiTrust Digital Library,* hdl.handle.net/2027/nyp.33433068232887.]

Saint Agapetus, Martyr (✝ 274) — August 18

Since the Acts of life of Agapetus are false, his memorial is left for the particular calendars.

Saint Agapetus suffered a cruel martyrdom at Praeneste, now called Palestrina, twenty-four miles from Rome in his youth. He had dared to reproach for his cruelty towards the Christians, one of Emperor Aurelian's favorites, who immediately gave the order to arrest him. He was flogged with leaden-tipped straps and scorpions; his constancy and prayer under torture converted five hundred pagans, who declared themselves Christians and were executed at once. The young martyr was thrown into a horrible prison where a heavenly vision fortified him. After a second questioning, he was again scourged, then laid upon the rack that his body might be torn with iron nails.

He still lived and was again ordered to sacrifice to Apollo; his refusals won for him still more torments: live coals on his head, suspension by his feet, boiling water poured over him. His courage was superhuman, his answers admirable. Wild beasts in the arena spared him and lay down at his feet, and still more pagans were converted. He was finally beheaded, and the Christians buried his body in a field where they found a new tomb prepared as though for his sepulcher. Two churches in Palestrina and others in various places are dedicated to God under his name.

[Guérin, Abbé (Paul), François Giry, and Simon Martin. *Les Petits Bollandistes: Vies Des Saints De L'Ancien et du Nouveau Testament.* Translated by the Monastère du Magnificat. Paris: Bloud et Barral, 1882. *HathiTrust Digital Library,* hdl.handle.net/2027/nnc1.0036694380.]

Saint Timothy, Martyr († 311) — August 22

All that is known about Timothy, apart from his name, is that he was buried on the Via Ostiensis on August 22. His memorial is left for particular calendars.

In the time of Saint Melchiades, the pope came to Rome from Antioch, a man of quality called Timothy, very learned and skilled in the holy scriptures and zealous in the service of God. So he lodged in the house of Sylvester, who afterward was pope, and baptized the emperor, Constantine. Timothy, being in Rome, began to be famous for his blameless life and excellent learning, confirming the faithful in the faith of Christ converting many Gentiles by his preaching and illuminating them with the light of the gospel.

He employed himself a year in these holy exercises and at last was taken by the governor Tarquinius, who seeing he could by no means draw him from the confession of Christ, commanded him to be cruelly whipped three times. After that, he afflicted him with long and hard imprisonment, dislocated his members upon the rack Equuleus, and rent his body by other torments, and he caused him to be beheaded. Sylvester carried his body to his own house. Afterward, a worthy matron, called Theodora, buried it in her garden in the Way of Ostia, near the tomb of the apostle Saint Paul, in whose church it was afterward honorably placed. The Church makes commemoration of Saint Timothy upon the day of his martyrdom, which was the 22nd of August, in the year of our Lord, 311.

[Ribadeneyra, Pedro de. "The Life of St. Timothy, Martyr." *The Lives of Saints, With Other Feasts of the Year, according to the Roman Calendar. Written in Spanish by the Reverend Father Peter Ribadeneyra, Priest of the Society of Jesus. Translated Into English by W.P. (William Petre) Esq; The Second Edition Corrected and Amended,* vol. 2, p. 202. London. Printed by B.S., 1730. *HathiTrust Digital Library,* hdl.handle.net//2027/nyp.33433003053000.]

Saint Symphorianus, Martyr († 180) — August 22

The veneration of Symphorianus, who suffered martyrdom by the Aedui[97], is not a part of the Roman tradition. His memorial, placed on the Roman calendar in the thirteenth century, is left to the particular calendars.

About 180, a grand procession in honor of the Roman goddess Ceres was organized at Autun in southern

---

[97] A tribe of Roman-allied Celts who lived in the area between the current Saône and Loire rivers.

France. Among the crowd was one who refused to pay the ordinary marks of worship. That non-conformist was therefore dragged before the magistrate and accused of sacrilege and sedition. When asked his name and condition, he replied, "*My name is Symphorianus. I am a Christian.*" He was the son of a noble Christian family, still young and so innocent that he was thought to converse with the holy Angels. Moreover, the Christians of Autun were few and little known, and the judge could not believe that the youth was serious in his purpose.

Nevertheless, he caused the laws enforcing pagan worship to be read, expecting ready compliance. The young man replied that it was the law of the King of kings that he must obey. "*Give me a hammer,*" he said, "*and I will break your idol into pieces.*"

He was scourged and thrown into a dungeon. Some days later, this son of light came from the darkness of his prison, haggard and worn but full of joy. He despised the riches and honors offered to him as he had despised torments. He died by the sword and went to the court of his heavenly King. The mother of Saint Symphorianus stood on the city walls and saw her son taken out to die. She knew the honors he had refused and the dishonor of his death, but she esteemed the approval of Christ better than all the riches of the earth, and she cried out to him, "*My son, my son, keep the living God in your heart; look up to Him who reigns in heaven!*" Thus, she shared in the glory of his passion, and her name lives with his in the records of the Church. Many miracles spread the glory of Saint Symphorianus and Christ, the King of all Saints.

[Shea, John G. *Little Pictorial Lives of the Saints, with Reflections for Every Day of the Year; Compiled from "Butler's Lives."* New York: Benziger, 1894. *HathiTrust Digital Library,* hdl.handle.net/2027/nyp.33433068232887.]

Saint Philip Benizi, Servite Priest (1233-1285) — August 23

The memorial of Philip, who died on August 22, 1285, entered the general calendar in 1690. His feast is now left to the particular calendars since he is not of universal significance.

Saint Philip Benizi was born in Florence on the Feast of the Assumption, 1233. That same day the Order of Servites was founded by the Mother of God. As an infant one-year-old, Philip spoke in the presence of these new religious and announced the Servants of the Virgin. Amid all the temptations of his youth, he longed to become a Servant of Mary, and it was only the fear of his unworthiness that made him yield to his father's wish and begin to study medicine. As a result, he received the bonnet of a doctor of medicine at Padua.

After long and weary waiting, his doubts were solved one day by Our Lady Herself, who, in a vision during a Mass in Florence offered in the Servite Chapel, bade him enter Her Order. Still, Philip dared only show himself as a lay brother, saying nothing of his studies. He strove to do penance for his sins in this humble state. Two Dominican Fathers traveling with him one day recognized the great talents, wisdom, and knowledge he had succeeded in concealing. They talked to his Superiors and told him to prepare for the priesthood. As a priest, he did immense good. He pacified many dissensions common among the city-states of those days. One day he met a leper, almost naked and without money, and gave him his tunic. When the leper put it on, he was instantly cured.

After that, honors were accorded him in rapid succession; he became General of the Order, and only by flight did he escape elevation to the Papal throne; he retired to a grotto in the mountains until the conclave had ended. His preaching restored peace to Italy, which was wasted by civil wars. He was sent not only to various cities of that country but to the Netherlands and Germany, where he converted many, not without opposition and even a flogging by rebels. At the Council of Lyons, he spoke to the assembled prelates with the gift of tongues. Yet, amid all these favors, Philip lived in extreme penitence, constantly examining his soul before God and condemning himself as only fit for hell.

Even though Saint Philip was free from every stain of mortal sin, he was never weary of imploring God's mercy. From the time he was ten years old, he prayed the Penitential Psalms daily. On his deathbed, he recited verses of the *Miserere,* his cheeks streaming with tears; during his agony, he went through a terrible contest to overcome the fear of damnation. But a few minutes before he died, all his doubts disappeared and were succeeded by a holy trust. He uttered the responses to the final prayers in a low but audible voice; when the Mother of God appeared before him at last, he lifted his arms with joy and breathed a gentle sigh as if placing his soul in Her hands. He died on the Octave of the Assumption, 1285.

[Shea, John G. *Little Pictorial Lives of the Saints, with Reflections for Every Day of the Year; Compiled from "Butler's Lives."* New York: Benziger, 1894. *HathiTrust Digital Library,* hdl.handle.net/2027/nyp.33433068232887.]

Saint Zephyrinus, Pope, and Martyr († 217) — August 26

No reason exists to consider Zephyrinus a martyr (217), nor is August 26 the day of his death. His memorial, a thirteenth-century addition to the Roman calendar, is abolished.

Saint Zephyrinus, a native of Rome, succeeded Victor I in the pontificate in the year 198. In 202, Septimus Severus, a military despot, raised the fifth and most bloody persecution against the Church for nine years until the emperor died in 211. Until this furious storm ended, the holy pastor remained concealed for the sake of his flock, supporting and comforting the distressed disciples of Christ. He suffered by charity and compassion that every confessor underwent. The triumphs of the martyrs were indeed his joy, but his heart received many deep wounds from the fall of apostates and heretics. Nor did this latter affliction cease when peace was restored to the Church. The holy Pope had the affliction of witnessing the fall of Tertullian. However, he saw to his joy the conversion of Natalis, who had become a heretical bishop, when he lapsed into the Theodotian heresy. God, wishing to bring him back to the Church, sent him a solid correction which opened his eyes, and he came to kneel at the feet of the Vicar of Christ, wearing a hair shirt and humbly asking pardon for his revolt.

Eusebius tells us that this holy Pope exerted his zeal so strenuously against the heretics' blasphemies that they treated him with the utmost contempt. To his glory, however, they also called him the principal defender of Christ's divinity. Saint Zephyrinus governed the Church for nineteen years, dying in 217 as a martyr under Antoninus Caracalla. He was buried in his cemetery on the 26th of August.

[Guérin, Abbé (Paul), François Giry, and Simon Martin. *Les Petits Bollandistes: Vies Des Saints De L'Ancien et du Nouveau Testament.* Translated by the Monastère du Magnificat. Paris: Bloud et Barral, 1882. *HathiTrust Digital Library,* hdl.handle.net/2027/nnc1.0036694380; Shea, John G. *Little Pictorial Lives of the Saints, with Reflections for Every Day of the Year; Compiled from "Butler's Lives."* New York: Benziger, 1894. *HathiTrust Digital Library,* hdl.handle.net/2027/nyp.33433068232887.]

Saint Hermes, Martyr († 132) — August 28

Only the name of Hermes is known because he was buried on the Via Salaria on August 28. His memorial is left for particular calendars.

Among the Roman Gentry was Hermes, a very noble and wealthy man and Governor of the City of Rome; who, having seen his son raised from death to life, illuminated with light from heaven, received holy baptism, together with his wife and children, and sister, Theodora, and all his family, which consisted of one thousand two hundred and fifty persons. Moreover, he gave liberty to his slaves and the poor, his servants a good part of his wealth, and his son the government of his house, preparing him for martyrdom. The conversion of Saint Hermes made a great noise throughout the city because he was a person of such note and quality and so well known.

Prefect Aurelius[98] commanded him to be apprehended with Saint Alexander and committed him to the charge of Quirinus, tribune or master of the camp. They had a daughter, Balbina, who was very sick of the king's evil. Quirinus, compassionating Saint Hermes, said to him that he wondered if a man of such quality, and so high dignity, who has held for so a wife and discreet a man as he was, would suffer himself to be so abused; and for a foolish superstition would lose such great honor, nobility, riches, and be basely fettered in a filthy prison: for seeing the happiness of man ended with his life, he was only once to be born and once to die; and whereas he could enjoy the pleasures and goods of this life, he would instead make a choice of the sufferings and miseries he endured, which could avail and profit him nothing.

---

[98] Aurelius Heraclianus, † 268.

Saint Hermes answered that he had been in the same error, but Saint Alexander had freed him from it and had also restored life to a son of his and sight to his servant and nurse. Moreover, he solved his arguments and agreed that if Saint Alexander, who was bound in chains in another prison, should come that night to visit Hermes, Quirinus should embrace the faith of Christ. Quirinus, his doubled fetters and guards upon Saint Alexander, that he might not get out of prison and come to see Hermes. But, Saint Alexander, conducted by an angel, who appeared to him with a torch in his hand, in the shape of a child, of about five years old, came to the house of Quirinus, visited Saint Hermes, and cured Balbina, Quirinus's daughter, of the king's evil.

Whereas upon Quirinus and all his family, illuminated by the light of heaven, made themselves Christians and were all of them afterward martyrs of the Lord. For the prefect, Aurelian, having understood what had passed, commanded all those baptized to be put into a ship and, with stones tied to their necks, to be cast out into the deep sea. So Quirinus was diversely tormented and, at last, beheaded. Saint Hermes passed the same sentence, whose body his sister, Saint Theodora, took and buried in the way called Via Salaria, not far from Rome.

The martyrdom of Saint Hermes was upon the 28th of August, upon which the holy church celebrates it, and happened in the year of our Lord, 132 A.D., with Hadrian being emperor. Pelagius, the second pope of that name, adorned and illustrated the place where Saint Hermes was buried. All the Martyrologies make mention of his martyrdom, especially that of Ado, which treats more largely of it, taking out the acts of Saint Alexander, martyr, what is there written concerning it, which acts are in the third tome of Surius.

[Ribadeneyra, Pedro de. "The Life of St. Hermes, Martyr." *The Lives of Saints, With Other Feasts of the Year, according to the Roman Calendar. Written in Spanish by the*

Reverend Father Peter Ribadeneyra, Priest of the Society of Jesus. Translated Into English by W.P. (William Petre) Esq; The Second Edition Corrected and Amended, vol. 2, pp. 229-230. London. Printed by B.S., 1730. *HathiTrust Digital Library,* hdl.handle.net//2027/nyp.33433003053000.]

Saint Sabina, Martyr († 126) — August 29

The Acts of the life of Sabina are entirely legendary. Nevertheless, her memorial is left on the calendar of her titular church on the Viale Aventino.

She was a wealthy widow of high birth and lived in the province of Umbria in Italy. She had a servant called Seraphia, a native of Antioch in Syria, who was a zealous Christian and served God in the holy state of virginity. The religious deportment of this virtuous maidservant had such an influence over the mistress that she was converted to the Christian faith; and so powerfully did the great truths of our holy religion operate on her soul that her fervor and piety soon rendered her name illustrious among the great lights of the church, at the beginning of the second century. The persecution of Hadrian began to rage, and Beryllus, governor of the province, caused Sabina and Seraphia to be apprehended and the latter to be beaten to death with clubs. Sabina was discharged out of regard to her quality and friends, but her zeal procured her the crown of martyrdom the year following. She suffered at Rome, as the Bollandists have proved. She is honored on the 29th of August and again with Saint Seraphia on the 3rd of September because, on that day, as Ado informs us, a famous ancient church was dedicated to God in Rome, under the patronage of those two saints, in 430. It, at present, bears only the name of Saint Sabina. In it was kept the first among the stations in Lent, till, in the last century, the public prayers of forty hours succeeded the devotion of the stations, equally being the general assembly of the city in the same church to join in prayer.

[Shea, John G. *Little Pictorial Lives of the Saints, with Reflections for Every Day of the Year; Compiled from "Butler's Lives."* New York: Benziger, 1894. *HathiTrust Digital Library,* hdl.handle.net/2027/nyp.33433068232887.]

Saints Felix and Adauctus, Martyrs († 303) — August 30

Only the names of Felix and Adauctus are known, and the date of their burial (August 30) in the cemetery of Commodilla (Catacomba di Commodilla) on the Via Ostiensis. Their memorial is left to the particular calendars.

In the time of the emperors Dioclesian and Maximian, there were in Rome two holy brother priests, both called Felix[99], which means *happy*, and they were so no less in life than name. The elder of the two brothers was apprehended by the command of the emperors and carried to the Temple of Serapis[100] to adore the false gods. But the saint looking upon the statue and idol of metal in the temple breathed in the face of it, and it fell and broke into pieces. The same happened in the Temple of Mercury[101] and in that of Diana[102]. So the judge commanded him to be cruelly tormented on the rack of

---

[99] From a Latin word meaning "happy or lucky".

[100] In Ancient Rome, the Temple of Serapis was a sanctuary dedicated to the god Serapis and the goddess Isis. The temple was built on an unknown date, but it was known to exist during Caracalla's reign. It was known as Quirinal Hill's most monumental temple.

[101] The Temple of Mercury was a sanctuary dedicated to the god Mercury on the Aventine Hill in Ancient Rome. The temple was established in 495 BC. It was one of Rome's oldest temples. It was still known to exist in the third century.

[102] The Temple of Diana was an edifice in ancient Rome that was built in the 6th century BC during the reign of King Servius Tullius, according to the early semi-legendary history of Rome.

Equuleus[103], to know of him by what sorcery he had thrown down and broken into pieces their gods. And the saint answered, "*What I have done, I have not done it with the help of a devil, but by the power and virtue of God.*" So the judge, in fury and rage, caused him to be carried out of the city by the Via Ostiensis, where there was a very high tree consecrated to the devils and close by a temple they intended Felix to offer sacrifice.

The saint came to the tree, made his prayer, and with great confidence (as if he was speaking to somebody) said to it, "*I command thee in the name of my Lord Jesus Christ, that plucked up by the roots, thou fall upon this temple hereby and break into pieces the altar or statue which is in it that henceforward no souls may be deceived by thee.*" He had no sooner said that the tree fell upon the temple and ruined it and broke the idol into pieces that one could not say there had been one before. The judge, having understood, commanded him to be beheaded and his body to be left in the fields to be eaten by the wolves and dogs.

Another Christian, unknown to men but well-known to God, saw him go to his execution, and understanding that he went to die for Christ, inflamed with love for the same Christ, began to say in a loud voice, "*According to the same law that this man lives, do I live also. He confesses Jesus Christ for God, and so do I*". The ministers of justice hearing this laid hold of him, and by their permission, he went first to Saint Felix and gave him the kiss of peace, with him beheaded.

Not knowing his name, the Christians called him in Latin, Adauctusbecause he had joined himself to Saint Felix as his companion so that he might receive the crown of martyrdom with him in heaven. And in the night, they

---

[103] The rack was known as Equuleus in Roman sources; the word fidicula (torture instrument), more commonly the name of a small lyre or stringed instrument, was used to describe a similar torture device, though its exact design has been lost.

buried their holy bodies in a significant hole that the great tree had left when it fell upon the temple by the prayer of Saint Felix. The Gentiles would have taken them out thence, but the devil entered them and tormented them. And afterward on that place was built a fair church, which becoming decayed was repaired by Saint John, pope, as is to be seen in the Book of the Bishops of Rome. The Church celebrates the feast of these martyrs upon the thirtieth of August, the day of their martyrdom in the year 302, Dioclesian and Maximian emperors. What has been related is taken from Ado's Martyrology. Other Martyrologies and those of Bede and Usuardus also make mention of these saints.

[Ribadeneyra, Pedro de. "The Lives of the holy martyrs, Felix and Adauctus." *The Lives of Saints, With Other Feasts of the Year, according to the Roman Calendar. Written in Spanish by the Reverend Father Peter Ribadeneyra, Priest of the Society of Jesus. Translated Into English by W.P. (William Petre) Esq; The Second Edition Corrected and Amended, vol. 2, pp. 235-236.* London. Printed by B.S., 1730. *HathiTrust Digital Library,* hdl.handle.net/2027/nyp.33433003053000.]

Saint Raymund Nonnatus, Religious of Our Lady of Mercy and Cardinal (1204-1240) — August 31

The memorial of Raymond, who died in Cerdanya, Spain, in 1240, was listed in the Roman calendar in 1669. It is now left to the particular calendars since he is not considered among those saints of universal significance.

Saint Raymund Nonnatus was born in Catalonia, Spain, in 1204. Motherless from infancy, in his childhood, he seemed to find pleasure only in his devotions and serious duties. He chose the Blessed Virgin for his mother almost as soon as the light of reason made this choice available to him. His father, perceiving an inclination to the religious state and unwilling to give up his son, took him from school and sent him to care for a farm he owned in the country. Raymund readily obeyed and, to enjoy holy solitude, kept the sheep and spent his time in the mountains and forests in holy meditation and prayer. He found there an ancient hermitage containing a portrait of his Blessed Mother and made this his asylum. There the devil found him and, assuming the disguise of a shepherd, attempted to turn him away from his devotions, but Raymund turned his back on his visitor and called Mary to assist. The sole name of the Mother of God caused the demon to disappear, and the hermit prostrated himself and blessed Her for Her assistance.

Sometime afterward, he joined the new Order of Our Lady of Mercy for the redemption of captives. He was admitted to the profession at Barcelona by the holy founder, Saint Peter Nolasco. Within two or three years after his profession, he was sent into Barbary with a considerable sum of money; in Algiers, he purchased the liberty of many slaves. When all his treasure was exhausted, he gave himself up as a hostage for the ransom of others, according to the Rule of his Order. This magnanimous sacrifice only exasperated the Moslems, who treated him with uncommon barbarity until they began to fear that if he died in their hands, they would lose the ransom which had been asked for his deliverance. A crier announced in the streets that anyone who mistreated him would answer for it if he died.

Therefore, he was permitted to go abroad in the streets, which he utilized to comfort and encourage the Christians in chains and convert and baptize certain Moslems. Learning of this, their pasha, furious, condemned him to be impaled, but his severe sentence was commuted at the insistence of those who had an interest in the ransom payments for the slaves he was replacing. Instead, he underwent a cruel bastinade, but that torment did not daunt his courage. So long as he saw souls in danger of perishing eternally, he thought he had yet done nothing.

Saint Raymund had no more money to employ to release poor captives and converse with those of the local beliefs about religion meant death. He enjoyed sufficient liberty nonetheless to continue the same endeavors, and he did so, hoping either for success or martyrdom. The governor, enraged, ordered our Saint to have his lips pierced and padlocked, then to be imprisoned until members of his Order would bring his ransom. He remained in jail for eight months before his brethren arrived with the required sum, sent by Saint Peter Nolasco.

Upon his return to Spain, he was nominated Cardinal by Pope Gregory IX, and the Pope called him to Rome. The Saint was on his way but had gone no farther than Cardona when he was seized with a violent fever. He died on August 31, 1240, in his thirty-seventh year. His face in death became beautiful and radiant like that of Moses when he descended from the mountaintop, where he had spoken with God. A heavenly fragrance surrounded his body, and cures were affected on behalf of those who came and touched him.

[Shea, John G. *Little Pictorial Lives of the Saints, with Reflections for Every Day of the Year; Compiled from "Butler's Lives."* New York: Benziger, 1894. *HathiTrust Digital Library,* hdl.handle.net/2027/nyp.33433068232887.]

SEPTEMBER

Saint Giles, Abbot (640~720) — September 1

The account of Giles's life is legendary, and his memorial, a twelfth-century addition to the general calendar, is left for particular calendars.

Saint Giles, whose name has been held in great veneration for many centuries in France and England, was born in the year 640 in Athens and was of noble extraction. Particular remarkable works of medicine and poetry are attributed to him, but his knowledge was primarily that of the Saints.

As a young man, he met a poor beggar who was sick and half-naked. He was moved with compassion and gave him his splendid tunic; the moment the beggar put it on, he found himself in perfect health. Through this miracle, Giles understood how pleasing almsgiving is to God. Shortly afterward, he distributed all his goods to the poor and entered a life of poverty, suffering, and humility. But Jesus Christ did not let Himself be outdone in generosity, and soon miracles multiplied so greatly in his wake that the world's admiration surrounded him. It became impossible for him to profit in his own country from obscurity and retirement, which he desired more than anything else. He, therefore, went to France and chose for his hermitage the open spaces of the south, near the mouth of the Rhone.

Soon he was known there, too, by the miracles his kindness brought down from heaven. So he moved again, and this time Providence brought him near Saint Veredemus, a hermit of Greek origin like himself; then, the two rejoiced in the ordinary life of God's love. So for two years, they remained together until the invasion of their solitude caused Giles to migrate to a deep forest in southeastern France, in the diocese of Nimes.

He spent many years in this intense solitude, living on wild herbs or roots and clear water and conversing only with God. He was nourished there by a doe of the forest. One day, being pursued by Visigoths[104] hunting in the woods, she fled for refuge to the Saint and lay down at his feet. Being moved to tears, he prayed for God to spare the innocent animal's life. But, unfortunately, an arrow the hunters had sent in her direction came and lodged in his hand, making a wound that would never heal. When the hunters found the animal there and saw the bleeding wound of the gentle hermit, they begged his pardon on their knees, and the chase was ended. The Visigoth king came to visit this holy hermit, accompanied by the bishop, who afterward ordained Giles, a priest.

The reputation of the sanctity of Saint Giles was constantly increased by his many miracles, which rendered his name famous throughout France. He was highly esteemed by the pious king but could not be prevailed upon to leave his solitude. Finally, he accepted several disciples and established excellent discipline in the monastery the king built for them. Destroyed during the invasions of the Moslems who had entered Spain, it was rebuilt during the lifetime of the founder and his disciples when they returned after the torment. In succeeding ages, it became a flourishing abbey of the Benedictine Order, which bore his name.

[Shea, John G. *Little Pictorial Lives of the Saints, with Reflections for Every Day of the Year; Compiled from "Butler's Lives."* New York: Benziger, 1894. *HathiTrust Digital Library,* hdl.handle.net/2027/nyp.33433068232887; Jaud, Leon. *Vie Des Saints Pour Tous Les Jours De L'annee: Avec Une Pratique De Piete Pour Chaque Jour.* Translated by the Monastère du Magnificat. Tours: A. Mame, 1950. Print; Guérin, Abbé (Paul), François Giry, and Simon Martin. *Les Petits Bollandistes: Vies Des Saints De L'Ancien et du Nouveau Testament.* Translated by the Monastère du Magnificat.

---

104 The Visigoths were an early Germanic people who, along with the Ostrogoths, formed the two major political entities of the Goths within the Roman Empire during the Migration Period.

Paris: Bloud et Barral, 1882. *HathiTrust Digital Library,* hdl.handle.net/2027/nnc1.0036694380.]

Saints Twelve Holy Brothers, Martyrs († 258) — September 1

The Acts of the lives of the twelve brothers are legends. They were not actually brothers and died at different places in Apulia. Their memorial, added to the Roman calendar in the thirteenth century, is abolished.

On the same day the Church celebrates the feast of Saint Giles, she makes a commemoration of twelve brothers, martyrs, who were by country, Africans, natives of a city in Latin called, Hadrumetum[105]; which they say at present is called, Sissa, although some call it Toulb, and others, Macometa. The names of these brave soldiers of Christ were: Donatus, Felix, Arontius, Honoratus, Fortunatus, Sabanian, Septimius, Januarius, Felix the Second, Vitalis, Satyrus, and Repositus

They were of noble parentage and well instructed in human and divine literature. They were apprehended in Africa and afterward carried into Italy to the city of Beneventum, where they ended their course of glorious martyrdom. However, on different days, Valerian was emperor of Rome: before they were put to death, they were tormented with many cruel torments.

Alfanus[106]wrote their martyrdom in heroic verses in the seventh tome of Surius. Anastasius Bibliotbecarius also wrote of them, as Petrus Gelisinus in his annotations

---

[105] Hadrumetum, also known by several different spellings and names, was a Phoenician colony that existed before Carthage. It went on to become one of the most important cities in Roman Africa before being destroyed by Vandal and Umayyad conquerors.

[106] Saint Alfanus I, also known as Alfano I, was the archbishop of Salerno from 1058 until his death in 1085. He was well-known as a translator, writer, theologian, and physician.

on his martyrology. The *Roman Martyrology* also, and Cæsar Baronius[107] mentions them in his annotations.

[Ribadeneyra, Pedro de. "The Lives of Twelve Holy Brothers, Martyrs." *The Lives of Saints, With Other Feasts of the Year, according to the Roman Calendar. Written in Spanish by the Reverend Father Peter Ribadeneyra, Priest of the Society of Jesus. Translated Into English by W.P. (William Petre) Esq; The Second Edition Corrected and Amended,* vol. 2, p. 238. London. Printed by B.S., 1730. *HathiTrust Digital Library,* hdl.handle.net//2027/nyp.33433003053000.]

Saint Lawrence Justinian, First Patriarch of Venice (1381-1455) — September 5

The memorial of Lawrence, who died in Venice on January 8, 1455, was added to the Roman calendar in 1690. However, it is left to the particular calendars since this saint is not of universal significance.

Lawrence, born in 1381, longed to be a Saint from childhood. Then, when he was nineteen years of age, he was given a vision of the Eternal Wisdom in the form of a beautiful and noble Lady who told him to seek the only repose he would ever know in Her, the Eternal Wisdom of God. All earthly things paled in his eyes before the ineffable beauty of this sight, and as it faded away, a void was left in his heart that none but God could fill. So, refusing the offer of a brilliant marriage, at the age of nineteen, he fled from his home in Venice and joined the Canons Regular of Saint George[108] in their monastery, situated on a little island about a mile from Venice, where his uncle was a priest.

---

[107] Caesar Baronius [Cesare Baronio] (August 30, 1538 – June 30, 1607) was an Italian cardinal and Catholic Church historian. His most famous work is the *Annales Ecclesiastici,* which was published in twelve folio volumes. Pope Benedict XIV bestowed the title of Venerable on him.

[108] The Canons Regular of San Giorgio in Alga (*Congregatio Canonicorum Sancti Georgii in Alga Venetiarum*) were a congregation of canons regular who were influential in the 15th and 16th century reform movement of monastic life in northern Italy. Canons used to dress in white with a turquoise vest, earning the titles 'Turchini,' 'Azzurini,' or even 'Celestini.'

When Lawrence first entered religion, a nobleman went to dissuade him from the folly of thus sacrificing every earthly prospect. The young monk listened patiently to his friend's affectionate appeal, which soon changed into scorn and violent abuse. But, calmly and kindly, he then replied. He pointed out the shortness of life, the uncertainty of earthly happiness, and the incomparable superiority of the prize he sought to any pleasures his friend had named. The latter could make no answer; he felt in truth that Lawrence was wise and he was the fool. And he, too, left the world, became a fellow novice with the Saint, and eventually died a holy death.

As a monk, the mortification of Saint Lawrence was exemplary; he never drank outside of meals and, when urged to do so, replied: If we cannot endure a little heat on earth, how will we bear that of Purgatory? He underwent two painful operations without saying any word except the holy name of Jesus. Before the second intervention, when the surgeon's hand trembled, he said, cut with vigor; your instrument cannot match the iron hooks used to tear the sides of the martyrs.

Ordained a priest, then elected Superior and General of his Order, Saint Lawrence strengthened his brethren. Humility keeps silent and does not become inflated in prosperity, whereas in adversity, it is elevated, generous, and full of joy and invincible courage. Few know what this virtue is; it is possessed only by those to whom God has given it by infusion as a reward for their persevering efforts and their spirit of prayer. He encouraged frequent Communion, saying that the person who does not strive to become united with Him as frequently as possible has very little love for Jesus Christ. When he was consecrated bishop of his diocese in 1433, he thoroughly reformed his see in the face of slander and insult. He founded fifteen monasteries and many churches, and his cathedral became a model for all of

Christendom. His door was never closed to the poor, but he lived like a poor monk.

His zeal led to his being appointed the first Patriarch of Venice, but he remained in heart and soul a humble priest, thirsting for the vision reserved for heaven. He had just finished writing his last work, *The Degrees of Perfection*, when finally, the eternal day began to dawn. Are you preparing a bed of feathers for me? he said. No, my Lord was stretched on a hard and painful tree. Laid upon straw, he exclaimed in rapture, Good Jesus, behold, I come. He died in 1455, at the age of seventy-four.

[Guérin, Abbé (Paul), François Giry, and Simon Martin. *Les Petits Bollandistes: Vies Des Saints De L'Ancien et du Nouveau Testament.* Translated by the Monastère du Magnificat. Paris: Bloud et Barral, 1882. *HathiTrust Digital Library,* hdl.handle.net/2027/nnc1.0036694380; Shea, John G. *Little Pictorial Lives of the Saints, with Reflections for Every Day of the Year; Compiled from "Butler's Lives."* New York: Benziger, 1894. *HathiTrust Digital Library,* hdl.handle.net/2027/nyp.33433068232887.]

Saint Adrian (of Nicomedia), Martyr († 306) — September 8

Adrian is an unknown Eastern martyr whose cult was introduced because of the dedication of a church in his honor in the Roman Forum. His memorial is left to the particular calendars.

This saint was an officer in the Roman army, who, having persecuted the Christians in the reign of Maximian Galerius, was so moved by their constancy and patience, that he embraced their faith and suffered many torments and a glorious martyrdom for the same at Nicomedia, about the year 306, in the tenth or last general persecution. His relics were conveyed to Constantinople, thence to Rome, afterward into Flanders, where they were deposited in the Benedictine abbey of Decline, dedicated in honor of Saint Peter, in the time of the first abbot, Severald. Baldwin VI., earl of Flanders, surnamed of Mons, because he married the heiress of that county, bought of a wealthy lord, named Gerard, the village of Hundelghem[109], in which stood a famous chapel of our Lady. The count founded there, in 1088, the town now called Giersbergen or Gerard's Mount[110], on which, by a famous charter, he bestowed great privileges. Besides many pious donations to that place, he removed this abbey of Saint Peter, which has since taken the name of Saint Adrian, whose relics, which it possesses, have been rendered famous by many miracles. Geersberg, called in French Grammont, stands upon the Dender, in Flanders, near the borders of Brabant and Hainault. Saint Adrian is commemorated in the Martyrologies, which bear the name of Saint Jerome, and in the Roman, on the fourth of March, and chiefly on the eighth of September, which was the day of the translation of his relics to Rome, where a very ancient church bears his name.

[Butler, Alban. *The Lives of the Fathers, Martyrs, and Other Principal Saints. Compiled from Original Monuments and Authentic Records*. Dublin: James Duffy, 1866. *HathiTrust Digital Library,* catalog.hathitrust.org/Record/001941109.]

Saints Gorgonius, Dorotheus, and Companions, Martyrs (✝ 304) — September 9

All that is known about Gorgonius is his name and the date of his burial in the cemetery of the Laurels on the Via Labicana on September 9. His memorial is left for particular calendars.

---

[109] *Hundelgem* is a village in East Flanders with a population of 612. Hundelgem is located northeast of Munkzwalm and southeast of Dikkele.
[110] *Giersbergen* is a North Brabant hamlet. Giersbergen is located in the Netherlands, northwest of Zandkant and northeast of Springheuvel.

Dorotheus was the first chamberlain to the emperor Dioclesian; Gorgonius and Peter were under chamberlains. They were the three principal eunuchs of the palace; they had sometimes borne the weight of the most challenging affairs of state and been the support of both emperor and his court. When the palace of Nicomedia was set on fire, probably by the contrivance of Galerius, who unjustly charged the Christians with it, Dorotheus, Gorgonius, and several others under his dependence were very cruelly tortured and at length strangled. Peter had refused to sacrifice, was hung up naked in the air, and whipped on all parts of his body. After the executioners had torn his flesh in such a manner that the bones started, without being able to shake his constancy, they poured salt and vinegar into his wounds; then had a gridiron brought, and a fire made, on which they broiled him as we do meat, telling him while he should continue in that condition if he would not obey. Still, he was resolute to the last and died under torture. The bodies of Saint Dorotheus and his companions were cast into the sea by order of Dioclesian, lest the Christians should worship them as gods, as Eusebius mentions, which mistake of the heathens could only arise from the reverence that Christians paid to the relics of martyrs. The martyr Gorgonius, whose name was famous in Rome, seems different from the former. The Liberian Calendar, published by Bucherius, mentions his tomb on the Via Labicana[111], and he was honored with an office in the sacramentary of Pope Gelasius. Sigebert in his chronicle on the year 764, Rabanus Maurus in his martyrology, and others relate that Saint Chrodegang obtained from Rome, of Pope Paul, the relics of Saint Gorgonius, and enriched with that treasure his great monastery of Gorze, situated two leagues from Metz. Among the poems of Pope

---

[111] The Via Labicana was an ancient Italian road that ran east-southeast from Rome.

Damasus is an epitaph of Saint Gorgonius [of Nicomedia].

The martyrs show by example that a faithful Christian is invincible in virtue and fortitude; as Saint Gregory Nazianzen says, he looks upon misfortunes and crosses as the seeds of the most heroic virtues; therefore, he delights in adversity. Torments do not discompose the serenity of his countenance; much less do they change the steadfastness of his heart. Nothing can pull him down; everything yields to the generosity and wisdom of this philosopher. If he is stripped of the goods and conveniences of life, he has wings to raise him even to heaven. He flies even to the bosom of God, who abundantly makes him amends for all and is to him all things. He is in the world with a body like a pure spirit. Amid passions and sufferings, he is as invincible as if he were impassible: he lets himself be vanquished in everything except in courage; where he submits, he triumphs by humility, patience, and constancy, even in torments and in death itself. Do we maintain this character even under the fair trials we meet?

[Butler, Alban. *The Lives of the Fathers, Martyrs, and Other Principal Saints. Compiled from Original Monuments and Authentic Records.* Dublin: James Duffy, 1866. *HathiTrust Digital Library,* catalog.hathitrust.org/Record/001941109.]

Saint Nicholas of Tolentino, Confessor (1245- 1310) — September 10

The memorial of Nicholas, who died at Tolentine in 1305, entered the Roman calendar in 1585. It is left to the particular calendars since he is not of universal significance.

This Patron of the Universal Church was born in 1245, in answer to the prayer of a holy mother, and was vowed before his birth to the service of God. His parents had made a pilgrimage across Italy to visit the shrine of Saint Nicholas of Myre and ask his intercession to obtain a child; the infant granted them was given the same name in his honor.

Saint Nicholas of Tolentino never lost his baptismal innocence. His austerities as a very young religious were conspicuous even in the austere Order to which he belonged, the Hermits of Saint Augustine. He only replied to the remonstrances of his superiors, *"How can I be said to fast, while every morning at the altar I receive my God?"* The demons undertook a war against his spirit of prayer, going as far as to beat him and leave him inert on the floor, but they could not separate his soul from his Lord. He did, however, remain lame for life. He conceived an ardent charity for the holy souls of purgatory, so near and yet so far from their Savior. After his Mass, it was often revealed to him that the souls for whom he had offered the Holy Sacrifice had been admitted to the presence of God.

Saint Nicholas frequently went out of his monastery to beg for aid for the poor. He visited prisoners and the dying to administer the Last Sacraments. And this great Saint resurrected over one hundred children, on one occasion bringing back to life several who had been under water for several days.

During an illness, he was ordered to eat meat by a physician, which he had made a vow never to do. A plate containing well-prepared fowl was brought to him. In the presence of several witnesses, he made the sign of the cross over it, and the bird flew away out the window.

During the year preceding his death, a star always appeared over the altar where he said his Mass; afterward, it would conduct him to his cell, or lead him back again, later, to the altar. Amid his loving labors for God and man, he was haunted by thoughts of his unworthiness.

The heavens, said he, is not pure in the sight of Him whom I serve; how then shall I, a sinful man, stand before Him? Then, one day, as he pondered on the greatness of God and his nothingness, Mary, Queen of all Saints, appeared before him. "*Fear not, Nicholas,*" She said, "*all is well with you: My Son bears you in His Heart, and I am your protection.*" Then his soul was at rest.

At the hour of his death, which occurred on September 10, 1310, he heard, it is said, the songs which the Angels sing in the presence of their Lord. He died and was buried in the chapel where he was accustomed to offer the Holy Mass and say his prayers. He was canonized in 1446 by Pope Eugene IV. Three hundred and one miracles were recognized during the process. His tomb has become renowned by many more, even though his relics have been lost, save for two arms from which blood still exudes when a great danger menaces the Church. This occurred, for example, when infidels took over the island of Cyprus in 1570. The religious of Saint Augustine continue to maintain the service of the large basilica of Saint Nicholas in Tolentino. Saint Nicholas of Tolentino, like Saint Joseph, the virginal father of Jesus, has been declared a Patron of the Universal Church.

[Shea, John G. *Little Pictorial Lives of the Saints, with Reflections for Every Day of the Year; Compiled from "Butler's Lives."* New York: Benziger, 1894. *HathiTrust Digital Library,* hdl.handle.net/2027/nyp.33433068232887.]

Saints Protus and Hyacinth, Martyrs († 257–9) — September 11

Apart from their names, all that is known about these martyrs is the date and place of their burial in the cemetery of Basilla on the Via Salaria on September 11. Their memorial is left for particular calendars.

The Saints whose victory the church commemorates on this day are honored among the most illustrious martyrs that ennobled Rome with their blood when the emperors of the world attempted, with the whole weight of their power, to crush the little flock of Christ. Their epitaph, among the works of Pope Damasus, calls them brothers and informs us that Hyacinthus sustained the first conflict but that Protus obtained his crown before him. In the Acts of Saint Eugenia, they are said to have been eunuchs and retainers to that virtuous lady and martyr, who is honored on the 25th of December. Their martyrdom, and that of Eugenia, is placed in these acts under Valerian in 257. Still, the Liberian Calendar assures us that Saint Basilla, who seems to have been a companion of Saint Eugenia, received her crown on the 22nd of September, in the persecution of Dioclesian, in 304, and was buried on the Via Salaria. Saint Avitus, of Vienna, about the year 500; Fortunatus and others mention Saint Eugenia among the most celebrated virgins and martyrs. The ancient calendar, drawn up in the pontificate of Liberius, says the festival of Saints Protus and Hyacinthus on the 11th of September, as celebrated at their tomb on the old Via Salaria, in the cemetery of Basilla, who lay buried at some distance. Her name ought to be written *Bassilla*, as it is in the Liberian Calendar, for it is derived from Bassus. This cemetery was afterward comprised under that of Saint Priscilla, who was buried not far off on the new Via Salaria. Saints Protus and Hyacinthus are honored in the sacramentary of Saint Gregory, in the ancient martyrology, published by F. Fronto, and in those of Bede, Usuard, Vandelbert, etc. Pope Damasus, in 366, removed the earth which hid the tomb of these two martyrs from the view of the faithful; and, during his pontificate, a priest named Theodorus built over it a church, as appears from an ancient epitaph published by

Baronius. Anastasius relates that Pope Symmachus afterward adorned it with plates and vessels of silver. Pope Clement VIII., in 1592, caused the sacred remains of Saints Protus and Hyacinthus to be removed from this church into the city and to be deposited in the church of Saint John Baptist, belonging to the Florentines; of which translation an account is given us by Sarazanius, an eyewitness, in his notes on the poems of Pope Damasus. A considerable part of their relics was given to the Benedictine abbey at Mühlheim, now called Seligenstadt[112] —*i.e.,* the seat of the blessed, in the diocese of Mentz, in 829, as Eginhard and others relate; part to the church of Saint Vincent, at Metz, about the year 972, etc.

What words can we find sufficiently to praise the heroic virtue and invincible fortitude of the martyrs! They stood out against the fury of those tyrants whose arms had subdued the most distant nations, whose yoke almost the whole known world was subject, and whose power both kings and people revered. Standing alone, without any preparation of war, they appeared undaunted in the presence of those proud conquerors, who seemed to think that the very earth ought to bend under their feet. Yet, armed with virtue and divine grace, they were an over-match for all the powers of the world and hell; they fought with wild beasts, fires, and swords; with courage and remarkable cheerfulness, they braved the cruelest torments, and by humility, patience, meekness, and constancy, baffled all enemies, and triumphed over men and devils. How glorious was the victory of such an invincible virtue! Yet, having before our eyes the examples of so many holy saints, are we as cowardly as to shrink

---

[112] Former Benedictine Abbey of Seligenstadt. A close adviser to Charlemagne founded the abbey and gardens around 830. The abbey was expanded in the 11th and 12th centuries, and Benedictine monks worked and studied there until 1803 when it was closed. Seligenstadt is located approximately 10 miles east of Frankfurt, Germany.

under temptations or lose patience under the most ordinary trials?

[Butler, Alban. *The Lives of the Fathers, Martyrs, and Other Principal Saints. Compiled from Original Monuments and Authentic Records.* Dublin: James Duffy, 1866. *HathiTrust Digital Library,* catalog.hathitrust.org/Record/001941109.]

Feast of the Holy Name of Mary (Established in 1683) — September 12

This feast was included in the Roman calendar in 1684 to celebrate the victory over the Turks at Vienna 1683. Since it duplicates the feast of the Birth of Mary, it is now suppressed.

This feast was established by Pope Innocent XI in 1683 that the faithful may in a particular manner recommend to God on this day, through the intercession of the Blessed Virgin, the necessities of His Church, and return Him thanks for His gracious protection and numberless mercies.

What gave occasion to the institution of this feast was the desire of all Christendom for a solemn thanksgiving that would commemorate the deliverance of Vienna, obtained through the intercession of Our Lady, when the city was besieged by the Turks in 1683. An army of 550,000 invaders had reached the city walls and threatened all of Europe. John Sobieski, King of Poland, came with a much smaller army to assist the besieged city during the octave of the Nativity of the Blessed Virgin and made ready for a great battle. This religious prince began with a Mass celebrated, which he desired to serve, his arms in a cross. Then, after receiving Communion with fervor, he rose at the close of the sacrifice and cried out, *"Let us march with confidence under the protection of Heaven and with the aid of the Most Holy Virgin!"* His hope was not disappointed; the Turks were struck with a sudden panic and fled in disorder. Since that time, the feast day has been celebrated during the octave of the Nativity of Our Lady.

[Jaud, Leon. *Vie Des Saints Pour Tous Les Jours De L'annee: Avec Une Pratique De Piete Pour Chaque Jour.* Translated by the Monastère du Magnificat. Tours: A. Mame, 1950. Print; Shea, John G. *Little Pictorial Lives of the Saints, with Reflections for Every Day of the Year; Compiled from "Butler's Lives."* New York: Benziger, 1894. *HathiTrust Digital Library,* hdl.handle.net/2027/nyp.33433068232887.]

Saint Nicomedes, Martyr († 90) — September 15

In addition to his name, all that is known of Nicomedes is his burial on September 15 in the cemetery that bears his name on the Via Nomentana. His memorial is left for particular calendars.

When the glorious virgin, Saint Petronilla, to conserve her virginity for her most dear spouse Jesus Christ, refused to marry Count Flaccus and besought to her Lord to take her to himself entire and pure, a holy priest Nicomedes came to her house and said Mass and communicated to her. She, upon receiving God, gave up her soul to him. The holy virgin had in her company another young maid, Felicula, very like her in her sanctity, beauty, and good manners. Count Flaccus, having seen his marriage to Saint Petronilla had not succeeded, cast his eyes upon Felicula and ensured her that she would accept him for her husband. When he could not win her consent through fair means, he resolved to obtain that by force which he could not get by kindness, telling her that she must choose one of the two, either take him for her husband or else offer sacrifice to the gods. Felicula answered him with great freedom, *"I will not be thy wife because I am espoused to Jesus Christ, not will I offer sacrifice to the gods because I am a Christian.*" Flaccus was enraged above measure and delivered her up to his vicar so that he might examine her cause.

And in fine, after they had shut her up seven days in a dark chamber without giving her anything to eat and had kept her there as many other days amongst the vestal virgins (where she would not eat of their meats because they had been offered up to their goddess Vesta[113]), they tormented her upon the rack Equuleus[114]. Afterward, they threw her into a filthy sink, where she gave up her soul to God.

Saint Nicomedes, a priest (who administered the Blessed Sacrament to Saint Petronilla at the hour of her death), being alerted of it, went out of a cave where he had hidden and, in the night, took the body of Saint Felicula and buried it about a mile from Rome on the Via Ardeatina. Hearing of this great work of charity that Nicomedes had done, Flaccus commanded him to be apprehended and used all the art he possibly could to persuade him to sacrifice to the gods. Still, the saint laughing at all his promises and threats, commanded him to be cruelly whipped that in the torment, he rendered up his soul to the Lord. The judge commanded his body to be cast into the Tiber River, but a clergyman called Justus (who was no less just in deed than by name) fought for it, found it, and buried it in his garden near the wall of the city on the Via Nomentana.

There came many Christians, and by his own merits obtained of God great favors. He died on the 15th of September, during which the Church celebrates his feast. He had a church and burying place of his name in

---

[113] In Roman religion, Vesta is the virgin goddess of the hearth, home, and family. She was rarely depicted in human form, preferring to be symbolized by the fire of her temple in the *Forum Romanum*. Only her priestesses, the Vestal Virgins, were allowed to enter her temple, where they guarded sacred objects, prepared flour, and sacred salt (*mola salsa*) for official sacrifices, and tended Vesta's sacred fire at the temple hearth.

[114] A type of rack used in Roman antiquity to extort confessions from suspects or accused people.

Rome. The Martyrologies write of Saint Nicomedes, the Roman, and those of Bede, Usuard, Ado, and Cardinal Baronius in his Annotations.

[Ribadeneyra, Pedro de. "The Life of St. Nicomedes, Priest, and Martyr." *The Lives of Saints, With Other Feasts of the Year, according to the Roman Calendar. Written in Spanish by the Reverend Father Peter Ribadeneyra, Priest of the Society of Jesus. Translated Into English by W.P. (William Petre) Esq; The Second Edition Corrected and Amended, vol. 2, pp. 251-252.* London. Printed by B.S., 1730. *HathiTrust Digital Library*, hdl.handle.net/2027/nyp.33433003053000.]

Saint Euphemia, Virgin and Martyr (✝ 307) — September 16

The Acts of Life of Euphemia, a celebrated virgin and martyr from Chalcedon, are legendary, and her memorial, although widely observed for many centuries, is left to the particular calendars.

The City of Chalcedon[115] was the theatre of her glorious martyrdom; she suffered in the persecution continued by the successors of Dioclesian, about the year 307. The eminent sanctity of this holy virgin, loaded with the fruits of all Christian virtues, excited the devil's rage and his instruments, the persecutors. Still, all the efforts of their malice only rendered her virtue the more triumphant and glorious. Having embraced the holy state of virginity, she, by the black or dark-colored garments which she wore, declared to all men her steady purpose of taking no share in the earthly pleasures and amusements which fill the hearts, set an edge on the passions, and take up the most precious part of the time of worldlings. The exercises of penance and religion were the serious occupations to which she devoted herself. As

---

[115] Chalcedon was a Bithynian maritime town in Asia Minor. It was almost directly opposite Byzantium, south of Scutari (modern Üsküdar), and is now a district of Istanbul known as Kadıköy.

the love of God reigned in her heart, it was her constant study to walk always before him, to labor in all her actions to please him, and, by the humility of her heart and whole deportment, by the mortification of her senses, by the constancy and zeal of her devotion, by the heavenliness of her conversation. The activity of her enthusiasm and charity to make continually higher advances towards heaven. Whatever was not God appeared to her empty and contemptible; she found no pleasure or delight but in what tended to unite her heart increasingly to him here by love; and she thirsted after his presence and fruition in the kingdom of his glory, panting, and longing to be dismissed from the pilgrimage of this world, and the corruptible tabernacle of the body. God was pleased to hear her sighs and crown her humble desires. She was apprehended by the persecutors and cruelly tortured by the command of an inhuman judge named Priscus. The torments she underwent were represented most movingly in a famous picture kept in the great church at Chalcedon, accurately described by Saint Asterius. While one soldier pulled her head back, another with a mallet beat out all her teeth and bruised her mouth so that her beautiful tender face, hair, and clothes were covered with blood. After suffering many other torments, she was laid in a dungeon, where prayer was her whole comfort, joy, and strength. Being at length condemned to be burnt alive, she ascended the pile with such an admirable cheerfulness in her countenance as bespoke the interior sweet joy of her soul going to eternal life. Thus, she finished her course.

She is honored as one of the chief martyrs of the Grecian church, and her festival is a holy day in almost all the east. Four churches in Constantinople formerly bore her name. One at Chalcedon was exceedingly spacious and famous, in which the fourth general council condemned Eutyches in 451. The fathers in it acknowledged the church much indebted to the intercession of this holy virgin for the happy issue of that affair. Evagrius, the historian, testifies that emperors, patriarchs, and all ranks of people resorted to Chalcedon to be partakers of the blessings God abundantly conferred on men through her patronage, and those manifest miracles were there wrought. These relics were translated into the great church of Saint Sophia at Constantinople; and, above all other such holy treasures, excited the rage of Constantine Copronymus, as Theophanes, Zonaras, and Cedrenus relate. In what manner they were then concealed and afterward recovered is recorded by Constantine, bishop of Tio, in Paphlagonia, in an oration on that subject. The sacred remains of Saint Euphemia are now preserved at Syllebria, a metropolitical see on the Propontic shore between Constantinople[116] and Adrianople[117], as Prince Cantemir informs us. Still, a portion is possessed by the church of the Sorbonne at Paris, which was a present made by a great master of Rhodes. Saint Euphemia had a church in Rome at the time of Saint Gregory the Great, probably the same standing, and was repaired by Urban VIII.

[Butler, Alban. *The Lives of the Fathers, Martyrs, and Other Principal Saints. Compiled from Original Monuments and Authentic Records.* Dublin: James Duffy, 1866. *HathiTrust Digital Library,* catalog.hathitrust.org/Record/001941109.]

---

[116] Now Istanbul, Turkey.
[117] Now Edirne, Turkey.

Saints Lucy and Geminianus (also known as Geminian, or Gimignano), Martyrs under Dioclesian († 300) — September 16

Although of ancient origin, the memorial of Lucy and Geminianus is abolished since it constitutes a duplication of the December 13 feast of Lucy. Geminianus, mentioned in the account of Lucy's death, is fictitious.

Saint Lucy was a virtuous matron who lived most holy to the seventy-fifth year of age after her husband's death. She had a son called Euprepius, very lewd and vicious and, above all, an enemy of the Christians. The devil got so far power over this young man that, forgetting all his obligations to his mother, he accused her before the emperor Dioclesian that she was a Christian. The emperor commanded her to be apprehended and cast into prison, where she was comforted by our Lord. The next day, they brought her to judicature, and finding her constant in the confession of Jesus Christ, the emperor caused her to be most cruelly whipped. Suddenly, there arose a whirlwind, and a terrible earthquake, by which the temple of Jupiter was thrown down and so ruined that of that building there remained not one stone upon another.

The emperor, enraged to hear that commanded a great brass cauldron to be brought, filled with melted pitch and burning lead, and the saint to be bast into there to be boiled. But the virtue of the Almighty protected her, and she was in the vessel three days praising God as if she had been all the while in a soft bed. After this, they led her through the city in an embarrassing manner, loaded with irons and lead. And passing the gate of the house of a principal man, called Geminian, where there was a significant number of idols, a pigeon more white than snow came down from heaven, and fate upon the head of Geminian—who moved by what he saw, and illuminated with a heavenly light cast himself at the feet of the saint, and demanded baptism, and received it from the hand of a priest called Protafius, who was admonished by an angel, that he should go to the prison to baptize him.

Diocletian committed Lucy and Geminian into the hands of the cruelest judge that he should torment them and make an end of them. But, when they were torturing and beating them with cudgels, the chamber where the judge was fell and killed him. Another judge, Abofrasius, succeeding him, invented new torments to put them to (as if the former had not been sufficient).

Seventy-five persons converted by seeing the wonders God wrought in his saints. And they all received the crown of martyrdom. Moreover, the judge had no cause to boast, for going on horseback over a bridge, he fell into the river and drowned, and his body was never found. At last, the blessed Saint Lucy and Saint Geminian suffered death by the sword, by the command of Megalius, who had been sometime consul, upon the 16th of September, in the year of our Lord, 303. Their bodies were taken up by a holy woman called Maxima, who buried them with great reverence and devotion.

[Ribadeneyra, Pedro de. "The Lives of St. Lucy and St. Geminian, Martyrs." *The Lives of Saints, With Other Feasts of the Year, according to the Roman Calendar. Written in Spanish by the Reverend Father Peter Ribadeneyra, Priest of the Society of Jesus. Translated Into English by W.P. (William Petre) Esq; The Second Edition Corrected and Amended,* vol. 2, pp. 259-260. London. Printed by B.S., 1730. *HathiTrust Digital Library,* hdl.handle.net//2027/nyp.33433003053000.]

The Stigmata of Saint Francis (†1224) — September 17

The memorial of the stigmata of Francis (1224), placed in the Roman calendar in 1585, suppressed in 1602, and restored in 1615, is left for the particular calendars. It duplicates the feast of Francis on October 4.

Saint Bonaventure, the biographer of Saint Francis of Assisi, wrote that he had been praying on Mount Alverno two years before his holy death in a solitary retreat, where he had gone to fast for forty days in honor of the Archangel Michael. No one ever meditated more than Francis on the Passion of his Lord. During his retreat, he beheld in vision a six-winged Seraph attached to a cross and received at the same time a painful wound of the heart, which seemed to transpierce it. When the vision ended, his hands and feet bore the marks of the angelic crucifixion he had seen in the vision. He understood by his vision that the soul must come to resemble Christ by the ardors of its interior fire rather than by any physical, exterior means. Reproduced here is a meditation of the saintly 19th century Abbot, Dom Guéranger of Solemnes in France:

The Feast of the Stigmata of Saint Francis, whom we will soon honor again on his feast of October 4th, is not only to glorify a Saint; it commemorates and signifies something which goes beyond the life of any single man, even one of the greatest of the Church. The God-Man never ceases to live on in His Church, and the reproduction of His mysteries in this Spouse whom He wants to be like Himself is the explanation of history.

In the thirteenth century, it seemed that charity, whose divine precept many no longer heeded, concentrated in a few souls the fires which had once sufficed to inflame multitudes. Sanctity shone as brilliantly as ever, but the hour for the cooling of the brazier had struck for the peoples. The Church itself says so today in its liturgy at the Collect: "*O Lord Jesus Christ, Who when the world was growing cold, didst renew the sacred marks of Thy Passion in the flesh of the most blessed Francis, to inflame our hearts with the fire of Thy love; mercifully grant, that by his merits and prayers we may always carry the Cross, and bring forth worthy fruits of penance.*" The

Spouse of Christ had already begun to experience the long series of social defections among the nations, with their denials, treasons, derision, slaps, and spittings in the very praetorium, all of which conclude in the legalized separation of society from its Author. The era of the Passion is advanced; the exaltation of the Holy Cross, which for centuries was triumphant in the eyes of the nations, acquires in the sight of heaven, as the Angels look down upon it, the aspect of an ever-closer resemblance with the Spouse to the sufferings of her crucified Beloved.

Saint Francis, loved today by all who know of him — and few there are who do not — was like precious marble placed before an expert sculptor. The Holy Spirit chose the flesh of the seraph of Assisi to express His divine thought, thus manifesting to the world the particular direction He intends to give to souls after that. This stigmatization offers a first example, a complete image, of the new labor on which the divine Spirit is meditating — total union, on the very Cross of Christ itself, of the mystical Body with the divine Head. Francis is honored by this importance of choice, but after him, the sacred sign will be received by others who also personify the Church. From this time on, the Stigmata of the Lord Jesus will always be visible here and there on this earth.

[Guéranger, Prosper L. P. *L'Annee Liturgique: Le Temps après la Pentecote 1-6*. Translated by the Monastère du Magnificat. Tours: Mane, 1919.]

Saint Joseph of Cupertino, Franciscan Priest (1603-1663) — September 18

The memorial of Joseph, who died at Osimo in 1663, was entered into the Roman calendar in 1769. It is left for particular calendars since he is not a saint of universal significance.

Joseph Desa was born in the little city of Cupertino, near the Gulf of Taranto, in 1600. It is said in the acts of the process of his canonization that at the age of five, he already showed such signs of sanctity that if he had been an adult, he would have been revered as a perfect man. Yet, already in his youth, he was ravished in ecstasies that tore him away from the earth; it has been calculated that perhaps half of his life for some sixty years was literally above the ground. But much remains to be said of Saint Joseph, apart from his visible divine favors.

He almost died at seven from an internal abscess, which only his prayer to Our Lady cured. He learned to be a shoemaker to earn his living but was often absent in spirit from his work. He treated his flesh with singular rigor. The Cardinal de Lauria, who knew him well for long years, said he wore a coarse hair shirt and never ate meat, contenting himself with fruits and bread. He seasoned his soup, if he accepted any, with a dry and bitter powder of wormwood. At seventeen, he desired to become a conventual Franciscan but was refused because he had not studied. He entered the Capuchins as a lay brother, but the divine favors he received seemed everywhere to bring down contempt upon him. He was in continuous contemplation and dropped plates and cauldrons. He would often stop and kneel, and his long halts in places of discomfort brought on a tumor of the knee, which was very painful. It was decided that he lacked aptitude and health and was sent home. He was then regarded everywhere as a vagabond and a fool, and his mother was harsh, as had been her custom for long years. She did, however, obtain permission for him to take charge of the stable for the conventual Franciscans, wearing the habit of the Third Order.

Saint Joseph proved himself many times to be perfectly obedient. His humility was heroic, and his mortification most exceptional. His words bore fruit, wakened the indifferent, warned against vice, and generally were seen to come from a very kind and virtuous man. He was finally granted the habit. He read with difficulty and wrote with more problems, but the Mother of God was watching over him. When he had been admitted to minor Orders by the bishop's intervention, he desired to be a priest but knew well only one text of the Gospel. By a special Providence of God, that was the text he was asked to expound during the canonical examination for the diaconate. The bishop charged with hearing candidates for the priesthood found that the first ones answered exceptionally well. He ordained them without further hearings, thus passing Joseph with the others. He was ordained in 1628.

He retired to a hermitage, apparently in nearly continuous ecstasy or at least contemplation. He kept nothing for himself save the tunic he wore. Rejoicing being poor, he felt entirely free also. He obeyed his Superiors and went wherever he was sent, wearing sandals and an old tunic which often came back with pieces missing; the people had begun to venerate him as a Saint and had cut them off. He was accused of failing in poverty when he did not notice what was happening. The humble Brother wanted to pass for a sinner; he asked for the lowest employments and transported the building materials for a church on his shoulders. He begged for the community. At the church, he was a priest; elsewhere, he was a poor Brother.

Toward the end of his life, all divine consolations were denied the Saint, including his ecstasies. He fell victim to unceasing aridity and could find no savor in any holy reading. Then the infernal spirits inspired terrible visions and dreams. He shed tears amid this darkness and prayed to his Savior to help him but received no answer. When the General of the Order heard of this, he called him to Rome, and there he recovered from the fearful trial, and all his joy returned.

He still had combats with the enemy of God to bear, just like when the demons took human form to attempt to injure him physically. Other afflictions were not spared him, but his soul overcame all barriers between himself and God. He died on September 18, 1663, at 63, in the Franciscan convent of Osino. He had celebrated Holy Mass, including the day before his death, as he had foretold he would do.

[Guérin, Abbé (Paul), François Giry, and Simon Martin. *Les Petits Bollandistes: Vies Des Saints De L'Ancien et du Nouveau Testament.* Translated by the Monastère du Magnificat. Paris: Bloud et Barral, 1882. *HathiTrust Digital Library,* hdl.handle.net/2027/nnc1.0036694380.]

Saint Januarius (and Companions), Bishop and Martyr († 541) — September 19

In keeping with Jerome's martyrology and Carthage's calendar, this should only be a memorial of Januarius without mentioning his companions.

Saint Januarius was the bishop of the city of Beneventum, which is in the kingdom of Naples. A holy confessor called Sosius, being in prison for the persecution of Dioclesian, Maximian, and Saint Januarius, visited him to comfort him and to encourage him to suffer martyrdom. Timothy, the president, commanded him to be apprehended and brought before him and endeavor to pervert him and to draw many words and false reasons to the adoration of his vain gods. But perceiving it was a lost time, he caused an oven to be heated for three days; and Saint Januarius to be cast into it. But our Lord so preserved him that he came out of the oven, without having a thread of his garment, or a hair of his head, singed by the fire.

The tyrant was yet more enraged, seeing the flames spared him, whom he desired to make an end of, and commanded the martyr to be so cruelly tormented that all his members were disjointed. Accordingly, Festus, deacon, and Desiderius, lector, came to visit him; and are known to be Christians, were taken, and led with their bishop, Saint Januarius, loaded with iron chains before the couch of the president to the city of Pozzuoli[118]. There, they were all cast into the same prison, in which were prisoners, Socius, deacon of the city of Mycenae, and two of the laity called Eutyches and Acutius; who had all been condemned to be torn in pieces by wild beasts, and were expecting the execution of their sentence of condemnation. But, instead, the day following, they were all cast to the beasts, who forgot their natural fierceness, and threw themselves at the feet of Saint Januarius and his companions as if they had been such tame sheep.

The president, attributing this miracle of our Lord to sorcery and magic, gave a sentence against them and commanded them to be beheaded. Still, instantly he lost his sight and, by the prayers of Saint Januarius, recovered it again. This miracle converted nearly five thousand persons. The favor the wicked judge had received was insufficient to assuage his fury and make him acknowledge the mighty hand of God, which wrought in his saints. Still, seeing so many people's conversion and fearing the emperors' anger, he pronounced a sentence of death against these holy martyrs. They led them to the place of their martyrdom and cut off their heads.

Their bodies were carried to different places: that of Saint Januarius having been first at Beneventum; and afterward in the monastery called the *Mountain of the*

---

[118] Pozzuoli is a city and comune of the Metropolitan City of Naples in Campania, Italy. It serves as the capital of the Phlegrean Peninsula.

Virgin, which was translated to Naples in the time of Pope Alexander VI, and placed in the cathedral church; where it is honored with great devotion and reverence by all that city, who take him for their patron and receive tremendous and continual favors by his means.

Two miracles amongst others our Lord have wrought through the merits of Saint Januarius. The first is that he has delivered the city and kingdom of Naples from the burning of the mountain called Vesuvius; which is not far from Naples, and casts forth fire, and sometimes an abundance of fire comes out of it that one would think that it would consume and burn up all those countries; as it happened in the time of the emperor Titus; in which burning Pliny the second died, for he went nearer it than he should have done, out of curiosity to see it.

But another time the fire came out of the mountain, was so dreadful and terrible that it seemed all Europe was to be turned into ashes; for it broke forth so often, and with such violence, that it reached even to Constantinople, and it ceased by the prayers of Saint Januarius; and the Grecians instituted a feast in his honor, and every year made two solemn processions, giving thanks to God for having delivered them from that danger, and beseeching Him to preserve them for the future. Upon this occasion, the devotion to Saint Januarius increased in the people who visited his holy relics and founded many churches in diverse places in his honor.

The other miracle is perpetual and lasts to this very day. They have at Naples the sacred head of Saint Januarius, and a glass vial apart, full of the blood of the same saint congealed, and joining it with the head, or putting it before it, immediately the blood begins to melt and dissolve, and to become liquid as if it were newly shed.

The martyrdom of Saint Januarius was upon the 19th of September, in the year of our Lord 305, in the reign of the above-said Diocletian and Maximian. His Holiness Sixtus V, in the first year of his popedom, which was the year 1585, on the 27th of January, commanded Saint Januarius to be served with a single office. And afterward, Pope Gregory XIV ordained that his feast should be kept in the city and kingdom of Naples and that he should be served there with a double office and in the rest of the Christendom with a semi-double.

John the Deacon wrote the *Martyrdom of Saint Januarius and His Holy Companions*, and Surius recounts it in his fifth tome, and the Roman Martyrologies, and those of Bede, Usuard, and Ado, as also other authors, Latin and Greek, who write the lives of the saints, make mention of them.

[Ribadeneyra, Pedro de. "The Life of Saint Januarius, Bishop and Martyr." *The Lives of Saints, With Other Feasts of the Year, according to the Roman Calendar. Written in Spanish by the Reverend Father Peter Ribadeneyra, Priest of the Society of Jesus. Translated Into English by W.P. (William Petre) Esq; The Second Edition Corrected and Amended*, vol. 2, pp. 271-272. London. Printed by B.S., 1730. *HathiTrust Digital Library*, hdl.handle.net//2027/nyp.33433003053000.]

Saint Eustachius and Companions, Martyrs (✝ 118) — September 20

The account of the death of [Eustachius] is entirely legendary. His memorial, in the Roman calendar since the twelfth century, is abolished.

The remarkable story of Saint Eustachius, named Placidus before his conversion, is a lesson given by God Himself on the marvels of His Divine Providence. At the beginning of the second century, he was a distinguished and very wealthy officer of the Roman army under the emperor Trajan. He practiced generous charity to the poor, although he had not yet perceived the errors of idolatry.

One day, while this distinguished officer was vainly pursuing a deer, the animal suddenly stood immobile in the light of a hilltop, and he perceived a luminous cross between its horns. On the cross was the image of the crucified Savior, and a voice said to him, "*I am the Christ whom you honor without knowing it; the alms you give to the poor has reached Me.*" So, like Saint Paul, he fell from his horse and remained inert for a time. Then, coming to himself, he said interiorly, *What is this voice I have heard? You who speak to me, who are you, that I may believe in you?* And the Lord told him interiorly that He was the Creator of the light, of the seasons, of man and all things visible, that he had suffered to save mankind, died, and been buried, but had risen the third day.

This was sufficient, and the officer went home to fulfill the prescription he had received to be baptized with his wife and two young sons. His spouse had received a similar revelation at the same time as himself, and they all went to the Christian authority of the region in secret to be baptized the same night.

In a short time, he lost all his possessions through natural catastrophes and robbers. But he had been advised beforehand that the Lord wanted to make of him another Job, that the ancient enemy had already plotted against him, and that he was not to allow any thought of blasphemy to arise in his heart amid the sufferings that were awaiting him. So he prayed for strength and retired from the region after the calamities with his wife and children. When by unforeseeable and extraordinary accidents, his wife and children were also taken from him, and he believed the children dead, he was close to despair and wished his life might end. Still, the warning of the Lord returned to his mind, and he entered the service of a landowner of a village called Badyssus to tend the fields. He remained for fifteen years in this occupation. During this time, his loved ones were well and safe, all spared in the difficult circumstances which had removed them from his sight but separated, each one like himself, from the three others.

In those days, the empire suffered greatly from the ravages of barbarians and sank under the assaults. The emperor Trajan had Eustachius sought out and, when found, had him clothed in splendid garments to give him command over the troops he intended to send against the invaders. During the celebration of his return, he related to the emperor all that had occurred to him. When the troops were being assembled, his sons were conscripted. Seeing them, he noticed them as young men taller than most and of great nobility of bearing and countenance and kept them near him without yet recognizing them. One of the two, while on bivouac near the very house of his mother, who, like Eustachius, had taken employment in the garden of a landowner, related the confused memories of his childhood to his companion. Suddenly, the two brothers recognized one another and embraced in an outflow of joy.

Their mother, by delicate attentions of Providence, had chanced to overhear them and, reflecting on what she heard, became confident they were her sons. She went to the captain of the campaign to inquire about them and immediately recognized him. Not wishing to startle him, she began to relate her story, identifying herself as the wife of a certain Placidus and saying she believed she was now in the presence of her two sons from whom she had been separated and whom she had not seen for long years. One must imagine the captain's sentiments on hearing this narration, the reunion which followed, and the prayers of thanksgiving sent to God by the family and the troops, who joined them in their joy and prayers.

Returning to Rome victorious, Eustachius was received in triumph and greatly honored, but he refused when commanded to sacrifice to the false gods during the celebration. The enraged Emperor Hadrian — for Trajan had died — ordered him to be exposed to a starved lion with his wife and children. But instead of harming these servants of God, the beast came up to them, lowered its head as if in homage, and left the arena. More furious, the emperor caused the martyrs to be shut up inside a brazen bull, under which a fire was to be kindled, that they might be roasted to death. Saint Eustachius prayed aloud and thanked God, asking Him who had reunited them to cause their lives to end at the same time so that they might be received together by Him into the happiness of His presence. They expired, but neither their bodies nor even their hair was injured. They were found entire the next day, and it was believed they were still alive at first. Many believed in Christ through this final miracle, which to us today seems perhaps less miraculous than the story of their existence while alive. A church in honor of the martyrs still exists in Rome: Saint-Eustachius *in Thermis.*

[Guérin, Abbé (Paul), François Giry, and Simon Martin. *Les Petits Bollandistes: Vies Des Saints De L'Ancien et du Nouveau Testament.* Translated by the Monastère du Magnificat. Paris: Bloud et Barral, 1882. *HathiTrust Digital Library,* hdl.handle.net/2027/nnc1.0036694380.]

Saint Thomas of Villanova, Bishop of Valencia (1488-1555) — September 22

The memorial of Thomas, who died in Valencia, Spain, on September 8, 1555, was placed in the Roman calendar in 1659. He is not a saint of universal significance, and his memorial is left to the particular calendars.

Saint Thomas, the glory of the Spanish Church in the sixteenth century, was born in the diocese of Toledo in 1488. His mother was a Christian of extraordinary tenderness for the poor. God worked a miracle for her one day when her servants had given away all the flour in their storeroom. When another beggar came to the door, she told them to go back and look again, and they found the storeroom filled with flour. Her little son followed his mother's example and one day gave away to six poor persons in succession, the six young chicks following the hen around in the yard. When his mother asked where they were, he said, "*You did not leave any bread in the house, Mama, so I gave them the chicks! I would have given the hen if another beggar had come.*"

At the age of fifteen years, he began his studies and succeeded so well that he was judged fit to teach philosophy and theology in a college of Alcala[119] and then at Salamanca[120]. When his father died, he returned to Villanova to dispose of his inheritance. He made his house into a hospital, keeping only what was needed for his mother, and gave the rest to the poor. At twenty-eight, he entered the Order of the Hermits of Saint Augustine[121] at Salamanca, becoming professed in 1517.

When ordained a priest three years later, he continued his teaching of theology but also began to preach so remarkably well that he was compared with Saint Paul and the prophet Elias. The city was reformed, and after Emperor Charles V heard him once, he returned and often mingled with the crowd to listen, finally making Saint Thomas his official preacher.

---

[119] *Alcalá de Henares University* or *College of San Ildefonso,* Alcalá de Henares, Spain (1630-1785).

[120] *Monastery of Santa María de Trianos,* a monastery of Augustinian Canons at Salamanca, Spain (pre-1125–1835).

[121] The Augustinian Hermits, also known as the Austin Friars (officially the Order of the Hermit Friars of Saint Augustine; O.S.A.), were one of the four major mendicant orders of the Middle Ages. Following the Vandal invasion of northern Africa (c. 428), a number of congregations of hermits following St. Augustine's Rule established monasteries in central and northern Italy.

He became Prior of his Order in three cities, then three times a Provincial Superior. His sanctity continued to increase, and he was nominated archbishop of Valencia in 1544; he had refused a similar offer sixteen years earlier but was obliged to accept. After a long drought, rain fell when he assumed his new office. He arrived as a pilgrim accompanied by one fellow monk and was not recognized in the convent of his Order when the two travelers came asking for shelter during the rain. He was obliged to reveal his identity when the Prior, who wondered where the awaited archbishop might be, asked him if perchance it was.

The new Archbishop was so poor that he was given money for furnishings but took it to the hospital for the indigent. On being led to his throne in church, he pushed the silken cushions aside and, with tears, kissed the ground. His first visit was to the prison. Two-thirds of his episcopal revenues were annually spent on alms. He fed five hundred needy persons daily, made himself responsible for bringing up the city's orphans, and sheltered neglected foundlings with a mother's care. During his eleven years of the episcopate, not one poor maiden was married without alms from the archbishop. Spurred by his example, the rich and the selfish became liberal and generous. And when, on the Nativity of Our Lady, 1555, after one week of illness, Saint Thomas was about to breathe his last, he gave his bed to a poor man and asked to be placed on the floor. It has been said that at his death, he was probably the only poor man in his see.

[Guérin, Abbé (Paul), François Giry, and Simon Martin. *Les Petits Bollandistes: Vies Des Saints De L'Ancien et du Nouveau Testament.* Translated by the Monastère du Magnificat. Paris: Bloud et Barral, 1882. *HathiTrust Digital Library,* hdl.handle.net/2027/nnc1.0036694380.]

Saint Maurice and the Theban Legion, Soldiers and Martyrs († 286) — September 22

There are many historical difficulties in the account of the martyrdom of Maurice and his companions at Agaunum[122], and their veneration does not form a part of the Roman tradition. Therefore, this memorial, which dates from the eleventh century in the Roman calendar, is left to the particular calendars.

The Roman Legion of Christians, called the Theban Legion[123], under the presidency of their General, Maurice, numbered more than six thousand men. They marched from the East into Gaul, which was in revolt. They were camped near the Lake of Geneva when they received orders to join the others in a solemn sacrifice to the gods. They retired a little farther away, to a site today called Saint Maurice d'Augaune, to abstain, but were told to return and join the festival with the others. They found themselves in the sad necessity of disobeying the command. It was not an act of felony for these brave soldiers, who had already fought many battles, but of heroic loyalty. Nonetheless, the brutal prince gave the order to decimate the Legion. It would seem the emperor's messengers might have feared a forced resistance, but the disciples of Jesus Christ hoped for nothing but a peaceful victory over the world and the demon with all his false gods.

The names of the soldiers were written on papers and placed in the caps of the centurions, for 600 were destined to perish as examples. These embraced their comrades, who encouraged them and even envied their

---

[122] In modern-day Switzerland.
[123] According to the hagiographies of Saint Maurice, the Legion's chief saint, the Theban Legion is a Roman legion from Egypt — "six thousand six hundred and sixty-six men" — who converted en masse to Christianity and were martyred together in 286, according to Christian hagiography.

fate. The plain soon flowed with the blood of the martyrs. The survivors persisted in declaring themselves Christians, and the butchery began again; the blood of another 600 reddened the waters of the Rhone. The others persevered in their faith, and Saint Maurice sent the tyrant an admirable letter, saying: Emperor, we are your soldiers; we are ready to combat the enemies of the empire, but we are also Christians, and we owe fidelity to the true God. We are not rebels but prefer to die innocent rather than live guilty. The emperor, seeing himself defeated, ordered them all to be massacred. As the massacre began, these generous soldiers deposed their weapons, offered their necks to the sword, and suffered from being butchered in silence.

[Jaud, Leon. *Vie Des Saints Pour Tous Les Jours De L'annee: Avec Une Pratique De Piete Pour Chaque Jour.* Translated by the Monastère du Magnificat. Tours: A. Mame, 1950. Print.]

Saint Linus, Pope and Martyr († 76) — September 23

The memorial of Linus, an eleventh-century addition to the Roman calendar, is abolished since the date of his death is unknown, and it appears that he was not a martyr.

Saint Linus was converted to Rome in the days when Saint Peter was preaching the Gospel there. This nobleman, originally from Volterra in Tuscany, left his father and renounced his heritage to practice the doctrine of Our Lord Jesus Christ with greater perfection. He soon gave admirable proofs of his zeal, learning, and prudence, and the first Vicar of Christ employed him in preaching and administering the Sacraments.

He crossed into Gaul and became the bishop of the city of Besancon. The number of faithful increased daily by the conversion of many idolaters. The Saint one day attempted to turn some of those away from the celebration of a festival in honor of their gods, telling them that these idols were but statues without breath or sentiment and represented only human beings whose vices were public knowledge. He urged them to turn to the unique God, Creator of the heavens and the earth, to whom alone man owes the homage of sacrifice. A prodigy followed his words; a column of their temple crumbled and caused the fall of an idol, which broke into a thousand pieces. The worshipers, unmoved by this, drove the Saint out of the city of Besançon[124], as the city's tradition still attests.

He returned to Rome and was there when the prince of the Apostles was martyred. He wrote an account of the double martyrdom of Saints Peter and Paul and was judged worthy of replacing the first Vicar of Christ. The register of his reign records the creation of fifteen bishops and eighteen priests. The Roman breviary says that the faith and sanctity of this blessed Pope were so great that he drove the demons from many possessed persons. He had governed the Church scarcely a year before he shed his blood for his Savior. His body was buried in the Vatican near Saint Peter. Only in the 17th century did his tomb reappear, marked *Linus* when Pope Urban VIII had the work on the *Confession of Saint Peter*[125] completed in the Basilica bearing his name.

[Guérin, Abbé (Paul), François Giry, and Simon Martin. *Les Petits Bollandistes: Vies Des Saints De L'Ancien et du Nouveau Testament.* Translated by the Monastère du

---

[124] Besançon is a city in eastern France near the Swiss border.

[125] Saint Peter's church in the Vatican, which had fallen into disrepair, was rebuilt under Pope Julius II in 1506 and dedicated by Pope Urban VIII in 1626. The richest treasure of this venerable place, however, are the relics of Saints Peter and Paul, which are housed in a sumptuous vault beyond the middle of the church towards the upper end, beneath a magnificent altar, at which only the pope says Mass unless he commissions another to do so. This sacred vault is known as *The Confession of Saint Peter*, or the *Threshold of the Apostles (Limina Apostolorum)*, to which pilgrims have flocked since the beginning of time.

Magnificat. Paris: Bloud et Barral, 1882. *HathiTrust Digital Library,*
hdl.handle.net/2027/nnc1.0036694380.]

Saint Thecla, First Virgin Martyr († First Century) — September 23

The memorial of Thecla, placed in the general calendar in the same century, is abolished because there is no basis for her veneration other than the apocryphal Acts of the lives of Paul and Thecla.

Saint Thecla is one of the most ancient, as she is one of the most illustrious Saints in the calendar of the Church. At Iconium[126], Saint Thecla heard the preaching of Saint Paul, who kindled the love of virginity in her heart. She had been promised in marriage to a young man who was rich and generous, but after hearing the discourses of the Apostle's word, she died to all thought of earthly espousals. However, she forgot her beauty; she was deaf to her parent's threats, fled from a luxurious home, and followed the Apostle at the first opportunity.

The rage of her parents and her suitor followed hard after her, and the Roman power did its worst against the virgin Christ had chosen for Himself. First, she was stripped and placed in the public theater, but her innocence shrouded her like a garment. Then the lions were let loose against her; they fell crouching at her feet and licked them like a house pet. Even fire could not harm her. Torment after torment was inflicted upon her, until finally the divine Spouse of virgins spoke the word of deliverance and called her to Himself, with the double crown of martyrdom and virginity upon her head.

---

[126] The Latin name for Konya, Turkey's ancient city, is Iconium. Since the 1st century, the city of Iconium in Lycaonia has been a Christian bishopric under the Ecumenical Patriarchate of Constantinople. Although the area had never been professedly Catholic, a Roman Catholic titular archbishopric (*Archidioecesis Iconiensis*) was established in 1662.

[Shea, John G. *Little Pictorial Lives of the Saints, with Reflections for Every Day of the Year; Compiled from "Butler's Lives."* New York: Benziger, 1894. *HathiTrust Digital Library,* hdl.handle.net/2027/nyp.33433068232887.]

Our Lady of Ransom or Mercy (Her Order's establishment 1218) — September 24

Since this memorial, which entered the Roman calendar in 1696, reflects the extraordinary devotion of the Order founded by St. Peter Nolasco[127] for ransoming captives, it is now left to the particular calendars.

The story of Our Lady of Ransom is, at its outset, that of Saint Peter Nolasco, born in Languedoc about 1189. At age twenty-five, he took a vow of chastity and made over his vast estates to the Church. After making a pilgrimage to Our Lady of Montserrat, he went to Barcelona, where he began to practice various works of charity. He conceived the idea of establishing an Order for the redemption of captives seized by the Moors on the seas and in Spain itself; they were being cruelly tormented in their African prisons to make them deny their faith. He spoke of it to the king of Aragon, James I, who knew him well and already respected him as a Saint, for the king had already asked for his prayers when he sent out his armies to combat the Moors, and he attributed his victories to those prayers.

In effect, all the Christians of Europe, and above all of Spain, were praying a great deal to obtain from God the remedy for the great evil that had befallen them. The divine Will was soon manifested. On the same night, August 1, 1218, the Blessed Virgin appeared to Saint Peter, his confessor, Raymund of Peñafort, and the king, and through these three servants of God, he established a

---

[127] Mercedarian Order.

work of the most perfect charity, the redemption of captives.

On that night, while the Church was celebrating the feast of Saint Peter in Chains, the Virgin Mary came from heaven and appeared first to Saint Peter, saying that She indeed desired the establishment of a religious Order bearing the name of Her mercy. Its members would undertake to deliver Christian captives and offer themselves, if necessary, as a gage. Word of the miracle soon spread over the entire kingdom, and on August 10th, the king went to the cathedral for a Mass celebrated by the bishop of Barcelona. Saint Raymund went up into the pulpit and narrated his vision with admirable eloquence and enthusiasm. The king besought the bishop's blessing for the heaven-sent plan, and the bishop bestowed the habit on Saint Peter, who emitted the solemn vow to give himself as a hostage if necessary.

The Order, thus solemnly established in Spain, was approved by Gregory IX under the name of *Our Lady of Mercy*. The Order spread rapidly through God's grace and under His Virgin Mother's protection. Its growth was increased as the charity and holiness of its members were observed; they very often followed Her directive to give themselves up to voluntary slavery, when necessary, to aid the good work. Thanks to God and the Blessed Virgin, it was to return that a feast day was instituted and observed on September 24th, first in this Order of Our Lady, then everywhere in Spain and France. It was finally extended to the entire Church by Innocent XII.

[Guérin, Abbé (Paul), François Giry, and Simon Martin. *Les Petits Bollandistes: Vies Des Saints De L'Ancien et du Nouveau Testament.* Translated by the Monastère du Magnificat. Paris: Bloud et Barral, 1882. *HathiTrust Digital Library,* hdl.handle.net/2027/nnc1.0036694380; Shea, John G. *Little Pictorial Lives of the Saints, with Reflections for Every Day of the Year; Compiled from "Butler's Lives."* New York: Benziger, 1894. *HathiTrust Digital Library,* hdl.handle.net/2027/nyp.33433068232887.]

Saint Cyprian and Saint Justina, Martyrs († 314) — September 26

These persons did not exist, and this thirteenth-century addition to the Roman calendar is abolished.

The detestable superstitions of Saint Cyprian's idolatrous parents delivered him from infancy to the devil. He was brought up in all the impious mysteries of idolatry, astrology, and black magic. Having learned all the extravagances of these schools of error and delusion, Cyprian hesitated at no crime, blasphemed Christ, and committed secret murders.

In the time of the emperor Diocletian, a young Christian called Justina lived at Antioch, of high birth and great beauty. A pagan nobleman fell in love with her, finding her modesty inaccessible and her resolution to evade him invincible. He applied to Cyprian for assistance. Cyprian tried every secret he was acquainted with to overcome her resolution. Justina, perceiving herself vigorously attacked, armed herself by prayer, watchfulness, and mortification against all his demonic artifices and the power of his spells. Cyprian, realizing a superior power was besting him, began to recognize the weakness of the infernal spirits and resolved to quit their service and become a Christian himself. Agladius, the suitor of the holy virgin, was likewise converted and baptized.

When the persecution of Diocletian broke out, Cyprian and Justina were seized and presented to the same judge. She was inhumanly scourged, and Cyprian was torn with iron hooks. After this, they were sent in chains to Diocletian, who commanded their heads to be struck off. This sentence was executed at Nicomedia[128] in the year 304.

[Shea, John G. *Little Pictorial Lives of the Saints, with Reflections for Every Day of the Year; Compiled from "Butler's Lives."* New York: Benziger, 1894. *HathiTrust Digital Library,* hdl.handle.net/2027/nyp.33433068232887.]

Feast of the Dedication of St Michael the Archangel, (a.k.a., "Michaelmas") (est. Fourth Century) — September 29

The memorials of Gabriel and Raphael are added to this celebration, now called: Michael, Gabriel, and Raphael, Archangels.

MI-CA-EL, or *Who is like unto God?* was the cry of the great Archangel when he smote the rebel Lucifer in the conflict of the heavenly hosts. From that hour, he has been known as Michael, Captain of the armies of God, the archetype of divine fortitude, the champion of every faithful soul in strife with the powers of evil. What is more, we see him in Holy Scripture as the special guardian of the children of Israel, their comfort and protector in times of sorrow or conflict. It is he who prepares their return from the Persian captivity when the prophet Daniel prays for that favor: *And he said to me: Fear not, Daniel: for from the first day that thou didst set thy heart to understand, to afflict thyself in the sight of thy God, thy words have been heard: and I am come for thy words. But the prince of the kingdom of the Persians resisted me one and twenty days: and behold Michael, one of the chief princes, came to help me, and I remained there by the*

---

128 Nicomedia (modern İzmit) was an ancient Greek city in modern-day Turkey. Nicomedia was chosen by the emperor Diocletian, who ruled in the east, to be the Roman Empire's eastern and most senior capital city in 286, a position it held throughout the Tetrarchy system (293–324).

king of the Persians. (Daniel 10:12-13); who leads the valiant Maccabees to victory in battle, after the prayer of Judas Maccabeus: *O Lord, when they that were sent by king Sennacherib blasphemed thee, an angel went out, and slew of them a hundred and eighty-five thousand: Even so destroy this army in our sight today, and let the rest know that he hath spoken ill against thy sanctuary: and judge thou him according to his wickedness. And the armies joined battle on the thirteenth day of the month Adar: and the army of Nicanor was defeated, and he himself was first slain in the battle. And when his army saw that Nicanor was slain, they threw away their weapons and fled. (1 Maccabees 7:41-44)*.

Since its foundation by Jesus Christ, the Church has venerated Saint Michael as her special patron and protector. She invokes him by name in her *Confiteor* when accusing her faults; she summons him to the side of her children in the agony of death and chooses him as their escort from the chastening flames of purgatory to the realms of holy light. Lastly, when Antichrist shall have set up his kingdom on earth, Michael will unfurl the standard of the Cross once more. This we know from a prophecy of Scripture which states clearly that in those days, the great prince Michael will rise to protect the children of God.

But at that time shall Michael rise up, the great prince, who standeth for the children of thy people: and a time shall come such as never was from the time that nations began even until that time. And at that time shall thy people be saved, every one that shall be found written in the book. And many of those that sleep in the dust of the earth, shall awake: some unto life everlasting, and others unto reproach, to see it always. But they that are learned shall shine as the brightness of the firmament: and they that instruct many to justice, as stars for all eternity. But thou, O Daniel, shut up the words, and seal the book,

even to the time appointed: many shall pass over, and
knowledge shall be manifold. (Daniel 12:1-4)

During the plague in Rome in the 6th century,
Pope Gregory the Great saw Saint Michael in a vision
sheathing his flaming sword to show that he would end the
scourge ravaging the city. In 608, a church was erected in
thanksgiving to Saint Michael for the help he gave.

[Shea, John G. *Little Pictorial Lives of the Saints, with Reflections for Every Day of the
Year; Compiled from "Butler's Lives."* New York: Benziger, 1894. *HathiTrust Digital
Library,* hdl.handle.net/2027/nyp.33433068232887.]

OCTOBER

Saint Remigius, Bishop, and Confessor (✝ 533) — October 1

*The memorial of Remigius, who died at Rheims on
January 13, 533, was entered into the Roman calendar in
the thirteenth century. Since he is not a saint of universal
significance, this observance is left to the particular
calendars.*

Saint Remi or Remigius was born to noble and
pious parents in the middle of the fifth century. His
mother, Saint Celine, had birthed two sons before him;
the eldest, Saint Principius, became the twelfth bishop of
Soissons, and the second was the father of Saint Lupus,
the thirteenth bishop of the same see. Saint Remi was
given to his parents many years later, miraculously; a blind
hermit named Montanus, afflicted by the state of religion
in the churches of Gaul, was told three times,
supernaturally, to advise his worthy parents that they
would have a son who would be the light of the Francs,
and would bring these new conquerors out of the idolatry
in which they were plunged.

418

The child born to them in fulfillment of the prediction was at the age of twenty-two, acclaimed Archbishop of Rheims, despite his humble doubts about his competence. He was unusually tall, and his countenance manifested a blend of majesty and serenity; his bearing was gentle, humble, and retiring. He was learned and eloquent, and his pity and charity were boundless. In his labors, he knew no weariness. His body was the outward expression of a noble and holy soul, breathing the spirit of humility and compunction.

Moreover, the archbishop received the gift of miracles. When a great fire threatened the city of Rheims with total ruin, he arrested it by his presence; he faced it with a crucifix and made the sign of the cross, and the flames retired as he advanced. Moreover, he resurrected a young woman, increasing his fame.

God had a particular and great work in store for His predestined servant. The south of France was in the hands of Arians, and in the last years of the 5th century, the pagan Franks were seizing the north from the Romans. But Saint Remigius was loved by Clovis, the fifth of the Merovingian kings. The king was converted and baptized by him in 496, after winning the famous battle of Tolbiac, to fulfill his promise to adopt the religion of his Christian wife if he repulsed the invading armies. Unfortunately, a vast army of invaders, which had cast all of France into panic, fled in disarray when the small army of Clovis attacked, and their leader was slain.

Clovis had married the noble Christian maiden known to us as Saint Clotilda, and these three acting concertedly gained virtually the entire nation to the Christian religion. Saint Remi and his assistants baptized the army simultaneously as Clovis. The Saint threw down the altars of the idols, built churches, and appointed bishops. He silenced the Arians and presided at the

Catholic First Council of Orleans[129]. Eventually, he converted so many that he left France a Catholic kingdom; its king was also the first crowned son of the Church and, at that time, the only one. Ever since Saint Remi, Catholic France has rejoiced in its title of the *eldest daughter of the Church.*

After an episcopate of seventy-four years, the longest on record, Saint Remi died in 533, leaving to France his famous *Testament,* predicting God's graces of predilection for this blessed kingdom, if its Heads remained faithful to Him, with the most severe chastisements if the contrary ensued. As the nation's Catholic historians affirm, the prophecy has already been fulfilled three times for the three royal dynasties.

[Guérin, Abbé (Paul), François Giry, and Simon Martin. *Les Petits Bollandistes: Vies Des Saints De L'Ancien et du Nouveau Testament.* Translated by the Monastère du Magnificat. Paris: Bloud et Barral, 1882. *HathiTrust Digital Library,* hdl.handle.net/2027/nnc1.0036694380; Shea, John G. *Little Pictorial Lives of the Saints, with Reflections for Every Day of the Year; Compiled from "Butler's Lives."* New York: Benziger, 1894. *HathiTrust Digital Library,* hdl.handle.net/2027/nyp.33433068232887.]

Saint Placidus, and of his Companions, Martyrs († 541) — October 5

The 1961 revision of the monastic calendar distinguishes Placid, a disciple of Benedict, from an unknown martyr of Sicily of the same name. This memorial, added to the Roman calendar in 1588, is abolished.

At that time, the glorious patriarch Saint Benedict shined in the world. He enlightened it by his most holy life and miracles, and by the institution of his holy Order, there lived in Rome one Tertullus, a very honorable and

---

[129] By order of Clovis, the First Council of Orleans (*Conciliumn Aurelianense*) was held on July 10, 511.

wealthy lord, next to emperors in dignity. This gentleman had four children, Placidus, Eutychius, Victorin, and Flavia. And as he was not less pious, he was rich and potent, understanding the great and wonderful works God brought by Saint Benedict, and desiring that his son Placidus (the eldest) should be brought up in all virtue. Therefore, in the holy fear of our Lord, he offered him to Saint Benedict when he was seven years old, beseeching him that he would instruct him and teach him the direct way to happiness.

Placidus lived with his holy master and was so docile and well inclined that he began presently in that tender age to profit much in virtue. He loved abstinence and took delight in watching, fasting, and austerity. He was humble and punctual in obedience, modest, silent, bashful, mature in understanding, and grave in manners and comportment. Saint Benedict bore him a particular affection for his nobility, good condition, and much more because he had profited so much in all perfection in a few years.

Tertullus was not content to have offered his son to the saint, but having understood that he founded a monastery at Mount Cassin[130], he gave him certain fair lands and lordships, which he had thereabouts. Besides these, he gave him eighteen villages, or hamlets, in Sicily, with their ports, woods, rivers, fishing places, and mills. So great was the holiness of this gentleman, and so persuaded he was, that so liberal a donation, made for the founding of the monasteries, and sustentation of the servants of God, was pleasing and acceptable to our Lord, who had given him those goods.

When it was known in Sicily what Tertullus had given to the monks, there wanted not those who out of

---

[130] The Abbey of Montecassino (*Abbazia di Montecassino*) was founded in 529 by Saint Benedict of Nursia on the site of an ancient tower and an Apollo temple. Located 516 meters above sea level, it has had an alternate history of destruction, looting, earthquakes, and subsequent reconstructions.

covetousness endeavored to possess themselves of those inheritances and to hold them by force and violence; because they were given to religion, or as if God our Lord made no account of the injuries done to his servants. Therefore, when Saint Benedict noticed what had passed in Sicily, he resolved to send thither Placidus. For although he was only twenty-one, yet for his great piety and prudence, and for that he was the son of Tertullus, he judged he would be better able than any other to defend those goods and to get them out of their hands, who now unjustly had seized on them.

Like a child of obedience, the holy young man accepted the journey and, accompanied by Gordian and Donatus, his two familiar friends, departed from Mount Cassin, upon the 20th day of May, in the year of our Lord 536. He came to Capua, where he was received with much charity by Saint German, bishop of the same city, and from thence, he followed on his way to Canosa (in the province of Apulia) by Rioly until he came to Sicily. All along the way, he wrought great miracles: he cured a secretary of the church of Capua, called Zofas, who had a great pain of the head; and a blind man, making a sign of the cross upon his eyes; and a child that was dying; and a young maid that was blind, deaf, and dumb. He cast many devils out of the bodies they possessed; by his prayers, he cured many sick of diverse diseases whose health was despaired. Insomuch that Saint Placidus was renowned wherever he passed.

And so, when he came into Sicily, he received great reverence and admiration as an angel from heaven. And, on the same island of Sicily, he also wrought many great miracles in favor of the inhabitants of that place. Upon arriving at the city of Messina, a prime gentleman called Messalinus, a great friend of his father, entertained him at his own house. Still, he would stay only one day in it, saying that monks ought not to lodge in a place of seculars because the manner of conversation of the one and the other were different.

He agreed with those that had usurped the lands and lordships, which had belonged to his father, but now belonged to his Order, in such sort that they might keep a good conscience, and his Order might not be injured. So he began there in the haven of Messina to build a monastery for his religious, an oratory to Saint John the Baptist, which the bishop of Messina consecrated, and the monastery was finished in the fourth year after he came into Sicily.

The life of Saint Placidus was so perfect, and his words so burning with divine love, that accompanied by the miracles which God wrought by him, they enflamed the hearts of many, that despising the vanities of the world, and hurtful delights and contentments of the flesh, they gave themselves freely to God. Saint Placidus employed himself in continual prayer and meditation and recreated his spirit in our Lord, shedding many tears.

During Lent, on Sundays, Tuesdays, and Thursdays, he fasted with bread and water; the rest of the days, he ate nothing and drank no wine throughout the year. He wore a haircloth next to his skin. He slept sitting instead of lying, and his sleep was short and light. He was meek, grave, and courteous and was never seen angry. He spoke not, but only when necessity required it, either to comfort his monks or the poor or for some urgent or charitable business. By this, his so austere and perfect life, he drew many to religion, and in a short time were gathered to him thirty other religious, who flourished with a great example of sanctity; and the Order of the holy father Saint Benedict went on increasing in the world.

It was published in Rome, how Saint Placidus was in Sicily, the life he led, the monastery he founded, and the miracles God wrought by him; and his brothers Eutychius and Victorin, and his sister Flavia, desirous to see him (for they had not seen him since their father Tertullus had delivered him to the care of Saint Benedict) sailed into Sicily, where they found him, and were received by him with singular joy and contentment, praising our Lord for having given them such a brother, who did so genuinely serve Him. They stayed some days in that monastery; and that we might understand the ways which God takes to bring men to heaven, and to crown them with glory, he permitted that a Moor, called Mamucha, captain to Abdala, an African king, should come at this time to infest the coasts of Sicily, and to make war upon the Christians. He brought a Navy of one hundred ships and sixteen thousand eight hundred fighting men in those vessels. They entered the haven of Messina, and the monastery of Saint John the Baptist, being near the sea, fell suddenly upon it and, by brutal violence, broke the gates and put chains upon all that were in the monastery.

Saint Placidus, with his brethren Eutychius, Victorin, and Flavia; and with Faustus and Firmatus, deacon, and thirty monks, were carried in chains before Mamucha, a cruel and vicious man and fiercer than a tiger. Who after that by threats and frights, he could not persuade them to renounce our Lord Jesus Christ, he commanded them to be cruelly whipped, and then to be shut up in prison, and that nothing should be given them there to eat, but that they should be cudgeled and whipped, and be hung up by their feet, and have smoke placed under them. After this torment, he commanded a little barley and water to be given to everyone, to be kept alive so that they might be tormented longer.

They all suffered their torments with great patience, constancy, and joy, praising our Lord to see that they should suffer for His love and the confession of His faith, Saint Placidus, like a brave captain going before them, animating them by his example. So also, the holy virgin Flavia, his sister, amongst the rest, showed tremendous grit and heavenly valor; for holding her naked and lifted in the air, and tearing in pieces her flesh, the heartless tyrant asking her, how, being so noble a person. A Roman, she could endure that ignominy and nakedness? She answered *That for the love of Jesus Christ, all torments were sweet to her, and death was life.* And, seeing he could not overcome her by afflictions, he would have specified that his most shameless and impudent soldiers ravish her and give her the greatest torments that the holy virgin could receive. But she prayed to God, and our Lord, who is such a friend to chastity, did so defend her, that all that went about to meddle with her became lame and senseless, and for this, they let her alone.

Mamucha commanded the saints to be brought before him daily and put to new torments. And because he saw one time that Saint Placidus was very jocund in his sufferings and praised God, he commanded many blows to be given upon the mouth with a stone. And seeing this was not sufficient to make the saint leave off the praises of God, he caused his tongue to be cut out; but after it was cut out, he spoke better and went on the praises of the Lord, giving Him thanks for what he suffered for His sake.

They were hung up one night with anchors and stones of great weight tied to their legs. Finally, the tyrant commanded them to be beheaded, declaring in a sentence their condemnation that he put them to death because they adored and held for God Christ, who was crucified. They were carried to the seaside, and Saint Placidus made his prayer to our Lord, beseeching Him for the merits and intercession of his master, Saint Benedict, to give them constancy to pass that gulf of death, and bring them to the haven of bliss. All his companions answered, *Amen,* they offered their necks to the sword and were beheaded, and their bodies remained there for four days without burial.

The barbarians destroyed the monastery, not leaving one stone upon another, yet they touched not the church of Saint John the Baptist, and entering their ships, they departed to go on their voyage. But the Lord immediately sent such a vehement and terrible storm that there in the mouth of the haven and strait between Messina and Calabria, the hundred ships were sunk, and the sixteen thousand eight hundred persons were sunk that were in them were drowned. Afterward, Gordian, one of the two companions who came with Saint Placidus from Mount Cassin and alone had escaped (being young and near to a back door when the barbarians came), buried the body of Saint Placidus in the Church of Saint John the Baptist; and the bodies of the other thirty-three martyrs, in the place where they were beheaded. Both in one place and the other, God wrought many miracles, curing the sick from all parts to beg health through the intercession of Saint Placidus and his blessed companions.

Their martyrdom was upon the 5th of October, in the thirteenth year of the reign of Justinian, in the year of our Lord 541, according to Gordian, who was the author of this history, and according to Cardinal Baronius, in his corrected annotations. Saint Placidus was twenty-six years old when he died. When the glorious father, Saint Benedict, heard of the martyrdom of his dear child, and his holy companions, he rejoiced extremely and gave thanks to our Lord that had given him such a son and had crowned him with the crown of martyrdom and put him for an example and pattern for his Order, and in the whole Church.

Of Saint Placidus, write all the Martyrologies, and Leo Ostiensis, Cassian, Trithemius, and Cardinal Baronius in his Annotations upon the Martyrology and the seventh tome of his Annals. And Pope Sixtus V, in the year of our Lord 1588, which was the fourth of his popedom, commanded his feast to be celebrated in the whole Catholic Church, with a single Office, and in the church of Messina of Saint John the Baptist, where his relics reside, with a double Office.

[Ribadeneyra, Pedro de. "The Life of Saint Placidus, and his Companions, Martyrs." *The Lives of Saints, With Other Feasts of the Year, according to the Roman Calendar. Written in Spanish by the Reverend Father Peter Ribadeneyra, Priest of the Society of Jesus. Translated Into English by W.P. (William Petre) Esq; The Second Edition Corrected and Amended*, vol. 2, pp. 324-326. London. Printed by B.S., 1730. *HathiTrust Digital Library*, hdl.handle.net//2027/nyp.33433003053000.]

Saint Mark, Pope, and Confessor (✝ 336) — October 7

The memorial of Mark, who died in Rome in 336, is now left for the particular calendars. This saint does not have universal significance.

Saint Mark was by birth a Roman and served God with such enthusiasm among the clergy of that church that, advancing continually in sincere humility and the knowledge and sense of his weakness and imperfections, he strove every day to surpass himself in the fervor of his charity and zeal, and in the exercise of all virtues. The persecution ceased in the West, upon the abdication of Dioclesian and Maximian, at the beginning of the year 305 but was revived for a short time by Maxentius in 312. Saint Mark abated nothing of his watchfulness but endeavored to redouble his zeal during the church's peace; knowing that if men sometimes cease openly to persecute the faithful, the devil never allows them any truce, and his snares are generally most to be feared in the time of calm. The saint contributed much to advance the service of God during the pontificate of Saint Sylvester; after his demise, he was himself placed in the apostolic chair on the 18th of January, 336. He held that dignity for only eight months and twenty days, dying on the 7th of October. According to the Pontifical published by Anastasius, he built two churches, one on the Via Ardeatina, where he was afterward buried; another within the walls, near the capitol. He was interred in the Via Ardeatina, in the cemetery of Balbina, a holy martyr buried there. It was initially called Prætextatus, probably from some illustrious person of that name. It was situated without the Ardeatine gate, not far from the cemetery of Calixtus, on the Via Appia. Saint Mark had very much beautified and adorned this burial place out of respect to the martyrs there interred, and he is buried there from that time bore his name. Pope Damasus, in his epitaph, extols his extraordinary disinterestedness and contempt of all earthly things and his remarkable spirit of prayer, by which he drew down on the people abundant spiritual blessings. His name occurs in the Liberian Calendar, compiled soon after his death, and in all other Martyrologies of the Western church. A church bore its name in Rome in the fifth century. His remains were translated into it by order of Gregory VII. The pontificals mention that the church was repaired by Hadrian I, Gregory IV, and Paul II. This last pope built near it a palace which was the summer residence of the popes till Sixtus V preferred the Quirinal Hill[131] or Monte Cavallo[132].

It was by constant watchfulness over themselves, assiduous self-denial, and humble prayer that all the saints triumphed over their spiritual enemies. They never laid down their arms. So a Christian should be afraid of no enemy more than himself, whom he always carries about with him, and whom he cannot flee. He, therefore, never

---

[131] The Quirinal Hill is one of Rome's Seven Hills, located north of the city center. It is the official residence of the Italian president, who resides in the Quirinal Palace.

[132] *Monte Cavallo* is a comune in the Province of Macerata, Marche, Italy, about 50 miles southwest of Ancona and 28 miles southwest of Macerata.

ceases to cry out to God: Who will preserve me from falling through myself! Not my strength. Unless thou, O Lord, art my light and support, I watch in vain.

[Butler, Alban. *The Lives of the Fathers, Martyrs, and Other Principal Saints. Compiled from Original Monuments and Authentic Records.* Dublin: James Duffy, 1866. *HathiTrust Digital Library,* catalog.hathitrust.org/Record/001941109.]

Saints Marcellus and Apuleius, Martyrs († third or fourth century) — October 8

The memorial of Marcellus, martyred at Capua, was placed on the Roman calendar in the thirteenth century. His cult is not a part of the Roman tradition and is left to the particular calendars. The Acts of the life of Apuleius are legendary, and his memorial, which entered the Roman calendar in the eleventh and twelfth centuries, is abolished.

These two martyrs mentioned in the Gelasian Sacramentary today, whom a legend describes as having been disciples of Simon Magus at Rome, were, in fact, inhabitants of Capua.

Marcellus is one of a group that includes Castus, Emilius, and Saturninus. We do not find the name of Apuleius, who appears in our Missal, in any ancient list, and it is merely a medieval tradition that asserts that he was the servant of Marcellus and shared the crown of martyrdom with his master.

Apuleius is unknown even to the ancient hagiography of Capua; no writer ever mentions him, nor is his picture to be found in the mosaics of Saint Priscus dating from the fifth or sixth century, where at least thirty-two saints are represented, the more significant part of whom belong to the Province of Campania.

Because of this, a doubt arises whether the name Apuleius has not been derived from an error in copying the topographical indication in the Martyrology today: *in Apulia, Natale Casti et Emeli, Marcelli (in Apulia, the birthplace of Castus and Emelius, Marcellus).*

The following lines may still be read on the Lombard façade of the Church of Saint Marcellus at Capua[133]:

MARCELLVS · SANCTVS · COMTEMNENS ·
CAESARIS · ACTVS
EST · CAPVAM · LATVS · PRO · CHRISTO ·
DECAPITATVS

"Saint Marcellus, because he despised the command of Caesar, was brought to Capua and beheaded here for Christ's sake."

[Schuster, Ildefonso, 1880-1954, W. Fairfax-Cholmeley, and Arthur Levelis-Marke. "Saints Marcellus and Apuleius, Martyrs". *The Sacramentary: (Liber Sacramentorum): Historical & Liturgical Notes on the Roman Missal*, vol. 5, p. 163. London: Burns, Oates & Washbourne, 1924-30. *HathiTrust Digital Library*, hdl.handle.net/2027/uc1.b3008500.]

Saints Sergius and Bacchus, Martyrs (✝ 303) — October 8

A twelfth-century addition to the Roman calendar, the memorial of Sergius is abolished. The cult of this Syrian martyr is not a part of the Roman tradition. Likewise, the Acts of the life of Bacchus are legendary, and his memorial, which entered the Roman calendar in the eleventh and twelfth centuries, is abolished.

---

[133] *Chiesa di San Marcello*, 81043 Capua, Province of Caserta, Italy.

The fame of these two martyrs can only be compared with that of the Anargyroi[134], Cosmas, and Damian. The tomb of Saint Sergius was at Resafa[135]. It was the object of such continual pilgrimages from all parts of the Eastern world that Emperor Justinian surrounded the city with walls to defend the sanctuary and its treasures from the barbarians. The name of Resafa was changed to that of Sergiopolis in honor of the celestial patron of the city.

Tradition joins the name of the martyr Sergius, but according to Antoninus of Piacenza[136], the former saint was buried in another place. *In civitate Barbarisso.*

Saint Gregory of Tours relates the numerous miracles at Resafa, on account of which many churches and monasteries were dedicated to Saint Sergius. Moreover, the nomadic tribes of Syria honor him as their special patron.

In Rome, several churches were also named after these celebrated Eastern martyrs. However, the Convent of Saints Sergius and Bacchus *post formam aquaeductus* at the Lateran had been left empty. They abandoned it when Paschal I caused it to be restored and, endowing it once more, established a monastic community whose duty was to chant the day and night Offices in the Lateran Basilica.

The Vatican likewise possessed an oratory dedicated to the martyrs Sergius and Bacchus; we know that it was restored by Gregory II, who added to the sanctuary a *diaconia* with a hospital for the poor.

---

[134] *Agioi Anargyroi* is a Greek suburb in the north-central agglomeration of Athens. It gets its name from the "Holy Unmercenaries," who were saints who were not paid for their medical services.

[135] Resafa, also spelled Rusafa, was a city in the Roman province of Euphratensis, in modern-day Syria. It was known in the Byzantine era as Sergiopolis and briefly as Anastasiopolis. It is an archaeological site located southwest of Raqqa and the Euphrates River.

[136] Saint Antoninus of Piacenza is the patron saint of the Italian town of Piacenza. In the Roman Catholic Church, he is regarded as a saint and martyr, with a feast day on September 30. The saint was said to have been martyred at Piacenza or Travo during the Diocletian Persecution in 303 AD.

The Basilica of Saint Paul counted among the sanctuaries affiliated with it, the Church of Saints Sergius and Bacchus in Suburra, and the ancient monastery Canelicum[137], which is still in existence. Another basilica in honor of these Syrian martyrs rose at the foot of the Capitol, between the Arch of Septimius Severus[138] and the Julian Basilica[139]. It was restored in the thirteenth century by Innocent III, who attributed his elevation to the Papacy to the intercession of the martyrs. He caused the following inscription to be placed on the porch of the church:

POENE • RVI • QVASI • NVLLA • FVI •
SED • ME • RELEVAVIT • LOTHARIVS
PRIVS • POSTQVAM • RENOVAVIT •
DEQVE • MEO • PRAEMIO • SVMPTVS •
PATER • VRBIS
ET • ORBIS • HOC • TAMEN • EX •
PROPRIO • FECIT • MIHI • SIC •
RENOVOR • BIS

"I was almost in ruins and destroyed when Lotharius raised me up. After he had restored me, he received an immediate reward and became the Father of the City and the world. He performed this work at his own expense; thus, I have been twice renewed."

[Schuster, Ildefonso, 1880-1954, W. Fairfax-Cholmeley, and Arthur Levelis-Marke. "Saints Sergius and Bacchus, Martyrs". *The Sacramentary: (Liber Sacramentorum): Historical & Liturgical Notes on the Roman Missal,* vol. 5, pp. 163-164. London:

---

[137] *Santi Sergio e Bacco* is a Byzantine Rite Catholic church located on *Piazza Madonna dei Monti* in the *rione of Monti* in Rome, Italy. Sergius and Bacchus are said to be early fourth-century Roman military officers and Christian martyrs who were buried in Syria. The church was known as *Sergius and Bacchus in Callinico* in the 9th century, *Sergius and Bacchus de Suburra* in the Middle Ages, and *Madonna del Pascolo* from the 18th century forward.

[138] The Arch of Septimius Severus, located at the northeastern end of the Roman Forum, is a white marble triumphal arch dedicated in 203 A.D. to commemorate Emperor Septimius Severus and his two sons, Caracalla and Geta, in the Parthian campaigns of 194-195 A.D. and 197-199 A.D.

[139] The Basilica Julia was once a structure in the Roman Forum. During the Roman Empire, it was a large, ornate public building used for meetings and other official business. Its ruins have been studied.

Burns, Oates & Washbourne, 1924-30. *HathiTrust Digital Library,* hdl.handle.net/2027/ucl.b3008500.]

Saint Francis Borgia, Confessor (1510–1572) — October 10

The memorial of Francis, who died in Rome on September 30, 1572, dates from 1688 in the Roman calendar. It is now left to the particular calendars because of a lack of universal significance.

Saint Francis Borgia, named for Francis of Assisi at his birth in 1510, was placed under the tutelage of his uncle, Archbishop of Saragossa, after the death of his mother when he was ten years old. Soon he had to go to the court of Spain, as he was destined to be one of the great lords of that nation. There he remained Christian, modest, and virtuous. His noble and beautiful appearance soon brought him snares which he succeeded in escaping, setting for himself regimes of prayer and study to flee from the dangers. He wore a hair shirt and never would enter any of those games of chance which cause the loss not only of money but of time, the spirit of devotion, and peace of soul. The Empress arranged for him to marry Eleanor de Castro of Portugal, who, like himself, was very pious. They were blessed with eight children, five sons and three daughters, who continued to practice the virtue of their parents.

After becoming the Duke of Gandia after his father's death, he became one of Spain's wealthiest and most honored nobles. Then, in 1539, there was laid upon him the sad duty of escorting the mortal remains of his once beautiful sovereign, Empress Isabella, who had died still young, to the royal burial ground at Granada. The coffin had to be opened for him so that he might verify the body before it was placed in the tomb. So

433

unrecognizable, so astonishing a sight met his eyes that he vowed never again to serve any earthly sovereign subject to so drastic and terrible a change.

It was many years before he could follow the call of his Lord; the emperor named him Captain-General of Catalonia and sent him to bring to justice a group of bandits who had ravaged the countryside. The poor found in him strong protection against oppression. His ordinances banished vices; he endowed poor girls and assisted families ruined by misery and reversals; he delivered debtors from prisons by paying what they owed. He was, in effect, the very Christian Viceroy of the Emperor. Saint Francis was relieved of this duty when he asked the emperor to return and govern his subjects at Gandia after his father's death. In Gandia, he again did much public good; he built monasteries, founded hospitals, and helped the poor in every possible way. But suddenly, his wife was taken from him. God told him that this loss was for his and her advantage, and amid his tears, he offered his own life and that of his children if that would please the Eternal Master.

After making a retreat according to the Exercises of Saint Ignatius[140], under Blessed Peter Favre, he made the vows of a Jesuit privately until he could see to the establishment of his children. When he went to Rome with one of them, he was rumored to be made a cardinal like two of his brothers. But he wished to avoid all dignities and succeeded in doing so by leaving Rome as soon as possible. Saint Ignatius made him his Vicar General for Spain, Portugal, and the East Indies, and there was scarcely a city in Spain and Portugal where he did not establish colleges or houses of the Company of Jesus. At the death of Saint Ignatius two years later, the

---

[140] The Spiritual Exercises, written by Ignatius of Loyola, a 16th-century Spanish priest, theologian, and founder of the Society of Jesus, are a collection of Christian meditations, contemplations, and prayers.

Order chose him to be its General. Then his journeys became countless; narrating them all would be impossible.

The Turks were threatening Christendom, and Pope Saint Pius V commissioned two cardinal-legates[141] to go and assemble the European Christian princes into a league for its defense. The holy Pope chose Francis to accompany one of the Cardinals, and worn out as he was, the Saint obeyed at once. But unfortunately, the fatigues of the embassy exhausted what little life was left to him. Saint Francis died the same year as Saint Pius V, happy to do so in the service of God and the Church, when he returned to Rome in October 1572.

[Guérin, Abbé (Paul), François Giry, and Simon Martin. *Les Petits Bollandistes: Vies Des Saints De L'Ancien et du Nouveau Testament.* Translated by the Monastère du Magnificat. Paris: Bloud et Barral, 1882. *HathiTrust Digital Library,* hdl.handle.net/2027/nnc1.0036694380; Shea, John G. *Little Pictorial Lives of the Saints, with Reflections for Every Day of the Year; Compiled from "Butler's Lives."* New York: Benziger, 1894. *HathiTrust Digital Library,* hdl.handle.net/2027/nyp.33433068232887.]

The Divine Maternity of Mary (1751) — October 11

This is now included in the solemnity on January 1.

When Mary of Nazareth conceived in Her womb the Word of God, that conception was the effect of the fullness of Her grace and action of the Holy Spirit which occurred in Her soul first, thereby making Her flesh a tabernacle and a sanctuary. The dignity of the Mother of God is Her great sanctity. The incomparable grace raises Her above all the Angels, the grace in which She was predestined and created for this glorious purpose. By the

---

[141] The term "legate" is used in a variety of contexts in the Roman Catholic Church, but it always refers to the modern diplomatic and legal concept of "ambassador."

acts of Her blessed Maternity, She *bordered* on divinity while remaining entirely human. In this way, She seems to exhaust, as it were, the power of God — the fullness of the grace accorded Her cannot be surpassed. Therefore, it is easier for us to conceive of the greatness of Mary. However, when we consider Her maternity of the Mystical Body, the Church, like Herself, is entirely human and composed of persons far from being what our Savior was, a Divine Person incarnate.

We better understand what Mary is for the Church by listening to Saint Louis Mary de Montfort, Apostle of the Cross, and the Rosary of Our Lady. As Mary was necessary for God in the Incarnation of the Word, so She is necessary for Him to sanctify souls and bring about their likeness to Christ, and We much need her in our great infirmity:

The Holy Ghost gives no heavenly gift to men which He does not have pass through Her virginal hands, such is the sentiment of the Church and its holy Fathers. Mary, being transformed into God by grace and by the glory which transforms all the Saints into Him, asks nothing, wishes nothing, and does nothing contrary to God's eternal and immutable Will. When we read then in the writings of Saints Bernard, Bernardine, Bonaventure, and others, that in heaven and on earth everything, even God Himself, is subject to the Blessed Virgin, they mean that the authority which God has been well pleased to give Her is so great that it seems as if She had the same power as God; and that Her prayers and petitions are so powerful with God that they always pass for commandments with His Majesty, who never resists the prayer of His dear Mother because She is always humble and conformed to His Will. Suppose Moses, by the force of his prayer, stayed the anger of God against the Israelites in a manner so powerful that the most high and infinitely merciful Lord, being unable to resist him, told him to let Him alone that He might be angry with and punish those rebellious people. What must we not, with much greater reason, think of the prayer of the humble Mary, the worthy Mother of God, which is more powerful with His Majesty than the prayers and intercessions of all the Angels and Saints in heaven and on earth?

The sin of our first father has spoiled us all, soured us, puffed us up, and corrupted us. The actual sins we have committed, whether mortal or venial, pardoned though they may be, have nevertheless increased our desire, weakness, inconstancy, and corruption and left evil remains in our souls. We have nothing for our portion but pride and blindness of spirit, hardness of heart, weakness, and inconstancy of soul, revolted passions, and sicknesses in the body. Therefore, let us boldly say with Saint Bernard that we need a mediator with the Mediator Himself and that the divine Mary is most capable of filling that charitable office. It was through Her that Jesus Christ came to us, and through Her, we must go to Him if we fear to go directly to Jesus Christ, our God, whether because of His infinite greatness, our vileness, or our sins, let us boldly implore the aid and intercession of Mary, our Mother. She is good, and She is tender. She has nothing austere and forbidding, nothing too sublime and brilliant. She is so charitable that She repels none of those who ask Her intercession, no matter how great sinners they have been; for, as the Saints say, never has it been heard, since the world was the world, that anyone has confidently and perseveringly had recourse to our Blessed Lady and yet been repelled.

[Grignion, de M. L.-M. *True Devotion to Mary.* Bay Shore, NY: Montfort Publications, 1960. Print; Guérin, Abbé (Paul), François Giry, and Simon Martin. *Les Petits Bollandistes: Vies Des Saints De L'Ancien et du Nouveau Testament.* Translated by the Monastère du Magnificat. Paris: Bloud et Barral, 1882. *HathiTrust Digital Library,* hdl.handle.net/2027/nnc1.0036694380.]

Saint Edward III, King of England, Confessor (1001~1066) — October 13

The memorial of Edward, who died in London on January 5, 1066, was placed on the Roman calendar in 1679. It may now be added to particular calendars since this saint is not of universal significance.

Saint Edward, son of King Ethelred, whose kingdom of England fell to the Danish invaders, was unexpectedly raised to the throne of England in 1041 at the age of forty. God had shown Edward to a pious bishop in a vision as England's King, anointed by Saint Peter: Behold the one who will be King through My favor; he will be cherished by heaven, agreeable to men, terrible to his enemies, loving to his subjects, very useful to the Church of God. The English people, tired of being governed by foreign domination, decided in 1041 to reinstate the surviving son of their legitimate sovereign and, under the leadership of three noblemen, succeeded in crowning Edward on Easter Sunday of the year 1042. Edward had spent twenty-seven years of his forty in exile in Normandy, in the palace of his maternal uncle.

When he was raised to the throne, the virtues of his earlier years, simplicity, gentleness, humility, and tender charity, but above all, his angelic purity, shone with new brightness. By a rare inspiration of God, though he married to content his nobles and people, he preserved perfect chastity in the married state. So little did he set his heart on riches that when he saw a servant robbing his treasury three times, he let him escape, saying the poor man needed the gold more than he did. He loved standing at his palace gate, speaking kindly to the poor beggars and lepers who crowded about him, many of whom he healed of their diseases. The people rejoiced in having a Saint for their king.

Long wars had brought the kingdom to a sad state, but Edward's zeal and sanctity soon wrought a significant change. His reign of twenty-four years was one of almost unbroken peace. He undertook only one war, which was victorious, to reinstate Malcolm, legitimate king of Scotland. The country grew prosperous, the ruined churches rose again under his hand, the weak lived secure, and for ages afterward, men spoke with affection of the laws of good Saint Edward. The holy king delighted in building and enriching churches; Westminster Abbey was his last and noblest work.

He devoted to the holy Apostles Saint Peter and Saint John the Evangelist and promised never to refuse alms asked in the latter's name. One day when he had no money with him, a poor man reached out his hand in the name of the Apostle, and the king gave him a valuable ring he was wearing. Sometime later, Saint John appeared to two pilgrims returning from the Holy Land. He gave them a ring and said: Take it to the king; he gave it to me one day when I asked for alms in the habit of a pilgrim. Tell him I will visit and take him with me in six months to follow the unblemished Lamb. The King received it from them after hearing their relation to this incident and broke into tears. And Edward died six months later, on January 5, 1066. Many miracles occurred at his tomb. In 1102 his body was exhumed and found intact and flexible, with its habits perfectly preserved also, appearing to be new. He was canonized in 1161 by Pope Alexander III.

[Guérin, Abbé (Paul), François Giry, and Simon Martin. *Les Petits Bollandistes: Vies Des Saints De L'Ancien et du Nouveau Testament.* Translated by the Monastère du Magnificat. Paris: Bloud et Barral, 1882. *HathiTrust Digital Library,* hdl.handle.net/2027/nnc1.0036694380; Shea, John G. *Little Pictorial Lives of the Saints, with Reflections for Every Day of the Year; Compiled from "Butler's Lives."* New York: Benziger, 1894. *HathiTrust Digital Library,* hdl.handle.net/2027/nyp.33433068232887.]

Saint Peter of Alcantara, Confessor, Reformer (1499-1562) — October 19

Because it does not celebrate a saint of universal significance, this memorial is left to the particular calendars. Peter died at Alcantara, Spain, on October 18, 1562, and his feast was placed in the Roman calendar in 1670.

Saint Peter was born in 1499 near the Portuguese border of Spain. While still a sixteen-year-old, he left his home at Alcantara and entered a convent of Discalced Franciscans near Valencia. He rose quickly to high posts in the Order as a guardian, a definitor, and then Superior of the Province of Saint Gabriel. But his thirst for penance was still unappeased, and in 1539, being then forty years old, he founded the Congregation of Saint Joseph of the Strict Observance to conserve the letter of the Rule of Saint Francis. He suffered great tribulations to conserve that Rule in its integrity. Eventually, Saint Peter himself, the year before his death, raised it to the status of a province under obedience to the Minister General of the entire Seraphic Order. The Reform he instituted has since been extended even to the farthest Orient and the Indies; it is believed God ordained that it repair the ravages to the faith of the sixteenth century.

The modesty of Saint Peter remains proverbial in the Franciscan Order; never did he raise his eyes to look at the non-essentials of his interior life with God. His fast was constant and severe; he lived perpetually on bread and water alone, even during his illnesses. He devised a harness to keep him upright on his seat during the short hour and a half of sleep he took every day for forty years. He acknowledged to Saint Teresa of Avila that this mortification was the one that cost him the most. The cells of the friars of Saint Joseph resembled graves rather than dwelling places. That of Saint Peter himself was four and a half feet in length so that he could never lie down; his sackcloth habit and a cloak were his only garments; he never covered his head or feet. In the bitter winter, he would open the door and window of his cell so that, by closing them again, he might be grateful for the shelter of his cell. Among those whom he guided to perfection, we may name Saint Teresa, who fully appreciated this remarkable director. He read her soul, approved her spirit of prayer, and strengthened her to carry out her reforms.

Everywhere he could do so, he planted crosses, for the Passion of Our Lord was engraved in his heart. Wherever they were to be placed, even on mountains, and however heavy they might be, he went to the destined sites carrying them on his shoulders. From these heights, he would preach the mysteries of the Cross, afterward remaining in prayer there. Shepherds saw him several times in the air, at the height of the highest trees of the forests. He never went anywhere except on foot, even in his old age. He was often seen prostrated before a large crucifix, shedding torrents of tears, and he was found in ecstasy once at the height of the traverse of a crucifix. Saint Peter died at the age of sixty-three, repeating with the Psalmist, *I rejoiced when it was said unto me, let us go unto the house of the Lord!* The date was October 18, 1562; he was kneeling in prayer.

[Guérin, Abbé (Paul), François Giry, and Simon Martin. *Les Petits Bollandistes: Vies Des Saints De L'Ancien et du Nouveau Testament.* Translated by the Monastère du Magnificat. Paris: Bloud et Barral, 1882. *HathiTrust Digital Library,* hdl.handle.net/2027/nnc1.0036694380; Shea, John G. *Little Pictorial Lives of the Saints, with Reflections for Every Day of the Year; Compiled from "Butler's Lives."* New York: Benziger, 1894. *HathiTrust Digital Library,* hdl.handle.net/2027/nyp.33433068232887.]

Saint Hilarion, Patriarch of the Solitaries of Palestine († 372) — October 21

The memorial of Hilarion, who died in Cyprus about 371, is a thirteenth-century addition to the Roman Calendar. It is now left to the particular calendars since it does not commemorate a saint of universal significance.

Saint Hilarion was born to pagan parents near Gaza and was converted while studying grammar in Alexandria. He renounced games, the theater, and all the vain amusements of young people, to attend the reunions of his fellow Christians. He desired to see the great Saint Anthony in the desert and went to Egypt, where he remained near him for two months. He carefully observed everything in his life and conduct — his friendliness, gentleness towards others, and severity towards himself- then returned to Palestine with a few solitaries to settle his affairs. His father and mother had both died, and he kept nothing of his heritage for himself. At that time, he was only fifteen years old.

Despite his youth and delicate health, he retired to a desert; he practiced severe mortification, tempted continually by the demons expending all their efforts to make him abandon this life of total renouncement. Instead, he redoubled his austerities, tilled the ground, and, following the example of the Egyptian monks, made baskets of reeds and willow branches. He lived first in a cabin of reeds, then in one of clay, so low and narrow that it seemed more like a tomb than lodging for a young man. He learned all the Holy Scriptures by heart and repeated them with admirable devotion. When thieves approached him one day, he told them he did not fear them because he had nothing to lose, and death did not alarm him since he was ready to die. His answers so touched them they promised him to abandon their life of pillage.

He soon began to work miracles by his prayers, and visitors made their way to his former solitude. Several remained nearby to become his disciples and thus gave rise to the monastic life in Palestine, of which Hilarion is regarded as the founder. Saint Anthony esteemed him highly, sometimes wrote him letters, and sent the sick persons who came to him from Syria, telling them they did not need to take so long a journey. Saint Hilarion was a master exorcist and healer of all illnesses. Still, he refused all remuneration for his assistance, saying to his visitors from the city that they were better placed than he to distribute in alms the money they were offering him. Frequently, the scattered solitaries of Palestine came to him to listen to his instructions, and he also visited them. The pagans, too, gathered around him. His exhortations to abandon idolatry were so powerful that on one occasion, a group of Saracens promised to convert, asking him to send them a priest to baptize them and establish a church. One day, accompanied by three thousand people following him, he blessed the vine of a solitary who received him. The vine furnished a triple harvest, and all in the crowd were well nourished.

Saint Hilarion found his solitude transformed into a city and decided at sixty-five to go elsewhere. His Palestinian disciples attempted to change his mind without success, taking only forty monks with him. So he set out for Egypt on foot. Saint Anthony had recently died, and he wished to visit the places where he had dwelt. After spending some time in Egypt, he went with only two religions to a village a few days away from Babylon. He remained only a short time there, afterward going elsewhere and everywhere assisting those who had recourse to his prayers. In Sicily, he delivered a demoniac, and then a crowd came to surround him once again. In Dalmatia, he still worked miracles and saved a city from being engulfed by tidal waves raised by an earthquake.

These traditions are still alive in the regions where he passed. He tried many times to live unknown but never could succeed.

Saint Hilarion died in 372 on the island of Cyprus at the age of seventy years. His last words were: Go forth, my soul; why dost thou doubt? Nigh seventy years hast thou served God, and dost thou fear death? His body was found incorrupted afterward, and was transported to Palestine to his original monastery. Saint Jerome was his foremost biographer.

[Guérin, Abbé (Paul), François Giry, and Simon Martin. *Les Petits Bollandistes: Vies Des Saints De L'Ancien et du Nouveau Testament.* Translated by the Monastère du Magnificat. Paris: Bloud et Barral, 1882. *HathiTrust Digital Library,* hdl.handle.net/2027/nnc1.0036694380.]

Saint Ursula and her Companions, Virgins and Martyrs at Cologne († 383) — October 21

The memorial of Ursula and her companions, added to the calendar in the fourteenth century, is abolished because the accounts of their martyrdom are purely legendary. Not even the names of the "holy virgins" allegedly put to death at Cologne are known.

Saint Ursula was born in Great Britain to Christian parents; her father, Maurus, was king of Cornubia in Scotland. Ursula was sought in marriage by a young pagan prince but had already vowed her life and her heart to Jesus Christ.

In 383, she was boarded onto a boat with many young girls and Christian women whom a Roman conqueror wished to give as wives to his soldiers after having endowed them with rich terrains. But a storm arose during the crossing of the Channel, and the ships, instead of reaching western Gaul, were driven towards the mouth of the Rhine. The Huns, who at that time were ravaging Europe, saw the ships and were preparing to pillage them and inflict on these virgins and women a dishonor more dreaded by them than death. But, commanded by Ursula, they resisted heroically and so well that suddenly the sentiments of the barbarians changed. They took up their arms to be rid of this peaceful army. Soon the victims fell under the blows of the executioners, and their souls winged their way to heaven.

The prince of the Huns, struck by Ursula's beauty, spared her at first; he tried to console her for the death of her companions and promised to marry her. But, when she did not consent, he shot her with an arrow, and this consecrated virgin fell with the others. She was considered the leader of the eleven thousand brought by the Romans from Great Britain. Many churches have relics of this army of martyrs. Still, no region is more richly endowed than that of Cologne since it is to that city that the Christians of the area devotedly carried the mortal remains of the martyrs.

In the seventh century, a magnificent church rose over their tomb, whose walls served as reliquaries. This holy cemetery has been rendered illustrious by many miracles. Pilgrims and especially young girls have come from all over Europe to beg for protection for their virginity from Saint Ursula and her companions. The very arrow which pierced Saint Ursula is still conserved there. A religious, devoted greatly to these martyrs had fallen dangerously ill; a virgin appeared to him and said: I am one of the virgins you honor. To reward you for the eleven thousand *Our Fathers* you recited to honor us. You will have our assistance in the hour of death. And soon, the glorious troop came to escort his soul. Saint Ursula is the patron of young teachers, and many congregations of nuns dedicated to education bear her name.

[Jaud, Leon. *Vie Des Saints Pour Tous Les Jours De L'annee: Avec Une Pratique De Piete Pour Chaque Jour.* Translated by the Monastère du Magnificat. Tours: A. Mame, 1950. Print.]

Saint Raphael the Archangel (1921) — October 24

The feast of Raphael, placed in the general calendar in 1921, is now joined to the feast of Michael and Gabriel, celebrated on September 29.

This holy Archangel identified himself to the exiled Jew Tobias as *one of the Seven who stand before God (Tob.* 12:15). His name means *the healing of God,* and he is thought to be the Angel who came down and agitated the water of the pool of Bethsaida in Jerusalem. The sick, who always lay around the pool, strove to be the first to enter the water afterward because that fortunate one was always cured. We read this in the story of the paralytic healed by Jesus, who had waited patiently for thirty-eight years, unable to move when the occasion presented itself. (*cf.* John 5:1-9)

Saint Raphael is best known through the beautiful history of the two Tobias, father and son, exiled to Persia in the days of the Assyrian conquest in the eighth century before Christ. In their story, the Archangel plays a significant role.

The father Tobias was a faithful son of Jacob and was old and worn out by his manifold good works; for many years, he had assisted his fellow exiles in every possible way, even burying the slain of Israel during the persecution by Sennacherib and continuing this practice despite the wrath that king manifested towards him. Having been stripped of all his possessions, he desired to have his son recover a substantial sum of money he had once lent to a family member in a distant city. He needed a companion for the young Tobias. God if guide in the Archangel Raphael, whom the son met providentially one day, in the person of a stranger from the same area where he was to go, in the country of the Medes. Raphael, to all appearances, was a young man like himself, who said his name was Azarias *(Assistance of God)*. Everything went well, as proposed; the young Tobias recovered the sum and then was married to the virtuous daughter of another relative whom Providence had reserved for him during their stay in Media.

All aspects of this journey had been thorny with difficulties, but the wise guide had found a way to overcome them. When a colossal fish threatened to devour Tobias, camped on the shores of the Tigris, the guide told him how to remove it from the water, and the fish expired at his feet. Remedies and provisions were derived from this creature by the directives of Azarias. When the Angel led Tobias for lodging in the city of Rages to the house of his relative Raguel, father of the beautiful Sara, the young man learned that seven proposed husbands had died on the day of the planned marriage. How would Tobias fare? The Angel reassured him that this would not be his fate and told him to pray with his future spouse for three nights that they might be blessed with a holy posterity. Sara was an only daughter, as Tobias was an only son, and she was endowed with an immense heritage.

During the absence of the young Tobias, his father had become blind when the droppings of a pigeon had fallen into his eyes. So when the two travelers returned after an extended absence, which had cost his mother many tears, the young Tobias was deeply grieved to find his father unable to see him and his new daughter-in-law. But Raphael told the son how to cure his father's blindness using the fish's gall; after the remedy had proved productive, all of them rejoiced in their blessings.

When Tobias, the son, narrated his story and told his father that all their benefits had come to them through this stranger, both father and son wished to give Azarias half of the inheritance. Raphael declined and revealed his identity, saying he was sent to assist the man's family, who had never failed to obey and honor the blessed God of Israel. Raphael, before he disappeared, said to the family: It is honorable to reveal and confess the works of God. Prayer is good, with fasting and alms, more than to lay up treasures, for alms deliver from death, purge away sins, and cause the giver to find mercy and life everlasting. So when thou didst pray with tears and didst bury the dead, and didst leave thy dinner to hide the dead by day in thy house and bury them by night, I offered thy prayer to the Lord. And because thou was acceptable to God, trials needed to prove thee. I am the Angel Raphael, one of the seven who stand before the Lord.

[*The Holy Bible Translated from the Latin Vulgate: Diligently Compared with the Hebrew, Greek, And Other Editions in Divers Languages: The Old Testament First Published by the English College at Douay, A. D. 1609, And the New Testament First Published by the English College at Rheims, A. D. 1582.* Baltimore: John Murphy Company, 1914. Compilation reprinted courtesy of *Monastère des Apôtres,* Mont-Tremblant, Quebec, Canada. *HathiTrust Digital Library,* catalog.hathitrust.org/Record/008410632.]

Saint Chrysanthus and Saint Daria, Martyrs († 284) — October 25

Apart from their names, all that is known about Chrysanthus and Daria is that they were buried on the Via Salaria. Ancient documents place their memorial on different days, and this eleventh-century addition to the Roman calendar is left for the particular calendars.

Chrysanthus was the son of a Roman senator, born in Egypt. While still young, he went with his father to Rome, where his superior intelligence was quickly appreciated. Convinced of the vanity of idol worship, he undertook every means at his disposition to learn the truth and deliver his soul from the doubts afflicting him. An elderly gentleman was pointed out to him as a sage, and Chrysanthus went to him with his questions. The old man, a Christian, had no difficulty opening the eyes of the young neophyte; Chrysanthus instantly embraced the truth with ardor and became an apostle.

His father, at first astonished, became irritated and decided to bring his son back from what he called his superstitions and errors. But unfortunately, no means were adequate for this purpose. Thus, influenced by his associates, the father locked him in his palace and sent a courtesan to seduce his purity.

When the first one failed, others were commissioned for the infamous task. Finally, a vestal virgin, priestess of an idol regarded as the empire's bulwark, attempted every ploy to corrupt the young Christian. Instead, she became the conquest of grace. The two Christians saw themselves united by the bonds of faith, hope, and charity and determined to add to these holy chains those of a virginal marriage. This decision brought about liberty for Chrysanthus and gave him the means to continue his preaching of Christ. Many conversions among the officers of the Roman society with which he was already familiar were the fruit of the apostolate of the young spouses, including that of the tribune Claudius, with his household and seventy soldiers.

But complaints began to be addressed to the prefect of Rome, who arrested the young couple. After enduring torments, Chrysanthus was shut up in the Mamertine Prison, and Daria was sent to a house of ill fame. But the Lord watched over both as He had done over many others, and they surmounted their trials intact and pure. To be done with them, the irritated emperor had them buried alive. It appears this torment was chosen to inflict on Daria the death reserved for unfaithful vestals. The principal relics of Chrysanthus and Daria are in the Abbey of Saint Avold in the diocese of Metz.

[Guérin, Abbé (Paul), François Giry, and Simon Martin. *Les Petits Bollandistes: Vies Des Saints De L'Ancien et du Nouveau Testament.* Translated by the Monastère du Magnificat. Paris: Bloud et Barral, 1882. *HathiTrust Digital Library,* hdl.handle.net/2027/nnc1.0036694380.]

Saint Evaristus, Pope, and Martyr (✝ 108) — October 26

The memorial of Evaristus, added to the general calendar in the eleventh century, is now abolished. There is no reason to consider him a martyr, and the date of his death is unknown.

Saint Evaristus succeeded Saint Anacletus on the throne of Saint Peter, elected during the second general persecution under the reign of Domitian. That emperor no doubt did not know that the Christian pontificate was being perpetrated in the shadows of the catacombs. The text of the *Liber Pontificalis* says of the new pope:

Evaristus, born in Greece to a Jewish father named Juda, originally from the city of Bethlehem, reigned for thirteen years, six months, and two days under the reigns of Domitian, Nerva, and Trajan, from the Consulate of Valens and Veter (96) until that of Gallus and Bradua (108). This pontiff divided among the priests the titles of the city of Rome. By his constitution, he established seven deacons to assist the bishop and serve as authentic witnesses for him. During the three ordinations he conducted in December, he promoted six priests, two deacons, and five bishops destined for various churches. Evaristus received the crown of martyrdom. He was buried near the body of Blessed Peter in the Vatican on the sixth day of the Calends of November (October 25, 108). The episcopal throne remained vacant for nineteen days.

The Bollandists explain two passages of this text: Saint Anacletus had ordained twenty-five priests for the city of Rome; Saint Evaristus completed this institution by settling the boundaries of each of these titles and filling the vacancies which probably occurred during the persecution of Diocletian. As for the decree by which he ordains those seven deacons to make up the bishop's procession, we find in the first epistle of Saint Anacletus a text that helps us grasp and better perceive the discipline of the early Church. There existed amid the diverse elements which composed it in its first years, proud minds, envious souls, ambitious hearts which could not bear the yoke of obedience, and who by their revolts and incessant detraction fatigued the patience of the Apostles. The deacons were to be the Pope's guards against their ill-intentioned projects.

At the same time as Saint Ignatius, the illustrious bishop of Antioch, Pope Saint Evaristus gave his life by martyrdom. The acts of his martyrdom are lost, but we perceive that the same faith, heroism, and devotion united the churches of the East and the West. He is often represented with a sword because he was decapitated or with a crib. After all, it is believed that he was born in Bethlehem, from which his father migrated.

[Guérin, Abbé (Paul), François Giry, and Simon Martin. *Les Petits Bollandistes: Vies Des Saints De L'Ancien et du Nouveau Testament.* Translated by the Monastère du Magnificat. Paris: Bloud et Barral, 1882. *HathiTrust Digital Library,* hdl.handle.net/2027/nnc1.0036694380; Shea, John G. *Little Pictorial Lives of the Saints, with Reflections for Every Day of the Year; Compiled from "Butler's Lives."* New York: Benziger, 1894. *HathiTrust Digital Library,* hdl.handle.net/2027/nyp.33433068232887.]

NOVEMBER

Saints Vitalis and Agricola, Martyrs († 304) — November 4

Nothing is known about these martyrs of Bologna except that Ambrose found their relics in 393. This thirteenth-century edition of the Roman Calendar is left for particular calendars.

Saint Ambrose informs us that Agricola was a gentleman of Bologna whose behavior in the world had engaged the affection of the idolaters amongst whom he lived. Vitalis, his slave, learned from him the Christian religion and first received the crown, for the servant and the freeman are the same thing in Christ, nor is there any difference from their condition to their reward. They were both seized, probably in the year 304, and Vitalis was first put to torture. He ceased not to praise God so long as he had the use of his tongue and saw no part of his body left which was not covered with wounds and blood. He prayed to Jesus Christ to receive his soul and bestow the crown his angel had shown him on him. His prayer was no sooner ended than he gave up the ghost. Agricola's execution was deferred out of cruel compassion. That time and the sight of the sufferings of his faithful servant might daunt his resolution. But he was animated and encouraged by such an example. After which, the affection of the judges and people was converted into fury, and the martyr was hung on a cross, and his body pierced with so many huge nails that the number of his wounds surpassed that of his limbs. The bodies of the martyrs were laid in the burial place of the Jews. Saint Ambrose flying from the arms of the tyrant Eugenius, came to Bologna in 393 and there discovered these relics. He took some of the blood found at the bottom of the grave and the cross and nails, which were the instruments of Agricola's martyrdom. Juliana, a devout widow of Florence, invited him to dedicate a church she had built in that city and begged of him this treasure, which he was not able to refuse her, and the value of which he much extols to her three daughters, bidding them receive with respect these presents of salvation, which were laid under the altar.

[Butler, Alban. *The Lives of the Fathers, Martyrs, and Other Principal Saints. Compiled from Original Monuments and Authentic Records.* Dublin: James Duffy, 1866. *HathiTrust Digital Library,* catalog.hathitrust.org/Record/001941109.]

The Holy Four Crowned Brothers, Martyrs († 304) — November 8

There are many historical difficulties concerning these four martyrs, after whom a famous church was named in Rome. The ancient memorial is now left for particular calendars.

Four brothers in the persecution of Dioclesian, employed in offices of trust and honor at Rome, were apprehended for declaring against the worship of idols and whipped with scourges loaded with plummets of lead till they expired in the hands of their tormentors. They were buried on the Via Labicana, three miles from Rome, and were at first called the Four Crowned Martyrs: their names were Severus, Severianus, Carpophorus, and Victorious. Pope Gregory the Great mentions an old church of the four crowned martyrs in Rome. Pope Leo IV, in 841, caused the church to be repaired, and the relies of these martyrs to be translated thither out of the cemetery on the Via Labicana. When this church had been consumed by fire, Paschal II rebuilt it; upon which occasion, the relics of these martyrs were discovered under the altar in two rich urns, the one of porphyry, the other of serpentine marble, deposited in a stone vault. The new altar was built upon the same spot, and these relics were again found in the same situation under Paul V. This church is an ancient title of a cardinal priest. Five other martyrs, Claudius, Nicostratus, Symphorianus, Castorius, and Simplicius, who had suffered in the same persecution, were buried in the same cemetery. Leo IV translated their precious remains into the same church and are likewise honored there to this day. These martyrs are named in the martyrology of Bede and others. These five are said to have been put to death because they refused to make idols, being carvers by profession.

The rage of tyrants, masters of the world, spread the faith they vainly endeavored to extinguish by fighting against heaven. The martyrs, who died for it, sealed it with their blood and gave testimony to Jesus Christ, the strongest and most persuasive of all others. Other Christians, who fled, became the apostles of the countries whither they went. Whence Saint Augustine compares them to torches, which, if you attempt to put them out by shaking them, are kindled and flame so much more. So the martyrs, by the meekness and fervor of their lives, and their constancy in resisting evil to death, converted an infidel world and disarmed the obstinacy of the most implacable enemies of the truth. But what judgments must await those Christians who, by the scandal of their sloth and worldly spirit, dishonor their religion, blaspheme Christ, withdraw even the faithful from the practice of the gospel, and tempt a Christian world to turn infidel?

[Butler, Alban. *The Lives of the Fathers, Martyrs, and Other Principal Saints. Compiled from Original Monuments and Authentic Records.* Dublin: James Duffy, 1866. *HathiTrust Digital Library,* catalog.hathitrust.org/Record/001941109.]

Saint Theodore Tyro, Martyr in Asia Minor (✝ 304) — November 9

Nothing is known about Theodore, who died at Amaseia in Pontus. His memorial is left to the particular calendars.

Saint Theodore Tyro, one of the most celebrated Asian martyrs, was born of a noble family in the East and enrolled while still a youth in the imperial army. Early in 306, when he had just joined the legion and marched with its soldiers into the Pont, the Roman Emperor issued an edict requiring all Christians to offer sacrifice. The young man was faced with the choice between apostasy and death. He declared before his commander that he was ready to be cut into pieces and offer up every limb to his Creator, who had died for him. Wishing to conquer him by gentleness, the commander left him in peace for a while so that he might think over his resolution.

He profited from his liberty to fortify other confessors for martyrdom. In his ardor for the downfall of idolatry, he set fire to a temple dedicated to the goddess Cybele, called the mother of the gods. When arrested, he did not attempt to conceal his actions. Still, he admitted at once that he was the author of it and had undertaken it to prevent the sacrileges committed every day in that place of abomination. However, the judge could not persuade him to renounce this crime and adore the empire's divinities; he, therefore, had him cruelly whipped and then shut up in a solitary cell with the order to give him nothing to eat and let him die of hunger.

Our Lord visited him during the night and consoled him, and He told his servant He would nourish him invisibly. This visit filled him with joy that he began to sing; at that moment, Angels in white robes appeared in his prison to sing hymns of joy with him. The jailers and guardians witnessed this spectacle, as did the judge

Publius who had condemned him, but none of them were touched by it. On the contrary, they gave him an ounce of bread and a flask of water every day, only to prolong his martyrdom. The Saint refused these offerings.

When the authorities made him fine promises and attempted to persuade him to conform, he protested that he would never say one word or make one gesture contrary to the fidelity he owed to his sovereign Lord. He was again beaten and tortured with iron hooks, then burnt with torches, and condemned finally to be burnt alive to punish him for the fire he had ignited. Nevertheless, he made the sign of the Cross and, filled with faith, hope, and pure love of God gave up to Him his beautiful soul, victorious and laden with merits. The year was 304. The Christians saw his soul rise to heaven like a flash of light and fire.

[Guérin, Abbé (Paul), François Giry, and Simon Martin. *Les Petits Bollandistes: Vies Des Saints De L'Ancien et du Nouveau Testament*. Translated by the Monastère du Magnificat. Paris: Bloud et Barral, 1882. *HathiTrust Digital Library*, hdl.handle.net/2027/nnc1.0036694380; Shea, John G. *Little Pictorial Lives of the Saints, with Reflections for Every Day of the Year; Compiled from "Butler's Lives."* New York: Benziger, 1894. *HathiTrust Digital Library*, hdl.handle.net/2027/nyp.33433068232887.]

Saint Andrew Avellino, Confessor († 1608) — November 10

The memorial of Andrew, who died in Naples in 1608, was inscribed in the Roman calendar in 1725. Since this saint is not considered of universal significance, his feast is left for the particular calendars.

After a holy youth devoted to serious studies of philosophy and the humanities in Venice, Lancelot Avellino was ordained priest by the bishop of Naples. He was assigned to the chaplaincy of a community of nuns, sadly in need of reform; his fearless courage and perseverance finally overcame many difficulties, and regular observance was restored in the monastery. Certain irritated libertines, however, decided to do away with him and, waiting for him when he was about to leave a church, felled him with three sword thrusts. He lost much blood, but his wounds healed perfectly without any trace. The viceroy of Naples was ready to employ all his authority to punish the authors of this sacrilege; the holy priest, not desiring the death of sinners but rather their conversion and their salvation, declined to pursue them. One of them, however, died soon afterward, assassinated by a man who wished to avenge a dishonor to his house.

He was still practicing law, which he had studied in Naples; one day, a slight untruth escaped him in defense of a client, and he conceived such regret for his fault that he vowed to practice law no longer. In 1556, at thirty-six, he entered the Theatine Order, taking the name of Andrew out of love for the cross. After a pilgrimage to Rome to the tombs of the Apostles, he returned to Naples and was named master of novices in his community, a duty he fulfilled for ten years. He was also chosen to be Superior of the house there and then was sent out to found two houses elsewhere, at Milan and Piacenza. At the latter city, he again met the opposition of libertines, but the Duke of Parma, to whom letters accusing him were directed, was utterly charmed when he met him and regarded him as a Saint.

He became Superior of the Milan foundation, where his friendship with Saint Charles Borromeo took root; the two Saints often conversed together. And Saint Andrew, with his admirable simplicity, confided to the archbishop that he had seen Our Lord and that since that time, the impression of His divine beauty, remaining with him constantly, had rendered insipid all other so-called beauties of the earth. Petitions were presented to Pope

Gregory XIV to make him a bishop, but he declined that honor with firmness, having always desired to remain obedient rather than to command. When his term as superior ended, he successfully avoided the government of another Theatine residence for only three years, then became the superior at *Saint Paul of Naples.*

Once when Saint Andrew was taking the Viaticum to a dying person and a storm extinguished the lamps, a heavenly light surrounded him, guided his steps, and sheltered him from the rain. But he was far from exempt from suffering. His horse threw him one day on a rough road and, since his feet were caught in the stirrups, dragged him for a long time along this road. He invoked Saint Dominic and Saint Thomas Aquinas, who came to him, wiped his face covered with blood, cured his wounds, and even helped him back onto the horse. He attributed such episodes to his unworthiness, believing he was among the reprobate. Still, Saint Thomas once again came to him, accompanied by Saint Augustine, and restored his confidence in the love and mercy of God.

On the last day of his life, November 10, 1608, Saint Andrew rose to say Mass. He was eighty-eight years old and so weak he could scarcely reach the altar. He began the *Judica me, Deus,* the opening prayer, but fell forward, the victim of apoplexy[142]. Laid on a straw mattress, his whole frame was convulsed in agony while the ancient fiend, in visible form, advanced as though to seize his soul. Then, while the onlookers prayed and wept, he invoked Our Lady, and his Guardian Angel grabbed the monster and dragged it out of the room. A calm and holy smile settled on the features of the dying Saint and, as he gazed with a grateful countenance on the image of Mary, his holy soul winged its way to God.

---

[142] Apoplexy is the rupture of an internal organ and the symptoms that accompany it. Previously, the term referred to what is now known as a stroke.

[Guérin, Abbé (Paul), François Giry, and Simon Martin. *Les Petits Bollandistes: Vies Des Saints De L'Ancien et du Nouveau Testament.* Translated by the Monastère du Magnificat. Paris: Bloud et Barral, 1882. *HathiTrust Digital Library,* hdl.handle.net/2027/nnc1.0036694380; Shea, John G. *Little Pictorial Lives of the Saints, with Reflections for Every Day of the Year; Compiled from "Butler's Lives."* New York: Benziger, 1894. *HathiTrust Digital Library,* hdl.handle.net/2027/nyp.33433068232887.]

Saints Trypho and Respicius, Martyrs, and Nympha, Virgin († 250) — November 10

Nothing is known about Trypho, Respicius, and Nympha. Therefore, their memorial, placed in the general calendar in the eleventh century, is abolished.

Trypho and Respicius were natives of Bithynia, at or near Apamea. Upon the opening of Decius's persecution, 250 were seized, loaded with chains, and conducted to Nice, where Aquilinus, governor of Bithynia and East prefect, resided. After some days' confinement, they were brought to their trial before him. Upon their confession of their faith, an officer that stood by them told them that all who refused to offer sacrifice were to be burnt alive and urged them to have compassion for themselves. Respicius answered: "We cannot better have compassion on ourselves than by confessing Jesus Christ, the true judge, who will come to call everyone to an account for all their actions." Aquilinus told them they were old enough to know what they ought to do. "Yes," said Trypho, "and therefore, we desire to attain the perfection of true wisdom by following Jesus Christ." The judge ordered them to be put on the rack. The martyrs stripped themselves and stepped forward with surprising alacrity to express their readiness to suffer. They bore the torture for nearly three hours with admirable patience and tranquility. They only opened their mouths to invoke God, praise his mercy and power, and give the judge to understand the dangers he exposed himself by his blindness. When they were taken down from the rack, Aquilinus, who was going out on a party of hunting, ordered them to be tied to the tails of horses and led out into the fields, naked and torn and bruised all over as they were, that they might be exposed in that condition to the cold air; for it was winter, and the severity of the frost was so great that they were disabled from walking or standing without exquisite pain, for their feet were cloven by it. After this torment, the governor asked them if they did not yet relent and, finding their constancy invincible, ordered them again to prison, threatening that they should be treated with the utmost rigor. Soon after this, Aquilinus set out to make the tour of some other cities that were under his jurisdiction, and at his return to Nice, called for the two prisoners, and promising them great riches and honors if they complied, conjured them to consider their good before it was too late. The martyrs, who had only God before their eyes, replied: "We cannot better follow your advice, and consider our good, than by persevering firm in the confession of the name of Jesus Christ."

Aquilinus, finding himself defeated in all his attacks, in a fit of impotent rage, commanded their feet to be pierced with large nails and the martyrs to be dragged in that condition in the cold weather through the streets. He, the strength of martyrs, gave them courage superior to the enemy's malice. The governor, surprised and confounded at their meek patience, ordered them to be whipped, which was done until the executioners were wearied. This further enraged the judge, and he commanded their flesh to be torn with hooks and afterward lighted torches to be applied to their sides. The saints remaining the same during these torments, the governor cried out to the tormentors, bidding them to exert their skill in torturing the obstinate wretches most exquisitely. But the saints were invincible and prayed thus:

"Lord Jesus Christ, for whom we fight, suffer not the devil to conquer us: strengthen and enable us to finish our course. The combat is yours: may the victory be yours." The next day they were examined a third time, and, being as constant as before, they were beaten with plummets of lead and beheaded in the year 250.

The Roman Martyrology joins Saint Nympha with these two martyrs because her body reposes with theirs in Rome. She was a virgin of Palermo in Sicily and, in the invasion of the Goths, in the fifth century, fled into Italy, where she served God in great sanctity and died in peace at Suana in Tuscany. The Greeks honor Saint Trypho on the 1st of February, and there stood a church in Constantinople formerly near that of Sancta Sophia, which bore his name. The ancient church of Saint Trypho in Rome, being fallen to decay in 1604, was united to the church of Saint Augustine, which is now possessed of part of the relics of these three saints. But the principal parts of those of Saints Trypho, Respicius, and Nympha, repose under the high altar in the church of the Holy Ghost in Saxia, belonging to a great hospital in Rome. This street lying between Saint Peter's church and the Tiber is called Saxia, from a colony of Saxons whom Charlemagne, after he had defeated them in Germany, placed there so that they might be instructed in the faith.

[Butler, Alban. *The Lives of the Fathers, Martyrs, and Other Principal Saints. Compiled from Original Monuments and Authentic Records.* Dublin: James Duffy, 1866. *HathiTrust Digital Library,* catalog.hathitrust.org/Record/001941109.]

Saint Mennas, Martyr († 304) — November 11

Despite its antiquity, the cult of Mennas, a noted Alexandrian martyr, has not remained popular in the West as the centuries passed. Instead, his memorial is left for particular calendars.

Saint Mennas was an Egyptian and a soldier. A most famous martyr, who being in garrison in a city of the province of Phrygia, or the lesser Asia called Cotyæum (present-day Kütahya, Turkey), and understanding that there was published a very rigorous edict of the Emperors Dioclesian and Maximian against the Christians, leaving his military cincture and dignity and the service of the emperors, he retired to the desert where he remained for five years living a solitary life, and in great austerity, as if it were making proof of himself by fastings, prayers, and penances, to enter into the battle he expected, and to shed his blood for our Lord.

At the end of the five years, and God inspired him, he returned to the city upon a particular festival day, and when all the people were assembled in the theatre to see specific military exercises such as jostling or running at the tilt. Mennas entered the middle of the spectators in poor and ragged clothes as a pitiful man and, with a loud voice and a cheerful and grave countenance, began to say those words of the Prophet Isaiah, "*I have been found by those who fought me not and manifested to those who asked not after me*" (Isaiah 65:1), to give to understand that he came not by force, but of his own accord and voluntarily offered himself for martyrdom.

All those present instantly cast their eyes upon Mennas, wondering at his habit, boldness, and freedom. They laid hands on him and carried him to Pyrrhus, the president, confessing that he had previously been a soldier of the emperors and was a Christian. Pyrrhus commanded him to be taken to prison and (that he might not interrupt the feast they kept) to be brought before his tribunal the next day. The judge endeavored by flatteries, sweet words, offers, and promises, to allure the holy martyr and to draw him to deny Jesus Christ and to adore his false gods. Still, when all his arts and deceits had no success. The holy martyr answered him with great courage and freedom. He turned all that false kindness into cruelty and commanded him to be stretched on the ground and whipped with raw sinews[143] until he obeyed the commands of the emperors.

They beat him cruelly, and such abundance of blood flowed from his wounds that the place did swim with it. They lifted him upon the rack Equuleus, tore his flesh with iron hooks, burnt his sides with flaming torches, rubbed his wounds with a rough hair-cloth, dragged his body upon the ground strewn with brambles, beat him afresh with rods and whips plummeted with lead, and buffeted him sorely in the face. Nevertheless, the brave soldier of Christ endured all with a courageous and quiet heart and with gracious and smiling countenance (as it had not been he, but some other that had suffered) scoffing at their torments and begged of the impious executioners that they would increase them because he said all he had suffered and all that he could suffer was but little in comparison to what God deserved, and what he deserved to suffer for Him.

The judge, officers, and executioners were amazed to see such a strange constancy and great joy amidst such grievous pains. Some of his ancient friends went about to persuade him to leave that "obstinacy and folly" (as they called it), that he would not lose his life (which is so desirable) nor the honors or pleasures which he might enjoy. And as if they had been, the hissings of some venomous serpent stopped his ears against his words, holding all those for deadly enemies with the hopes that this frail and transitory life would deprive him of lasting and eternal life. Finally, the president feeling the constancy of this soldier of the Lord, pronounced the sentence of death against him, commanding that he should be beheaded and burnt.

---

[143] A tendon, particularly one that has been dressed for use as a cord or thread.

They carried him to a place called Potemia, and many people flocked together to see him. He, in his poor attire as one that made little account of all things here below, lifting his eyes to heaven and fixing his heart upon God, made his prayer and besought our Lord with great affection that he would favor him in that hour and give him the victory for his son Jesus Christ's sake, that free from the miseries of life he might see and adore him and forever enjoy his glorious presence. Then, having ended his prayer, he was beheaded, and his holy body was cast into the fire to be burnt. But it pleased our Lord that certain pious men should use such industry and care that they did gather out of the fire some of his precious relics and wrapped them in fine linen and sweet ointments and carried them into his own country as the saint himself before he died had charged them to do.

The martyrdom of Saint Mennas was upon the eleventh of November in the year of Christ 296, in the reign of Dioclesian and Maximian. God wrought many great miracles by this martyr after his death, which are recounted by Timothy, Archbishop of Alexandria, Metaphrastes, Lipoman, and Laurence Surius. Saint Mennas mention all the Martyrologies, the Roman, those of Bede, Usuard, and Ado, and the Greeks in their Menologium, Metaphrastes, and the rest that write the lives of the saint.

[Ribadeneyra, Pedro de. "The Life of St. Mennas, Soldier, and Martyr." *The Lives of Saints, With Other Feasts of the Year, according to the Roman Calendar. Written in Spanish by the Reverend Father Peter Ribadeneyra, Priest of the Society of Jesus. Translated Into English by W.P. (William Petre) Esq; The Second Edition Corrected and Amended, vol. 2, pp. 417-418.* London. Printed by B.S., 1730. *HathiTrust Digital Library,* hdl.handle.net/2027/nyp.33433003053000.]

Saint Didacus (or Diego), Confessor († 1463) — November 13

The memorial of Didacus, who died at Alcala, Spain, on November 12, 1463, entered the Roman calendar in 1588. Due to a lack of universal significance, it is left to the particular calendars.

Saint Didacus was born in Andalusia in Spain, near the beginning of the fifteenth century. He was remarkable from childhood for his love of solitude and conversations concerning holy things. When still young, he retired to live with a hermit not far from his village, where he spent several years in vigils, fasting, and manual work. Like the fathers of the desert, he made baskets and other objects with willow branches and gave them to those who brought alms to the two hermits.

God inspired him to enter the Order of the seraphic Saint Francis; he did so at the convent of Arrizafa, not far from Cordova. He did not aspire to ecclesiastical honors but to the perfection and inviolable observance of his Rule — an admirable ideal, the practice of which, according to Saint Thomas Aquinas, is equivalent to martyrdom in merit. He made himself the servant of all his brethren. Any occupation was his choice. All his possessions were a tunic, a crucifix, a rosary, a prayer book, and a book of meditations. These he did not consider his own and wanted them to be the most worn of all in the house. He found ways to nourish the poor who came to the convent, depriving himself of bread and other food that was given him, and if unable to do so, consoled them with such gentle words that they left with profit nonetheless.

At one time, he was sent by his superiors to the Canary Islands and went there joyfully, hoping to win the crown of martyrdom. Such, however, was not God's Will.

After making many conversions by his example and holy words, he was recalled to Spain. He was assigned to the care of the sick, and when he went to Rome for the Jubilee year of 1450, with 3,800 other religious of his Order, most of whom fell ill there, he undertook to care for them, succeeding in procuring for them all they needed even in that time of scarcity.

Saint Didacus one day heard a poor woman lamenting and learned that she had not known that her seven-year-old son had gone to sleep in her large oven; she had lighted a fire and lost her senses when she heard his cries. So he sent her to the altar of the Blessed Virgin to pray and went with a large group of persons to the oven; although all the wood was burnt, the child was taken from it without so much as a trace of burns. The miracle was so evident that the neighbors took the child in triumph to the church where his mother was praying, and the Canons of the Church dressed him in white in honor of the Blessed Virgin. Since then, many afflicted persons have invoked the Mother of Heaven there.

After a long and painful illness, Saint Didacus ended his days in 1463, embracing the cross he had so dearly loved his entire life. He died having on his lips the words of the hymn, *Dulce Lignum*[144]. His body remained incorrupt for several months, exposed to the faithful's devotion, ever exhaling a marvelous fragrance. He was canonized in 1588; Philip II, king of Spain, had labored to obtain that grace after his son was miraculously cured in 1562 by the Saint's relics when he had fallen from a ladder and incurred a mortal wound on his head.

[Guérin, Abbé (Paul), François Giry, and Simon Martin. *Les Petits Bollandistes: Vies Des Saints De L'Ancien et du Nouveau Testament.* Translated by the Monastère du Magnificat. Paris: Bloud et Barral, 1882. *HathiTrust Digital Library,* hdl.handle.net/2027/nnc1.0036694380; Shea, John G. *Little Pictorial Lives of the*

---

144 *Dulce lignum, dulces clavos, or "O sweet wood, O sweet nails,"* is a Good Friday chant. This is one of the few mass chant propers that does not come from Scripture; it is based on Fortunatus' 6th-century poem *Pange lingua, gloriosi*, specifically the *Crux fideles* section.

Saints, with Reflections for Every Day of the Year; Compiled from "Butler's Lives."
New York: Benziger, 1894. *HathiTrust Digital Library,*
hdl.handle.net/2027/nyp.33433068232887.]

Saint Gregory Thaumaturge (or Gregory the Wonderworker), Bishop and Confessor († 270) — November 17

The memorial of Gregory, who died at New Caesarea in Pontus, about 270, was placed in the Roman calendar in 1568. It is left for the particular calendars because he is not considered a saint of universal significance.

Saint Gregory was born in the Pont to distinguished parents who were still engaged in the superstitions of paganism. He lost his father at fourteen and began reflecting on idolatry's fables' folly. He recognized the unity of God and was becoming disposed to accept the truths of Christianity. His father had destined him for the legal profession, in which the art of oratory is essential, and in this pursuit, he was succeeding very well, having learned Latin. Accordingly, he was counseled to apply himself to Roman law.

Gregory and his brother Athenodorus, later to be a bishop like himself, had a sister living in Palestine at Caesarea. Not far from that city was a law school, and in Caesarea itself, another which the famous Origen had opened in the year 231 and in which he was teaching philosophy. The two brothers heard Origen there, and that master discovered in them a remarkable capacity for knowledge and, more important still, rare dispositions for virtue. He strove to inspire a love for truth in them and an ardent desire to attain a greater understanding and the possession of the Supreme Good, and the two brothers soon put aside their intentions to study law. Gregory also studied in Alexandria for three years after persecution drove his master, Origen, from Palestine, but returned there with the famous exegete in 238. He was then baptized and, in the presence of a large audience, delivered a speech in which he testified his gratitude towards his teacher, praising his methods and thanking God for being such an excellent professor.

When he returned to his native city of Neocaesarea in the Pont, his friends urged him to seek high positions, but Gregory desired to retire into solitude and devote himself to prayer. For a time, he did so, often changing his habitation because the archbishop of the region wished to make him Bishop of Neocaesarea. Eventually, he was obliged to consent. That city was very prosperous, and the inhabitants were corrupted by paganism. With Christian zeal and charity, Saint Gregory began to attempt to bring them to the light of Christ with the aid of the gift of miracles he had received. As he lay awake one night, an elderly man entered his room and pointed to a Lady of superhuman beauty who accompanied him, radiant with heavenly light. This elderly man was Saint John the Evangelist, and the Lady of Light was the Mother of God. She told Saint John to give Gregory the instruction he desired, at which point he gave Saint Gregory a creed that contained the doctrine of the Trinity in all its abundance. Saint Gregory consigned it to writing, directed all his preaching by it, and handed it down to his successors. This creed later preserved his flock from the Arian heresy.

He converted a pagan priest one day when the latter requested a miracle, and a considerable rock moved to another location at his command. The pagan priest abandoned all things to follow Christ afterward. One day the bishop planted his staff beside the river, which passed alongside the city and often ravaged it by floods. He commanded it never again to exceed the limit marked by his staff, and in the time of Saint Gregory of Nyssa, who wrote of his miracles nearly a hundred years later, it had never done so. The bishop settled a conflict about to cause bloodshed between two brothers when he prayed all night beside the lake whose possession they were disputing. It dried up, and the miracle ended the difficulty.

When the persecution of Decius began in 250, the bishop counseled his faithful to depart and not expose themselves to trials perhaps too severe for their faith; none fell into apostasy. He retired to a desert and was not seen by the soldiers when pursued. On a second attempt, they found him praying with his companion, the converted pagan priest, now a deacon; they had mistaken them the first time for trees. The captain of the soldiers was convinced this had been a miracle and became a Christian to join him. Some of his Christians were captured, including Saint Troadus, the martyr who merited the grace of dying for the Faith. The persecution ended at the death of the emperor in 251.

It is believed that Saint Gregory died in the year 270, on the 17th of November. Before his death, he asked how many pagans remained in the city and was told there were only seventeen. He thanked God for the graces He had bestowed on the population, for there had been only seventeen Christians when he arrived.

[Guérin, Abbé (Paul), François Giry, and Simon Martin. *Les Petits Bollandistes: Vies Des Saints De L'Ancien et du Nouveau Testament.* Translated by the Monastère du Magnificat. Paris: Bloud et Barral, 1882. *HathiTrust Digital Library,* hdl.handle.net/2027/nnc1.0036694380.]

Saint Felix of Valois, Confessor (1127-1212) — November 20

There are many historical difficulties in the documents about the life of Felix. His memorial, added to the Roman calendar in 1679, is left to the particular calendars.

Saint Felix was the son of the Count of Valois. His mother carried him to Saint Bernard at his monastery of Clairvaux to offer him there to God when he was three years old; she kept him, however, under her care and took particular care of him, permitting him, still young, to distribute the alms she was pleased to give to the poor. When the exiled Pope Innocent II sought refuge in France, the Count of Valois, father of Felix, offered his castle of Crépy to the Pontiff, who often blessed the young child he saw being trained in virtue. One day when Felix gave away his habits to a poor beggar, he found them that evening neatly laid on his bed; and he thanked God for this sign of His divine goodness, proving that one loses nothing when one gives to the poor.

When he was ten years old, he obtained grace for a prisoner condemned to death through his prayer and pleadings with his uncle, a lord of whom the man was the subject. Felix had a presentiment that this man would become a saint. But he retired into a deep solitude where he undertook severe penance and died the death of the just.

The unfortunate divorce of Felix's parents, and the ex-communication of his father, who had remarried and whose condemnation raised serious troubles in his domains, caused to mature in the young man a long-formed resolution to leave the world. Confiding his mother to her pious brother, Thibault, Count of Champagne, Felix took the Cistercian habit at Clairvaux. His rare virtues drew on him an admiration such that, with Saint Bernard's consent, he fled from it to Italy, where he began to live an austere life with an aged hermit in the Alps. For this purpose, he had departed secretly, and the servants his uncle sent believed him dead, unable to trace him; they published the rumor of his death. About this time, the old hermit procured the ordination of his disciple as a priest.

After his elderly counselor died in his arms, Saint Felix returned to France. He built a cell in the diocese of Meaux in an uninhabited forest; this place was later named Cerfroid. Amid savage beasts, he led an angelic life of perpetual fasting. Here God inspired him with the desire of founding an Order for the redemption of Christian captives. The Lord also moved Saint John of Matha, a young nobleman of Provence, to seek out the hermit and join him. The two applied themselves to the practice of all virtues. John overtly proposed to Saint Felix the project of an Order for the redemption of captives when his preceptor was already seventy years old. The latter gladly offered himself to God for that purpose, and after praying for three days, the two solitaries made a pilgrimage to Rome in the middle of winter. The Pope kindly received them after reading Bishop of Paris's recommendation. He, too, prayed and became convinced that the Holy Spirit inspired the two Saints, and he gave his approbation to the Trinitarian Order

Within forty years, the Order would have six hundred monasteries. Saint John, Superior General, left the direction of the convents in France to Saint Felix, exercised from the monastery the founders had built at Cerfroid. There Saint Felix died in November of 1212, at the age of eighty-five, only about six weeks before his younger co-founder. It is a constant tradition in the Trinitarian Order that Saint Felix and Saint John were canonized by Urban IV in 1260, though no bull has ever been found. In 1219, Saint Felix's feast was already kept in the entire diocese of Meaux. In 1666 Alexander VI declared that veneration of the servant of God immemorial.

[Butler, Alban. *The Lives of the Fathers, Martyrs, and Other Principal Saints. Compiled from Original Monuments and Authentic Records.* Dublin: James Duffy, 1866. *HathiTrust Digital Library,* catalog.hathitrust.org/Record/001941109; Guérin, Abbé (Paul), François Giry, and Simon Martin. *Les Petits Bollandistes: Vies Des Saints De L'Ancien et du Nouveau Testament.* Translated by the Monastère du Magnificat.

Paris: Bloud et Barral, 1882. *HathiTrust Digital Library,* hdl.handle.net/2027/nnc1.0036694380]

Saint Felicity (or Felicitas) of Rome, Martyr (✝ 165) — November 23

Since all we know about Felicity is her name and the date of her burial in the cemetery of Maximus on the Via Salaria, her memorial is left for the particular calendars.

One of the affections that those that have children ought to moderate and overcome is the love of the same children. For although naturally they love them and ought to love them, they ought to do it with stint and measure, and in such a manner that for the love of their children they do not lose the love of God which ought to be preferred before all things.

Also, it is diligently to be considered wherein the true love of children does conflict, for many persons desire and provide for their children the perishable and frail goods of life with such great anxiety and with such an insatiable thirst that all seems little and short to them in comparison of what they would do for their children. In this, they put the form and essence of their love, without taking care to adorn them with virtues, and to make them worthy of the goods which they procure them, and to teach them how they are to get the eternal and immense goods of glory which we hope for in comparison of which all earthly goods are but counterfeit and painted goods.

To teach parents this truth and to give them a rule and an example of what to do with their children, the holy Church today makes a commemoration of the blessed Saint Felicitas, a noble Roman matron who was a widow with seven children and lived irreprehensibly, endeavoring to serve God and to make her children serve Him. And, by her example and holy instructions, animated them and so grounded them in the love of God that all seven sons were martyred before the eyes of their blessed mother in the time of Antoninus, that were made an end by diverse kinds of torments and deaths, as was said on the day of their martyrdom which was on the tenth of July.

But after that, the glorious champions of Jesus Christ and sons of Saint Felicitas fought valiantly and obtained the victory. All the rage and fury of the emperor was turned against their holy mother because she had given strength and arms to her sons to fight by her words. For this cause, the tyrant commanded her to be cast into prison and would not have her die immediately, to the end that living she might every day increasingly resent the death of her children, for although she already saw them as citizens in heaven, she was content and rejoiced, yet as a mother, she could not feel her having lost them as to herself. On the contrary, however, she had gained them to God.

He kept her in prison for four months, the more to afflict and torment her, and in the end, seeing she constantly persevered in the faith of Christ, he commanded her to be beheaded. So of this blessed mother and pattern of Christian mothers, and as Saint Gregory says[145], *"As for this woman, I will not call her a martyr, but more than a martyr, since she died seven times before her own death, by each of the seven wages of love which she sent to precede her in the Kingdom. Came first to the torture but only succeeded in the eighth. The mother saw the death of her sons with great suffering, but without fear; she mixed the joy of hope with the pain of nature. She feared for them during their lives and rejoices for them at the moment of their death. She wished to leave none after her, lest she could not keep him as a companion to preserve one of them as a survivor."*

---

[145] Saint Gregory the Great in *Homily 3 on the Gospels*.

Saint Gregory also states, "*Consider this woman, my brothers, and consider what we will weigh in front of her, we who are virile by the body. Often, when we propose to do good, it is enough for a word, even insignificant, sprung against us from the mouth of a mocking so that our resolution to act bends immediately and that, disassembled, we recoil. In many cases, words keep us from doing good work, even when even the tortures could not relieve Felicity in her holy resolutions. We stopped by the light breath of a nasty word; it was by the sword that she flung herself into the Kingdom, neglecting nothing that stood in the way of her resolution. We do not want to abide by the commandments of the Lord by giving alms of our goods, even if we have too much; she not only brought her fortune to God, but she also gave himself her own flesh. When we lose our children by the divine will, we weep without being consoled; she would have cried them dead if she had not offered them.*"

And Saint Peter Chrysologus, Archbishop of Ravenna, says[146], "*Behold here a woman whom the life of her children made solicitous and their death made secure. Happy she has many lights in heaven as she had children upon earth. She was happy to bring them forth and most happy to send them to heaven. She went more delightfully among their dead bodies when the tyrant ordered them to be killed than when she suckled them in their cradles. For she considered with the eyes of her soul that as many as their wounds were, so many were to be the jewels of their victory, as many torments, so many rewards, and the harder their combats were, the more glorious were to be their crowns. What shall I say of this courageous woman, but that she is not a true mother, who knows not how to love her children as this mother loves hers.*"

---

[146] Saint Peter Chrysologus, *Sermon 134, De sancta Felicitate ('On saint Felicitas')*. Delivered in Latin at Ravenna (northern Italy), c. 450.

The martyrdom of Saint Felicitas was on the twenty-third of November in the year of our Lord 175. The *Roman Martyrology* and the rest make mention of her.

[Ribadeneyra, Pedro de. "The Life of St. Felicitas, Martyr." *The Lives of Saints, With Other Feasts of the Year, according to the Roman Calendar. Written in Spanish by the Reverend Father Peter Ribadeneyra, Priest of the Society of Jesus. Translated Into English by W.P. (William Petre) Esq; The Second Edition Corrected and Amended, vol. 2, pp. 444-445.* London. Printed by B.S., 1730. *HathiTrust Digital Library,* hdl.handle.net/2027/nyp.33433003053000.]

Saint Chrysogonus, Martyr (✝ 303) — November 23

The account of the martyrdom of Chrysogonus is fictitious, and no reason exists to consider him a Roman martyr. Nevertheless, his memorial is left on the calendar of the church that bears his name.

The Name of this holy martyr, who was apprehended at Rome, but beheaded at Aquileia in the persecution of Dioclesian, occurs in the Canon of the Mass and is mentioned in the ancient Calendar of Carthage of the fifth century, and all Western Martyrologies since that time. The church in Rome, of which he is the titular saint, is mentioned in a council held by Pope Symmachus, and in the epistles of Saint Gregory the Great, it gives the title to a cardinal priest. The head of Saint Chrysogonus is shown there is a rich case, but his body is in Venice.

[Butler, Alban. *The Lives of the Fathers, Martyrs, and Other Principal Saints. Compiled from Original Monuments and Authentic Records.* Dublin: James Duffy, 1866. *HathiTrust Digital Library,* catalog.hathitrust.org/Record/001941109.]

Saint Catherine of Alexandria, Virgin, and Martyr († 305) — November 25

Not only are the Acts of the life of Catherine legendary, but it is impossible to assert anything about her at all. Her memorial, added to the calendar during the thirteenth century, is abolished.

Catherine was a noble virgin of Alexandria, born in the fourth century. Before her Baptism, she saw in a dream the Blessed Virgin asking Her Son to receive her among His servants, but the Divine Infant turned away, saying the waters of Baptism did not yet regenerate her. Nevertheless, she made haste to receive that sacrament. Afterward, when the dream was repeated, Catherine saw that the Savior received her with great affection and espoused her before the court of heaven with a fine ring. She woke with it on her finger.

She had a very active intelligence, fit for all matters, and she undertook the study of philosophy and theology. At that time, there were schools in Alexandria for the instruction of Christians, where excellent Christian scholars taught. She made significant progress and could sustain the truths of our religion against even very subtle sophists. At that time, Maximinus II was sharing the empire with Constantine the Great and Licinius and had as his district Egypt. This cruel Christian-hater ordinarily resided in Alexandria, the capital of the province. He announced an enormous pagan sacrifice, such that the air would be darkened with the smoke of the bulls and sheep immolated on the altars of the gods. Catherine, before this event, strove to strengthen the Christians against the fatal lures, repeating that the oracles vaunted by the infidels were a pure illusion, originating in the depths of the lower regions.

She foresaw that soon it would be the Christians' turn to be immolated when they refused to participate in the ceremonies. She, therefore, went to the emperor himself, asking to speak with him, and her singular beauty and majestic air won an audience for her. She told him that it was strange that he should, by his example, attract so many people to such a horrific cult. By his high office, he was obliged to turn them away from it since reason itself shows us that there can be only one sovereign Being, the first principle of all else. She begged him to cease so great a disorder by giving the true God the honor due Him, lest he reap the wages of his indifference in this life and the next. The consequences of her hardy act extended over a specific time; he decided to call in fifty sophists of his suite to bring back this virgin from her errors. A large audience assembled to hear the debate; the emperor sat on his throne with his entire court, dissimulating his rage.

Catherine began by saying she was surprised that he obliged her to face, alone, fifty individuals. Still, she asked his grace that if the true God she adored rendered her victorious, he would adopt her religion and renounce the cult of the demons. He was not pleased and replied that it was not for her to lay down conditions for the discussion. The head of the sophists began the orations and reprimanded her for opposing the authority of poets, orators, and philosophers, who unanimously had revered Jupiter, Juno, Neptune, Minerva, and others. He cited their writings and said she should consider that these persons were far anterior to this new religion she was following. She listened carefully before answering, then spoke, showing that the ridiculous fables which Homer, Orpheus, and other poets had invented concerning their divinities and the fact that many offered a cult to them, as well as the terrible crimes attributed to them, proved them to be gods only in the opinion of the ignorant and gullible.

And then she proved that the prophecies of the Hebrew Scriptures had clearly announced the time and the circumstances of the life of the future Savior and that these were now fulfilled. Prodigy, the head of the sophists, avowed that she was correct and renounced his errors; the others said they could not oppose their chief. Maximinus had them put to death by fire, but the fire did not consume their remains. Thus, they died as Christians, receiving the Baptism of blood.

The story of Saint Catherine continues during the time of the emperor's efforts to persuade her to marry him; he put to death his converted wife and the captain of his guards who had received Baptism with two hundred of his soldiers. He delivered Catherine to prison and tortured her because of her firmness in refusing his overtures. The famous wheel of Saint Catherine — several interacting wheels — which he invented to torment her was furnished with sharp razor blades and sharp points of the iron; all who saw it trembled. But as soon as it was set in motion, it was miraculously disjointed and broken into pieces, and these pieces flew in all directions and wounded the spectators. The barbaric emperor finally commanded that she be decapitated, and she offered her neck to the executioner after praying that her mortal remains would be respected.

The story of Saint Catherine continues with the discovery of the intact body of a young and beautiful girl on Mount Sinai in the ninth century, four centuries later. The Church, in the Collect of her feast day, bears witness to the transport of her body. Moreover, several proofs testified to the identity of her mortal remains found in the region of the famous monastery existing on that mountain since the fifth century. Her head is today conserved in Rome.

[Guérin, Abbé (Paul), François Giry, and Simon Martin. *Les Petits Bollandistes: Vies Des Saints De L'Ancien et du Nouveau Testament.* Translated by the Monastère du

Magnificat. Paris: Bloud et Barral, 1882. *HathiTrust Digital Library*, hdl.handle.net/2027/nnc1.0036694380.]

Saint Sylvester Gozzolini, Abbot (1177–1267) — November 26

The memorial of Sylvester, who died at Fabriano in 1267, was inscribed in the Roman calendar in 1890. It is left for the particular calendars since the veneration of this martyr is not a part of the Roman tradition.

[Institutor of the Sylvestrin Monks.] This saint was born of a noble family at Osimo or Osmo, about fourteen miles from Loretto, in 1177. He studied the laws and theology at Bologna and Padua and was instituted to a canonry at Osimo, made prayer, pious reading, and the instruction of others his whole employment. His zeal in reproving vice made him enemies, and his bishop, whom he admonished of certain neglects to discharge his office, declared himself his persecutor. These trials served to purify the heart of the servant of God and prepared him for the grace of the pure love of God. The sight of the carcass of a man who had been admired in his lifetime for his beauty and significant accomplishments completed his loathing and contempt of this treacherous world so that, deploring its scandals and blindness, he left the city privately and retired into a desert thirty miles from Osimo, being then forty years old. To satisfy the importunity of others, in 1231, he built a monastery upon Monte Fano, two miles from Fabriano, in the marquisate of Ancona. In this house, he settled the rule of Saint Bennet without any mitigation: and, in 1248, obtained Innocent IV., who was then at Lyons, the confirmation of his institute. He lived to found twenty-five monasteries in Italy, and leaving his disciples heirs of his double spirit of penance and prayer, he departed to the Lord on the 26th of November in 1267, at ninety years old. God was pleased to work several miracles at his tomb, and his name is inserted in the Roman Martyrology.

[Butler, Alban. *The Lives of the Fathers, Martyrs, and Other Principal Saints. Compiled from Original Monuments and Authentic Records.* Dublin: James Duffy, 1866. *HathiTrust Digital Library,* catalog.hathitrust.org/Record/001941109.]

Saint Peter of Alexandria, Patriarch, and Martyr († 310) — November 25

That is his honor, the "seal of the martyrs," because he is the last martyr of Egypt under great persecution. The feast was added to the Roman calendar in the twelfth century. It is left for the particular calendars since the veneration of this martyr is not a part of the Roman tradition.

The Church of Alexandria, founded by the Evangelist Saint Mark in the name of the Apostle Saint Peter, was the head of the churches of Egypt and several other provinces; it lost its Metropolitan when Saint Thomas of Alexandria died at the end of the third century. Saint Peter, a priest of that city, replaced him and soon governed the church amid the terrors of the persecution by Diocletian and Maximian. Two bishops and more than six hundred Christians were in irons and on the verge of torture; he sent them pastoral letters to animate them to zeal and perseverance and rejoiced to learn that several of them had won the grace of martyrdom.

Many, however, had preferred apostasy to a cruel death. Saint Peter was obliged to instigate penances for them to return to the communion of the faithful. When he deposed a bishop who had incensed an idol during the persecution, his act of justice acquired the hostility of a certain Arius, the bishop's favorite, who became the author of a schism and an instrument of the cruel emperor Maximian who persecuted the Christians. He animated this tyrant against Saint Peter. The sentence of ex-communication, which Saint Peter was the first to pronounce against the two schismatics, Arius and Melitius, and which he strenuously upheld despite the united efforts of influential members of their parties, is proof that he possessed firmness as well as sagacity and zeal.

The Patriarch was soon seized and thrown into prison. There he encouraged the confessors imprisoned with him to sing the praises of God and pray to their Savior in their hearts without ceasing. Saint Peter never ceased repeating to the faithful that, in order not to fear death, it is necessary to begin by dying to oneself, renouncing our self-will, and detaching ourselves from all things. He was soon to give proof of his perfect detachment in his glorious martyrdom.

While in prison, he was advised in an apparition about his successors in the Alexandrian church, and he recognized that the day of his eternal liberation was at hand. He informed these two faithful sons that his martyrdom was imminent. In effect, the emperor passed a sentence of death on him, even though a crowd of persons had come to the prison to attempt to prevent by force the martyrdom of their patriarch; they remained all night for fear he might be executed in secret. But Saint Peter delivered himself to his executioners and died by the sword on November 26, 310. His appearance on the scaffold was so majestic that none dared to touch him; it was necessary to pay one of them in gold to strike the fatal blow.

[Guérin, Abbé (Paul), François Giry, and Simon Martin. *Les Petits Bollandistes: Vies Des Saints De L'Ancien et du Nouveau Testament.* Translated by the Monastère du Magnificat. Paris: Bloud et Barral, 1882. *HathiTrust Digital Library,* hdl.handle.net/2027/nnc1.0036694380; Shea, John G. *Little Pictorial Lives of the Saints, with Reflections for Every Day of the Year; Compiled from "Butler's Lives."*

New York: Benziger, 1894. *HathiTrust Digital Library,* hdl.handle.net/2027/nyp.33433068232887.]

Saint Saturninus, Bishop and Martyr (†ca. 70 A.D.) — November 29

Apart from his name, all that is known about Saturninus is the date of his burial in the cemetery of Thraso (Catacomba di Trasone) on the Via Salaria on November 29. His memorial is left for particular calendars.

Saint Saturninus was a contemporary and a disciple of Our Lord Jesus Christ; he came to Palestine from Greece, attracted by the reputation of Saint John the Baptist, which had echoed even to the northern Mediterranean region. He then followed our Savior, heard His teaching, and was a witness to many of His miracles. He was present in the Cenacle when the Holy Spirit descended at Pentecost upon the Mother of Christ, the Apostles and Disciples assembled in the number 120. (*Acts of the Apostles* 1:15) He departed to teach Christianity under Saint Peter's authority, evangelizing the lands east of Palestine and going as far as the region of the Persians and Medes and their neighboring provinces. He cured the sick, the lepers, and the paralytics and delivered souls from the demons, and before he left, he gave written instructions to the new Christians concerning what they should believe and practice.

When Saint Saturninus went with Saint Peter to Rome, the Apostle was inspired to send out several fervent evangelists to the West to dissipate the darkness in which the light of Christ still plunged those regions. Saturninus was directed to go to what is now southern France, to Toulouse in particular. Saint Peter consecrated him as a bishop so that he might form and ordain native priests for the future Christian churches of Gaul. He was given for his companion Papulus, later to become Saint Papulus the Martyr.

The two companions acquired at Nimes, an ardent assistant in the person of Honestus. At Carcassonne, when the three announced Christ, they were thrown into a prison, where they suffered from hunger; but the Lord sent an Angel to deliver them, and they continued their way to Toulouse, preaching the doctrine and the name of Christ publicly. In this large and wealthy city, where idolatry was entrenched, the idols became mute when the missionaries arrived. This caused great astonishment, and the cause of the silence was sought. Saint Saturninus, in the meantime, was working miracles that produced a strong impression on the witnesses; among them, the cure of a woman with advanced leprosy. The sign of the cross he made over crowds often cured many sick persons simultaneously, and he baptized those who showed themselves ready for the sacrament. For a time, he left his two disciples there and continued elsewhere, preaching in the cities of what is now Auch and Eauze. A Spaniard heard of him and crossed the Pyrenees; this man, by the name of Paternus, advanced so rapidly on the paths of virtue that Saint Saturninus ordained him and then established him as bishop of Eauze. He returned to Toulouse and sent Honestus to Spain to preach. When the latter returned to ask him to come with him to Spain, he left his disciple Papulus in charge for a time at Toulouse.

At Pampeluna (Pamplona), his preaching brought thousands to the truth, delivering these former idolaters from the heavy yoke of the ancient enemy. But, while he continued his apostolic labors elsewhere, Toulouse persecution broke out against Papulus, and the faithful Christian obtained the crown of martyrdom by a violent death. At once, Saint Saturnin returned to Toulouse when he learned of it.

The idols again became mute. One day a great multitude was gathered near a pagan altar, where a bull stood ready for the sacrifice. A man in the crowd pointed out Saturninus, who was passing by, as the cause of the silence. There is the one who preaches everywhere that our temples must be torn down and dares to call our gods devils! It is his presence that imposes silence on our oracles! He was chained and dragged to the summit of the capital, situated on a high hill, and commanded to offer sacrifice to the idols and cease to preach Jesus Christ. An Angel appeared to him to fortify him, and the terrible flagellation he endured could not alter his firmness. I know only one God, the only true one; to Him alone, I will offer sacrifice on the altar of my heart. How can I fear gods who you say are afraid of me? A rope tied him to the bull, driven down the stairs to the capitol. His skull was broken, and the Saint entered the beatitude of the unceasing vision of God. His body was taken up and buried by two devout young women. Tradition conserved the memory of the place of his burial, where later a church was built.

[Guérin, Abbé (Paul), François Giry, and Simon Martin. *Les Petits Bollandistes: Vies Des Saints De L'Ancien et du Nouveau Testament.* Translated by the Monastère du Magnificat. Paris: Bloud et Barral, 1882. *HathiTrust Digital Library,* hdl.handle.net/2027/nnc1.0036694380.]

DECEMBER

Saint Bibiana (or Viviana), Virgin and Martyr († 363) — December 2

Nothing is known about "Vivian" except her name, under which the title Pope Simplicius (468-483) dedicated a church on the Esquiline hill in Rome. Her memorial, placed in the Roman calendar in the eleventh century, is left to the basilica that bears her name.

Saint Bibiana was a native of Rome, born in the fourth century, the daughter and sister of martyrs. Flavian, her Christian father, was apprehended during the reign of Julian the Apostate, branded on the face as a slave, and banished to Tuscany, where he died of his wounds a few days later. Her mother, Dafrosa, was beheaded two weeks later. Their two daughters, Bibiana and Demetria, were stripped of all they had in the world after their parent's death and then imprisoned with orders to give them no food. But on the other hand, the Roman praetorian offered them rewards if they would abandon their faith and threatened a cruel death if they would not conform. Still, they replied courageously that the goods and advantages of this world had no attraction for them and that they would endure a thousand deaths rather than betray their faith and their Savior. After having pronounced this ardent defense, Demetria fell to the ground and expired at her sister's side; she is inscribed in the Roman martyrology on June 21st.

The officer ordered that Bibiana be placed in the custody of a woman named Rufina, who was commanded to corrupt or mistreat her. But the martyr made prayer her shield and remained invincible. Then, enraged by the courage and perseverance of the young virgin, the persecutor ordered her to be tied to a pillar and whipped until she expired, with scourges tipped with leaden plummets. The Saint underwent this punishment cheerfully and died at the hands of the executioners. A holy priest buried her at a site where afterward, a chapel and then a church was built above her tomb. In 1628 the church was splendidly rebuilt by Pope Urban VIII, and in it, he placed the relics of the two sisters and Saint Dafrosa, their mother.

[Shea, John G. *Little Pictorial Lives of the Saints, with Reflections for Every Day of the Year; Compiled from "Butler's Lives."* New York: Benziger, 1894. *HathiTrust Digital Library,* hdl.handle.net/2027/nyp.33433068232887; Guérin, Abbé (Paul), François Giry, and Simon Martin. *Les Petits Bollandistes: Vies Des Saints De L'Ancien et du Nouveau Testament.* Translated by the Monastère du Magnificat. Paris: Bloud et Barral, 1882. *HathiTrust Digital Library,* hdl.handle.net/2027/nnc1.0036694380.]

Saint Barbara, Virgin, and Martyr († 235) — December 4

The Acts of the life of Barbara are legendary, and historians disagree over the site of her martyrdom. The twelfth-century memorial of this saint is abolished.

A pagan father, Dioscorus, brought up Saint Barbara. Intending to protect her beauty, he kept her jealously secluded in a lonely but very luxurious tower that he built for that purpose, for in his way, he loved her. In her forced solitude, this very gifted young girl undertook to study religion and soon saw all the vices and absurdities of paganism; her clear mind realized that there could be only one supreme Creator-God and that He is entitled to the worship of His reasonable creatures. Divine Providence, by its wonderful ways, contrived to obtain for her the means to send a message to Origen, the famous exegete, asking for knowledge of the Christian faith. That teacher of Alexandria immediately sent to her, at Nicomedia, a disciple named Valentinian. Soon she was baptized, and Our Lord appeared to her, as He would appear to others, such as Saint Catherine of Alexandria and Saint Teresa of Avila, to tell her He had chosen her to be His spouse. Saint Barbara, rejoicing, hoped to be able to communicate her precious new faith to her father but would soon discover that hope was vain.

When she was of the age to marry, many requests for her hand came to her wealthy father. She was his only heiress, and he rejected her expressed wish not to accept any such offer, although she said she wished to remain his consolation for his declining years. When she continued to refuse every suitor's demand, and when Dioscorus returned from a journey to find all the idols he had placed in her tower broken in pieces and scattered about, he was furious. Discovering his daughter's conversion, he was beside himself with rage. She escaped and dwelt for a time in a cavern concealed by the vegetation growing at the entrance. But finally, her father's threats of chastisement, which he made known during his searches for anyone who might be concealing her, caused some local shepherds who knew of her whereabouts to reveal her retreat.

Her father denounced her to the civil tribunal, and Barbara was horribly tortured twice and finally beheaded. Her father, merciless to the last, asked to deal her the fatal blow himself. God, however, speedily punished her persecutors. While the Angels were bearing her soul to Paradise, a flash of lightning struck Dioscorus and Marcian, the civil prefect, and both were summoned in haste to the judgment seat of God.

Saint Barbara is beloved by the Spanish-speaking people. She is the special protectress of the region of Metz in France, where a magnificent church, later destroyed, was built in her honor in the 1500s. She is invoked against sudden and unprovided death and invariably answers all requests for the favor of receiving the Last Sacraments. A famous instance of her intervention on behalf of a Saint who was on the verge of death can be read in the life of Saint Stanislaus Kostka.

[Guérin, Abbé (Paul), François Giry, and Simon Martin. *Les Petits Bollandistes: Vies Des Saints De L'Ancien et du Nouveau Testament.* Translated by the Monastère du Magnificat. Paris: Bloud et Barral, 1882. *HathiTrust Digital Library,* hdl.handle.net/2027/nnc1.0036694380; Shea, John G. *Little Pictorial Lives of the Saints, with Reflections for Every Day of the Year; Compiled from "Butler's Lives."* New York: Benziger, 1894. *HathiTrust Digital Library,* hdl.handle.net/2027/nyp.33433068232887.]

Saint Sabas (or Sabbas the Sanctified), Patriarchal Abbot in Palestine (439-531) — December 5

The memorial of Sabbas, who died near Jerusalem on December 5, 532, was entered into the general calendar in the twelfth century. However, since he is not a saint of universal significance, it is now left to the particular calendars.

Saint Sabas, one of the most renowned patriarchs of the monks of Palestine, was born in 439 near Caesarea. At the age of fifteen, in the absence of his parents, he suffered under the conduct of an uncle and, weary of the world's problems, decided to forsake the world and enter a monastery not far from his family home. After he had spent ten years in religious life, his two uncles and his parents attempted to persuade him to leave the monastery to which he had migrated in Palestine. He replied: Do you want me to be a deserter, leaving God after placing myself in His service? If those who abandon the militia of earthly kings are severely punished, what chastisement would I not deserve if I abandoned that of the King of heaven?

When he was thirty years old, desiring greater solitude, he began to live a divine life so far above nature that he seemed no longer to have a body. *As Saint Euthymius called him Abbot of a nearby monastery, the young sage* dwelt in a cavern on a mountain near Jerusalem, where he prayed, sang Psalms, and wove baskets of palm branches. He was forty-five years old when he began to direct those who came to live as hermits, as he did, and he gave each of them a place to build a cell; soon, this was the largest monastery in Palestine. He left the region when certain agitators complained about him, for he considered himself incapable of maintaining good discipline. The Patriarch of Jerusalem, Sallustus, did not easily credit the complaints and instead ordained Sabas a priest so that he might say Mass for his disciples — for they had been displeased by his lack of desire for that honor. He was at that time fifty-three years old. The Patriarch presented him to them as their father, whom they should obey and honor, making him superior to all the Palestine monasteries. But several monks remained obstinate, and Saint Sabas again went elsewhere, to a cavern near Scythopolis.

As the years passed, he oversaw seven monasteries; but his influence was not limited to Palestine. The heresies afflicting religion were being sustained by the emperor of Constantinople, who had exiled the Catholic Patriarch of that city, Elias. Saint Sabas converted the one who had replaced Elias and wrote to the emperor that he should cease to persecute the Church of Jerusalem and impose taxes on the cities of Palestine, which they were unable to pay. In effect, the people were reduced to extreme misery. The emperor died soon afterward, and the pious Justin replaced him. Justin restored the true faith by an edict and recalled the exiles, re-establishing the exiled prelates in their sees.

When Saint Sabas was ninety-one years old, he made the long journey to Constantinople to ask Justinian, successor to Justin, not to act with severity against the province of Palestine, where a revolt had occurred by the non-submission of a group of Samaritans. The emperor honored him highly and wished to endow his monasteries with wealth. Still, the holy Patriarch asked him to use the riches he was offering to build a hospice for pilgrims in Jerusalem, decorate the unfinished Church of the Blessed Virgin, build a fortress where the monks could take refuge when barbarians invaded the land, and finally, to re-establish preaching of the true Faith, by edicts proscribing the various errors being propagated. The holy Abbot lived

to be ninety-two years old and died in 531 in the arms of
the monks of his first monastery.

[Guérin, Abbé (Paul), François Giry, and Simon Martin. *Les Petits Bollandistes: Vies
Des Saints De L'Ancien et du Nouveau Testament.* Translated by the Monastère du
Magnificat. Paris: Bloud et Barral, 1882. *HathiTrust Digital Library,*
hdl.handle.net/2027/nnc1.0036694380.]

Saint Melchiades, Pope (✝ 314) — December 10

*The memorial of Melchiades, who died in Rome on
January 10, 314, entered the Roman calendar during the
thirteenth century. It is left for observance by particular
calendars. There is no reason to consider him a martyr;
he died after the peace of Constantine, and his name (also
called Miltiades) appears in the Depositio Episcoporum.*

Melchiades, or Miltiades, succeeded Eusebius in
the see of Rome, being chosen on the 2d of July, 311, in
the reign of Maxentius. Constantine vanquished that
tyrant on the 28th of October in 312 and soon after issued
edicts, allowing Christians the free exercise of their
religion and the liberty of building churches. To soothe
the minds of the pagans, who were uneasy at this
innovation, when he arrived in Milan at the beginning of
the year 313, he, by a second edict, ensured to all religions
except heresies liberty of conscience. Among the first laws
he enacted in favor of Christians, he passed one to exempt
the clergy from the burden of civil offices. On Sundays,
he obliged all his soldiers to repeat a prayer addressed to
the one only God, and no idolater could scruple at such a
practice. He abolished the pagan festivals and mysteries in
which lewdness had a share. Unnatural impurity being
almost unrestrained among the heathens, the Romans,
when luxury and debauchery arrived at the highest pitch
among them, began to shun marriage so that they might

be more at liberty to follow their passions. After which, laws obliged Augustus to encourage and command all men to marry, inflicting heavy penalties on the disobedient. The Christian religion restrained the abuses more effectually than they could have been by human laws. Constantine, in favor of celibacy, repealed the Poppæan law. This emperor also made a law to punish adultery with death.

The good pope rejoiced exceedingly at the prosperity of God's house and, by his zealous labors, very much extended its pale. Still, he had the affliction to see it torn by an intestine division in the Donatist schism, blazed with great fury in Africa. Mensurius, bishop of Carthage, being falsely accused of having delivered up the sacred scriptures to be burnt in the time of the persecution, Donatus, bishop of Cassanigra in Numidia, most unreasonably separated himself from his communion and continued his schism when Cecilian had succeeded Mensurius in the see of Carthage and was joined by many jealous enemies of that good prelate, especially by the powerful lady Lucilla, who was personally piqued against Cecilian while he was a deacon of that church. The schismatics appealed to Constantine, who was then in Gaul, and implored him to commission three Gaulish bishops, whom they specified, to judge their cause against Cecilian. The emperor granted them these judges they demanded but ordered the bishops, as mentioned earlier, to repair to Rome, imploring Pope Melchiades to examine the controversy, together with these Gaulish bishops, and to decide it according to justice and equity. The emperor left the decision to the bishops of this affair because it regarded a bishop. Pope Melchiades opened a council in the Lateran Palace on the 2d of October 313, at which both Cecilian and Donatus of Cassanigra were present; the former was pronounced by the pope and his council innocent of the whole charge that was brought against him. Donatus of Cassanigra was the only person condemned on that occasion; the other bishops who had adhered to him were allowed to keep their sees upon their renouncing the schism. Saint Augustine, speaking of the moderation the pope used, calls him an excellent man, a true son of peace, and a true father of Christians. Yet the Donatists, after his death, had recourse to their usual arms of slander to asperse his character and pretended that this pope had delivered the scriptures into the hands of the persecutors, which Saint Augustine calls a groundless and malicious slander. Saint Melchiades died on the 10th of January, 314, having sat two years, six months, and eight days, and was buried on the Appian Road in the cemetery of Calixtus; he is named in the Roman Martyrology and those of Bede, Ado, Usuard, etc. In some calendars, he is styled a martyr, doubtless on account of his sufferings in preceding persecutions.

This holy pope saw a door opened by the church's peace to the conversion of many, and he rejoiced at the triumph of the cross of Christ. But with worldly prosperity, a worldly spirit too often broke into the sanctuary itself. The zealous pastor sometimes had a reason to complain, with Isaiah, *"Thou hast multiplied the nation, and hast not increased my joy."* Under the pressures of severe persecution, the true spirit of our holy religion was maintained in many among its professors during the first ages; yet, amidst the holiest examples, and under the influence of the strongest motives and helps, avarice and ambition insinuated themselves into the hearts of some, who, by the abuse of the most extraordinary graces, became of all others the most abandoned to wickedness; witness Judas, the apostate in the college of the apostles; also several amongst the disciples of the primitive saints, as Simon Magus, Paul of Samosata, and others. But with temporal honors and affluence, the love of the world, though most severely condemned by Christ, as the capital enemy to his grace and holy love and the source of all vicious passions, crept into the hearts of many, to the utter extinction of the Christian spirit in their souls. This, indeed, reigns, and always will, in many chosen souls, whose lives are often hidden from the world, but in whom God will always provide for his honor faithful servants on earth, who will praise him in spirit and truth. But so deplorable are the overflowing of sensuality, avarice, and ambition, and such the lukewarmness and spiritual insensibility which has taken root in the hearts of many Christians that the torrent of evil example and a worldly spirit ought to fill everyone with alarms and oblige everyone to hold fast and be infinitely upon his guard that he be not carried away by it. It is not the crowd that we are to follow, but the gospel: and though temporal goods and prosperity are a blessing, they ought extremely to rouse our attention, excite our watchfulness, and inspire us with fear, being fraught with snares, and by the abuse which is frequently made of them, the ruin of virtue.

[Butler, Alban. *The Lives of the Fathers, Martyrs, and Other Principal Saints. Compiled from Original Monuments and Authentic Records.* Dublin: James Duffy, 1866. *HathiTrust Digital Library,* catalog.hathitrust.org/Record/001941109.]

Saint Anastasia, Martyr († 304) — December 25

[Deleted from the calendar without comment.]

This saint enjoys the distinction, unique in the Roman liturgy, of having a special commemoration in the second Mass on Christmas day. This Mass was initially celebrated not in honor of the birth of Christ but to commemorate the martyr, and towards the end of the fifth century, her name was inserted in the Roman Canon of the Mass.

Anastasia was married to a gentleman of prime quality and great birth, called Publius, who was a fierce and cruel man and much given to the adoration of his false gods; and for this cause, hated Saint Anastasia because she was a Christian and always employed herself in doing good, and succoring the holy Confessors, who in the bloodiest persecution of Dioclesian and Maxima were kept in prison, and put to torments for the faith of Jesus Christ. Nevertheless, Metaphrastes says that Saint Anastasia conserved her virginity and that Publius, her husband, did not come near her but afflicted her beyond measure, shut her up in a chamber of his house, giving her a certain stint of meat, that she might soon end her days, and treating her so unmercifully, that the saint was compelled to write two letters to Saint Chrysogonus, Martyr, who at that time was also a prisoner in Rome, beseeching him that he would help her by his prayers to the Lord; and Saint Chrysogonus answered her by two other letters, which we have put down in his life; and comforted her, and animated her to the crown of martyrdom.

But it happened at the very time she was thus straightened and afflicted. The emperor Dioclesian sent Publius, her husband, as an ambassador to the King of Persia; when he departed from Rome, he left her in the same prison, intending to put her to death when he should return from Persia. But, by the will of God, he fell sick by the way and died, paying with temporal and eternal death, his dangerous and tyrannical usage of Saint Anastasia. So she became free and had the command of herself and her means, which she wholly employed in the service and sustentation of the poor, especially of the holy confessors and martyrs, as she had promised.

It was a wonderful thing to see the zeal and affection with which this blessed widow and virgin busied herself in visiting prisons that were full of holy martyrs, and how she comforted and refreshed them, and cleansed their wounds, and alleviated their pains, and interred their dead bodies, and in all things conversed with them as their servant or slave. But while she was attending to these holy works, our Lord, who had freed her from her husband, would give her the reward of them; and not that she, who with great charity and humility, served the martyrs should want the crown of martyrdom.

She was apprehended by a certain prefect and cast into a brutal and horrid prison, where Saint Theodota (who had accomplished her martyrdom and reigned in heaven with Christ) sustained her two months of food brought from heaven. Then, in the end, she blessed Saint Anastasia and was put into a ship with two hundred men and seventy women (Usuard and Ado say seven hundred), all Christians, to be drowned in the sea. But the boat, guided by the providence of the Lord, arrived on the island *Palmaria*, where Saint Anastasia was tied to stakes and lifted a little from the earth. After that, they put fire underneath her, and so her body was burned, and her blessed soul purified, which was more on fire, and radiant with the flames of divine love than her body was with the flames of that other material fire, with which it was burnt and consumed.

All the other saints that came with her died for our Lord by diverse torments and death, amongst which there was one called Eutychian, a straightforward man without any malice. He was wealthy. They took away all his goods from him, but he gave no sign of being anything troubled at it, for he had his heart fixed where his treasure was, and to all questions, they asked him, he answered nothing but this: *They shall not take away Christ from me, although they take away my head.* A certain matron, called

Apollonia, took the body of Saint Anastasia, half-burnt, and kissing it many times with great tenderness, and anointing it with precious ointments, wrapped it in moist pure linen, and buried it in a garden of her own house, where a little after was built a church, and her name called it.

The martyrdom of Saint Anastasia was on the twenty-fifth of December, in the reign of Dioclesian and Maximian, in the year of Christ 304. This saint was very famous in Rome, where she had a church, which is the title of a Cardinal. Of her do mention the martyrologies, the Roman, those of Bede, Usuard, and Ado; and Metaphrastes, in the acts of the other Anastasia, yet more ancient, which are received by Lipoman, in his fifth tome, and by Surius in his sixth of the Lives of Saints.

[Ribadeneyra, Pedro de. "The Life of Saint Anastasia, Martyr." *The Lives of Saints, With Other Feasts of the Year, according to the Roman Calendar. Written in Spanish by the Reverend Father Peter Ribadeneyra, Priest of the Society of Jesus. Translated Into English by W.P. (William Petre) Esq; The Second Edition Corrected and Amended,* vol. 2, pp. 554-555. London. Printed by B.S., 1730. *HathiTrust Digital Library,* hdl.handle.net//2027/nyp.33433003053000.]

List of Roman Emperors

The Roman Empire was a powerful and terrifying global force for over a millennium. Its ascension signaled the end of the ancient Roman era, and its fall ushered in the European Renaissance. During this time, the Roman Empire was ruled by nearly 200 emperors, some more successful — and famous — than others. Consider the following list of Roman emperors from 27 B.C. to A.D. 1453. [✝ indicates periods of great Christian persecution.]

The Principate: The Principate was the name given to the early period of the Roman Empire (27 B.C. to A.D. 284). A single emperor ruled the Roman Empire at the time (the *princeps*). While the Roman Empire attempted to uphold the traditions of the earlier Roman Republic, the people of Roman rule resembled an autocracy in which the emperor wielded the majority of political power. Check out this list of the Principate Roman Emperors.

The Julian-Claudian Dynasty: Julius Caesar is most likely the first image that comes to mind when you think of a Roman emperor. *Caesar*, on the other hand, was not an official Roman emperor. Many people mistake *Julius Caesar* for the first Roman emperor because the title Caesar later became an honorific title meaning "successor of the emperor." The Julian-Claudian Dynasty began in 27 B.C. when *Augustus* became the first and best Roman emperor (according to many historians). This period also includes Nero, widely regarded as the worst Roman emperor by historians.

- Augustus (27 B.C.-A.D. 14)
- Tiberius (A.D. 14-37)
- Caligula (A.D. 37-41)
- Claudius (A.D. 41-54)
- Nero (A.D. 54-68) ✝

The Year of the Four Emperors: The Roman Empire experienced a brief period of unrest after Nero Claudius Caesar committed suicide in A.D. 68. It saw four emperors ascend in a year, three of whom died before the end of 69. (Galba and Vitellius were killed shortly after taking power; Otho committed suicide after being defeated by Vitellius). Vespasian, the period's final emperor, reigned for ten years and established the Flavian Dynasty.

- Galba (June 68-January 69)
- Otho (January 69-April 69)
- Vitellius (April 69-December 69)
- Vespasian (December 69-79)

The Flavian Dynasty: At the end of the first century, the Flavian Dynasty ruled for nearly 40 years. Emperor Titus, Vespasian's son, ruled during Vesuvius' eruption in A.D. 79. Domitian, his brother, ruled for 15 years before being assassinated, ushering in Marcus Cocceius Nerva.

- Vespasian (A.D. 69-79)
- Titus (A.D. 79-81)
- Domitian (A.D. 81-96) ✝

The Nerva-Antonine Dynasty: The Nerva-Antonine Dynasty's first five emperors are known historically as the Five Good Emperors. They were considered more moderate and less oppressive than previous Roman emperors. Many people thought the Five Good Emperors shared this trait because they were all adopted, not blood heirs to the throne, and chosen for their benevolence rather than military loyalty.

- Nerva (A.D. 96-98)
- Trajan (A.D. 98-117) ✝
- Hadrian (A.D. 117-138)
- Antoninus Pius (A.D. 138-161)

- Marcus Aurelius (A.D. 161-180) ✝
- Lucius Verus (ruled with father-in-law Marcus Aurelius from A.D. 161-169)
- Commodus (A.D. 180-192)

The Year of the Five Emperors: Following the Five Good Emperors came the Year of the Five Emperors, in which five different men vied for power following the assassination of Commodus in A.D. 192. Pertinax was chosen but assassinated soon after; his successor, Didius Julianus, was assassinated in less than three months by Septimus Severus, who had claimed the title for himself. Following Pertinax's death, Pescennius Niger and Clodius Albinus claimed the title of Emperor but were rejected by the Senate.

- Pertinax (January-March 193)
- Didius Julianus (March-June 193)
- Septimius Severus (April 193-211) ✝

The Severan Dynasty: The Severan Dynasty ended the civil war that had erupted during the Year of the Five Emperors. This dynasty's empresses strongly influenced the emperors (the Julias of Rome). This emperor line would be the last of the Principate, which ended with Maximinus Thrax's assassination of Alexander Severus.

- Septimius Severus (A.D. 193-211) ✝
- Caracalla (A.D. 211-217)
- Geta (ruled with brother Caracalla from A.D. 211-212)
- Macrinus (A.D. 217-218)
- Diadumenian (May-June 218)
- Elagabalus (A.D. 218-222)
- Severus Alexander (A.D. 222-235)

The Dominate: The Principate republic gave way to the Dominate period's despotism, in which emperors seized power violently and lost it just as quickly. These rulers were more authoritarian, hence the name *Dominate* ("to master or control" in Latin). Continue reading for a list of Dominate period Roman emperors.

The Crisis of the Third Century: The Principate ended with the Third Century Crisis (A.D. 235-284), which threatened to destroy the Roman Empire due to political instability and unrest. It included the Year of the Six Emperors in A.D. 238 when five emperors were assassinated in quick succession, followed by a series of emperors who only held power until someone took it away.

- Maximinus Thrax (A.D. 235-238) †
- Gordian I (March 238-April 238)
- Gordian II (ruled with his father from March 238-April 238)
- Puplenus (April 238-July 238)
- Balbinus (led with Puplenus from April 238-July 238)
- Gordian III (July 238-244)
- Philip the Arab (A.D. 244-249)
- Phillip II (ruled with father Philip from A.D. 247-249)
- Decius (A.D. 249-251) †
- Herennius Etruscus (June 251)
- Hostilianus (June 251-November 251)
- Trebonianus Gallus (A.D. 251-253)
- Volusianus (ruled with father Trebonianus Gallus from A.D. 251-253)
- Aemilianus (July 253-September 253)
- Valerian (A.D. 253-260) †

- Gallienus (ruled with father Valerian from A.D. 253-260, then alone from A.D. 260-268)
- Saloninus (shortly ruled with his father Gallienus from January 260-September 260)
- Claudius Gothicus (A.D. 268-270)
- Quintillus (A.D. April 270-May 270)
- Aurelian (A.D. 270-275)
- Tacitus (A.D. 275-276)
- Florianus (June 276-September 276)
- Probus (A.D. 276-282)
- Carus (A.D. 282-283)
- Carinus (A.D. 283-285)
- Numerianus (ruled with brother Carinus from A.D. 283-284)

The Tetrarchy: When Diocletian was proclaimed Emperor in A.D. 284, the Roman Empire was forever changed. He declared in A.D. 293 that the Roman government would be governed by two emperors (a*ugustuses*) and two junior emperors (*caesares*). This resulted in multiple emperors reigning simultaneously and, eventually, the territorial division of the Roman Empire into East and West.

The Tetrarchs: Diocletian, Maximian, Galerius, and Constantius I were the Four Tetrarchs. The first two emperors were known as *Augustuses*, while the next two were *Caesares*. Galerius would eventually rule as Augustus until A.D. 311 when a power struggle over his throne would erupt. Constantius later established the great Constantinian Dynasty.

- Diocletian (ruled with Maximian from A.D. 284-305) ✝
- Maximian (ruled with Diocletian from A.D. 286-305)

- Galerius (served as Caesar from A.D. 293-305, then ruled as Augustus from 305-311)
- Constantius I (served as Caesar from A.D. 293-305, then ruled as Augustus from 305-306)
- Severus (A.D. 306-307)
- Maxentius (A.D. 306 -312)
- Licinius (A.D. 308-324)
- Maximinus Daza (A.D. 308-313)
- Valerius Valens (A.D. 316-317)
- Martinian (July 324-September 324)

The Constantinian Dynasty: Constantine I, the son of Constantius I, ruled the fourth century for 30 years. He was instrumental in converting the Roman Empire to Christianity. Constantine I also established the Byzantine city-state of Constantinople, laying the groundwork for the Byzantine Empire. Constantine II, Constans, and Constantius II, his three sons, would rule for another 20 years.

- Constantius I the Great (served as Caesar from A.D. 293-305, then ruled as Augustus from A.D. 305-306)
- Constantine I (A.D. 306-337)
- Constantine II (A.D. 337-340)
- Constans (A.D. 337-350)
- Constantius II (A.D. 337-361)
- Vetranio (March 350-December 350)
- Julian the Apostate (A.D. 361-363)
- Jovian (A.D. 363-364)

The Valentinian Dynasty: This line of emperors, also known as the Valentinianic Dynasty, was in charge of the Roman Empire's western regions. Galla, Valentinian I's daughter, married Theodosius the Great, Emperor of the

Eastern Territory. The brief dynasty ended when two usurpers, Magnus Maximus and Eugenius, gained control of the West with Senate approval.

- Valentinian I (A.D. 364-375)
- Valens (A.D. 364-378)
- Gratian (A.D. 375-383)
- Valentinian II (A.D. 375-392)
- Magnus Maximus (usurper in the West; ruled from A.D. 383-388)
- Victor (A.D. 387-388)
- Eugenius (usurper in the West; ruled from A.D. 393-394)

The Theodosian Dynasty: The Theodosian Dynasty was the Roman Empire's final dynasty. Theodosius I was the last emperor of the united Roman Empire; after his death, his sons, Honorius and Arcadius, took control of the empire's western and eastern regions. From then on, the Roman Empire would be divided and ruled separately.

- Theodosius I the Great (A.D. 379-395)
- Honorius (ruled in the West from A.D. 395-423)
- Arcadius (ruled in the East from A.D. 395-408)
- Theodosius II (ruled in the East from A.D. 408-450)
- Constantine III (usurper in the West; ruled from A.D. 409-411)
- Constans II (ruled in the West from A.D. 409-411)
- Constantius III (ruled in the West from February 421-September 421)
- Joannes (ruled in the West from A.D. 423-425)

- Valentinian III (ruled in the West from A.D. 425-455)
- Marcian (ruled in the East from A.D. 450-457)

The Last Western Roman Emperors: In its final years, the Roman Empire's western territories began to shrink. Western Roman Emperors ruled over smaller regions for shorter periods, and the Roman Empire's eastern half frequently ignored them. Some historians attribute the deposition of Romulus Augustulus, the last Western Roman Emperor, to the fall of the classical Roman Empire.

- Petronius Maximus (March 455-May 455)
- Avitus (A.D. 455-456)
- Majorian (A.D. 457-461)
- Libius Severus (A.D. 461-465)
- Anthemius (A.D. 467-472)
- Olybrius (July 472-November 472)
- Glycerius (A.D. 473-474)
- Julius Nepos (A.D. 474-475)
- Romulus Augustulus (A.D. 474-476)

The Rise of the Byzantine Empire: Following the fall of the Western Roman Empire in A.D. 476, the Eastern Roman Empire evolved into what is now known as the Byzantine Empire. Many historians believe that the Byzantine Empire began with the Constantinian Dynasty in A.D. 306, but others believe it began with the fall of Rome. Zeno (A.D. 474-491), Basil II (A.D. 976-1025), and Constantine XI (A.D. 1405-1453), who was killed when the Byzantine Empire fell to the Ottoman Empire in 1453, were notable Byzantine emperors.

The Holy Roman Empire: The power of the Roman emperors resurfaced in the early Middle Ages. It was inherited by the Holy Roman Emperors, the monarchs of Italy, and later Germany. From A.D. 800 to 814, Charlemagne was the first emperor of the Holy Roman Empire, which spanned Western and Central Europe. Otto I of the Ottonian Dynasty (A.D. 962-973), Charles V (A.D. 1519-1556), and Francis II (A.D. 1792-1806), the last emperor before the fall of the Holy Roman Empire in the Napoleonic Wars, were all notable Holy Roman Emperors.

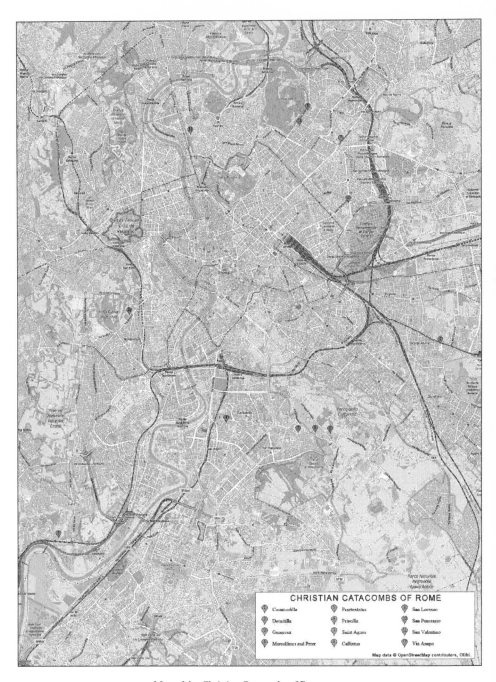

Map of the Christian Catacombs of Rome

Christian Catacombs of Rome

The below list identifies the ancient Christian catacombs of Rome along with their Roman location (in parentheses), modern street addresses, and geo coordinates:

1. **Catacombs of Commodilla** (Via Ostiensis): These catacombs on the Via Ostiensis contain one of the earliest images of a bearded Christ. They originally held the relics of Saints Felix and Adauctus. Excavations on the Commodilla were conducted by Franciscan archaeologist Bellarmino Bagatti (1933-34). [Via delle Sette Chiese, 42, 00145 Roma RM, Italy] [41.86123501234728, 12.48351840910371]

2. **Catacombs of Domitilla** (Via delle Sette Chiese): Discovered in 1593, these catacombs, which are more than 15 kilometers long, owe their name to the granddaughter of Vespasian. [41.858889, 12.505556]

3. **Catacombs of Generosa** (Via Campana): Located on the Campana Road, these catacombs are said to have been the resting place, perhaps temporarily, of Simplicius, Faustinus, and Beatrix, Christian Martyrs who died in Rome during the Diocletian persecution (302 or 303). [Museo delle Catacombe di Generosa; Via delle Catacombe di Generosa, 41, 00148 Roma RM, Italy] [41.83586493853041, 12.432115385758191]

4. **Catacombs of Marcellinus and Peter** (Via Labicana): These catacombs are situated on the ancient Via Labicana, today Via Casilina in Rome, Italy, near the church of Santi Marcellino e Pietro ad Duas Lauros. Their name refers to the Christian martyrs Marcellinus and Peter, who,

according to tradition, were buried here near the body of St. Tiburtius. [Mausoleum of Saint Elena Tor Pignattara; Catacombe SS. Marcellino e Pietro e Mausoleo di S.Elena: Via Casilina, 641, 00177 Roma RM, Italy] [41.878339036837325, 12.548695961253355]

5. **Catacombs of Praetextatus** (Via Appia): These are found along the Via Appia and were built at the end of the 2nd century. They consist of a vast underground burial area, first in pagan use and then in Christian use, housing various tombs of Christian martyrs. In the oldest parts of the complex may be found the "cubiculum of the coronation," with a rare depiction for that period of Christ being crowned with thorns, and a 4th-century painting of Susanna and the old men in the allegorical guise of a lamb and wolves. [Praetextatus Catacombs; Catacombe di Pretestato: Via Appia Pignatelli, 11, 00178 Roma RM, Italy] [41.8587436977285, 12.51535088581553]

6. **Catacombs of Priscilla** (Via Salaria): The Catacomb of Priscilla, situated at the Via Salaria across from the Villa Ada, probably derives its name from the name of the landowner on whose land they were built. The Benedictine nuns of Priscilla look after them. These hold some frescoes important to art history, such as the first representations of the Virgin Mary. [Via Salaria, 430, 00199 Roma RM, Italy] [41.92972394564594, 12.508645014766493]

7. **Catacombs of Saint Agnes** (Via Nomentana): After being a martyr because of her Christian faith, Sant'Agnese was buried in the catacombs that subsequently bore her name. [Via Nomentana,

349, 00162 Roma RM, Italy] [41.92264359741693, 12.518638601235825]

8. **Catacomb of Callixtus** (Via Appia Antica): Sited along the Appian Way, these catacombs were built after AD 150, with some private Christian hypogea and a funeral area directly dependent on the Catholic Church. It takes its name from the deacon Saint Callixtus, proposed by Pope Zephyrinus in the administration of the same cemetery on his accession as pope. He enlarged the complex, which soon became the Roman Church's official one. The arcades, where more than fifty martyrs and sixteen pontiffs were buried, form part of a complex graveyard that occupies fifteen hectares and is almost 20 km (12 mi) long. [Via Appia Antica, 110 - 00179 Roma RM, Italy] [41.858927, 12.510808]

9. **Catacomb of San Lorenzo**: Built into the hill beside *San Lorenzo fuori le Mura*, these catacombs are said to have been the final resting place of St. Lawrence. The church was built by Pope Sixtus III and later remodeled into the present nave. Sixtus also redecorated the shrine in the catacomb and was buried there. [Piazzale del Verano, 3, 00185 Roma RM, Italy] [41.909343296421376, 12.520886808124686]

10. **Catacomb of San Pancrazio (also called of Ottavilla)**: Established underneath the San Pancrazio Basilica, which Pope Symmachus built on the place where the body of the young martyr Saint Pancras, or Pancratius, had been buried. In the 17th century, it was given to the Discalced Carmelites, who completely remodeled it. The catacombs house fragments of sculpture and pagan and early Christian inscriptions. [Piazza di

S. Pancrazio, 00164 Roma **RM**, Italy] [41.88496904853874, 12.454088824555377]

11. **Catacombs of San Sebastiano** (Via Appia Antica): These 12-kilometer-long catacombs owe their name to San Sebastiano, a soldier who became a martyr for converting to Christianity. Together with those of San Callisto, they are the best that can be visited. [Via Appia Antica, 136, 00179 Roma RM, Italy] [41.85580694898332, 12.515841293203325]

12. **Catacombs of San Valentino** (Via Flaminia): These catacombs were dedicated to Saint Valentine. In the 13th century, the martyr's relics were transferred to the Basilica of Saint Praxedes. [Viale Maresciallo Pilsudski, 00197 Roma RM, Italy] [41.92462203333131, 12.4729058980611]

13. **Catacombs of Via Anapo**: On the Via Salaria, the Catacombs of Via Anapo are datable to the end of the 3rd or the beginning of the 4th century and contain diverse frescoes of biblical subjects. [Via Anapo, 6, 00199 Roma **RM**, Italy] [41.92639543496073, 12.506009898317199]

Determining Easter

The date of Easter is determined each year through a calculation known as *computus* (Latin for "computation"). Easter is observed on the first Sunday following the Paschal full moon, which occurs on or after March 21 (a fixed approximation of the March equinox). Determining this date in advance necessitates a correlation between the lunar months and the solar year, as well as considering the Julian or Gregorian calendar month, date, and weekday. The algorithm's complexity stems from the desire to associate the Easter date with the Jewish Passover feast, which Christians believe is when Jesus was crucified.

On the first Sunday after the Passover feast, Jesus rose from the dead. (Technically, he arose Saturday night, but that still counts as Sunday in the Jewish calendar, which starts each day at sunset rather than midnight.)

The Passover date is a complicated subject. In theory, the date should be the 14th of Nisan, the Jewish month, and it should correspond to a full moon (the Jewish calendar being partly lunar). In practice, however, this was not always the case. The month-moon cycles became uncoordinated, and feasts were sometimes held on a "liturgical" full moon that was not an astronomical full moon. As a result, rabbis had to announce when Passover would be observed regularly.

Christians did not like being reliant on rabbinic pronouncements for how to celebrate Christian feasts, so they devised another method of determining the date. They decided to celebrate Easter on the first Sunday following (but never on) the Paschal full moon.

The Paschal full moon is the first full moon that occurs on or after the spring equinox. This day, however, can be counted in a variety of ways. One method is to look at the sky, which produces the astronomical spring equinox. However, because this varies yearly, most people adhere to the calendrical spring equinox, observed on March 21.

Easter is the first Sunday after the Paschal full moon, the first full moon on or after March 21 on the Gregorian calendar. As a result, Easter is always between March 22 and April 25.

To find Palm Sunday (the sixth Sunday of Lent), begin with the date of Easter and move back one week: it is the Sunday before Easter Sunday. Start with the date of Easter Sunday, then back up six weeks (giving you the first Sunday of Lent), and then back up four more days: Ash Wednesday is the Wednesday before the first Sunday of Lent.

Bibliography

Bouyer, Louis, and Peter Kwasniewski. *The Memoirs of Louis Bouyer: From Youth and Conversion to Vatican II, the Liturgical Reform, and After.* Translated by John Pepino, English Lang. Ed., Kettering, OH: Angelico Press, 2015. Print.

Bugnini, Annibale. *The Reform of the Liturgy, 1948-1975.* Translated by Matthew J. O'Connell. Collegeville: Minnesota, Liturgical Press, 1990. Print.

Butler, Alban. *The Lives of the Fathers, Martyrs, and Other Principal Saints. Compiled from Original Monuments and Authentic Records.* Dublin: James Duffy, 1866. *HathiTrust Digital Library,* catalog.hathitrust.org/Record/001941109.

Benedict XIV. *The Roman Martyrology: Published by Order of Gregory XIII, Revised by Authority of Urban VIII and Clement X, Augmented and Corrected in 1749 by Benedict XIV.* Revised ed. Baltimore: John Murphy, 1916. archive.org/details/romanmartyrology00cathuoft.

Cekada Anthony. *Work of Human Hands: A Theological Critique of the Mass of Paul VI.* Philothea Press 2010.

Goñi, Beásoain P. J. A. *La Reforma Del Año Litúrgico Y Del Calendario Romano Tras El Concilio Vaticano II.* Roma: Ed. Liturgiche, 2011. Print.

Guérin, Abbé (Paul), François Giry, and Simon Martin. *Les Petits Bollandistes: Vies Des Saints De L'Ancien et du Nouveau Testament.* Translated by the Monastère du Magnificat. Paris: Bloud et Barral, 1882. *HathiTrust Digital Library,* hdl.handle.net/2027/nnc1.0036694380.

Guéranger, Prosper L. P. *L'Annee Liturgique: Le Temps après la Pentecote 1-6.* Translated by the Monastère du Magnificat. Tours: Mane, 1919.

Guéranger, Prosper, and Lucien Fromage. *The Liturgical Year.* Translated by Laurence Shepherd. Dublin: J. Duffy,

1867-1890. *HathiTrust Digital Library,*
catalog.hathitrust.org/Record/012192952.

Hellriegel, Martin B. "The Lord Our Coming King, Hasten to
Adore Him!" [Collegeville, Minnesota]. *Orate Fratres
1927-12-25: Vol 2 Iss 2,* 25 Dec. 1927. *Internet Archive,*
archive.org/details/sim_worship_1927-12-25_2_2.

Herbermann, Charles G, Edward A. Pace, Condé Bénoist Pallen,
Thomas J. Shahan, John J. Wynne, and Andrew A.
MacErlean. *The Catholic Encyclopedia: An International
Work of Reference on the Constitution, Doctrine,
Discipline, and History of the Catholic Church: in Fifteen
Volumes.* New York: Robert Appleton Co., 1907. *Internet
Archive,* archive.org/details/07470918.1.emory.edu.

Hoever, Hugo H. *Lives of the Saints: For Every Day of the Year.*
New York: Catholic Book Pub, 1955. Print.

The Holy Bible Translated from the Latin Vulgate. Baltimore: John
Murphy Company, 1914. *HathiTrust Digital Library,*
catalog.hathitrust.org/Record/008410632.

Jaud, Leon. *Vie Des Saints Pour Tous Les Jours De L'annee: Avec
Une Pratique De Piete Pour Chaque Jour.* Translated by
the Monastère du Magnificat. Tours: A. Mame, 1950.
Print.

Kwasniewski, Peter A. "The Sanctoral Killing Fields: On the
Removal of Saints from the General Roman Calendar."
New Liturgical Movement, Church Music Association of
America, 16 Nov. 2020,
www.newliturgicalmovement.org/2020/10/the-sanctoral-
killing-fields-on-removal.html.

Levy, Rosalie. *Heavenly Friends a Saint for Each Day.* Boston: Saint
Paul Editions, 1958. Print.

Grignion, de M. L.-M. *True Devotion to Mary.* Bay Shore, NY:
Montfort Publications, 1960. Print.

Marmion, Columba, and the Nuns of Tyburn convent. *Christ in His
Mysteries.* London: Sands: 1923. Print.